The Poor Belong to Us

WITHDRAWN

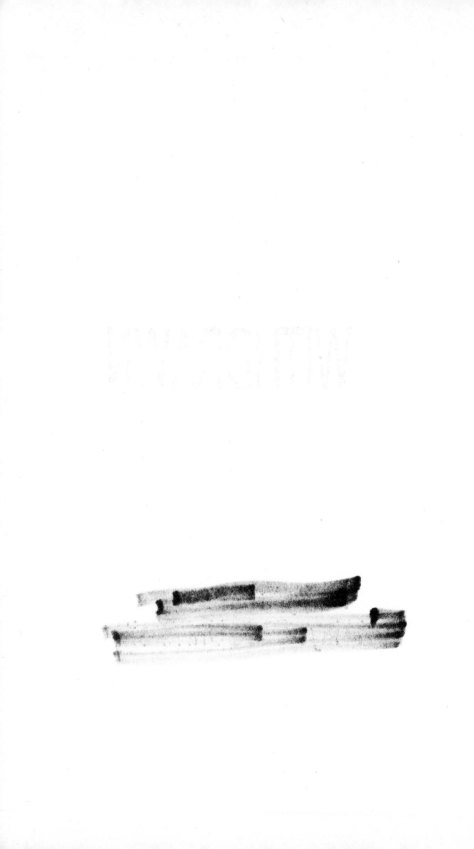

The Poor Belong to Us

∾ CATHOLIC CHARITIES AND
AMERICAN WELFARE

DOROTHY M. BROWN

ELIZABETH McKEOWN

HARVARD UNIVERSITY PRESS
Cambridge, Massachusetts, and London, England   1997

Copyright © 1997 by the President and Fellows of Harvard College
All rights reserved
Printed in the United States of America
Second printing, 2000

First Harvard University Press paperback edition, 2000

Library of Congress Cataloging-in-Publication Data

Brown, Dorothy M. (Dorothy Marie), 1932–
   The poor belong to us : Catholic charities and American welfare /
Dorothy M. Brown, Elizabeth McKeown.
       p.   cm.
   Includes bibliographical references and index.
   ISBN 0-674-68973-9 (cloth)
   ISBN 0-674-00401-9 (pbk.)
   1. Church work with the poor—United States—History.
   2. Church work with the poor—Catholic Church—History.
   3. Catholic Church—United States—Charities—History.
   4. Public Welfare—United States—History.
   5. United States—Church history—19th century.
   6. United States—Church history—20th century.
   7. United States—Social conditions.   I. McKeown, Elizabeth.   II. Title.
BX2347.8.P66B76   1997
361.7′5′08822—dc21   97-25736

Contents

Acknowledgments   *vii*

Introduction   *1*

1   The New York System   *13*

2   The Larger Landscape   *51*

3   Inside the Institutions: Foundlings, Orphans, Delinquents   *86*

4   Outside the Institutions: Pensions, Precaution, Prevention   *120*

5   Catholic Charities, the Great Depression, and the New Deal   *151*

Conclusion   *193*

Sources   *199*

Notes   *201*

Index   *279*

Acknowledgments

We are grateful for the help of many archivists and colleagues in this venture. At the Catholic University of America, Dr. Anthony Zito and his able staff of Sister Ann Crowley, John W. Shepherd, and Lynn Conway worked with us for four years. Rev. Paul Thomas, archivist of the Archdiocese of Baltimore; Rev. Edward F. McSweeney of the Diocese of Pittsburgh; Don Buske of the Archdiocese of Cincinnati; Rev. William Graf of the Diocese of Rochester; Sister Patricia Hodge, Director of Archives, Pittsburgh Sisters of Mercy; the archivists of the Sisters of Charity of Cincinnati, Mt. St. Joseph, Ohio; Sister Mary Hayes, archivist of Trinity College, Washington; and Paul Robichaud, C.S.P., of the Paulist archives were generous with their time and assistance. Msgr. James W. Murray, executive director of Catholic Charities of the Archdiocese of New York, graciously shared the records available at the Central Office; Sister Marguereta Smith provided us with several documents from the Cardinal Hayes papers in the archives of the Archdiocese of New York. Marty Beringer of Special Collections and Jon Reynolds and his staff at the Georgetown University archives introduced us to the important Tierney-*America* collection, and Kathleen Lyons and the staff of interlibrary loan services at Georgetown's Lauinger Library have been unfailingly helpful. The archivists at the National Archives and Federal Records branch at Suitland and the staff of the Bureau of Public Assistance in Baltimore also aided this research. Dorothy Abts Mohler shared materials from her records of the National School of Social Service, and Catholic University historian C. Joseph Nuesse reviewed our section on the university's School of Social Work. Christopher J. Kauffman, Jon Wakelyn, R. Emmett Curran, S.J., Paul Robichaud, C.S.P., Dolores Liptak, R.S.M., Timothy Meagher and William Portier—colleagues in the CLIO, an informal group of scholars interested in American Catholic history and culture—were helpful with their comments on a paper on the New York System. Carol Hurd Green of Boston College and Christopher J. Kauffman of the Catholic University of America read and provided valuable suggestions on the entire draft, and Jean Parlett provided editorial suggestions as we worked to meld our writing styles. Landegger and Keck fellowships supported our research, as did two Georgetown University summer grants.

The Poor Belong to Us

Introduction

Catholics have played a crucial but largely undocumented role in the evolution of American welfare. The burgeoning numbers of Catholic immigrants in the mid-nineteenth century commanded the attention of Protestant charity workers and reformers, who labored to succor and discipline their new neighbors. Galvanized both by the condition of their coreligionists and the practices of Protestant reformers, Catholics in the last quarter of the nineteenth century developed an extended network of institutions and services aimed at taking care of "their own." They also learned to leverage their position in "charity" to win a voice in local, state, and national policy-making and to gain access to the public purse. Charity became a primary emblem of Catholic identity in American culture and the chief means by which the church established a public voice. Small wonder then that in the midst of the New Deal debates over social security, a Catholic bishop rose to the floor to mark the territory. "The poor belong to us," Bishop Aloisius Muench defiantly reminded his colleagues. "We will not let them be taken from us!"

This proprietary Catholic claim to the poor was sustained by decades of labor on the part of religious communities of women, by diocesan welfare organizations, and by the investment in institutions and services that fueled a growing Catholic presence in the formation of local and state welfare policy. By 1935 Catholics were in position to significantly shape new social legislation for families and children. As New Deal and Great Society programs enlarged state responsibility for welfare over succeeding decades, Catholic charities maintained a consistent, if complicated, course as both a partner in government programs and as an advocate for the poor. By the 1990s the umbrella organization, Catholic Charities, U.S.A., represented the largest system of private social provision in the nation.

The Poor Belong to Us analyzes the local origins and national development of Catholic charities from the Civil War to World War II. It was as clients of charity that Catholics made their initial appearance in American welfare history, and nowhere were they more visible and troubling than in New York City. In 1852 the Protestant New York Association for Improving the Condition of the Poor (AICP) reported that three-quarters of its assistance went to Catholics. Ten years later in the wake of the Civil War draft riots, the AICP underscored the Irish-Catholic character of New York's "dangerous classes," insisting that seventy percent of the inmates of public almshouses and fifty percent of the city's criminals were born in Ireland. AICP leadership believed that a taint of "Irish blood" was also present in the native-born paupers and criminals of New York and referred to the children of Irish-Catholic immigrants as "accumulated refuse."[1] The preponderance of Catholic dependency remained a regular feature of AICP reports. As late as 1914, AICP social worker Katherine M. Dinan indicated that ninety percent of the women receiving "widows' pensions" from her agency were Catholic, and that Catholics still constituted three-quarters of AICP's clientele.

Although New York's Catholic bishop, John Hughes, chose to discount the poverty among Catholics in his diocese, Catholic indigence and delinquency was openly acknowledged among his coreligionists. In a formal statement in 1866, the entire body of Catholic bishops of the United States admitted that Catholic delinquency had assumed alarming proportions. "It is a melancholy fact, and a very humiliating avowal for us to make," they confessed, "that a very large portion of the vicious and idle youth of our principal cities are the children of Catholic parents."[2] A half century later, the situation seemed unrelieved. Catholic social workers pointed to a "deplorable percentage of children of Catholic parentage and baptism appearing as delinquents in the courts; to the number of applications by destitute Catholic families to non-Catholic agencies; to the out-of-proportion percentage of Catholic girls in reformative agencies and institutions; to the figures on illegitimacy; [and] to the number of Catholic women in the police courts."[3]

Interim local reports reinforced the point. Pittsburgh Catholic child workers produced statistics from the first decade of the century indicating that between forty-five and sixty percent of the children coming before the new juvenile court were Catholics.[4] Baltimore Catholics found the same situation. In 1915, for instance, 475 of the 830 children committed to reformatories by the courts there were Catholics. In St. Paul Catholic agents reported that Catholic children were being arrested on charges ranging from arson and assault with a dangerous weapon to violations of tobacco and poolroom laws.[5] That same year New York City's Charity

Organization Society noted that five thousand of its eight thousand cases were Catholic.[6] Charity organization societies in four other cities reported that Catholic families totaled between twenty-five and fifty percent of their annual budgets. In two cities the Catholic total was more than seventy percent.[7]

These self-reported accounts of Catholic dependency and delinquency were provided by individuals and groups who began to take an active part in efforts to remedy the situation. Confronting the obvious need of the Catholic poor and the pressure of public opinion, Catholic providers began to claim "their own" after the Civil War. Religious congregations and lay volunteers developed a collection of local institutions that eventually included schools, hospitals, foundling homes, orphanages, settlement houses, industrial schools, remedial institutions, and shelters for women. Catholic charities workers also initiated noninstitutional service programs that included housing and employment registries, probation and recreation services for youth, outdoor relief, family casework, and home nursing services.

A variety of motives sustained these efforts. Catholic providers believed caring for the poor was the true test of their own progress toward eternal salvation. They were also spurred by the activities of Protestant "child-savers," who labored diligently in the nineteenth century to rescue poor children from what they considered the baneful and antidemocratic control of the Catholic church and from the poverty and degeneracy of their parents. Catholics, not surprisingly, denounced these marauding Protestant charity workers and responded by creating large child-caring institutions that sheltered needy children under Catholic auspices. The leading motive was to save the souls of the children and their parents, but the importance of material provision and service was never undervalued. Salvation and social security blended seamlessly in the rhetoric of Catholic leaders, who were also aware that left unattended, the situation of the poor would be charged against them as a failed civic responsibility and would exacerbate anti-Catholic and nativist sentiments in the culture.

From its inception American Catholic social provision was anchored in child-care. In addition to the growing system of parochial schools, congregate institutions for children in major cities housed hundreds, even, in the case of New York City, thousands of infants and children.[8] Most of the residents were not orphans but children whose parents could not provide adequate care, or who regarded the institutions as a superior alternative to their own domestic situations and to the opportunities provided by local public schools. Operated primarily by religious congregations of women, these child-caring institutions became the hallmark of Catholic social provision.[9]

New York City had the greatest number of Catholic poor and bore the largest costs for dependent and delinquent children during the period of this study. And, as Catholics gained power in the Democratic party, the city became the site of a significant new "politics of charity." Family ties and neighborhood connections joined Catholic charities and Tammany Hall. The sisters who staffed the New York Foundling Asylum, the New York Catholic Protectory, and the large orphan asylums could count on the unwavering support of their coreligionists in New York Democracy. Hundreds of female and male lay volunteers also served New York Catholic charities as fund-raisers, informal advisers, institutional board members, and parish visitors.

Catholic charities workers soon extended their political reach beyond City Hall to influence legislation at the state level. After Protestant reformers engineered the passage of the Children's Law in the New York legislature in 1875, Catholic lobbyists added a rider stipulating that the religious background of dependent children must be honored in any plans for their care. The act provided a legislative guarantee of public funding to Catholic institutions caring for poor children. To the chagrin of its original sponsors, the new law resulted in the creation of a public revenue stream that enabled the managers of Catholic child-caring institutions to provide a safety net for thousands of impoverished parents and their children. After 1875 the number and size of Catholic institutions expanded under "the New York system" at a rate that set off loud alarms among the city's non-Catholic citizens.[10]

For decades after the passage of the Children's Law, these critics joined forces with political reformers in an attempt to overcome Tammany's influence in city government and to overturn the New York system of public support for private charities. The success of the Fusion campaign of Catholic mayoral candidate John Purroy Mitchel in 1913 raised reform hopes that a disinterested public authority could now effectively dismantle the New York system. But the Mitchel administration badly mishandled an investigation of private children's institutions in the city and lost City Hall to Tammany in the 1917 mayoral election. The Mitchel investigation did trigger a strong move toward diocesan centralization on the part of Archbishop Patrick Hayes, who attempted to exercise more direct control over the hundreds of independent institutions and organizations in his diocese in order to insure compliance with public regulations and to guarantee the steady flow in the per capita payments for children in Catholic institutions.[11]

As the agents of charity contended in New York, reformers in other cities also pressed for improvements in public child-care. The "home first" campaign of Progressive reformers marked a new course in efforts to increase public responsibility for dependent youngsters. No longer convinced that they should attempt to save poor children by rescuing them from their families and placing them in middle-class Protestant care, reformers now wished to promote a pension plan to keep children in their own homes under supervised parental care. The pension plan received strategically tendered support from leading New York Catholics at the White House Conference on the Care of Dependent Children in 1909. Meanwhile the creation of juvenile courts opened a door for more extended public intervention in the lives of poor children, charity organization societies in U.S. cities exercised growing influence over local social provision, and business leaders began to demand consolidated fund-raising campaigns for private charities.

Moved by the scope of these developments, Catholics began to experiment with "cooperation" in welfare work. They joined local charity federations and community chest campaigns, began to serve on city and state welfare boards, became visible as members and officers in the National Conference of Charities and Corrections, and took steps to prepare their coreligionists for the new civil service exams that would permit them to gain public employment in welfare positions. In spite of their growing interest in public developments, however, Catholic provision for children remained anchored in their institutions. In 1910, 445 Catholic institutions (not including day nurseries) cared for 88,860 dependent children.[12] From this strong institutional base, Catholics enlarged their activities to include day care and adoption services, and Catholic workers became involved in public debates over desertion, divorce, alcohol consumption, illegitimacy, and the growing attraction of birth control.

Internal sponsorship for Catholic charities reform came from a number of constituencies. Catholic University in Washington, D.C., had begun to train its priest-students in the new social sciences at the turn of the century, and most of the major clerical figures in reform had some association with that institution. Officers of the Society of St. Vincent de Paul (SVPS) in New York and Baltimore began to promote relationships with non-Catholic social welfare organizations and leaders, and Baltimore's SVPS led the way in the movement to coordinate and centralize Catholic charities by creating a citywide organization in 1907. A constituency of growing importance, Catholic laywomen with practical or academic training in social work became increasingly involved in both Catholic and secular welfare practices. As social work began to take on the aspects of a profession with special educational requirements and standards for accreditation, women with professional training and aspirations began to enter Catholic work. To prepare themselves they took advantage of the social work classes offered after 1912 by Jesuit schools of Loyola, Chicago, Boston College, and St. Louis University and sought advanced degrees from the secular universities and from non-Catholic schools of social service.

These groups began the sensitive task of reforming Catholic charities and of bringing a larger Catholic presence into the current practices of public welfare at the state and national levels. They publicly accepted a program of "scientific charity" in 1910 with the founding of their own NCCC, the National Conference of Catholic Charities.[13] Convened largely at the urging of New York Catholics, the NCCC was a voluntary lay movement in the years before World War I. Its predominantly female membership was composed largely of married and single lay volunteers, who aspired to provide a national organization to supplement local Catholic charities efforts. They pooled information on the level of Catholic need, especially in northern urban areas, and on existing Catholic responses. NCCC members also became informed on non-Catholic public and private welfare initiatives (mothers' pensions and community chest funding, for instance) and evaluated the methods and standards of non-Catholic social work and social reform. As they took up the task of making their practices more acceptably "scientific," however, these Catholic activists continued to use the language of charity to characterize Catholic social provision. The rhetoric of charity preserved a sense of distinction in the culture, even as Catholics became a growing force in the shaping of American public welfare.

The drive for consolidation at the diocesan level was soon taken up by local Catholic bishops, who responded to the demand for charities reform in the early decades of the twentieth century by assuming direct control of diocesan charitable institutions, services, and funding. They created new central bureaucracies of charity, to which they assigned priests as full-time administrators. Local bishops also appointed financial advisory boards of well-placed Catholic laymen and began to staff their new bureaus with professional social workers. The development of these central bureaus of charity greatly altered the original character of Catholic charities, reducing the influence of the independent lay boards that sustained most charitable institutions and the freedom of the religious orders that founded and staffed them.

The presence of female social workers in the new charities bureaus was also decisive in the modernization of Catholic charities. These women worked in an unfamiliar terrain located somewhere between motherhood and priesthood and in a fledgling profession that was struggling to establish its credentials.[14] Lacking the cachet of consecrated religious women and often stigmatized for earning a living by serving the poor, the social workers displaced traditional volunteers, challenged the pre-eminence of religious women and of institutional charities, and created considerable animosity among pastors accustomed to having the sole authority in matters pertaining to the welfare of dependent children and needy families in their parishes. Their gender, education, and professional status made them a sizable concern to these traditional authorities as they entered the sensitive area of Catholic family life.

Catholic social workers also began to gain positions in state and nonsectarian welfare organizations. Drawn by higher salaries and wider opportunities, they generally maintained their commitment to Catholic teaching and their loyalty to the Catholic community. Their presence added a significant Catholic dimension to state boards of charity and to professional associations, to municipal welfare organizations, and eventually to New Deal programs. New York Catholic social worker Jane Hoey, for example, was appointed to direct the Bureau of Public Assistance of the Social Security Board and to approve state plans for Aid to Dependent Children. Her colleague Mary Irene Atkinson became the director of the Child Welfare Division of the Children's Bureau. From their new federal positions, administrators like Hoey and Atkinson supported the growing role of the state in welfare provision but retained a strong emphasis in the parental and mentoring relationship characteristic of both Catholic charities and professional social work in the period.

Mastering the intricacies of special interest and reform politics on the national level represented a new challenge for Catholic charities. Although they had fared well enough when American politics was largely a local matter, the Great Depression of the 1930s confronted them with initiatives that heralded a growing involvement of state and federal government in the lives of individuals and families. Catholic charities organizations learned to advance their interests in these new circumstances and attempted to play a role in the formation and administration of federal welfare policies.[15] The clergy who headed the diocesan charities organizations used the strategy they had honed earlier at the local and state level, presenting Catholic charities as the protector of the religious rights of Catholic welfare recipients in order to make a place for their agencies in the new public programs. Conceding the need for federal funding for social welfare, they sought legal protections for the religious identity of dependent children in the new public programs and attempted to establish Catholic agencies as administrators of federal and state welfare funds.

Two programs received special attention. During the early New Deal, Catholic charities workers hoped to have their agencies approved as administrators of Federal Emergency Relief Administration (FERA) programs. They were disappointed when FERA administrator Harry Hopkins blocked the formal participation of private welfare organizations in 1933, ruling that all public moneys had to be distributed by public agencies. In the wake of Hopkins' decision, however, several local Catholic charities organizations arranged for their units to be delegated as public agencies and qualified as administrators of FERA funds. In Chicago, Pittsburgh, Baltimore, and St. Louis, Catholic charities remained a central part of the FERA effort. Meanwhile the Catholic Charities of New York found an alternative way to participate in the distribution of public relief. The agency began to loan its staff to the city during the crisis, and Catholic Charities social worker Mary Gibbons became director of the city's home relief program. Catholic agencies also continued to contract with local and/or state public welfare departments for care of dependent and handicapped children in their institutions and for special family casework.

Short-term relief was not the only focus of concern. Catholic charities leaders also actively shaped the child-caring programs of the Social Security Act. When Roosevelt's cabinet-level Committee on Economic Security met to draft the Social Security bill in 1934, the National Conference of Catholic Charities engaged in a significant effort to shape the provisions of Aid to Dependent Children (ADC) and Child Welfare Services in that legislation. The NCCC secured a change in the child welfare service proposal of the Children's Bureau, specifically eliminating the possibility of *mandated* state participation in the financing of child welfare services—an outcome that would have threatened the established local patterns of funding for Catholic child-care where state laws prohibited the allocation of state funds to private institutions.

Behind a blitz of letter-writing from diocesan agencies and aided by connections with Catholic congressmen, they also succeeded in limiting the scope of Aid to Dependent Children to those dependent children who lived with their parents or with relatives within the second degree of kinship. The ADC "kinship" clause, which confined federal and state funding to the blood relatives of dependent children, forestalled a situation in which local governments providing per capita support for children in institutions would have a significant financial incentive to move children from institutions into foster families where they would be supported by ADC revenues rather than from the local public purse. Although Catholic agencies remained barred from dispensing ADC funds directly to Catholic families, the final form of the social security legislation prevented ADC from being used for foster care and left traditional agencies responsible for the care of needy children who were unable to be sheltered by close relatives.

The influence of the Catholic charities network expanded and then contracted again during the New Deal as these massive government programs reconfigured public and private social provision. By the end of the decade, economic relief became the clear responsibility of the new federal and state agencies. The poor were now directly eligible for old-age and child-assistance programs, and the white male workforce and their widows would benefit from the emerging public insurance programs for unemployment and old age. The federalization of welfare policy under the Social Security Act prevented the kind of direct influence on the formation and administration of state welfare policy that Catholics had enjoyed in the New York system. Moreover, the Catholic women employed as administrators and social workers in the new public bureaucracies defended the rule of public administration for public funds and championed the role of the professional social worker in the lives of recipients of public assistance. Although the Catholic social workers believed that faith was a peerless asset in social life, they were also aware of the solid increase in the material security provided to poor Catholics by the state and enjoyed their own role in that improvement.

Between World War II and the War on Poverty, the Catholic charities network worked to establish itself as both advocate for the poor and as service provider. Following the Catholic population into the middle class, the energies of diocesan agencies were devoted to casework for families and services for youth and the elderly, until the Great Society programs and the social concerns of the Vatican Council (1962–1965) directed their attention to the needs of a "new" and largely non-Catholic poor. In the context of the War on Poverty, Catholic charities agencies took major steps to reconstruct themselves as "justice" workers, committed to advocacy and service to the poor irrespective of race or creed. In 1994 the local agencies affiliated with Catholic Charities, U.S.A.—the successor of the National Conference of Catholic Charities—spent $1.86 billion in emergency and social service programs that served eleven million persons. It also benefited from the talents of nearly 200,000 volunteers.[16] Its ability to continue to attract financial and human resources and to sustain grassroots services and legislative advocacy makes the Catholic charities network a significant asset for the poor in contemporary America and underscores the importance of the private sector in American welfare.

There is clear gain in adding this Catholic study to the rich mix of contemporary welfare scholarship. Theda Skocpol's recent study of state policy, *Protecting Soldiers and Mothers: The Political Origins of Social Policy in the United States,* offers a complex analysis of the factors retarding and promoting American social provision and invites further investigation of the role Catholics played in patronage and pension systems.[17] Catholic political bosses were a major element in the party system that awarded pensions and responded to the demands of poor constituents. This study develops that connection by reconstructing the relationship between Tammany Hall and Catholic charities in New York. It also details the efforts of the Catholic charities leaders who joined the push for mothers' pensions.

In *Mother-Work: Women, Child Welfare, and the State, 1890–1930* (1994), Molly Ladd-Taylor has produced a sophisticated study of maternalism, feminism, and the politicization of motherhood. In the present study, "the child" anchors Catholic claims to the poor and to the work of women in complex ways. Equally evident is the singular quality of Catholic "maternalism"—anchored as it was in Mother Church and in the work of single religious and professional Catholic women. These women learned from the organized efforts of Protestant women's organizations and secular reformers, but their "maternal" interests were shaped by a religious concern for saving souls and by their roots in the working class.

Recent significant analyses of Protestant women's personal service, commitment to saving their "sisters," and organizations for moral reform are provided by Peggy Pascoe's *Relations of Rescue: The Search for Female Moral Authority in the American West, 1874–1939* (1990); Regina G. Kunzel's *Fallen Women, Problem Girls: Unmarried Mothers and the Professionalization of Social Work, 1890–1945* (1993); and Mary E. Odem's *Delinquent Daughters: Protecting and Policing Adolescent Female Sexuality in the United States, 1885–1920* (1995). Our study provides an important complement to this research. In the extensive institutional work of religious congregations in foundling and maternity homes and houses of the Good Shepherd and in the prevention and reclamation efforts of Catholic diocesan bureaus of charity, Catholic charities offer a contrasting cultural response to rescue and control efforts of the period.[18]

Robyn Muncy's excellent study of the creation of the Hull House—University of Chicago—Children's Bureau network of women professionals in *Creating a Female Dominion in American Reform, 1890–1935* (1991) provides background for our efforts to detail the Catholic connections to this network, as Catholic women made their way from local to state to national administrative positions. Linda Gordon's *Pitied But Not Entitled: Single Mothers and the History of Welfare, 1890–1935* expands her important efforts to address the role of gender and race in welfare history.[19] Her discussion of the emergence of a two-track, entitlement-assistance pattern of state welfare offers another framework in which to measure the Catholic impact on the development of American welfare.

Committed to the principle of a "family wage," Catholic charities leaders both advanced and contested the two-track welfare state. On the one hand, charities leaders were eager to win entitlements for poor and working-class Catholics. They also supported the development of Aid to Dependent Children, and Catholic social worker Jane Hoey administered the program through its first two decades. On the other hand, Catholics traditionally resisted the distinction between needs and rights that the two-track system implied. Catholic charities advocates insisted that, absent a male breadwinner or a living wage, poor families still had a strong claim on both the private and the public resources of the community. Arguing that "human needs constitute the primary title to material goods," Catholics urged their agencies to become advocates for the poor in the emerging state system and to defend their right to assistance and to due process.[20] Although they accepted and encouraged "means-testing" and no doubt would have imposed their own version of "morals-testing" had they become directly involved in the administration of ADC, their belief that "needs create rights" did not easily lend itself to the unfortunate distinction between "entitlement" and "assistance" that began to characterize American public welfare during the New Deal.[21]

The Catholic presence in American welfare clearly underscores the composite nature of the American welfare system and provides important evidence of what Peter Mandler has called "the uses of charity." Catholics were prominent among the poor of the nineteenth-century cities, and the development of Catholic institutions and services supported by a combination of private contributions and public revenues is an important episode of "self-help" in the American welfare system. The mixed nature of these developments also demonstrates what Michael Katz has called "the blurred boundaries between public and private" in American welfare.[22]

Though the history of Catholic charities can add significantly to the discussions of maternalism, social (indeed, spiritual) control, gender, and welfare, at the same time it resists theoretical bracketing. The Catholic church is not monolithic; it is the most pluralist of all of the denominations in America. Its history is rooted in the local parishes and dioceses and is driven by divisions of class, ethnicity, and generation. Historians of Catholic social provision have addressed this complexity in recent volumes. Christopher J. Kauffman has given a nuanced reading of Catholic healthcare policies and practice in *Ministry and Meaning: A Religious History of Catholic Health Care in the United States* (1995), and Mary J. Oates offers an important socioeconomic overview in *The Catholic*

Philanthropic Tradition in America (1995). The Catholic church is also an international organization, as recent scholarship on European welfare systems reminds us. Anchored in programs for child-care, the present study of American Catholic charities helps to foster a comparative approach to the study of welfare.[23]

Our work on organized Catholic charities and American welfare builds on this rich welfare scholarship. The papers of the National Conference of Catholic Charities, still unaccessioned when we researched them, are our primary resource. The correspondence and reports of the NCCC are supplemented with archival materials from dioceses and institutions in Baltimore, Boston, Cincinnati, New York, Pittsburgh, Denver, Omaha, and Washington, D.C. Mindful of Michael Katz's caution against "taking voluntary agencies at their own word," we have used an array of journals, newspapers, private and public reports, and the records of the Social Security Administration and the United States Children's Bureau to provide additional material and to act as an outside check on Catholic sources.

The New York System

In July 1918 New York City conducted a public funeral that rivaled its biggest wartime extravaganzas. The deceased was the city's ex-mayor and latest war hero, John Purroy Mitchel, and the tribute offered a dramatic contrast to the bitterness of his defeat at the hands of Tammany Democrats in the municipal elections of 1917. Mitchel's political career had ended the previous November in the wake of a pitched battle with the Catholic church over the issue of public support for poor children in the city. Now a second and more spectacular fall had ended his life. Following his unsuccessful bid for reelection under the banner of New York's Fusionist reformers, Mitchel joined the Army Signal Corps. In the last week of his flight training program, his safety harness came loose and he fell five hundred feet from the open cockpit of his plane. The tragedy of his death softened the acrimony attached to his name, as official New York turned out for his funeral. Board of Aldermen President Alfred E. Smith, state senator Robert F. Wagner, and Tammany boss Charles F. Murphy paid their respects to the fallen flier at City Hall. Theodore Roosevelt and Nicholas Murray Butler served as honorary pallbearers during the procession to St. Patrick's Cathedral, where they joined worthies like Elihu Root, J. P. Morgan, and Jacob Schiff in the solemn requiem. The irony was apparent to many New Yorkers. During his years in New York politics, Mitchel had strenuously denounced Catholic connections to City Hall and won the approval of these same reformers and city leaders. Now the line that marched from City Hall to St. Patrick's reestablished that connection, as the forces of religion, politics, and reform in New York found common cause in the Mass of the Dead.

Mitchel's fall from political grace had begun in 1916 when a simmering battle over the city's charitable institutions for children had exploded into open war. Determined to reduce the numbers of children sheltered in Catholic asylums at city expense, his administration demanded a full-scale public review of the web of child-caring interests that bound City Hall (and by extension, Tammany Hall) together with the State Board of Charities (SBC) and the archdiocese of New York. In the brawl that resulted, city papers ran lurid headlines indicting Catholic orphanages, and diocesan officials retaliated with a massive pamphlet campaign denouncing Mitchel and his reform-minded coworkers. Convinced that he was the victim of a Catholic conspiracy, Mitchel then instructed the New York police to place secret wiretaps on the telephones of those involved in the attack on his administration. The personal invective on both sides was vicious. Two of the supporters of Catholic institutions died during the proceedings, and the police officer in charge of the wiretaps attempted suicide. But the ultimate source of the 1916 charities war lay in the system itself.

New York's long-standing practice of providing public funding for private charitable institutions began to develop early in the nineteenth century under Anglo-Protestant auspices. Moved by evangelical calls to reform and the impress of civic duty, private groups took responsibility for tending to the material and social needs of New York's poor. In what was to become the signature of New York social provision, these volunteers financed their efforts with funding from the public treasury. The earliest ventures were in education. The private Free School Society was established in 1805 to serve poor children who were not enrolled in church-run schools. Noting that these youngsters suffered from "cold, hunger and wretchedness," the Society also supplied food and clothing for their pupils on an informal basis. Renamed the Public School Society in 1826, this private organization served as the funding conduit for New York's public schools after the passage of the Common Schools Act of 1813. Although two Catholic elementary schools received a share of these public funds for several years, no money was provided by the Society to any denominational school after 1825.[1]

Following the lead of the Public School Society, newly formed benevolent associations began to petition for public funding for a variety of social measures for New York's poorest children. Two nondenominational Protestant societies benefited from public assistance: The Society for the Reformation of Juvenile Delinquents received property from the city's Common Council and cash grants from the state legislature to establish the New York House of Refuge in 1824; and the Common Council gave the New York Orphan Asylum a portion of Public School Society funds in 1825.

The first objections to this practice were leveled by New York's Roman Catholic minority under the leadership of Archbishop John Hughes.

During the 1840s Hughes strenuously objected to the Protestant tone of the public schools and to the role of the Public School Society. When his demand for equal public funding for Catholic schools went unheeded, Hughes committed the meager resources of his immigrant church to the massive project of financing an independent parochial school system in the archdiocese.

New York Catholics were notably more successful in securing public support for institutions to house the children of the Catholic poor. Driven by violence and hunger, immigrants poured through the Port of New York, and the numbers of poor Catholics grew at an alarming rate. Concerned by this new and disturbing urban population, city and state leaders gradually began to provide public financing for children in Catholic orphanages. The Roman Catholic Orphan Asylum (RCOA) received its first small share of state funds in 1833, and in 1846 the Common Council leased property on Fifth Avenue and Fifty-first Street to the asylum to build a new institution. The RCOA also began drawing public school funds from the Board of Education and in 1859 received $5,875 from that source and an additional $4,000 grant from the state legislature.[2]

During the second half of the nineteenth century, Catholic institutions grew to the point that they received the lion's share of public support. The funding took a variety of forms: Land, excise tax moneys, and per capita payments came from the city; and until 1873 the state legislature also supplied cash support in response to the petitions of individual institutions. By 1900 nearly 20,000 children were cared for yearly in Catholic institutions with public support. After 1850 New York's Catholic poor also constituted a majority of the inmates of the public/Protestant House of Refuge and the New York Orphan Asylum, although the church did not establish its legal right to provide religious services to Catholic children in non-Catholic institutions until 1891.[3] This practice of using private agencies to administer public poor support became the basis of the "New York system" and was the aggravated issue that exploded into open conflict in the charities investigations of 1914–1916.

The character of the system was deeply influenced by the growing strength of the Democratic party in the city at mid-century. Irish immigrants quickly discovered the advantages of party politics in the United States and developed their potential as political brokers through membership in the Tammany organization. The Irish presence in New York Democratic politics offered a growing advantage for Catholic child-caring institutions in the pursuit of public funds. A determination to "take care of their own" united the managers and trustees of the institutions and their supporters in City Hall in the common cause.

As the Catholic advantage in the New York system grew, skirmishes and flare-ups over issues of control and funding pockmarked the land-scape of charity in the city. These engagements were generally initiated by the reformers from the (Protestant) Charity Organization Society (COS) and the (private) State Charities Aid Association (SCAA), who believed that waste, fraud, and pauperism were the inevitable result of what they called "indiscriminate poor relief." These organizations were led by two no-nonsense Yankees, Josephine Shaw Lowell and Louisa Lee Schuyler. Lowell and Schuyler and their coworkers argued that publicly funded provision of cash or material relief had a profoundly negative impact on the poor. It caused poor people to demand such support as a right and reduced their willingness to better their situations on their own accord. Following the lead of England, which banned public doles in 1834, Lowell and Schuyler backed legislation making public "outdoor relief" illegal in New York in 1867.

Emphasizing instead the importance of character development and cross-class monitoring, the COS developed programs of "friendly visit-ing" among the poor. They divided the city into local units and assigned volunteer visitors to each neighborhood, instructing them in techniques of home investigation and disinterested counsel. These "alms of good advice" were tendered with the hope that poor families might learn to imitate the practices and character of their benevolent visitors and benefit from their company. Meanwhile the volunteers of the SCAA devoted themselves to the task of visiting and inspecting public institutions for poor, sick, and criminal populations and advising the State Board of Charities on necessary reforms. Together the COS and the SCAA turned their attentions in the 1880s and 1890s to the institutional "homes" of Catholic child-care. They sponsored legislation designed to increase pub-lic control over the admissions policies and administration of Catholic child-caring institutions, and they stoutly supported the alternative prac-tice of placing needy children in private foster homes.

These activists took their cues from the work of the Children's Aid Society (CAS), a nondenominational private agency that enjoyed the support of New York's Protestant elite and funding from the city trea-sury.[4] Founded in 1853 by the Connecticut-born Charles Loring Brace, the CAS responded to growing apprehension among New York's middle-class citizens caused by thousands of roving "street children." The Society supplied shelter and industrial training for poor children, hoping to lead them to gainful occupations and remove the menace from the streets. But its signature agenda was a much more dramatic form of child-removal. The Children's Aid Society ultimately aimed to "send the children West" to farm families where they would benefit from the discipline of outdoor work and the ministrations of Protestant religion.

Brace was convinced that poor children could be saved from the cycle of poverty endured by their parents if they could be physically and emotionally separated from those parents and from the family environment in which he believed such poverty was bred. On farms in the Midwest they could escape from the influence of what he called "the dangerous classes of New York City" (comprised largely of their own parents and companions). Country air, hard work, religious training, and a role at the bottom of the hierarchy in a farm household or small business would save these children from lives of pauperism and dependency. Good yeoman habits, a deference to the master's authority, and a genuine sense of earning one's own bread would rescue the boys from the temptations of vagrancy, and the domestic arts of household service would provide CAS girls (far fewer in number) with skills and an ambition for homes of their own.[5]

The importance of breaking up poor families and reestablishing poor children in foster households was therefore the central premise of Brace's work and the basis of most of his fund-raising appeals. In his vivid descriptions, poor parents passively endured an unspeakably squalid existence. Shiftless, intemperate, and desperately "groaning and begging," they barely managed to stay alive long enough to breed. They brought not only pestilence and disease to the city but "broods of vagrants and harlots." "Many times I have come into their shanties on a snowy morning and found the people asleep with the snow lying thick on their bed-clothes," Brace wrote. Most of the parents in Brace's descriptions were women. What warmth they had came from a bottle. "Every woman drank hard, I suppose to forget her misery; and dreadful quarrels raged among them. . ." "Liquor prevailed," he told his supporters.[6]

A significant distance no doubt existed between Brace's child-removal rhetoric and the reality of his placement practices. Poor parents seem to have been able to use Brace's organization to forward interests of their own, particularly by allowing their children to be placed by the Society as a kind of informal indenture and then receiving them back home again in New York when circumstances permitted. But CAS records document the removal of tens of thousands of children permanently from their parents and from the city of New York.[7]

Catholics soon came to regard the Children's Aid Society as an unqualified menace that had caused thousands of Catholic children to lose their religion and thus their only hope of eternal salvation. Alert Catholic leaders used the threat of child-removal to build their case for new and enlarged Catholic child-caring institutions to which poor parents might turn to preserve their children from the reach of the Protestant child-placers.[8]

Brace was well aware of Catholic opposition to his work. Frustrated at their growing resistance, he reacted by charging New York's "child problem" directly to the failures of the Catholic church. He elided poor Catholics and the "dangerous classes of New York City" and complained of the difficulties entailed in his efforts to rescue the children of the "Romanist" poor. Claiming that ninety-nine hundredths of the wretched denizens of the alleys and holes of the city were Catholics, he charged that these "lowest poor of New York" were not properly cared for by the Catholic clergy. The latter spent their resources instead for handsome churches. "As one looks at the moral condition of the Roman Catholic poor, one can only sigh that that once powerful body has lost so much of the inspiration of Christ which once filled it," he lamented. He noted "the chilling formalism of the ignorant Roman Catholic" and believed that "[the] very inner ideas of our spiritual life of free love towards God, true repentance and trust in a Divine Redeemer, seemed wanting in their minds."[9] The alleged indifference of the church to its own poor became the warrant for the CAS's child-removal agenda.

Brace's full-length treatment of *The Dangerous Classes of New York* appeared in 1872, the year after the forces of reform had removed the notorious Tweed Ring from power in New York City. In the elections of 1868, Tammany Hall had added the statehouse to its list of offices, and Tammany boss William Marcy Tweed got himself elected state senator. The Tammany cohort in Albany quickly demonstrated its ability to tap the state treasury to supply funds for the city's charities. Tweed welcomed the political returns that charitable largess brought to Tammany. Although he declared himself to be "nothing" in religion, Tweed was very aware of the rising numbers of Catholic voters, and his extensive program of public aid to private institutions included generous funding for Catholics.[10]

As Tammany reestablished itself after the fall of the Tweed Ring, Catholic institutions continued to benefit from a close relationship between the archdiocese and the Hall. The Catholic church in New York was led after the Civil War by Cardinal John McCloskey, who replaced Archbishop Hughes in 1865. McCloskey's genial nature greatly softened the belligerent separatism of his autocratic predecessor, and his loose oversight of Catholic caring institutions gave them room to develop their own policies. The picture became even brighter in 1872, when McCloskey's friend John Kelly became Tammany's first Irish-Catholic boss.[11] Taking control in the aftermath of the Tweed Ring scandals, Kelly began a tradition of Catholic leadership in Tammany that continued until the New Deal. His childhood was like that of many of New York's poor children. His father died when he was eight years old and his mother was left to raise seven children alone in New York's lower East side. Kelly became a street-smart gangleader and a gifted organizer. He was a reasonably good platform speaker, polished enough to raise funds for charity by lecturing on such subjects as the Sisters of Charity and the early Jesuit missionaries to America.[12]

Kelly could also be stubborn and vindictive. His bitter quarrels with Democrats Samuel J. Tilden and Grover Cleveland became legendary in New York politics. In addition to his stint in the United States Congress (1856–1858), his public offices included terms as city alderman, New York County sheriff, and comptroller of New York City (1877–1880). Widowed in 1866, he judiciously removed himself from the mayoral campaign of 1868 and spent three years in Europe while William Tweed ruled New York Democracy. When he returned to the city in 1872, Kelly was relatively free of the taint of Tweed and ready to join the lawyers, businessmen, and financiers who took up the cause of Tammany reform. He imposed a new discipline on the Hall, developed a superb organization in the wards and precincts, recaptured the statehouse with Tilden in 1876, and in 1880 backed the election of the first Catholic mayor of New York, the wealthy shipping magnate, William R. Grace.

Although politics remained his primary concern, Kelly also developed an absorbing interest in the Catholic church. He was drawn to the company of priests and maintained a close connection with New York's ecclesiastical leaders. Accompanied on his three-year sojourn abroad by the vicar-general of the archdiocese, William Quinn, he became deeply involved in the romance of the Catholic tradition. And when he married again in 1878, his new bride was McCloskey's niece, Theresa Mullin; the wedding took place in the cardinal's private chapel. Kelly also made sure that the city was well-represented at the dedication of St. Patrick's Cathedral in 1879, Protestant critics notwithstanding.

The dedication of the new cathedral coincided with two other significant expressions of Catholic strength. Both reflected the importance of children's charities. One was the funeral of a notable Protestant charity worker who had taken an active interest in Catholic work. The other was an internal audit of public financing for Catholic charities. At ceremonies marking the death of Mary Townsend Connolly in April 1879, mourners recalled her many charitable interests and her well-known ability to supply those interests with "liberal appropriations" from the city treasury. A floral arrangement at the head of her coffin acknowledged Mrs. Connolly's special generosity to the New York Foundling Asylum. The tribute was presented by Foundling Asylum director Sister Mary Irene Fitzgibbon, whose asylum was already one of the largest child-caring enterprises in the city.[13] Sister Irene and her coworker Sister Teresa Vincent McCrystal were members of the religious community of the

Sisters of Charity, founded by New York convert Elizabeth Seton in 1813. After the Civil War, the Catholic female religious communities of New York experienced dramatic growth as their program proved attractive to thousands of young first- and second-generation immigrants. The majority of these orders were dedicated to some combination of educational and social welfare and represented an immense resource for poor Catholics of New York.[14]

The religious sisters frequently relied on the help of both Catholic and non-Catholic women outside the convent walls to support their welfare work. The Unitarian Mary Connolly and her daughter Mary Hutchings had helped the Sisters of Charity form the Foundling Asylum Society to tap the private and public resources of New York. "Sister, we must get an appropriation from the Legislature," Mary Hutchings wrote to Sister Irene, "and I believe I can safely promise you one this winter. I speak with confidence, as I already have the promise of one or two of the most influential Senators to that effect." Her mother seconded the idea and told Sister Irene that "Mr. Connolly [her husband] and I have been talking over the matter tonight, and we feel that you must have an *Institution*. The Legislature must be applied to for assistance, and as, no doubt you have many friends there, you will be successful."[15]

The Connolly women spoke with special authority on the matter of public revenues. Richard Barrett Connolly was a Tweed Ring insider who served as the Comptroller of the City of New York. Tammany's success in the state legislature that season gave the Connollys every reason to encourage the Sisters of Charity. On December 15, 1870, with approval from the state legislature, the Common Council of New York approved a ninety-nine-year lease of a tract of land that formed a full city block between Lexington and Third Avenues and Sixty-eighth and Sixty-ninth Streets. The rent was fixed at one dollar a year, and the Council supplied a cash appropriation of $100,000 for the building fund.[16] Sister Irene and her female coworkers drafted a men's building committee from among the husbands and sons of the women of the Foundling Asylum Society, and by November 1873 the massive new building on Sixty-eighth and Lexington was ready for occupancy.[17]

Mrs. Connolly was also gratefully remembered by the Board of Trustees of the Roman Catholic Orphan Asylum, which had benefited from her help in gaining appropriations from the City Council and the city's excise fund. Sponsored in 1817 by the Roman Catholic Benevolent Society and staffed by the Sisters of Charity, the Orphan Asylum was the oldest Catholic charitable institution in the city. After struggling to survive on private donations for nearly two decades, the Orphan Asylum began to receive a modest city stipend of $500 a year in 1834, and in

1846 the Common Council leased the Asylum managers a large tract of land lying between Fifth and Madison Avenues and Fifty-first and Fifty-second Streets for the nominal fee of one dollar a year. With the combined resources of church collections and public appropriations, the Orphan Asylum began a building program on the site that continued through the rest of the century and sheltered thousands of children before it ceased operations in 1918.[18]

Like most children in New York's institutions, the RCOA children were generally not "true orphans." As many as 80 percent of them had one or both parents, who for a variety of reasons sought the help of the child-caring services provided by Catholic religious orders. Unlike other large Catholic institutions, however, the RCOA did not receive a per capita payment from the city for its children, and by 1879 the RCOA's Committee on Admissions began to send children to other Catholic institutions where they could draw per capita funds for their maintenance.[19]

The largest of these "per capita" institutions for Catholic children was the New York Catholic Protectory, and its trustees were also present at the Connolly memorial service. The Protectory occupied 144 acres in Westchester County and was intended to shelter both destitute and delinquent boys and girls.[20] In 1865 the legislature approved a grant of $50,000 for the Protectory building fund, and the Society for Destitute Catholic Children raised an additional $100,000 at a fair in the spring of 1867. The city subsequently provided the Protectory a per capita allowance of $110 a year. By 1879 it had received something in excess of two million dollars from the public treasury and had provided care and training for more than 10,000 children, most of whom had been assigned there by the city magistrates on vagrancy and nuisance charges.[21] In the 1880s the population of the Protectory rose to over 2,000 inmates each year, and by 1900 there were 3,100 children a year under the care of the Society for Destitute Catholic Children.

In the early years, the Society's lay membership provided extensive support for the Protectory in both time and resources, serving as trustees and managers of the institution.[22] They worked with the religious communities who had internal responsibility for the institution. On the boys' side of the institution, the Christian Brothers created an extensive industrial training school, with a print shop and shoemaking, cabinet-making, chair caning, and box-making departments. The girls, under the care of the Sisters of Charity, were also given industrial and some commercial training. The income from their combined efforts was an important source of revenue for the institution.[23]

The second indicator of the growth of Catholic child-caring institutions in the spring of 1879 came in the form of a financial review of the emerging system. The report was galvanized by a scathing indictment of Catholic ambitions that appeared under the guise of an architectural review of St. Patrick's Cathedral. New York Catholics were outraged when art critic Clarence Chatham Cook wrote off their prized new building as an "unmitigated sham" and were further infuriated when Cook charged that the cathedral stood on land that church leaders had taken from the city by underhanded means.[24] "The city was jockeyed out of the finest site on the island by a crafty and unscrupulous priest [Archbishop John Hughes], playing upon the political hopes and fears of as base a lot of men [Tammany Democrats] as ever got the government of a great city into their power," Cook wrote. He noted that "for the consideration of one dollar," Archbishop Hughes had obtained the deed for the huge parcel of land "in the heart of the most fashionable part of the city," including the entire area bounded west and east by Fifth Avenue and Madison Avenue, and south and north by Fiftieth Street and Fifty-first Street.

Cook's allegations were deliberately misleading. The land in question belonged to the Roman Catholic Orphan Asylum and not to the cathedral. (City records showed that the land on which the cathedral was built had come into Catholic hands through private sale at the end of the eighteenth century.) Cook's accusations inspired Catholic journalist John R. G. Hassard to publish an extensive review of the record of public investments in Catholic child-caring institutions.[25] Hassard insisted that the custom of providing land and financial support to private charitable societies dated to the early part of the century and showed that the participation of Protestant societies in the public treasury far outdistanced that of Catholics until the 1870s. He reviewed the histories of the three Catholic institutions that had benefited from sizable grants of land: the Roman Catholic Orphan Asylum and the Foundling Asylum (both managed by the Sisters of Charity) and the St. Joseph's Industrial Home, where the Sisters of Mercy provided industrial training for girls. The latter had been built on city land on Madison Avenue and Eighty-first Street. Sixteen non-Catholic asylums had also received land grants in desirable areas of midtown Manhattan, but Hassard acknowledged that the Catholic sites were generally much larger than those granted to non-Catholic organizations.

Hassard also reviewed the substantial record of public revenues paid to Catholic institutions. He pointed out that many prominent non-Catholic New Yorkers supported the policy of public support for private child-caring institutions as a practical solution to the needs of its citizens. The system relieved the state of responsibility for the direct care of children and provided them with the necessary religious and moral training in institutions of their own faith at a cost that was demonstrably less than that of the public institutions already in place.

In the Catholic case, the argument from economy was enhanced by the clear evidence of the savings to the state resulting from the fact that the religious caregivers worked virtually for free. The managers of Catholic institutions allotted only a small sum each year for the support of the sisters, who received no salary. The maintenance paid the Christian Brothers was considerably higher than that for the sisters but still well below the level of salaried employees. Moreover the public money received by Catholic institutions did not begin to cover construction and maintenance costs, and the per capita received from the city for the children did not cover their expenses.[26] The city of New York was receiving the added benefit of private contributions to Catholic charity of both finances and personal services.

According to Hassard's careful calculation, the three "great charities" of the Catholic church—the Roman Catholic Orphan Asylum, the Foundling Asylum, and the Protectory—had received more than 3.5 million dollars in public funds by 1879. In gross receipts this sum nearly equaled the 3.6 million dollars paid to the three largest Protestant (quasi-public) institutions—the House of Refuge, the Juvenile Asylum, and The Nursery and Child's Hospital at Lexington and Fifty-first Streets. He argued that the Catholic institutions housed a much larger population than their counterparts and that the city thus received far more for its money from those institutions.

Hassard also charged that the public moneys received by Protestant institutions frequently went to societies who were using charity "as an auxiliary to the work of proselytism." He insisted that Protestant child-saving societies were in the business of "child-stealing" and that they used public money "to build up one creed at the expense of another."[27] Two Protestant child-placing associations—the Children's Aid Association and the American Female Guardian Society—had received more than 1.3 million dollars in public funds.

The level of public support for Catholic child-care that John Hassard disclosed in 1879 increased even more dramatically over the next three decades. It was fed by the effects of a new state law, the so-called Children's Law of 1875, and by the activities of a new child-saving group, the Society for the Prevention of Cruelty to Children (SPCC), whose agents preferred to commit dependent and delinquent children to Catholic institutions rather than to the western child-placing program of the Children's Aid Society. The Children's Law was the work of reformers who served as volunteer citizen-commissioners for the State Board of

Charities (SBC). Established in 1867, the Board was composed of commissioners from each judicial district. Its duties included the inspection of all charitable institutions receiving public moneys. From the beginning the Board established the custom of maintaining the regular presence of a Catholic commissioner who assumed informal oversight for Catholic institutions.[28]

In 1874 SBC Vice President William Pryor Letchworth made an extensive inspection tour of all state and county almshouses in the state to review the situation of children who were still being housed in these facilities. The following year Letchworth surveyed the public child-caring institutions of New York and then undertook an extensive survey of all children's institutions and agencies, public and private, in the entire state. As a result of his efforts, the state legislature passed the Children's Law in 1875. In its final form, the law prohibited the placement of children over the age of two in the public poorhouses and required the removal of those already in such facilities. The bill also stipulated that all needy children in the state must be placed in institutions "governed or controlled by officers or persons of the same religious faith as the parents of such child, as far as practicable."[29]

Commissioner Letchworth's legendary labors provided a detailed map of the state of social provision for children in New York in 1874–1876, and the Children's Law that resulted from his work set the course of the New York system of child-care for the next fifty years. Letchworth and his reform-minded colleagues preferred to think of child-caring institutions as a transitional stage between the child's own home and a proper foster placement. They did not imagine the magnitude of the institutional growth triggered by the Children's Law. The "religious clause" stipulating that all children committed to private institutions should be placed according to their parents' religion quickly defeated any hope of placing the majority of dependent children in private family homes. There simply were not enough Catholic families in a position to care for the thousands of children who needed help. The legal guarantee of public per capita support for Catholic child-caring institutions after 1875 sustained an accelerated growth rate in the numbers of children sheltered in these facilities and an increase in the number of institutions themselves through the first decade of the twentieth century. Using public funds and ongoing private support, Catholic institutions offered poor parents both interim and long-term care for their children. The fact that most of the children were returned to their parents on request also meant that the institutions tended to support long-term family integrity and provided some protection for parental rights.

The rapid growth of Catholic child-caring institutions under the New

York system after the passage of the Children's Law appalled New York's Protestant child-savers. Two figures dominated efforts to reform the New York system. Josephine Shaw Lowell's name became virtually synonymous with those efforts. Lowell opposed both the rising numbers of children in institutions and the practice of public "outdoor" poor relief. She led efforts to curb the influence of private child-caring institutions and encouraged the development of a network of volunteer friendly visitors under the auspices of the Charity Organization Society of New York. Lowell was also the first woman to be appointed a commissioner of the State Board of Charities. From the date of her appointment in 1876, she exercised a strong influence on the board and on its president, William Rhinelander Stewart, who came to share her view that the "institutional child" produced in the New York system was simply unprepared for responsible citizenship in a democracy.

The second leading opponent of the New York system was Homer Folks. Folks represented the first and perhaps best-known of the new professional workers who began to join volunteers like Letchworth, Lowell, and Brace in opposition to the New York system in the 1890s. These new workers generally had university credentials and career experience and were determined to bring a new "scientific" approach to bear on the problems of public social provision. With the cooperation of the New York Protestant elite, they formed a "charities trust" and drew heavily on the resources of the large new philanthropic foundations to support their child-saving and welfare agendas. Homer Folks arrived in New York City from the Children's Aid Society of Philadelphia in 1893 to become the secretary of the private State Charities Aid Association and made an immediate impact by throwing his efforts into Josephine Shaw Lowell's campaign against public funding for private child-caring institutions. He contributed heavily to the efforts of reformers to undo that system during the New York State Constitutional Convention in 1894 and subsequently mounted a successful attack against the so-called Destitute Mothers' bill (1897), which proposed to supply public pensions for mothers to enable them to keep their children out of institutions and in their own homes.

As the child-removal program of Charles Loring Brace had spurred Catholics to greater efforts to keep their needy children in the city, so the well-publicized agenda of the child-savers of the 1880s and 1890s captured the attention of middle-class Catholics, whose sense of religious and civic obligation pushed them forward into the public debate. Most of the Catholic men who volunteered as trustees of the Catholic institutions were members of the Catholic laymen's Society of St. Vincent de Paul. Founded in France in 1833, the "Vincentians" acted as home visitors, supplying both material relief and personal support for the poor in their parishes. The New York City Council of the Society was founded in 1848. Vincentians accepted the traditional Catholic understanding that the practice of charity was a form of meritorious service necessary to the salvation of their own souls. They believed that the "help" of charity was always mutual. Persons who were better-off supplied material necessities and words of advice and encouragement to the poor. In return the poor were expected to pray for their benefactors, thereby helping to redeem the souls of the prosperous along with their own.

The New York Vincentians were also up-and-coming citizens, and their charitable work anchored their determination to take a place in respectable society as business advisers, trustees, and men of affairs. Many of them had connections to New York politics, especially through Tammany Hall. Tammany figured largely in the success of many of these men, and the Society of St. Vincent de Paul offered a method for sharing that success.[30] In addition to parish relief work, the New York Vincentians visited Catholics who were confined in the city's institutions on Blackwell's and Randall's Islands and acted as trustees and patrons for the Roman Catholic Orphan Asylum, the New York Catholic Protectory, and the New York Foundling Asylum. The Vincentians also supported a child-caring project of their own—a large orphan asylum on Staten Island called the Mission of the Immaculate Virgin. This operation began in 1870 as the St. Vincent de Paul Home for Newsboys, a shelter modeled after the highly publicized Newsboys Lodging House run by the Children's Aid Society. The Home and its subsequent expansion on Staten Island were run by the popular New York priest Father John C. Drumgoole with Vincentian oversight. The Staten Island orphanage sheltered more than one thousand children by 1880 and received city per capita payments for each one. The crowded conditions and the lack of adequate programs at the Mission made it an ongoing target for reformers and a centerpiece in the 1916 battle over the New York system.

The undisputed leader of the New York Vincentians after 1890 was Thomas Maurice Mulry. Like most Irish-Catholic New Yorkers of the period, Mulry's background was immigrant and working class. His father and uncles arrived from Ireland in the 1840s and earned their way as "cellar-diggers," or construction workers. The senior Mulry acquired his own business, and in 1868 the firm of Thomas Mulry & Son built the foundations for the new Tammany headquarters on Fourteenth Street. Thomas M. Mulry came into the business at the age of seventeen. His father introduced him at the same time to the Society of St. Vincent de Paul in their home parish of St. Bernard's. A successful businessman and banker, the younger Mulry devoted extensive time and personal resources to Vincentian work. In the mid-1880s he was the president of his parish council and the secretary of the central or Superior Council of New York. He ultimately held office as city, regional, and national president in the organization and was widely regarded as the "voice" of Catholic charities in New York between 1895 and 1915.[31]

In a precedent-breaking move in the 1890s, Mulry began to participate in the reform activities sponsored by non-Catholic charities leaders. He was not the first New York Catholic to reach out to prominent non-Catholics, of course. Catholics of the city had entertained non-Catholics in fraternal and political gatherings on regular occasions since the Civil War. Vincentians John Crimmins and Morgan O'Brien welcomed Henry Ward Beecher, Joseph Choate, and Theodore Roosevelt, for instance, to the annual Friendly Sons of St. Patrick's dinners. On those occasions the focus stayed on common business and political interests. Religious and caste differences were temporarily set aside.

Mulry's initiatives featured a different dimension. Although he was vice president of Friendly Sons and enjoyed the camaraderie of their annual dinners, he also joined non-Catholic charitable and welfare organizations in order to assure a Catholic presence in the Protestant-dominated forums where social policy on poor families and children was being shaped by the city's charity leaders. Mulry intended to support the work of reform, but he also saw the opportunity to publicize Catholic efforts and to defend Catholic institutions.

Because he recognized its growing influence on social provision and was eager to insure a Catholic voice in its deliberations, Thomas Mulry joined Josephine Shaw Lowell's Charity Organization Society as a representative of the St. Vincent de Paul Society in 1891. Four years later he became the chairman of the Fourth District Committee (Gramercy) of the COS. Mulry shared Lowell's belief that the poor would be better served if charity were better organized and if providers found more ways to cooperate, and he remained a faithful member of the Central Council of New York's COS until his death in 1916.[32]

Mulry, however, persistently opposed Lowell's views on child-caring. She campaigned extensively against the New York system of child-caring institutions, thought it a "grave error" to provide public money for the support of dependents in private institutions, and was convinced that the New York system encouraged the managers of institutions to constantly increase the number of inmates "since a larger number can be proportionally more cheaply supported than a small number, and consequently a direct pecuniary gain follows upon the increased size of these institutions."[33] As the pattern of public support for private charities continued and the Catholic portion of those funds increased, Lowell's objections drew growing support from a number of interested parties, and Mulry found himself holding highly contested ground in his defense of Catholic institutions.

Catholic laywomen also continued to contribute their time and resources to children's provision in New York. Although most of their efforts were institution-specific like those of the Foundling Asylum Society, in 1902 Catholic women established a citywide federation of volunteers called the Association of Catholic Charities of New York.[34] The new organization was led by Teresa O'Donohue. She was a member of the O'Donohue family whose presence in New York Democratic politics and New York Catholic charities went back to the Tweed years. Her father, Joseph O'Donohue, a successful coffee and tea merchant, was originally a member of the Brooklyn Democratic machine. Like Thomas Mulry, Teresa and her mother were early and faithful members of Josephine Shaw Lowell's Charity Organization Society. The Association under the leadership of the O'Donohues attracted more than three thousand members by World War I and supported an impressive number of initiatives for children in infant and children's institutions, day care and foster care programs, and "girl work." The success of the women's Association of Catholic Charities ultimately provided the model that archdiocesan officials would borrow when they reorganized the Catholic charities of New York in the wake of the charities wars of 1916.

Although they worked willingly with New York's non-Catholic welfare organizations, the O'Donohue women and their coworkers were motivated by incentives that differed dramatically from those of Progressive reformers. Like the Vincentians and most other Catholics of their day, the O'Donohues hoped to realize a spiritual gain from their work. The highest spiritual incentive was the disinterested love of God, and many volunteers strove to realize this lofty purpose. But Catholic tradition also encouraged service to the poor on a more self-interested basis. The works of mercy opened the church's treasury of grace, and Teresa O'Donohue eagerly sought to bring that spiritual capital to the membership of the Association of Catholic Charities. Merits available to the Association included an array of indulgences granted by the Vatican and, as O'Donohue noted proudly, "This has been a great stimulus in the field of charity, as all members work with so much more zeal when they realize that all their deeds are bringing interest in the future Savings Bank of Charity and will be recorded on the last day." Among the incentives were plenary indulgences for joining and attending monthly meetings, and an indulgence at the hour of death (which was also available to all financial benefactors of the Association). There were also indulgences for each home visit or good work and for assisting at funeral masses.[35] Josephine

Shaw Lowell would have found herself in a strange land had duty required that she attend an Association of Catholic Charities meeting in return for the faithful contributions of the O'Donohues to her Charity Organization Society.

While reformers developed their programs of child provision and battled over principle, the deaths of Boss John Kelly and his friend Cardinal John McCloskey in 1886 brought new leadership to Tammany and to the Catholic church in New York. The new archbishop, Michael A. Corrigan, who served from 1886 to 1902, chose a more rigorist approach to ecclesiastical administration than had McCloskey. After Roman training and prior experience as the bishop of Newark, Corrigan became part of the inner circle of archdiocesan leadership in 1880 when the Vatican named him as McCloskey's coadjutor and designated successor. Corrigan became immediately involved in administration of the archdiocese, tightening episcopal control over the clergy and standardizing ecclesiastical practices in the diocese; and his incumbency was marred by strenuous battles with his diocesan priests and episcopal colleagues.[36] Although Corrigan cultivated the support of wealthy Tammany Catholics like John Crimmins, Frederic Coudert, and Bourke Cochran, party affiliation was not the overriding factor in his associations with the laity. Convert George P. Bliss, a Republican of impeccable patrician ancestry, was Corrigan's friend and legal adviser.

Boss Kelly's successor was Richard Croker, whose tenure as Tammany chief coincided almost exactly with Michael Corrigan's term as archbishop of New York. But in contrast to McCloskey and Kelly, the two new leaders of the Church and the Hall did not become friends. Corrigan's "sweet, almost feminine temperament" could not abide association with the rougher elements of New York politics.[37] Richard Croker, born of poor Irish-Protestant stock, had developed a serious reputation as a violent street fighter before Tweed Ring insider Richard Connelly sponsored him to a clerk's position in the municipal system and made him a city alderman in 1868. Croker subsequently managed to ingratiate himself with John Kelly, not least by marrying a Catholic and joining the church. As Kelly's lieutenant, he learned to curb his temper and develop his political skills. When he retired from Tammany in 1902, he cultivated his taste for high living with a castle in Ireland and a stable of racehorses.

In spite of their differences, however, Corrigan and Croker had common interests in the New York system. Their working relationship began immediately after they took the leadership of their respective organizations and made common cause during the election of 1886 when the candidacy of Henry George and the rebellion of the popular New York priest Edward McGlynn threatened both Tammany and the Catholic chancery. George's Workingmen's Party and single-tax plan captured the attention of New York's working class and the fervent support of the normally Republican McGlynn. The prolabor policies of the Workingmen's Party and the outspoken oratory of McGlynn caused both Tammany and the New York hierarchy to hear "the echo of tumbrels rolling over cobblestones," especially in the aftermath of Chicago's Haymarket Riot.[38]

Corrigan feared McGlynn because of the priest's political views and because his popularity challenged Corrigan's leadership. McGlynn attacked the church's role in the New York system of child-care and questioned the importance of New York's Catholic charitable institutions. He was convinced that they retarded the quest for justice among the laboring classes and that they improperly provided Tammany with Catholic support. "You may go on forever with hospitals and orphan asylums and St. Vincent de Paul Societies, but with them you can't cure the trouble," McGlynn insisted.[39]

The Hall welcomed Corrigan's help in defeating Henry George. In reply to an inquiry from Tammany's Committee on Resolutions, Corrigan's vicar-general, Thomas Preston, wrote, "I can state with confidence that the great majority of the Catholic clergy in this City are opposed to the candidacy of Mr. George. They think his principles unsound and unsafe and contrary to the teachings of the Church. . . I think there is no question as to the position of the Catholic clergy, and although we never interfere directly in elections, we would not wish to be misunderstood at a time when the best interests of society may be in danger."[40] Tammany was grateful for the disclaimer and published it widely during the campaign. The poor, they believed, belonged to the church and the Hall and not to radicals like George.[41]

Tammany's gratitude for the assistance of the Catholic chancery did not go unremarked by critics. The ghost of the 1886 campaign was resurrected by the New York press in 1894, when city papers renewed the charge that Corrigan had been influenced by Tammany Catholics in his actions toward the charismatic Edward McGlynn. The New York *World* named prominent lawyers Frederic Coudert, John D. Crimmins, and George Bliss, Judge Joseph Daley, banker Eugene Kelly, and businessman Joseph O'Donohue.[42] With the exception of Bliss, these men were indeed Democrats. They were also longtime supporters of Catholic child-caring institutions, and in the summer of 1894, those institutions were again the center of political controversy, this time at the New York State Constitutional Convention. In a memorable bipartisan effort led by Coudert and Bliss, institution supporters blocked the plans of reformers to remove public funding from private providers by constitutional amendment.

The charities issue in 1894 was tightly bound to the question of state aid for elementary education. From the time of their foundation in the 1840s, the public schools of New York had been a lightning rod for both Protestant and Catholic fears. The public schools had been nurtured by the privately controlled Public School Society, and Catholic leaders denounced the unfairness of the system which, so they argued, promoted Protestant goals with Catholic taxes. Had Archbishop Hughes succeeded in the 1840s in gaining similar support for schools sponsored by Catholics, the state's elementary educational system would have mirrored the New York system of provision for dependent children.

Unable to force the state legislature to accede to his wishes, Hughes had made the controversial decision to build a complete parochial school system with private funding, and his successors continued the program he had launched. New York's Catholics thus faced a double levy, taxed to pay for the public schools and tithed again to finance a separate Catholic system. Catholic pastors also felt the weight of Hughes' decision and understood that preference and promotion would depend on their success in supporting his initiative. Both the laity and the pastors responded, however, and by the end of the century approximately 80,000 children were enrolled in parochial schools.

In spite of this commitment to private revenues, Catholic success in garnering public financing for children's institutions prompted church leaders to continue efforts to win public funding for their schools.[43] Their efforts aggravated the suspicions many of their fellow citizens already held toward Roman Catholics. In the tough economic times of the early 1890s, these fears erupted in a campaign against the receipt of public revenues by sectarian institutions. The National League for the Protection of American Institutions (NLPAI) led the effort, which was designed to end public support for all Catholic institutions. Founded in Saratoga, New York, in 1889, NLPAI sought "to secure constitutional and legislative safeguards for the protection of the common-school and other American Institutions . . . and to prevent all sectarian or denominational appropriations of public funds."[44] Its particular animus against Catholics was evident in its effort to establish litmus tests for candidates for public office and its opposition to Catholic efforts to gain pastoral access to penal institutions under New York's "Freedom of Worship" law. NLPAI's chief goal, however, was to pass prohibitions against parochial aid by amending state constitutions across the country. New York was clearly first on its list of concerns. When state Republicans engineered a Constitutional Convention in 1894, NLPAI was there to testify against the Catholic menace and to demand a constitutional amendment prohibiting aid to all "sectarian institutions."[45]

Sectarian child-caring institutions were targeted along with parochial schools, and the NLPAI amendment found ample support from city reformers who were determined to back an amendment that would halt the explosive growth of Catholic child-caring institutions. Two committees were established to deal with the issues: the Committee on Education, chaired by Republican delegate and NLPAI representative Frederick W. Holls; and the Committee on Charities, chaired by another Republican, New York Jewish leader Edward Lauterbach.[46] The two committees met in joint session to hear critics and defenders of Catholic institutions. The Rev. James M. King of the Methodist Episcopal Church of New York led the testimony for NLPAI and its supporters; Democrat Frederic Coudert and Republican George Bliss responded for Catholic interests. They were joined in defense of the New York system by Myer Stern, a representative of New York's Jewish charities, and by the powerful founder of the Society for the Prevention of Cruelty to Children, Elbridge Gerry.

Under the combined leadership of Coudert, Bliss, Gerry, and Lauterbach, a compromise was arranged that reaffirmed the status quo—no public aid for parochial schools and no constitutional prohibition against public aid for charities. The notable bipartisan support for the compromise testified to the strength of the New York system, which continued to be regarded as both economically and politically prudent. Catholic leaders yielded for the moment to claims that funding for parochial schools was an impermissible violation of the separation of church and state. But they insisted that poor citizens had a legitimate claim on public resources and that successful child-nurture was possible only with the help of religion. Frederic Coudert and George Bliss convinced the majority of delegates that the state must meet its obligations by continuing to pay for the child-caring work of the churches.

The Constitutional Convention did inaugurate changes that would become significant in the landscape of child-care, however. In an effort to eliminate the confusions and inconsistencies in the state's charitable laws, the convention enacted a constitutional provision affirming the State Board of Charities' oversight responsibilities for charitable institutions.[47] The SBC employed a new staff of salaried inspectors to visit institutions on a routine basis—a far cry from the time twenty years earlier when William Letchworth toiled away at his own expense on behalf of the State Board.

The SBC's responsibilities included the entire range of administrative procedures and rehabilitative care in the institutions. Catholic institutions had long been accused of taking applicants without inquiring too deeply into their circumstances, of simply submitting lists of names to the city for payment in lieu of a full institutional accounting, and of failing to discharge children in a timely fashion. The volunteer commissioners of the SBC had not been an effective check on the system. Now the Board had a new constitutional mandate to correct these alleged abuses. Salaried SBC agents were to investigate applicants for admission and judge whether they qualified for public support. They had the power to assess the sanitary and dietary conditions of institutions and to establish requirements for elementary and industrial education. And the Board could back up its demands by recommending withdrawal of public moneys from institutions that did not comply with its standards.[48]

On the face of it, these provisions seemed a victory for the forces of reform. The reality, however, was more mixed. In the first place, the scope of the SBC's new responsibilities was so extensive that even with the best will and the most dedicated agents, the task was overwhelming. And even if an adequate bureaucracy were in place, two other aspects of the new State Board authority dampened the victory. First, the original draft of the amendment explicitly stipulated that the Board had the power to cover both public and private institutions, but in the negotiations over the issue, this clause was quietly dropped. Second, Catholics continued to develop their influence as volunteer and salaried agents of the public and semipublic supervisory agencies. The realities of New York politics made this development more or less inevitable. The citizen-volunteers who had acted as commissioners of the SBC since its inception in 1865 were appointed by the governor. The governor, who appointed one commissioner for each judicial district, was guided by the rule of balanced membership. Commissioners were appointed to represent both political parties and the three religious constituencies with a large investment in charitable institutions, namely Protestants, Catholics, and Jews. New York City Democrats, therefore, continued to insure that the First Judicial District was represented on the State Board of Charities by someone who held the interests of Catholic child-caring institutions close to his heart. In addition, Catholics were represented in growing numbers among the salaried agents of city charities, and their loyalties lay with the institutions and the religious sisters who staffed them.[49]

Catholic institutional growth was also sustained by the activities of the semipublic Society for the Prevention of Cruelty to Children (SPCC). The Society had been incorporated in 1875, the same year that saw the passage of the Children's Law. The SPCC's president from 1879 to 1900 was Elbridge Gerry, a wealthy Protestant attorney. He was also a Democrat and longtime friend of Tammany. Gerry supported the principle of religiously based institutional placements for children in need, and by the time he testified at the Constitutional Convention on behalf of private child-caring institutions, his name was synonymous with his organization. The Gerry Society's paid agents attended the proceedings of the Magistrates' Courts and investigated cases of destitution and delinquency involving children, and they had police powers to reinforce their work. The Society's advice on the disposition of dependent and delinquent children became the informal law in the city's lower courts until the establishment of the Juvenile Court in 1903.[50]

The SPCC drew the wrath of Josephine Shaw Lowell and her supporters, who recognized that the Gerry Society had become a major element in the growth of the New York system. Lowell regularly complained that public officials had virtually lost control of children to the agents of SPCC and to the institutions, and her colleague Homer Folks estimated that by 1890 the Society controlled the lives of more than fifteen thousand children a year and consequently controlled the distribution of the one-and-one-half million dollars in public money that went to their support in the institutions. Folks agreed with Lowell that the SPCC was a "feeder" for the child-caring institutions and that it created a most serious obstacle to his campaign for foster care. In 1900, for instance, the Society had placed six children in private homes. During the same period, 2,407 children were placed in institutions on its recommendation. Folks lamented the "general failure" of the Society to urge the benefits of adoption. He also opposed an early form of mothers' pension legislation, the Destitute Mothers bill, which was scheduled to be administered through the Gerry Society. Submitted in the state legislature by Senator John F. Ahern in 1897, the bill would have empowered the SPCC to supervise the return of institutionalized children to their mothers and to approve the stipends awarded to the mothers by the city comptroller. Folks argued that the Ahern Bill gave the Gerry Society too much power and engineered its veto in New York City.[51]

In the wake of the 1894 Constitutional Convention, the State Board of Charities made an attempt to establish its authority over the SPCC, and the SPCC retaliated in 1898 with a lawsuit against the SBC. The Society argued that it was not included in the constitutional amendment granting the Board supervisory powers over child-caring institutions and therefore should not be subject to review by the SBC. Although the SPCC was aware that the reality of Board supervision was much weaker than its constitutional empowerment suggested, Elbridge Gerry believed that any degree of Board authority over SPCC work would threaten the Society's authority. The case was reviewed by the state Supreme Court, by the Appellate Division of the Supreme Court, and ultimately by the Court of Appeals. The Court of Appeals, in a highly controversial decision, reversed the judgment of the Appellate Court and supported the SPCC's claim that it was not subject to the jurisdiction of the State Board.

The 4–3 decision of the Court of Appeals was delivered by the Catholic Tammany Democrat, Justice Morgan J. O'Brien.[52] The SPCC, whose actions effectively controlled millions of dollars of public money, was thereby released by the Court from SBC supervision and remained free to continue to "feed" the Catholic institutions.[53]

Meanwhile city officials joined the private agents of the SPCC in supporting Catholic charitable institutions. In 1897 the voters of New York approved plans for the consolidation of the metropolitan area. Effective January 1, 1898, Greater New York encompassed nearly one hundred new municipalities, including Brooklyn and the Bronx. This enlarged setting greatly increased the importance of the new City Comptroller, Bird S. Coler. Coler was a banker who had come into New York politics through the Brooklyn Democratic machine, where he had supported consolidation against considerable Brooklyn opposition.[54] Now a Tammany man, Coler assumed responsibility for the financing and management of city contracts and budgetary oversight for New York charities. His influence as budget officer for the city's charities was greatly enhanced by the successful battle for "home rule" in Albany, where the state legislature had followed a time-honored practice of appropriating charity subventions from city treasuries.

In 1899 Tammany engineered the passage of the "Stranahan bill" in Albany. The bill removed the power of the charities' purse from the state legislature and placed it exclusively with the city's own budgetary authority, the Board of Estimate, of which Coler was a leading member. This "home rule" legislation greatly strengthened the city's role in the oversight of child-caring institutions in Greater New York.[55] Comptroller Coler's approach to the issue of subsidies for private charities acquired enlarged significance in this context.

Coler's first official report on the financial health of Greater New York included an adroit assessment of "municipal subsidies to private charities." He appeared to support the arguments of Josephine Shaw Lowell and her colleagues by calling for reform of the New York system. Echoing the chief criticisms of the reformers—that subsidies encouraged the practice of institutionalizing children, that large institutions were often detrimental to children, and that the private system made public supervision difficult at best—Coler abolished all lump-sum subsidies to private institutions from the city treasury and replaced them with per capita payments. He also proposed uniform standards for admissions and for practice in private institutions receiving public dollars.[56]

But the city was not at all interested in dismantling the New York system, and Coler remained skeptical of the agenda of reformers. He was also profuse in his praise for the religious caregivers in the institutions.

"It is not likely that public employees could be obtained who would rear children as economically, as efficaciously or with the same devotion and self-denial as is the case with religious orders and associations now performing this work, in many respects so successfully." Neither the supervisory powers of the state nor home rule in Greater New York would seriously interfere with established Catholic child-caring practices in New York at the turn of the century.[57]

Reformers did not give up their campaign to overturn the system, however. When Seth Low's Fusion campaign turned Tammany out of City Hall in 1901, they had a chance to make a more direct assault. In the face of concentrated pressure from the anti-institutional forces, Mayor Low chose Homer Folks as his City Commissioner of Charities.[58] For the next two years, Folks attempted to install measures that would give public officials more control of institutional admissions and practices. His chief effort went toward the creation of a separate city Bureau of Dependent Children, a move that Josephine Shaw Lowell had been advocating for nearly two decades. The office employed hundreds of agents and inspectors to reevaluate per capita commitments each year. Folks' goal was to document the status of each child under care in order to reduce the institutional population and lower public costs for child-care. Folks was able to show a clear decline in the institutional population in the non-Catholic New York Juvenile Asylum over the term of his office, and he claimed to have broken the power of the Society for the Prevention of Cruelty to Children over child-placement in New York City. But he was not successful in lowering the population in Catholic child-caring institutions, and he did not fundamentally alter the character of the New York system itself.[59]

Seth Low was defeated for reelection in 1903 by George B. McClellan, and the comptroller's office returned to Democratic control. A battle against foster care was soon initiated in that office under the new Catholic comptroller, Herman Metz. The child-removal program of the Children's Aid Society had provided the basis for an ideological alternative to institutional care, and the entire cluster of societies and agencies opposed to the institutions favored instead the idea of foster care in private homes. As with institutional placements, the law required that foster care be provided in homes that reflected the religion of the parents "where practicable." But in contrast to the institutional situation, this requirement did not result in huge public subsidies for Catholic work. Part of the reason for the difference was the simple difficulty in finding homes for large numbers of needy children among the Catholics of New York, but the foster care alternative was also impeded in Catholic circles by the popularity of the institutions and of the religious sisters who staffed them. Parents and the courts overwhelmingly preferred the institutional setting for the children who needed care.

Aware of the place held by foster care on the reform agenda, Comptroller Metz specifically targeted a program that had been initiated by Josephine Shaw Lowell and Homer Folks. In 1898 Homer Folks' State Charities Aid Association and the Association for Improving the Condition of the Poor established a Joint Committee on the Care of Motherless Infants to develop a model for the boarding-out of dependent babies. The Joint Committee directed its efforts toward high-risk infants in the public institutions on Randall's Island and developed a set of standards to improve the chances for their survival. Under committee rules no family could accept more than one infant, each placement was the subject of regular visitation by committee agents, and each boarding home was inspected and licensed by the New York City Department of Health. The city continued to pay the cost of boarding the children.[60]

Their project was designed not only to save foundlings at the city's nursery on Randall's Island but also to demonstrate the superiority of child-placing over the system of institutional care for dependent children. In 1905, however, the Tammany-controlled administration declared the Joint Committee illegal because it was not properly chartered and incorporated; the comptroller's office announced that it would withdraw city funding from the project. When Homer Folks countered by having the duly incorporated State Charities Aid Association take complete responsibility for the work of the Joint Committee, Comptroller Metz insisted the SCAA had improperly incorporated for the work of placing foundlings. Metz also characterized Folks' placement program as "professional philanthropy in its . . . most reckless form" and alleged that the Joint Committee was an unsavory organization that operated through "a hired female clerk, with a basket in her arm, peddling a live baby around the city." Institutions for children, the comptroller believed, were vastly preferable to the foster program of the SCAA.[61]

The attack on the Joint Committee was managed by Herman Metz's assistant, Daniel C. Potter. An ordained Baptist minister, Potter was Chief Examiner of Accounts of Charitable Institutions in the comptroller's office from 1904 to 1910. His politics and his child-caring preferences were consistently Democratic and institutional. Potter argued that the city got far better value for its investment from the institutions, especially because they guaranteed that the children in their care would be trained in religion. He scoffed at the idea that private institutions were "waxing fat on public funds." Trustees and directors, he pointed out, were always "passing the hat among themselves" to meet the needs of their institutions.[62] Potter praised the Catholic sisters abundantly, extolling their willingness "to wear themselves out in caring for the uncared." Their leaders were "women of rare executive ability" whose years of experience in child work gave them a great advantage. "I have found them everywhere alert for improvement," Potter stated, "and ready, within conservative lines, to experiment for betterment and progress . . . in the twenty-three Catholic children's asylums, hospitals and homes in this city."[63] Potter's involvement with the Catholic institutions and their managers continued formally and informally until his death in the aftermath of the charities investigation of 1916.

Meanwhile, the contest over poor children inevitably drew Thomas Mulry and Homer Folks together. The two met in the heat of the battle at the Constitutional Convention in 1894, and both men participated in the activities of the New York City Conference of Charities, sponsored jointly by the COS and the Association for Improving the Condition of the Poor. They continued to develop a relationship as members of the National Conference of Charities and Corrections and during Mulry's service from 1900 to 1907 on the State Charities Aid Association's Central Commission.[64] Mulry and Folks also participated in founding the New York State Conference of Charities and Corrections in 1900, and in 1909 both men served as conveners and vice presidents of the White House Conference on the Care of Dependent Children.

Although they shared a conviction about the importance of cooperation across religious and ethnic lines in the work of charity, the relationship between Folks and Mulry was increasingly impaired by their differences over the value of the New York system of child-caring. With Josephine Shaw Lowell, Folks argued that institutions were deeply harmful to children. Like Charles Loring Brace before him, Folks did not believe that most poor parents were best-suited to raise their own children, and he insistently promoted the cause of placing children in foster homes.

He also championed the role of the state in the care of children and was especially eager to see the State Board of Charities actively extend its constitutionally mandated powers of supervision to include the private as well as public charities.[65] Though a Republican, Folks did not entirely equate "the state" with the state legislature at Albany. Republican control of the state legislature was certainly a consistent feature of New York politics until World War I, and Republican power in Albany could frequently override the agendas of Tammany in New York City. But there was a reciprocity in politics as there was in charity. Tammany sage George Washington Plunkitt put the matter succinctly: "When Tammany's on top I do good turns for the Republicans. When they're on top they don't forget me."[66]

The informal understanding between Republican and Democratic bosses drove Folks to join independent reform movements in order to assist "the state" to realize its potential as an agent of human welfare. He helped form the Citizen's Union in 1897 and became a prominent member of the City Club, where he associated with other citizens interested in reform. His position with the State Charities Aid Association also allowed him to become "the leading evangelist among those preaching the gospel of placing- and boarding-out" of children.[67] Each of these gestures contained overt and implied criticisms of Catholic child-caring practices and put him at odds with his colleague Thomas Mulry and the other Catholic leaders of the city.[68]

Mulry did acknowledge that there was some merit in the arguments of Folks and Lowell in favor of child-placing, and in 1898 he marshalled the resources of the Society of St. Vincent de Paul and organized the Catholic Home Bureau to find foster placements for needy and orphaned Catholic children. Mulry was president of the Bureau's Board of Managers for the first eight years of its existence. The organization of the Catholic Home Bureau reflected Mulry's conclusions in his 1899 report on the care of destitute children for the National Conference of Charities and Correction. On behalf of the committee, he offered a carefully phrased endorsement of good foster homes when the child's circumstances warranted it. Religion headed Mulry's list of desirable traits, and "good homes" therefore meant Catholic homes for the great majority of New York's destitute children. Knowing that it was impossible to find homes in the number needed, Mulry reemphasized the importance of child-caring institutions for that large majority of children who could not be successfully placed. And he cautioned child-placers about the dangers of leaving children in homes without adequate supervision.[69]

Mulry's 1899 report was hailed as a landmark in the politics of child-saving. Reformers applauded the fact that Mulry, a Catholic, seemed to endorse the goals of the opponents of the child-caring institutions. The reality was more complicated. The Catholic Home Bureau placed fewer than three hundred children a year, whereas the major Catholic institutions for children in the city continued to shelter more than 20,000. Child-placing efforts by non-Catholic agencies continued to be frustrated by Catholic demands for religiously based placements. And although Mulry was sincere in his belief that "the home is the natural place to properly develop the child," he cautioned against the assumptions of Folks and the other child-placers. He especially liked to tell a tale about a man suffering from "institution-phobia," who wanted to close every institution and board out every child. "He lies awake at night," Mulry teased, "his mind filled with dreadful pictures of institution life. When he sleeps, he dreams of the institution walk, of the institution look and he talks at all times of the piece of machinery, in the shape of a human being, which the institution turns out."[70] Mulry and his Catholic colleagues believed that the reformers were deliberately creating a boogeyman called the "institutional child" to swing public opinion away from the benefits of the New York system.

The reformers' proposal to board children out for pay drew special criticism from Catholics. In addition to the potentially mercenary motives of caregivers and the insuperable obstacles in the way of proper state supervision, Thomas Mulry raised the question of the rights of the children and their parents. "Suppose it were possible to place all such children in homes, have the children no rights? What is the State? Is it not an aggregation of families bound together for mutual protection? I say the State has no right to exercise such sweeping powers."[71]

He was convinced that Catholic institutional care gave families a better deal. The religious sisters and brothers provided discipline and education for truant children until they were ready to be restored to their homes as good citizens. They sheltered destitute children until their families were again in a position to support them. And the fundamentals of their religion were there to make the task possible. Though he deplored the poverty that made institutions necessary, Mulry found no reason to "stand idly by, waiting for the millennium, when there will be no further need of them."[72]

Thomas Mulry remained an effective champion of Catholic child-care and an influential participant in the charities and corrections network of New York City and in the state. In 1907 Governor Charles Evans Hughes appointed him to the State Board of Charities as Commissioner for the Eastern Judicial District. His position on the SBC gave him even broader responsibility and influence in public and private welfare institutions in Greater New York, and he remained on the Board until his sudden death during the wrenching charities investigations of 1916. In the meantime his national stature was acknowledged when he became president of the National Conference of Charities and Correction in 1907 and convener and vice president of the White House Conference on the Care of Dependent Children in 1909. In 1910 he brought the fruit of his experience with Progressive reformers to bear as a founder of the National Conference of Catholic Charities.

In 1910 New York's anti-institutionalists also gained an important new foothold in the city's politics of charity. Their agent was a Catholic attorney with longtime family connections to Tammany, John Purroy Mitchel. Although the mayor's office remained in Democratic hands in the municipal elections of that year, reformers under the Fusion banner won key victories. Chief among them was the election of Mitchel as president of the Board of Aldermen—the elected officials who represented the boroughs of Greater New York. Mitchel was no newcomer to New York politics. As a young investigator in the office of the city's corporation counsel during the second McClellan administration, Mitchel had earned the praise of reformers when he caused Manhattan borough President John F. Ahern to be dismissed on charges of incompetence. Mitchel also lodged similar charges against the borough presidents of the Bronx, Queens, and Brooklyn, although he did not succeed in removing them from office. A defiantly anti-Tammany Catholic, Mitchel worked to disable the machine permanently.[73] He gained a seat on the powerful Board of Estimate in 1908 and used the position to promote business efficiency and professional expertise in city administration.

Soon after his election as Board of Aldermen president in 1910, Mitchel was in the thick of the fight of the reformers to challenge the system of support for child-caring institutions. With Mitchel on the Fusion ticket was longtime Republican and Catholic William A. Prendergast, who won the newly elective position of city comptroller. The two Fusionists immediately began to review the records of the comptroller's office, seeking to prove that there had been collusion between Catholic institutions and Tammany comptrollers during the two McClellan administrations (1903–1909). The Chief Examiner of Charitable Accounts, Daniel Potter, inadvertently provided the Fusionists with an excuse to widen their investigation.

In 1907 some of Potter's Catholic friends had decided to pay him a tribute to honor his contribution to their institutions, and Monsignor Dennis McMahon, the director of Catholic charities in Manhattan, suggested that the institutional managers make contributions to a purse for the Chief Examiner. A disgruntled employee later provided a stolen check voucher as evidence that McMahon received $500 for the Potter purse from the St. Vincent de Paul's Mission of the Immaculate Virgin on Staten Island, forcing McMahon to issue a sworn affidavit denying that he gave the money to Potter. The charities director claimed that he simply rolled the donation into his own discretionary fund and used it for Catholic institutions.

McMahon's protest notwithstanding, Mitchel and Prendergast used the check voucher to suggest the presence of widespread graft and collusion between the city and the institutions and arranged to have the city's Board of Estimate launch an investigation. When the Board sent agents into the charitable institutions of the city armed with letters demanding access to the books of the institutions, Catholics indignantly pointed out that inspectors from the comptroller's office already had

access to their institutional books under the rules established by Comptroller Coler ten years earlier. But the investigators were not content
merely to see that public per capita payments matched the numbers of
children committed by the city to the institution. They were determined
to uncover evidence showing that, with the collusion of city agents, the
Catholic sisterhoods made a profit on the children, taking more children
than they could care for in order to boost the income of their communities. They demanded to see the private accounts of the religious congregations as well as their public books.[74]

The institutional managers and their supporters protested strenuously,
and the ensuing uproar prompted officials of the archdiocese to spend
$83,000 for a professional accounting firm to review records of the
Catholic child-caring institutions for the years 1906–1909. The firm of
Patterson, Teale, and Dennis declared that it could find no evidence of
misuse of public funds.[75] Archdiocesan officials and the comptroller's
office then worked out a compromise. City investigations were halted,
the archdiocese agreed to adopt a more rigorous process of accounting,
and the comptroller's office increased its staff of auditors to improve its
budgetary oversight of the institutions.

The compromise did not heal the antagonism between the supporters
and the critics of the New York system. Instead the entire episode left
suspicion and a bitter taste in the mouths of Catholics and reinforced the
determination of the reformers to challenge the institutions. They soon
had a chance to do just that. In 1913 John Purroy Mitchel ran for mayor
on the Fusion ticket. Supported by some of the most powerful Protestants
and Jews in the city, he had defeated the candidate of Tammany Hall,
and his victory led a sweep of city offices. The opponents of the New
York system were in position to launch a full-blown review of the
charitable institutions of the city.

Mitchel appointed as his Commissioner of Charities the former assistant secretary of the State Charities Aid Association, John Adams Kingsbury. The new commissioner was determined to institute more effective
city supervision of charitable institutions, both public and private. Not
content with the 1910 agreement to improve accounting processes and
budgetary oversight, Kingsbury wanted to set standards of administration and care in the institutions and to develop the city's capacity to inspect and enforce those standards. His goal was to replicate under city
authority the mandates of the State Board of Charities. In contrast to the
loose oversight of the SBC, however, reformers led by the Commissioner
of Charities would be in charge of setting city standards and enforcing
city requirements.

Kingsbury's plans were abetted by his former boss, the secretary of the

State Charities Aid Association, Homer Folks. Associated with them were reformers whose names were linked with the most powerful non-Catholic charity organizations in the city. These included Edward T. Devine, who had replaced Josephine Shaw Lowell as president of the Charity Organization Society and who was also dean of the New York School of Philanthropy; Fulton Cutting, who was president of the Association for Improving the Condition of the Poor (Kingsbury had also worked as Cutting's assistant); and attorney Robert W. de Forest, who exercised a large influence over the agenda of the Russell Sage Foundation.[76] The Sage Foundation provided major revenues for these charity organizations, and their interlocking boards of directors formed the "charities trust" of New York City. Their views on the care of dependent and delinquent children were a potent ingredient in the New York City charities, and they weighed heavily in the institutional standards adopted by city officials during the Mitchel administration.

Armed with proposals for child-care reform and backed by these powerful interests, John Kingsbury launched another review of the city's private child-caring institutions during 1914–1915. His lieutenant in these investigations was his Catholic deputy commissioner, William J. Doherty. Doherty was the former secretary of the Catholic Home Bureau and a protégé of Thomas M. Mulry. Like Kingsbury, Doherty had lived in an orphanage. Placed by his widowed mother, he had spent most of his boyhood in St. John's Home in Brooklyn under the care of the Sisters of St. Joseph. Already resentful because the sisters at St. John's had not provided him with the college education they offered to other bright boys (they claimed his health was too poor), Doherty's antagonism to the New York system grew during his tenure at the Catholic Home Bureau when he realized that the managers of child-caring institutions were deliberately blocking his efforts to place dependent children in private homes. In the heat of the 1916 battles, his old mentor from St. John's openly claimed "That the Sisters of various institutions foiled him [Doherty] on many occasions is to their credit."[77] Their resistance and his own ambitions led Doherty to embrace the anti-institutional agenda of the reformers. The combination of Catholic background and reform ideology made him an ideal lieutenant for Commissioner Kingsbury.

Kingsbury instructed his new deputy to inspect thirty-eight of the private institutions to which the city committed dependent children. Doherty was assisted by a committee of three private citizens, one representing each of the three religious denominations in child-caring work. Ralph Reeder, the Superintendent of the New York Juvenile Asylum, represented Protestants, and Ludwig Bernstein, director of the Hebrew Sheltering Guardian Society, was the Jewish member. The third institutional voice was Christian Brother Barnabas McDonald, director of the New York Catholic Protectory's new cottage-style agricultural village at Lincolndale. Kingsbury authorized the four-man committee to set standards, to make inspection tours to see if those standards were being met, and to send in paid agents to supervise the follow-up.

Doherty and his committee cited twenty-four private institutions for failure to meet the standards they had established. Twelve of these were run by Catholic women.[78] Charges against the deficient institutions ranged from head lice to child labor. In publishing their findings, the city investigators picked another fight with the State Board of Charities by deliberately breaking with the long-standing policy of the Board to avoid harmful publicity about institutions if the latter were actively working with the Board to correct their deficiencies. Commissioner Kingsbury's 1914 publicly issued annual report graphically detailed the failings identified by his committee: "beds alive with vermin," antiquated methods of discipline and punishment, and institutions that "educated the children in little more than religious matters."[79]

William Doherty also carried the report to a national audience at the annual meeting of the National Conference of Charities and Corrections in the spring of 1915. In a paper later published by the Department of Child-Helping of the Russell Sage Foundation, Doherty added the State Board of Charities to his list of deficiencies in the New York system, along with institutional managers and corrupt former municipal administrations. In his view the SBC had not kept abreast of "the modern acceptation of what is adequate institutional care of dependent children." Painting his own efforts in glowing terms, he concluded that "[p]roper social vision of the welfare of dependent children . . . gradually is replacing the gloom and haze of dreary decades of barren institutionalism."[80]

Commissioner Kingsbury's 1914 annual report concluded by charging that SBC inspectors were either incompetent or in collusion with the institutions. They "had apparently gone through their inspection[s] with both eyes closed or with one auspicious and one drooping eye," he wrote. Following the publication of these charges, the Mitchel administration and State Charities Aid Association secretary Homer Folks urged Republican Governor Charles Whitman to establish a state commission to investigate the State Board of Charities. Whitman complied with the pressure from Kingsbury and Folks, and in November 1915 appointed New York insider and City Club President Charles H. Strong to investigate Kingsbury's charges against both the private institutions and the SBC.[81] The Strong Commission heard testimony during the winter and spring of 1916. Although non-Catholic institutions were also charged, the most sensational allegations centered around Catholic work. William

Doherty singled out a favorite target of the reformers. At the Mission of the Immaculate Virgin on Staten Island, he claimed, his inspectors saw soup served in greasy pails by unwashed boys and lapped up by many children who used no spoons. The pigs in the yard were fed the scraps from those same greasy pails. In the MIV lavatories, according to Doherty, two hundred boys shared one toothbrush and one piece of soap. In another Catholic institution, St. Joseph's Home for Girls in Manhattan, other inspectors testified that they observed girls kept at work for long hours in the institutional laundry, while St. Joseph's gave its children unclean bedclothes and rusty silverware. They also cited the asylum of the Dominican Sisters at Blauvelt in Westchester County for failure to provide adequate medical supervision and dental care.[82]

The testimony against the institutions was intended to reflect badly on the SBC, which had granted annual certificates of approval to the institutions under attack. Although stormy rebuttals from institution supporters challenged the validity of Doherty's standards and the accuracy of his reports, Doherty and Kingsbury injected a new dimension into the case against the State Board of Charities. Both testified that leading members of the SBC had improperly attempted to interfere with their work. They charged SBC Commissioner Thomas M. Mulry and Board secretary Robert W. Hebberd with pressuring Deputy Commissioner Doherty to "go easy on the sisters" and to consider conducting the investigation by himself without the presence of other inspectors.[83] Witnesses also accused Mulry and Hebberd of contacting prominent Jewish leaders in order to have the Jewish representative Ludwig Bernstein removed from Doherty's committee and of successfully pressuring the Christian Brothers to assign Brother Barnabas McDonald to a post in upstate New York where he would not be available to participate in the ongoing investigation.

Perceiving these charges to be a full-scale attack on the New York system, Catholic supporters of the system soon retaliated. In mid-February a Brooklyn priest named William B. Farrell, whose mother was Thomas Mulry's godmother, signed an open letter to Governor Whitman characterizing the Strong investigation as a "public scandal."[84] The charges contained in the Farrell pamphlet were incendiary. It suggested that the Strong Commission hearings were part of a conspiracy against the Catholic church and its supporters on the State Board of Charities orchestrated by Homer Folks, "an open and ardent enemy of the State Board of Charities," and by COS President Edward Devine. Devine in fact had earlier charged that the New York system originated with "a well organized Catholic interest, whose power and influence with the public officials is such that they dare not deny them anything," and John Kingsbury made the impolitic admission that he had deliberately selected William

Doherty "because he was a Catholic and might be able to cope with the opposition of the Catholic Church."[85]

Convincing evidence was later offered at the Strong hearings that Father Farrell did not write this broadside and its equally aggressive sequels by himself. Associated with him in the effort were Daniel C. Potter, State Board of Charities Secretary Robert Hebberd, Thomas Mulry, and the chancellor of the archdiocese of New York, Monsignor John J. Dunn.[86] Dunn arranged for the distribution of 700,000 copies of the first pamphlet from the steps of all Catholic churches of New York. Backing Dunn was the auxiliary bishop of New York, Patrick J. Hayes, who would succeed Cardinal John Farley to the see in 1918 and make his own reputation as "the cardinal of charities." Subsequent Farrell pamphlets responded to specific Kingsbury charges, defending the institutions and the sisters who ran them, even as they accused Deputy Commissioner William Doherty and Mayor John Mitchel of disloyalty to the church.

Immediately after the first Farrell pamphlet was issued in February 1916, there was a counterattack from the anti-institutionalists, who published an unsigned twenty-four-page booklet featuring a collection of eye-popping reproductions of newspaper headlines and editorial excerpts from the New York press. This pamphlet was assembled by a single agent, the public relations man for Homer Folks' State Charities Aid Association, Edward A. Moree. The costs of the publication were covered by John Kingsbury, and the pamphlet was distributed by the State Charities Aid Association. It was designed to create an image of the Dickensian conditions in New York orphanages by massing the press reports of the testimony of Kingsbury and Doherty. The cover of the Moree pamphlet featured a subtly altered version of the original charge against the Mission of the Immaculate Virgin—"ORPHANS AND PIGS FED FROM THE SAME BOWL!" Inside were comments from the *New York Evening Post,* the *New York Herald,* the *Brooklyn Times,* and most of the upstate dailies. The *New York Times,* which had battled the New York system for years, called Doherty's revelations "shocking, almost incredible." "Worse than anything in 'Oliver Twist'," echoed the *New York World.* Randolph Hearst's *New York American* featured cartoons depicting the beneficiaries of New York charity as porcine adult males, gathered around ample victuals at an institutional high table, while the ranks of skeletal orphans arrayed around them stared at bowls of meager gruel. "The orphaned poor get for their care and support what PENNIES are left when a swarm of grafters have divided the DOLLARS," the Hearst daily sermonized.[87] The identity of these "charity officials" was left deliberately ambiguous. The cartoon characters could be politicians, clerics, or institutional trustees like Thomas Mulry.

The editors of the Jesuit weekly, *America,* soon entered the pamphlet wars to take up the defense of Catholic charities for children. They solicited comments from State Board of Charities Secretary Robert Hebberd, who sustained the charge that the main forces behind the investigations were "the representatives of the State Charities Aid Association and some of their immediate allies." Hebberd's remarks revealed that there had been trouble between himself and Homer Folks for at least a decade. Brooklyn Catholic Charities Director Monsignor James J. Higgins also wrote for *America,* accusing Charles Strong of allowing unsupported allegations against Catholic institutions to run unchecked in the hearings and in the press. He too denounced the Strong Commission for its "sinister allied interests"—the SCAA, the Russell Sage Foundation, the Charity Organization Society, and the City Club. Jesuit editor Richard H. Tierney reviewed the role of Homer Folks in the appointment of Charles Strong and argued that Kingsbury's comments on the Mission of the Immaculate Virgin were based on hearsay and libelously inaccurate. He also forcefully condemned John Purroy Mitchel's role in the affair.[88]

The attacks on Mayor Mitchel led to a further sensation when the Farrell group found themselves charged with conspiracy to disrupt the Strong Commission hearings. Evidence for the charge came from highly controversial telephone wiretaps. With the approval of Mayor Mitchel, city police listened in on conversations between Monsignor Dunn, Father Farrell, Daniel Potter, and Robert Hebberd. The wiretaps became public knowledge when city counsel William H. Hotchkiss used the transcribed conversations to interrogate witnesses at the Strong hearings.[89]

The wiretapping caper was poor political judgment on Mitchel's part. Confronted with hundreds of thousands of Farrell pamphlets and the growing indignation of New York Catholics, Mitchel grew enraged and authorized the wiretapping in an attempt to prove that the archdiocese was illegally attempting to subvert the official business of city and state. Between March 18 and March 28, 1916, city police listened to more than one hundred telephone conversations among Farrell, Dunn, Hebberd, and Potter. These were indeed filled with bitter recriminations against Strong and the "charities trust." The transcripts from the wiretaps also made it plain that the collaborators were very anxious to send one of their number, Daniel Potter, away from New York and out of the reach of the investigation before he was called to testify.

Aware of the contents of the transcripts, Commissioner Kingsbury publicly condemned Potter in an address to the International Child Welfare League. Although Kingsbury had himself played a central role in the publication of the notorious Moree pamphlet, the personal attacks and sensational charges of conspiracy and anti-Catholicism in the Farrell broadsides infuriated him. The charities commissioner complained that he had been the subject of constant harassment ever since joining the Mitchel administration and implied that his enemies came from Tammany Hall and the Catholic church. Specifically he charged that Tammany had instigated a grand jury investigation of his Department of Public Charities in retaliation for his investigation of the children's institutions. "We [indicating city counsel William Hotchkiss who was present in the audience] subpoenaed the secretary of that grand jury the other day and confirmed our suspicions that Dr. D. C. Potter had been before that grand jury telling them what to do," Kingsbury told his audience. He alleged that Potter and SBC secretary Robert Hebberd colluded to influence the grand jury against his office and concluded by characterizing Potter as "one of the most despicable individuals in this community."[90]

One member of the Farrell group did not live to hear of the wiretaps. On March 10, shortly before he was scheduled to testify before the Strong Commission on charges that he had illegally interfered with William Doherty's investigation of the children's institutions, Thomas M. Mulry collapsed in his home. He died the next day, after being ministered to by Cardinal Farley himself and by four of his own sons who were priests. His unexpected death was a huge blow to the supporters of Catholic institutions in New York. In Brooklyn where Mulry's godmother, Mrs. William Farrell, wept at the news, her son again took up his pen. The "heart-breaking tragedy" of Mulry's death was brought on, Father Farrell charged, by the proceedings of the Strong Commission. Farrell alleged that Mulry had been secretly followed by city investigators in the weeks before his death. "He was simply sinking from the shameless attacks on his motives and honor [and] these wounds were made by a creature of his bounty [William Doherty]. . ."[91]

Although Mulry's death was the most shocking loss, the "charities wars" also levied other serious costs. Robert Hebberd resigned his position as secretary of the State Board of Charities as grand jury indictments for conspiracy were handed down against Potter, Dunn, Farrell, and himself. Felony charges were also lodged against Kingsbury and his counsel, William Hotchkiss, for instigating the wiretapping. By the time the Strong Commission brought its investigation to a conclusion in May, the large dailies had turned strongly against John "Paulpry" Mitchel, accusing him of abusing the powers of his office and violating the Constitution of the United States by authorizing the wiretaps. Mitchel completely lost control of himself in a public hearing, shouting out portions of the incriminating evidence gathered from the suspect wiretaps over the objections of commissioners conducting the hearing. He justified his wiretapping by charging it was necessary to prove the Catholic church guilty of an attempt to seize control of the city government.[92]

The charges against both sides were ultimately dismissed by the courts for lack of evidence. Daniel Potter died suddenly in August, two months before Commissioner Strong issued his final report on the affair. After all the fireworks, Strong's conclusions were notably conservative. Pronouncing the New York system so deeply entrenched that there was no practical way to eliminate it, he offered his own review of the controversy. In 1916 New York City cared for nearly one-third of the 110,000 dependent children in private institutions in the country. Of the 25,397 children receiving public aid in private institutions in the city, 15,912 were Catholic, 5,794 were Protestant, and 3,691 were Jewish. Private institutions in the city also cared for approximately 5,000 other children who were not supported by public funds. Strong estimated that the cost of public aid to children in the state of New York was $100 million a year, of which more than $60 million was spent in New York City.[93]

Strong rejected Kingsbury's depiction of child-caring institutions as "unfit for human habitation" but conceded that at least seven institutions were "a scandal and a public disgrace," citing their lack of industrial training and adequate recreation; the indescribable conditions of their toilets; the long hours of hard labor endured, especially by girls in institutional kitchens and laundries; poor mortality rates in at least one asylum for infants; and antiquated forms of discipline. The report also censured the State Board of Charities for its gradualist approach to the enforcement of its requirements. It failed to issue certificates of noncompliance and permitted faults and serious failings "to remain unattended for years" in the institutions subject to its inspection. Strong recommended that the State Board be completely reorganized, replacing the voluntary commissioners with a paid board of professionals.[94]

The charities wars subsided in the fall of 1916 as New Yorkers turned their attention increasingly to the war in Europe and to the issue of American "preparedness." But one year later John Mitchel paid the price. The mayoral campaign in the fall of 1917 placed Mitchel in a bitter contest for reelection against Democratic, Republican, and Socialist candidates. Condemned by many Catholics and derided by poor voters as a tool of the privileged classes, Mitchel turned to national security issues as the cornerstone of his campaign and ran against "Hearst, Hylan, and the Hohenzollerns." He also suggested, however, that he meant to defeat "Murphy, Cohalan, O'Leary, and all the Tammany brood. . ." He further antagonized working-class voters by charging that state senate leader Robert F. Wagner was "working more in the interests of Prussia than of the United States" and by sending police to break up demonstrations of

Irish nationalists on the streets of New York.[95] There were ample reasons for his failure, therefore, when he received only 23.2 percent of the vote in the November election. But his spectacular mishandling of the potent issues of charity and child-care in New York was the major ingredient in his fall.

The 1916 battle over children's institutions also had major repercussions for New York Catholic charities. The ease with which the anti-institutional forces were able to stir up Dickensian images in the public imagination made an enduring impression on New York's Catholics and heightened their determination to defend their own interests. The leadership privately admitted, however, that the outcry did not arise entirely from misguided prejudice. Catholic child-caring institutions were overcrowded and underequipped, and their inability to meet new public standards created a serious handicap for the church in the contest over the character and direction of social provision in the city. After World War I, therefore, archdiocesan leaders launched a massive internal reorganization of Catholic charities that brought the hitherto independent institutions and the hundreds of smaller charitable initiatives under the direct control of the archbishop and his agents. Professional social workers were employed to revise institutional practices and to offer home services to needy families with an eye toward lowering the institutional population. The newly centralized operation was financed by a new annual citywide Catholic Charities campaign, created by professional fund-raisers and modeled after the successful wartime drives. The size of the archdiocese and the scope of the centralization program in New York guaranteed that it would exercise a notable influence on the development of social provision, both Catholic and public, around the country in the next two decades.

The Larger Landscape

The struggles over child-care in New York were a bellwether for Catholic charities agencies in the first decades of the twentieth century, as public surveys and annual reports confirmed that Catholics continued to be heavily overrepresented on the relief rolls and in the correctional institutions of American cities. While older Irish and German enclaves began to migrate from the cities to the suburbs, new populations of Catholics from southern and eastern Europe changed urban demographics and demanded new forms of pastoral care. These population shifts frequently left downtown parishes with only meager means for assisting the newcomers and exacerbated the already existing imbalance between Catholic needs and Catholic resources. Catholic charities leaders were acutely aware of the growing influence of non-Catholic welfare agents and programs and of rising demands for new standards of "scientific" social provision in caring for these new poor. Professional social work, the increased regulatory authority of city and state boards of charity, and the very real clout of charity organization societies and community chest initiatives prompted them to cautiously experiment with new forms of organization and practice.

Structural reform led the list of Catholic responses. Consolidation of independent local initiatives under diocesan control and the development of modernized diocesan bureaus of charity were the dominant concerns of charities leaders between 1900 and 1930. Diocesan bishops began to tighten their organizations and establish new controls over many of the "secular" aspects of church practice.[1] Local pastors and institutional managers whose predecessors had enjoyed a considerable degree of independence in the nineteenth century became subject to new regulations and forms of accountability, and the lay volunteers who had taken the first steps toward creating central charities offices in the early years of the century were displaced by a new clerical leadership.

The bishops were especially eager to extend their control over church finances—which in most dioceses had been left to the discretion of individual parishes and institutions and were in many cases in a state of chaos—and to consolidate the charities of the dioceses under their direct supervision. They redesigned their legal relationships with parishes and institutions, introduced modern management practices, and more closely regulated financial affairs in their dioceses. These steps were deemed necessary both to defend Catholic interests and to meet the needs of dependent and delinquent Catholics. This marriage of church welfare and poor welfare paid dividends. By World War II, all of the major urban dioceses had centralized their welfare services and established new forms of fiscal and professional accountability. Most dioceses had also become active participants in the formation of local and state welfare policy and had insured revenue streams for Catholic charities from community chests and public welfare funds.[2]

The pace of consolidation varied according to local conditions, but the pattern was basically the same in each diocese. The bishop announced plans to bring all work under his direct supervision and appointed a priest to act as the executive director of charities. The priest-director opened a new central charities office (and branch offices in smaller cities of the dioceses), hired staff, and laid plans for coordinating the delivery of services in his diocese. With the help of lay financial advisers, the local bishop and his charities director also centralized the charities budget and consolidated fund-raising efforts.

The new clergy-directors of charity were faced with the tricky task of establishing their authority over the traditionally independent institutions and agencies of social provision in each diocese without alienating the volunteers who had created and managed these activities. When the institutions were operated by religious communities, the bishop and his agents could rely on ecclesiastical command, although the degree of authority exercised over individual orders varied with their canonical status. But the laity were not strictly required to donate their time and money to the social work of the diocese, and although bishops persuaded leading laymen to contribute financial expertise in campaign drives and recruited women to manage the canvassing, many of the traditional volunteers simply walked away from the process of consolidation and professionalization of charities and left the work to the new "central bureau." Sporadic efforts were made to win back the volunteers, but the record indicates that although Catholic social provision gained efficiency and financial stability in the process of consolidation, the very important asset of collective volunteer participation was severely damaged.[3]

The detail provided by individual dioceses lends texture to the general landscape as Catholic social provision underwent these significant changes. In all dioceses child-care anchored the Catholic program. Each diocese followed its own particular path from child work to other initiatives, including foster care programs, family casework, health and housing initiatives, and elder care.[4] And in each diocese, the parochial school system functioned as an important dimension of Catholic social provision and consumed a large portion of the human and financial resources of the diocese.

With 1,400,000 Catholics in more than three hundred parishes and a host of programs and institutions, the Catholic population of New York City was the largest in the country in 1918, and institutions, social services, hospitals, and schools that constituted New York Catholic social provision made it both the flagship and the largest challenge.[5] At the time that auxiliary bishop Patrick Hayes became archbishop of New York in 1919, Catholic charities were still decentralized. Hayes' authority over institutions was limited because they were independent corporations controlled by the private boards of managers and the religious orders that ran them. With the lessons of the charities wars freshly in mind, Hayes immediately engineered a reorganization of charities under a new archdiocesan bureaucracy.

He began his campaign by learning from the enemy. He commissioned his own investigation of all diocesan work, employing the instrument of the social survey, which had been widely adopted by secular reformers since the late nineteenth century and had become a staple of social reform efforts.[6] Comprehensive surveys supplied information on all institutions and relief services and identified the methods, funding sources, personnel, and results obtained by the various organizations. A well-executed survey gave diocesan officials strong leverage in their efforts to advance centralized planning and control.

Patrick Hayes knew that a comprehensive survey could not succeed without the archdiocesan clergy and lay charities leaders. He appeared at the annual retreat of his diocesan priests, informed the nearly one thousand retreatants of his intentions, and instructed them in their duty to cooperate.[7] He also met with superintendents of Catholic charitable agencies and representatives of parish conferences of the Society of St. Vincent de Paul to convey his plans and demand support. Stressing that the surveyors were not on a witch-hunt and that they would be acting as his personal representatives, he expected them to be given a cordial welcome from the institutions and to have every opportunity to observe and to learn.

The New York survey was completed by February 1920, and a carefully edited summary of the findings was released to the press for public relations purposes.[8] The confidential reports covered twenty-six hospitals; three clinics and dispensaries; four sisterhoods devoted to caring for the sick poor in their own homes; twenty institutions (with thirty-two branches) caring for dependent, defective, delinquent, and neglected children; twenty-four day nurseries; three institutions for delinquent girls; five homes for the aged; the Catholic Protective Society; the Society of St. Vincent de Paul; twenty-three women's auxiliaries; and ninety-three unaffiliated agencies.

Predictably the report concluded that the Catholic charities of the New York archdiocese needed better coordination of personnel, resources, and activities. The Society of St. Vincent de Paul, which had long claimed pride of place in New York Catholic social provision, was reported to be lagging. Parish councils of the Society existed in only 117 of 301 New York parishes. In spite of the notable falling-off of volunteer support, the survey could nevertheless claim that the church in New York made an important contribution to the social welfare of the city. In dollar terms the Catholic annual contribution for charity was $4,424,207 in 1919. Catholic agencies also received $2,622,245 in city and state funding during the year, but archdiocesan officials insisted that it was the city which stood in debt to the church for supplying the impressive sum of $4.5 million in personal charitable donations.

The survey paved the way for the installation of a new archdiocesan charities bureaucracy under the direction of the archbishop. Patrick Hayes immediately combined reorganization with an annual fund-raising campaign. He asked the firm of Harvey J. Hill, which had helped New Yorkers raise five million dollars for Catholic war work in 1918, to again supply professional help in planning the fund-raising.[9] Hayes shaped the outline of the charities campaign, insisting that it be based on an effort to recruit thousands of small donors to pledge an annual sum rather than concentrating on big money from the few very wealthy Catholics of the city. He called his fund-raising arm the Archbishop's Committee on the Laity and asked for 25,000 members. The drive for funds began in April 1920 and netted $503,274 from 125 parishes in its first week. In two weeks 16,668 volunteers visited 233,000 prospective donors and brought in $917,219.84.[10]

In May 1920 the office of the newly incorporated Catholic Charities of the Archdiocese of New York (CCNY) opened its doors. It featured separate divisions covering outdoor relief, child-care, health, protective care for delinquents, and social action. CCNY became a huge enterprise whose 212 separate agencies raised and spent millions of dollars in social provision.[11] Its clergy-executives and professional staff worked to establish uniform standards and practices among the institutions and foster programs of the dioceses, urged its component service providers to update their standards and equipment, and funded innovations like a venereal disease clinic in a Good Shepherd Home for delinquent girls and a psychiatric clinic at St. Vincent's Hospital.

In Pittsburgh Bishop Regis Canevin made an early attempt to impose a level of central control over charities in 1914 by appointing a commission of diocesan priests to assume oversight of charitable activities in the diocese. The indifferent results produced by this commission prompted Canevin to attempt a full-scale reorganization in 1919. Like his colleague Patrick Hayes, Canevin commissioned a social survey to support his plans. The Pittsburgh Catholic survey had significant historical precedent. The pioneering "Pittsburgh Survey" of 1909, sponsored by the Russell Sage Foundation, was the "first major attempt to survey in depth the entire life of a single community by team research."[12] Unlike Hayes, however, Bishop Canevin did not require his diocesan priests to take responsibility for the Pittsburgh Catholic survey. It was conducted and paid for by out-of-towners from the National Catholic War Council, the wartime social work organization of the Catholic church. The survey's director was Catholic University sociologist Rev. John O'Grady.

O'Grady began the Pittsburgh diocesan survey in the fall of 1919. In the heavily ethnic city, the surveyors concentrated their efforts on the Catholic children's institutions. Two hundred Catholic children were in foster homes and day nurseries. Two thousand more were cared for in large congregate institutions with independently determined policies and methods. With the help of students from Duquesne University's fledgling School of Social Work, O'Grady's team visited all twenty-seven child-caring institutions and their auxiliary organizations and provided a detailed assessment of Catholic child-care practices.[13]

They delivered the conclusions that Bishop Canevin sought. In their estimation the institutions and agencies of social welfare under Catholic auspices were "not cooperating fully for mutual benefit." They recommended that the entire social service work of the diocese be "carried on as a unit" and stipulated that in all dealings with both Catholic and public agencies, Catholic institutions and charitable associations should submit to central diocesan control.[14] The team provided an organizational chart for the central bureau, which featured a diocesan priest-executive and a professional staff and reduced the laity to an advisory financial role. The suggested bureaucracy strongly resembled that of the archdiocese of New York and included departments for relief, child-care, delinquency, health and hospitals, and social action.[15]

The plans materialized slowly. Regis Canevin died during the year after the survey and was replaced by his chancellor, Rev. Hugh Boyle. By 1921 the diocese could boast a central office of charity, with a paid staff and a sizable relief roll. But a confidential assessment written for Bishop Boyle by assistant bureau director, Rev. Edward J. Misklow, offers a graphic inside view of the sometimes violent prejudices and conflicting ambitions that dogged most efforts to centralize and rationalize Catholic social provision. Misklow was irate over persisting conditions in the bureau, and women bore the brunt of his anger. Likening its female employees to Frankenstein's body parts, Misklow predicted that Pittsburgh's Catholic charities bureau-monster would wreak havoc on the diocese that sponsored it.

Most of the women working in the bureau came from working-class backgrounds, and as Misklow's characterizations revealed, they were both poorly educated and underpaid. They compared unfavorably with their college-educated counterparts in the non-Catholic Children's Service Bureau of Pittsburgh; some had not even completed sixth grade. Their salaries averaged seventy-five dollars a month. Misklow offered particulars, complaining, for instance, that Children's Bureau supervisor Agnes McGary was "very defective." She permitted the placement of children without keeping records of where they were sent. The paperwork was incomplete in part because McGary had only one assistant—"a slow stenographer." Misklow invited Bishop Boyle to "imagine, if you can, two women of such inferior type taking over seven or eight hundred children from Juvenile Court. Imagine this department telling Pastor X what is right in child-placing!" He expressed sympathy for the Pittsburgh clergy: "These deficient women are set up as judges of extremely important problems of life. They dictate to the pastors of our parishes as to when a case of poverty is worthy, or when a children's case is to be solved by placement."[16]

In an obviously self-interested recommendation, Misklow urged Boyle to appoint a new director of charities to bring order to the bureau's "body parts." Supervising the female staff was "a man's work," he argued, and a full-time priest-executive would be required for the task. Misklow, not alone among his caste, believed that "women have not the brains necessary to superintend any big movement, much less one which constantly involves the use of philosophy, theology, and sociology."

Fittingly enough, however, the effective reorganization of Pittsburgh diocesan charities was accomplished only when Catholic social worker Luella Sauer became secretary of the Pittsburgh central bureau in 1931. Sauer came from stints in Catholic charities of Los Angeles and Cincinnati to lead Pittsburgh Catholics through the hardships of the Great Depression. She established the Conference of Catholic Charities of Pittsburgh as a competent provider of social services, and she became a well-known representative of Catholic charities at state and national levels.

In Boston a strong Catholic political presence reinforced the public role of the church after the turn of the century and provided assistance in the process of centralizing Catholic charities. The Catholic Charitable Bureau (CCB) was founded to supervise and coordinate the children's work of the archdiocese, and Catholics were regularly appointed to city and state welfare boards, where they looked after the interests of Catholic children cared for in Massachusetts' institutional and foster care systems. Between 1910 and 1916, Cardinal William O'Connell consolidated all Catholic social provision under the CCB. His control of the work of social provision became a central dimension of his unequivocal rule over all aspects of diocesan life.

In addition to its own internal programs, the CCB became a notable force in shaping welfare policy in Boston. The Boston Irish-Americans clearly remained suspicious of both their Yankee neighbors and the new social welfare measures of the period. Catholic leaders worried that Catholic motives and practices would become contaminated by exposure to secular standards, and they accused "the Harvard crowd" and "half-baked political economists from Harvard" of attempting to control public and private social provision in the city. Responding to Cardinal O'Connell's instructions, the CCB therefore began to establish itself as the defender of Catholic interests, monitoring the activities of private and public agencies in Boston and lobbying for favorable legislation in the state legislature.[17]

By 1921 Catholic charities leaders were willing to applaud the level of public welfare support available to Catholic families. Diocesan director Rev. George P. O'Conor expressed satisfaction with the care of the poor offered by his state's Department of Public Welfare and with the outdoor relief offered by the city of Boston. Tellingly, however, O'Conor still sought independence from non-Catholic influence, noting that when public resources were augmented by the work of the diocesan bureau and local Catholic institutions, Catholic Boston was able to handle its "portion of the adult poverty problem . . . without the necessity of our Catholic people any longer appealing to private or so-called non-sectarian societies for relief."[18]

While Boston's adult Catholic poor gained the advantage of public resources, dependent Catholic children remained a source of concern. Massachusetts law (1905) stipulated that every child had the right to be raised in the religion of his or her parents, but in 1922 George O'Conor still alleged that foster care provision remained the source of substantial "leakage" in the church and blamed the private non-Catholic child-placing agencies such as the Boston Children's Aid Society. He conceded that such agencies were "productive of the public good" and that they generally intended to be fair, but he insisted that the net result of their intervention was a loss of children to church membership. He preferred to deal exclusively with the "public authorities" in Massachusetts, believing they did a better job of "guarding the religious welfare of their charges."[19]

Although Boston's Yankee-Irish polarization was not repeated in more ethnically diverse dioceses around the country, the issues of assimilation presented in Boston were not unusual. The politics of charity in Boston highlights the complex pattern of accommodation and resistance that marked the development of social provision in American Catholic life. All around the country, charities offered Catholics a means of protecting their religious identities and pursuing their civic ambitions. The cause of the poor allowed them to cooperate with non-Catholics when it seemed advantageous and to justify the use of political muscle when it seemed warranted.[20]

When the Brooklyn-born George Mundelein became archbishop of Chicago in 1915, he immediately began the process of reorganizing the diocese. One of the great episcopal "bosses" of the period, Mundelein consolidated social provision and centralized diocesan finances under his own direct supervision.[21] Announcing that he "would rather help save the soul of a kiddie of the street than erect the finest monument in Chicago," Mundelein began to reform administration and systematize fund-raising in his Catholic charities. World War I delayed his efforts, but it also allowed Mundelein to establish himself with the leading men of the city and recruit support for his long-range plans. After experimenting with a lay board at the head of his new Associated Catholic Charities organization, the archbishop returned responsibility for both fund-raising and executive administration to his diocesan priests. His Central Charity Bureau organized adult and family relief, and a new Catholic Home Bureau began to move children out of institutions and into foster care and private adoptions.

Ethnic loyalties influenced the outcome of centralization efforts in Chicago as they did elsewhere. The smaller, nationally identified orphanages of the archdiocese remained essentially outside of Mundelein's control. These institutions were run by Poles and Bohemians and supported with proceeds from ethnic cemeteries and by donations from eastern European Catholics. Their institutional managers believed that the archdiocesan program favored the much larger "Irish" institution, St. Mary's Training School, and they resisted cooperation in diocesan fund-raising and opposed diocesan supervision.[22]

The national crisis of the 1930s also wore down Mundelein's long-standing resistance to citywide federated fund-raising efforts. Like Patrick Hayes, his counterpart in New York, Mundelein kept Catholics out of the United Charities appeals of the 1920s, but by 1930, under the pressure of the second winter of the Depression, he was ready to cooperate. His experience in the federation allowed him to position his diocesan charities agencies to act as a conduit for state funds from the Illinois Emergency Relief Commission and to remain an agent of the state under the New Deal's FERA program.[23]

Mundelein owed his successes to his financial acumen, his ability to adapt, and his willingness to use political pressure. The latter was apparent early in his Chicago term. In 1917 the Cook County Circuit Court ruled against "orphan-support," finding that public support to sectarian institutions violated the state constitution. The archdiocese appealed the decision to the Illinois Supreme Court and won after Mundelein mobilized Catholic opposition. Following the lead of Patrick Hayes, who in the wake of the charities wars of 1916 formed an organization composed of bishops from the six dioceses of his state and hired an Albany lawyer to represent Catholic interests in the legislature, Mundelein organized the Catholic bishops of Illinois and Catholic lay organizations to help him monitor Catholic interests at the 1920 state constitutional convention.[24]

In his political maneuvering, Mundelein sought the help of the most popular Catholic lay organization of the postwar period, the Knights of Columbus. The Knights had risen to popularity among working- and middle-class Catholic men who were interested in the order's fraternal and insurance features and drawn by the patriotic activism the Knights displayed in their war camp work during World War I.[25] Their popularity marked a strong contrast to the declining fortunes of the Society of St. Vincent de Paul. Although the Vincentians continued to organize men to provide parish relief and pursue special projects, their role in child investigation and placement ended with the rise of the diocesan bureaus, and their traditional independence was greatly diminished by new forms of ecclesiastical oversight. This loss of function, in turn, helped reduce the appeal and the membership of the organization.[26]

The experience of Baltimore's Vincentian leadership offers a graphic example of the internal struggles and bitter disappointments that accompanied the successes of centralized Catholic social provision in the 1920s. On the death in 1921 of its venerable cardinal-archbishop James Gibbons, the see of Baltimore was filled by the Irish-born bishop of St. Augustine, Florida, Michael James Curley. Curley's style and ambitions differed markedly from those of his predecessor, and he immediately asserted his will in the archdiocese, appointing Rev. Edwin Leonard as diocesan director of charities and instructing him to take charge of the independent work of Catholic charity.[27]

Leonard began by demanding that the leadership of the Society of St. Vincent de Paul submit to his authority. The Baltimore Vincentians resisted the mandate. They had compiled a notable record in charity work and were proud of their pioneering effort in creating the first central bureau of Catholic charities in 1907, the first to employ a full-time female social worker to provide family relief investigations.[28] In the postwar situation with a new bishop at the helm, the Vincentian leadership had expected to continue to act as Baltimore's Catholic "central bureau." But that was not Curley's intention. In the spring of 1923, Curley and Leonard forced the retirement of longtime Baltimore Vincentian president Robert Biggs.

The process was ugly. Rumors spread that Biggs was failing to perform his religious duties and unwilling to accept the lawful authority of his bishop. Biggs personally expressed his desire to cooperate with the new bishop but begged Curley not to destroy the Vincentian tradition in the city. Finally, in despair over Curley's intransigence, Biggs denounced the proceedings: ". . . I do want now to enter again a most earnest protest against the policy you are seeking to establish, against the manner in which you have attempted to establish that policy, against the conduct of the man you have designated as your representative [Leonard], and to say finally that you will find it extremely difficult to get Catholic gentlemen who have any sense of the nicer ethics of life to be willing to be connected in any way, officially or otherwise, with him."[29]

In the meantime other local Catholic bishops tried their luck in the new community financial federations. Citywide "charity endorsement committees" had begun to make an appearance before World War I and became the precursors of the community chests of the 1920s. Financial federations sponsored annual drives for charities and appointed committees of public-spirited citizens to review the applications of individual charitable organizations for a share in the proceeds of the local drives. The success of the massive public financial campaigns of World War I gave these local cooperative drives a huge boost and convinced some Catholic leaders that carefully monitored public cooperation was a reasonable policy.

Local Catholic opinion on cooperative funding reflected the degree to which individual dioceses prospered in independent fund-raising events. Medium-sized cities and dioceses, especially in the Midwest, were enthusiastic. By 1924 Duluth, Akron, Rochester, Detroit, Omaha, Kansas City, and St. Paul all reported positive experiences in the chest. The archdiocese of Cincinnati joined the chest in the 1920s and remained a fervent supporter through the New Deal.[30] Cleveland's diocesan director (later bishop) Hubert LeBlond thought Catholics had a right and a duty to participate in joint fund-raising and argued that if Catholic charities withdrew from participation, they would not only lose potential funding but would have to return to Catholic donors "and tax them all over again."[31]

Other Catholic charities leaders "praised the community chest with faint damns." Among the Catholic agencies that most strongly resisted joint financing in addition to New York were Chicago, Boston, St. Louis, and Baltimore, where a significant Catholic population had developed strong patterns of support for Catholic charities. New York City did not create a joint-financing drive for private welfare agencies until after Cardinal Hayes' death in 1939, and the District of Columbia did not organize a chest drive until 1928, due in part to the opposition of Catholic church leaders. This Catholic resistance was dictated by Archbishop Michael Curley, who also held Catholics out of the Baltimore drive until late in the decade.

The magazine of the National Conference of Catholic Charities, the *Catholic Charities Review,* also expressed skepticism about Catholic participation in the chest. Characterizing the chest movement as "a businessman's proposition," the *Review* suggested that social work professionals were controlled by people who managed the chests with an eye to economy and social control rather than the good of the poor. One writer bluntly concluded that "Who pays commands." Business was "getting a half-nelson on social work" and local welfare agencies were increasingly "hog-tied" by chest requirements. The writer urged Catholics to insist on representation on chest boards, where they should champion the interests of all the classes and not just the wealthy.[32] During the Depression, the *Review* editorialized about the indifference of the chests to the growing problems of relief and of "their preference for the elevation of the sensibilities of the middle classes." Its editors insisted that the chests were "essentially class organizations" and "do not appeal to the masses of the people."[33]

The *Catholic Charities Review* was the organ of the National Conference of Catholic Charities and had been ceded to the NCCC in 1917 by the Society of St. Vincent de Paul where, as the *St. Vincent de Paul Quarterly,* it had been the only national record of Catholic charities for two decades. In 1917 Catholic University social reformer Rev. John A. Ryan became its editor. Ryan continued to write for the magazine in the 1920s after editorial responsibilities had passed to NCCC secretary Rev. John O'Grady and his editorial assistant, Alice Padgett. Led particularly by O'Grady, these individuals played a significant role in the effort to extend the influence of Catholic charities to the national level.

The incentive to move beyond the local level and create a national forum for Catholic social provision was provided by the growth of non-Catholic national social and reform organizations in the Progressive period. The effort was sponsored before World War I by lay volunteers. Thomas Mulry of New York and Thomas Ring of Boston had inaugurated the tradition of national conferences for the Society of St. Vincent de Paul in the late nineteenth century; Catholic women in New York, Detroit, Pittsburgh, and Massachusetts had experimented with city and state federations and had even attempted one national meeting in conjunction with the Vincentians in 1908.[34] And growing numbers of the Catholic laity attended the annual meetings of the secular National Conference of Charities and Corrections.

Members of the Society of St. Vincent de Paul created an important precedent when they represented Catholic child-caring interests at the 1909 White House Conference on the Care of Dependent Children. Catholic delegates to that ground-breaking meeting included New Yorker Thomas M. Mulry, who was a convener and conference vice president, along with a dozen other Vincentians including New York City Comptroller Hermann Metz and United States Commissioner of Labor Charles P. Neill. Although they voiced careful support for the anti-institutional "home first" agenda of the White House Conference, the Vincentian delegates continued to champion child-caring institutions that anchored Catholic work. They recognized, however, that the work was undermined by chronic institutional problems: regimentation, overcrowding, lack of resources, and administrative rigidity and insularity. They also knew that the great majority of the Catholic poor remained beyond the walls of the institutions, crowding the courts, jails, and hospitals. The White House Conference had confirmed their sense of the importance of national organization, however, and the Vincentians issued a call to create the National Conference of Catholic Charities in the spring of 1910. Several hundred Catholic charities volunteers responded to the call and attended the inaugural meeting at Catholic University in Washington.[35]

As a first step, the newly organized National Conference of Catholic Charities made an inventory of Catholic work. Its members sought information on services, methods, and financing in local Catholic charities and attempted to chart the developing relationships between Catholics and state and local governments. Delegate surveys of local and state situations were incomplete and generally amateur, but the Conference succeeded in creating a general impression of the state of Catholic work.[36] In 1910 the tiny Catholic population of Atlanta boasted only three parishes and did little in the way of welfare work, whereas Brooklyn and Chicago each listed one hundred and eighty-five parishes and dozens of parish conferences of the Society of St. Vincent de Paul. NCCC leaders began to urge the reform of standards and practices across the board.

Delegates were also encouraged by reports that Catholic work was receiving a warm welcome from non-Catholics. Members from around the country testified that city and state boards of charity were committed to a spirit of "fair play" in their treatment of the religious interests of Catholics. This meant that in most instances state and city boards were willing to direct dependent Catholics to Catholic agencies and to support them with public funds. Catholic charity workers in most cities insisted that their relations with the local charity organization societies were friendly. As the numbers of Catholic delinquent children under municipal authority continued to increase, most Catholic workers also reported "cordial" and "very active" relations with the local juvenile courts and asked that more Catholic probation officers be assigned to the courts.[37]

Over the next decade, the NCCC established itself as an informal association led by lay volunteers and joined by a sprinkling of professional social workers and a few members of the clergy. Its members were drawn by a common interest in the welfare of dependent and delinquent Catholics and a civic-minded determination that Catholics should do their share in responding to the needs of their coreligionists. The leadership supplied by the Society of St. Vincent de Paul was supplemented by Catholic women, who dominated the early NCCC membership by a lopsided margin. Although religious communities of women involved in charities were virtually absent from Conference meetings until a special section was created for them in 1920, hundreds of laywomen representing individual societies and local and state Leagues of Catholic Women attended the Conference during the first decade.

In spite of the leadership role played by the lay volunteers, however, NCCC policies were ultimately dictated by the diocesan directors of charity who joined the Conference in the 1920s and 1930s. The clergy's participation was initially welcomed by the lay membership. The first executive secretary of the NCCC was Rev. William J. Kerby of the Catholic University of America, who held the post from 1910 to 1920.[38] Kerby's relationships with the lay membership of the Conference were notably cordial and collegial, and he articulated a compelling ideology for the modernization of Catholic social provision. Kerby acknowledged that "charity" was out of favor with many of his Progressive contemporaries, who insisted that the needs of the urban poor could not be met by the benevolent impulses of the advantaged classes. Reformers demanded "justice"—fair wages, child labor laws, public health measures, and social insurance against industrial accidents. Kerby embraced the language of justice and its progressive program, but he provided it with a foundation in the Catholic tradition of charity, arguing that justice was a moral and legal guarantee of the rights of individuals, based on the right to life. In his analysis the right to life became a fully developed social welfare agenda that included adequate wages, public health measures, and social insurance, and he urged Catholics to accept an enlarged role for the state in solving problems of social welfare.[39] Kerby was convinced, however, that by itself the calculus of distributive justice could not sustain the community. Justice required the foundation of charity. He championed a classic notion of charity that took the believer's love of God as its highest motive and expressed itself in daily and sustained attention to human needs. Arguing that charity provided the necessary context for the deliberate and impersonal machinery of justice, he urged his colleagues and students to create a movement that would reform the practices of charity for the sake of justice.

At the conclusion of World War I, when Kerby resigned as NCCC secretary, his departure marked the beginning of a major change in the movement to modernize Catholic charities. The collegial and informal tone of the first decade was transformed by a new leadership and new agendas. High on the list of precipitating factors behind Kerby's decision to remove himself from the leadership of the Conference was the presence of his ambitious understudy, Rev. John O'Grady. The Irish-born O'Grady was one of the many clerical students who benefited from Kerby's attentions at Catholic University. He arrived at the university in 1912 to begin his doctoral work in sociology and, with Kerby's support, received his degree in labor economics and a faculty appointment in the Department of Sociology at the university in 1915. In 1920 he replaced Kerby as NCCC secretary and remained in that office for the next forty years.

The contrast between Kerby and O'Grady was notable. Where Kerby was irenic, self-effacing, and deeply wedded to social courtesies, O'Grady was aggressively self-assured and largely indifferent to the sensibilities of others. Their relationship deteriorated in the 1920s as the younger priest pursued his own agendas in Catholic charities and became implicitly and explicitly critical of his mentor. It was O'Grady's personality and ambition that gave the NCCC its distinctive character during the 1920s and 1930s.[40] His ambitions became plain at the June 1919 meeting of the National Conference of Social Work (formerly the National Conference of Charities and Corrections) in Atlantic City. Nearly a hundred Catholic social workers at the secular conference gathered to hear his plans for "extending the influence" of the National Conference of Catholic Charities. O'Grady's first goal was to remove the lay volunteers from leadership positions in the NCCC and to replace them with professionals. William Kerby's departure cleared the way for O'Grady to implement his plan. A disappointed woman who had been part of the movement from the first decade of the century registered the dismay of the volunteers, and her assessment of the new secretary was pointed: "We regarded Dr.

O'G—as more or less of a well—not a joke exactly—makeshift perhaps pending the time when you would resume the task."[41] Aware of the mounting reaction from Vincentian leaders in the conference, O'Grady confided to a colleague: "We cannot change some of these old fellows. After I get full control, I expect to throw some of them overboard."[42]

To build a constituency of his own, O'Grady cultivated the diocesan directors of charity. Overshadowed by the volunteers in the first decade of the conference, these priests began to control NCCC policy in the 1920s, and as their power in the dioceses grew, they became the mainstay of O'Grady's leadership. In the 1930s these diocesan executives shaped the New Deal policy positions of the NCCC and gave O'Grady the financial backing that allowed him to open his own school of social work at Catholic University. Meanwhile several of them supported his early initiatives in the Conference. His plans received important support, for example, from the newly appointed director of Catholic Charities of New York, Rev. Robert F. Keegan, as New York City continued to play a leading role in the national Catholic charities movement.[43]

An inveterate traveler with a free railway pass always at hand, O'Grady became well-informed about local conditions in the dioceses. He spent a great deal of time with the directors and their staffs, and his correspondence reveals his persistent attempts to be involved in the work of diocesan centralization. Detroit leader James Fitzgerald (one Vincentian who remained an O'Grady supporter) noted admiringly that the secretary had "a nose for news." "He is a ferret for facts. Turn him loose in a city and he will know more about the charities of that city in less time than any contemporary."[44] In addition to becoming widely informed on diocesan conditions, O'Grady took care to cultivate his influence in Washington. He became the director of a new central office of Catholic charities in the city and entered eagerly into the local politics of social provision. He also prudently taught himself to play golf, joining the Congressional Country Club, where he met leading national figures and entertained his colleagues.

The United States' declaration of war in 1917 underscored the importance of moving on the national level to advance Catholic interests. The NCCC was still an informal network of volunteers and not well-positioned to play the role of national advocate. A new initiative, the National Catholic War Council, appeared to fill the vacuum and to coordinate Catholic participation in war work. The guiding hand behind the War Council was another New Yorker, John J. Burke. Burke was a member of Isaac Hecker's religious congregation, the Missionary Society of St. Paul the Apostle (Paulists) and was determined to adapt Hecker's vision of Catholic influence in American life to twentieth-century circumstances. He completed theological training at Catholic University before becoming the editor of the Paulist journal *Catholic World* in New York. Burke's connections to the city's Catholic leadership ran deep, and New York Catholics provided him with the financial backing to support his War Council program. His New York location also gave him a firsthand view of the changing landscape of social provision and the growing role of national associations in shaping American public policy. He witnessed the charities wars in the city and had learned the importance of strong representation in public circles. The creation of the Federal Council of Churches (FCC) in New York in 1908 had also impressed him. When the FCC created an effective General Wartime Commission of the [Protestant] Churches to influence wartime social policy in 1917, Burke set out to create a similar national organization for the Catholic church and persuaded bishops and lay leaders to create the National Catholic War Council (NCWC).[45]

With funding initially supplied by the New York Catholic War Drive and later by the $32-million Catholic portion of the federated United War Work campaign of 1918, the War Council became the dominant voice in the public work of the Catholic church during World War I. Its leadership developed goals well beyond the tasks of supplying spiritual and social services to Catholic troops. Burke and his coworkers promoted their agency as a watchdog for Catholic interests at state and national levels.

The laity supplied the labor for the NCWC's wartime agenda. The men's fraternal organization, the Knights of Columbus, provided services to soldiers in the camps and staffed employment and rehabilitation centers for returning servicemen, while organizations of laywomen staffed camp facilities and local community centers. Female volunteers operated under the direction of the Women's Committee of the NCWC. John Burke and his War Council associates recruited and trained women for war work at an old Washington, D.C., estate called Clifton.[46] After a six-week course, the volunteers were sent to camps and communities in the United States and in Europe, where they provided recreation for American troops and accommodations for discharged Army nurses and other female war workers.[47] They also became involved in supplying relief and social services for women and children in war-devastated regions of France and Belgium. There the American volunteers moved eagerly into a female Catholic culture of established traditions and volunteer service and absorbed the rituals of the French salon even as they opened welfare centers, nurseries, playgrounds, schools, and summer vacation facilities.[48]

Stateside, women's war work was organized for the NCWC by Margaret McGoorty Long, a social worker from the Cook County (Illinois) juvenile court.[49] As the field secretary of the Women's Committee, Long became intimately acquainted with Catholic resources for social work as she interviewed dozens of candidates for positions with the War Council in hospital and community work.[50] She also recommended sites for community houses, let contracts, reviewed programs, organized community funding drives, and promoted Women's Committee projects among local women's groups and business communities.

The Women's Committee goal was to create citywide social service networks in which volunteers and salaried War Council social workers would cooperate to serve immigrants and working women and their families. In contrast to the bureaucratic approach favored by the diocesan clergy, the focal point of these female service networks was to be the community center or settlement house, established with War Council funding and personnel and maintained by local coalitions of Catholic women, which would assume financial and administrative responsibility for the houses. The obstacles to this plan were large.

Catholics had not participated broadly in the prewar creation of settlement houses in immigrant neighborhoods, and those who did undertake settlement work were underfunded and poorly supported.[51] There were some notable exceptions, including Mary Workman at Brownson House in Los Angeles, Helen Phelan at Merrick House in Cleveland, and the highly visible Santa Maria Institute in Cincinnati staffed by Sisters of Charity Blandina Segale and her sister Justina.[52]

In the enthusiasm of wartime, the Women's Committee was determined to enter the field. In Cincinnati the committee arranged an invitation from the Bureau of Catholic Charities to establish a National Catholic Community House in the "over the Rhine" area, a Hungarian and German district. The project was housed in an abandoned saloon. The head secretary, Nelle Dowd, noted the congested housing conditions and commercial outlets in the neighborhood. Three ten-cent dance halls, soft drink saloons that served hard liquor, cheap and "questionable movies," and pool rooms competed with settlement house programs.[53]

In addition to neighborhood hazards, the pastors of the three local parishes remained decidedly skeptical about the project. One insisted that his parish already had a hall, clubs, a gymnasium, and swimming pool and that this was all his German-American congregation needed. He also pointed out that his parishioners would not associate with their Hungarian Catholic neighbors. A second pastor conceded that although he was unimpressed with new "fads," he would at least announce the Community Houses' dances to the youth in his parish. The pastor of the new Hungarian parish felt slighted when he was not consulted in the planning for the center.[54]

Dowd emphasized the need "to further convince the skeptical outsiders of the good of the work and the need of their unified co-operation." But the Cincinnati social worker was not able to convince her most important potential source of support. The settlement house had failed to win the cooperation of the Cincinnati Catholic Women's Association, which was busy planning its own housing project, a downtown hotel for women. Fearing competition and the expanding reach of the Bureau of Catholic Charities and its centralization agenda, local female volunteers refused to serve on the advisory board for the Community House for which the bureau served as sponsor.

The NCWC's Baltimore Community House fared better on all counts than did the beleaguered Cincinnati effort. Designed primarily to serve the Polish Catholic parishes in its neighborhood, the Baltimore settlement also managed to draw multi-ethnic support from the Irish of St. Patrick's, the Italians of St. Leo's, and the Germans of St. Michael's parishes. Head secretary Charlotte Ring adopted a gendered public relations strategy suggested by Catholic University's John Cooper. "Community improvement is a man's job," Cooper wrote. "The real dynamic force that comes from the neighborhood must be primarily masculine. The older, mature, middle aged men must be enlisted as the militant and dynamic power. It is they who have the necessary prestige and leadership in the neighborhood—they who have the interests of the neighborhood more at heart."[55] Ring created a men's club that drew the "masculine" backing that allowed the settlement to prosper.

The successful men's club guaranteed support and allowed Ring to devote her resources to work for girls and women. She acted as a home visitor, entering the homes of the younger girls to help them "make these homes a little more like real homes." She also organized classes in cooking, dressmaking, millinery, and, with the cooperation of the Red Cross, home nursing. When local pastors asked the settlement to provide a day nursery, Ring experimented with a nursery but found the need was seasonal. In the summer harvest months, the Polish mothers took their children with them to the fields or canneries; in the winter mothers took in sewing and so were at home with the children. Ring was also pressured to open a kindergarten at the Community House because many Catholic children went to the Methodist kindergarten and then went on to public school and lost contact with the local pastors.[56]

The "men's strategy" of the Baltimore Community House did not seem to deter the participation of local organizations of Catholic women, and Rev. Edwin Leonard, Baltimore diocesan director of charities, ultimately succeeded in persuading the citywide women's Sodality Union to assume financial responsibility for the house. However, they were instructed not to operate apart from the direction of the clergy. When Holy Rosary's pastor objected to the role of the Sodality and threatened to withdraw his support, diocesan director Leonard used the occasion to form an advisory council for the settlement that included three Polish pastors along with the Sodality Union officers. The lessons from Cincinnati and Baltimore suggested that the success of Catholic community service initiatives depended on winning the participation of local women's organizations in both financial assistance and direct services and providing an active oversight role for the clergy.

While the NCWC Women's Committee concentrated on reconstruction in U.S. cities and in Europe, male War Council leaders pursued their ambition to transform their national wartime organization into a permanent feature of Catholic and public life. The utility of a Catholic presence in Washington during the war created a powerful argument for a permanent organization in the capital, and in 1919 American bishops approved a shift from "war" to "welfare," translating the War Council into the National Catholic Welfare Conference (NCWC).[57]

"Catholic welfare" embraced a broad range of issues that included secularization, religious identity, and cultural difference. The NCWC wanted to become the voice of Catholic welfare in this expanded sense, defending Catholic views and promoting Catholic interests in the public culture. To advance its national agenda and buttress its claim, it employed a full-time Washington staff, arranged for its supporters among the hierarchy to form an administrative oversight committee, and sponsored an annual meeting for all American bishops. Although the NCWC lacked canonical authority, advocates deliberately promoted their organization as "the *bishops'* conference" and implied that its pronouncements and actions were underwritten by collective authority of the American hierarchy. John Burke retained his executive role as secretary of the National Catholic Welfare Conference and served in that capacity until his death in 1936. His ecclesiastical skills, reputation for personal propriety, and loyalty to church authority allowed him to protect the NCWC from internal opposition that threatened to destroy it in 1922. Under his leadership the NCWC also fought off legal challenges to Catholic schools and undertook a notable role in advancing church interests in Mexico.[58]

The welfare of the poor remained on the NCWC agenda, but social provision was subordinated to the larger concern of advancing Catholic interests in the public forum. Under the leadership of Rev. John A. Ryan, the NCWC's Social Action Department (SAD) was notable for its interest in labor legislation and its regulatory concerns. SAD offered to assist in diocesan charities reorganization efforts during the 1920s, and the NCWC leadership was also concerned to capture the loyalties of Catholic lay volunteers. Although it failed to bring Catholic men into the organization in any numbers, women responded with initial enthusiasm to the call for support. Under John Burke's tutelage, the NCWC sponsored the National Council of Catholic Women (NCCW).

Burke retained a controlling hand in the women's council, and Gertrude Hill Gavin, daughter of railroad financier James Hill and a member of Burke's New York inner circle, became its first president. The secretary and soul of the NCCW was Agnes Regan of San Francisco, who moved to Washington and spent the last two decades of her life in a valiant effort to make a success of the women's group. Both Gavin and Regan were heavily involved in financing the work of the NCCW, which was expected to be entirely self-supporting as it carried out the mandates of the parent organization.[59]

Efforts to encourage "girl work" on a national level dominated the NCCW agenda in the 1920s. The working conditions, family circumstances, travel and housing needs, and the dress and deportment of girls and young women drew the attentions of middle-class Catholics well before World War I.[60] The NCCW leadership now felt challenged to greater efforts by the successes of non-Catholic national organizations of women. They were well aware of the accomplishments of the General Federation of Women's Clubs and the Mothers' Congress, which had joined the professionals of Hull House and academics of the University of Chicago to lobby for mothers' pensions, child labor laws, and infant and maternal health measures. Two aspects of the work of the NCCW in the 1920s stand out. One was the organization's strenuous opposition to Margaret Sanger's birth control crusade. The other was the women's council's determined effort to create and support a new school of social work for Catholic women.

The birth control movement launched by Margaret Sanger in New York City in 1914 threatened Catholics at a fundamental level. Vowing to eliminate the need for orphanages and organized foster care, Sanger directed her early efforts to working-class women in heavily Catholic and Jewish areas of the city. Catholic leaders reacted by insisting that the promotion of contraception among the Catholic poor was a deliberate and especially obnoxious form of nativism. They linked "wage control" to birth control and made opposition to contraception a staple of Catholic public policy.[61]

Convinced that Catholic philosophical arguments against birth control would not deter the growing acceptance of the practice, John Burke believed that the organized opposition of Catholic women was the best defense.[62] At the inaugural convention of the National Council of Catholic Women in 1921, therefore, Burke asked NCCW delegates to endorse a resolution condemning birth control that had been drafted for them by

Rev. John A. Ryan of the NCWC's Social Action Department. The women willingly complied, and the resolution was given wide publicity. Although the NCCW delegates numbered less than 500, Margaret Sanger among others accepted the accompanying claim that this resolution represented the views of millions of Catholic women.[63] Agnes Regan became the chief NCWC/NCCW representative before Congress, and the organization could count on a large response from its local affiliates when it called for letters and telegrams of protest against attempts to sponsor federal legislation favoring birth control.[64]

The Sanger goad taught important lessons. Motivated in part by a desire to train women to "represent the Catholic viewpoint to the public," the NCCW launched its most demanding enterprise—a graduate school of social work. Plans for the National Catholic School of Social Service (NCSSS) in Washington originated, as did most Council initiatives, with John Burke, who saw the school as a necessary tool in "gearing up for battle." He announced to the NCCW's board of directors at its organizational meeting in 1920 that he wished them to assume responsibility for establishing and financing the school. Alarmed by the cost of buying a campus and of funding salaries and overhead for such an enterprise, the board hesitated at first but then yielded to his wishes and agreed to undertake the project. The school became the chief preoccupation of NCCW leadership, absorbing its energies and financial resources for the next quarter of a century.[65]

Burke remained deeply invested in the NCSSS. He insisted on serving as the school chaplain in spite of his many other duties and made it his home until his death in 1936.[66] He also chaired its Board of Managers, hired its directors and faculty, and dictated school policy down to the smallest details, recruiting faculty and students with strong religious motivations and establishing rules for the school that borrowed from convent life. Even though some NCSSS students were college-educated and even middle-aged, they were obliged to conform to religious and residential requirements that were strictly enforced throughout the twenty-five-year history of the school.[67] Most students accepted the rules with good grace, and alumnae were devoted to the maternal figure of NCCW secretary Agnes Regan, who remained the *de facto* director of the school.

The residential faculty of social work instructors and the regular presence of clergy from the Catholic University of America (CUA) supplemented the familial roles played by Regan and John Burke as heads of household and gave school life something of the flavor of a settlement house. After serious disagreements with successive lay administrators over the direction of the school, Burke prevailed upon his friend William

Kerby to act as nominal director for the school, while the popular Agnes Regan ran the program.[68] Several other CUA priests also took a proprietary interest in the NCSSS. These included moral theologian John A. Ryan and the Benedictine psychiatrist Thomas Verner Moore. CUA's Department of Sociology also provided two more school directors. Department graduates Francis Haas and Karl Alter took turns succeeding William Kerby in that capacity. Like so many of their counterparts in diocesan charities, both of these priest-directors moved on to become bishops.

Meanwhile John Burke and his colleagues failed to realize their initial aim to make the NCSSS a school for women who would return to their dioceses as volunteer organizers and workers. Virtually all of the women who applied for admission wanted to earn credentials that would qualify them for salaried employment.[69] Adjusting to that reality, the school awarded a diploma in social work for one year of full-time study. After two years of residence, students were eligible to receive a master of arts degree through the school's affiliation with Catholic University.

The NCSSS project responded to the growing demand for social workers in Catholic charities after World War I. With the exception of a few directors of citywide St. Vincent de Paul organizations and laymen in juvenile corrections work, the executives of the new diocesan charities bureaus were priests. Their success depended in large part on the work of the women who composed the supervisory, casework, and office staff of their agencies. The training of these workers became a prominent feature of the movement to consolidate and reform charities.

The effort to create Catholic schools of social work began before World War I. The first courses were generally composed of lectures arranged by local Catholic charities groups, and the early students were generally volunteer workers. But the importance of the new workers quickly led to more formal efforts. Under the inspiration of William Kerby, CUA's Department of Sociology endeavored to build "the social question" into its curriculum, and Kerby's influence also extended to neighboring Trinity College for Catholic women, where he served as a member of the faculty. Although some members of Trinity's lay advisory board fretted about the intrusion of this new social work "fad" in Trinity's liberal arts curriculum, others recognized "there are so many of our wealthier girls . . . who would like to [study social work] . . . it seems that if we do not offer it, we will not keep up."[70]

Between 1913 and 1936, the American Jesuit colleges made a serious commitment to social work education. Loyola University of Chicago began with a series of lectures in 1912 and developed a permanent course in 1913–1914, covering theoretical issues of the family and the state as well as practical material on social welfare and labor problems. The Jesuits later opened schools at Fordham (1916), St. Louis University (1930), and Boston College (1936).[71] A somewhat eccentric early training program was launched in Hot Springs, North Carolina, by Milwaukee priest and labor reformer Peter Dietz. Dietz opened the American Academy of Christian Democracy for Women in September 1915 with modest financial backing from a wealthy local Catholic convert, Katherine M. Safford. Although the school lasted only two years, Dietz' students found salaried positions in both public and Catholic charities, the latter usually with local leagues of Catholic women or citywide councils of St. Vincent de Paul. In the meantime Pittsburgh's League of Catholic Women initiated the training sessions for volunteers that became the precursor of the School of Social Service at Duquesne University in 1919.[72]

Patrick Hayes took the initial steps toward social work education in the New York archdiocese in the wake of the Strong Commission investigation. When city charities commissioner John Kingsbury issued orders that all city charities workers must have civil service qualifications, Hayes formed classes at the Cathedral School to train Catholics to pass the civil service exam and urged the Jesuits to organize social work classes at Fordham. Fordham offered a preliminary series of social work courses in the fall of 1916 and opened in the next year a permanent School of Social Service to train Catholic workers for the new work. Meanwhile several Catholic New Yorkers were already attending the New York School of Philanthropy (after 1919, the New York School of Social Work).[73] Students seeking graduate training in social work at the school included two priests who would figure largely in the reorganization of the child-caring institutions of the archdiocese. Rev. Robert F. Keegan became executive director of the new central organization, the Catholic Charities of the Archdiocese of New York, in 1920, and Bryan McEntegart became director of its Children's Division. Among their classmates was also a young Catholic woman, Jane M. Hoey, who was working for John Kingsbury in the new city Bureau of Child Welfare. In 1936 Hoey would become the chief of the massive Bureau of Public Assistance of the Social Security Administration with responsibility for administering the government's new Aid to Dependent Children program. Hoey, Keegan, and McEntegart would bring the experience of the New York system to the family welfare programs of the New Deal.

The reaction to the new Catholic workers was fretful at best and sometimes overtly hostile. The idea of paid workers was foreign and rather suspect to most Catholics. They readily adopted stereotypes of social workers as arrogant gossips and busybodies—compulsive "snoopers," who probed intrusively into the lives and secrets of the poor and the sick. Both volunteers and clergy assailed the ambitions and training of this new class of female worker. Some also argued that social work was still dominated by the agendas of Protestant charity organization societies. The Baltimore Sulpician John Fenlon insisted, "We Catholics were justified in our attitude toward many who came among our people bearing gifts, and we know that even yet not all the Danai are dead."[74] Two decades later the new rector of CUA, considering how best to deal with the School of Social Work on his campus, wondered aloud if social work still represented "something protestant."[75]

The gender of the workers was the source of even greater concern. When a new program in social work was announced at Pittsburgh's Duquesne University in 1919, its director made an effort to "clear away the sham and sentimentalism" that women brought to social work by enrolling "red-blooded men, men's men, with a spiritual outlook" in his school. Rev. John O'Connor believed that men were "especially well fitted for the larger and more constructive aspects of social work" and noted that "most of the contributions to economic and sociological theory are made by men." Males were also "particularly adapted for platform and other forms of social propaganda work." Advertisements for the school urged men to answer the church's call: "The good women will answer," he concluded, "but that will not be enough. It can be silenced [*sic*] only by the men."[76]

Across the state in Philadelphia, Rev. Francis X. Wastl was concerned that the new assessment techniques and surveillance practices gave female agents an unwelcome degree of control over the lives of the poor. The Catholic chaplain at the public almshouse at Blockley, Wastl charged Blockley's social workers with voyeurism, suggesting that they were particularly preoccupied with the "vice question" and that they used the new diagnostic tools to fish for evidence of sexual misconduct on the part of their patients. One particular social worker of his acquaintance had "a Wasserman obsession." (The Wasserman was a blood test for venereal disease.) "One cannot talk to her on any subject without hearing 'Wassermannn' every five minutes, like a refrain," Wastl reported. "When she meets her friends, I believe the countersign is 'Wasserman' and as she lies on her couch of death, I believe the last audible articulate sound will be a faintly murmured 'Wasserman'—her death gasp, her *'nunc dimittis.'*" "I do not know," he added archly, "what her first cry will be on the other side."[77]

Complaints about the gender of Catholic charity workers appeared regularly in the pages of *Catholic Charities Review* under the editorship of John O'Grady. At the end of the 1920s, the *Review* issued a dramatic call to Catholic charities to "Save the Men!" but concluded that the cause was already lost: "Of the total number of full time persons engaged in Catholic social work in the United States, only about twenty are men." The editor dryly suggested that the few survivors should be "accorded a special badge of honor" as they made their lonely way through offices and annual conventions filled with women. But even that gesture would be poor consolation: "If social work is women's work, we had better betake ourselves elsewhere."[78]

The suspicions and sour opinions of the male leadership underscored the importance of providing Catholic training programs for Catholic workers, and certain common concerns quickly dominated school curricula. Students learned to use new social work methods, including the family budget and the confidential exchange. They also learned to make social investigations of families before providing relief or awarding custody of dependent children and became conversant with the array of private and public social services available in their localities in order to act as resource providers for their coreligionists.[79]

The central focus of the new social casework was child-care and family service. Of course, marriage and the family were also the traditional bedrock of pastoral authority, and when the new Catholic social workers entered the homes and lives of Catholic families, they intruded on a sacred preserve. "We have been asked by social workers on all sides what could be done to make the clergy more sympathetic towards social work," announced the *Catholic Charities Review* in 1921. The editor's assessment made the problem plain: lay volunteers had been willing to work under the direction of the priest. The new professional workers appeared unwilling to do so.[80]

Because they very much needed the new workers, diocesan directors of charity often attempted to create a division of labor that would allow them to use their professional services without alienating pastors and other members of the clergy. One strategy was to confine the responsibilities of the female professionals strictly to relief work and foster placement and to keep them out of family and individual counseling situations. Omaha director Rev. James Borer insisted that the resolution of the material difficulties of the poor was relatively easy and could therefore be left to the female staff. The moral and spiritual problems of the poor, however, demanded ecclesiastical expertise. The pastor familiar with "theological laws and discipline" could deal with these problems much more efficiently than the social caseworker.[81] Acknowledging the threat to pastoral authority posed by the new workers, the *Catholic Charities Review* urged them to be especially careful to avoid usurping the role of the confessor: "The Catholic social worker who is well-grounded in the teachings of her religion will recognize the place of the confessional in Catholic life. She will not take unto herself the functions that belong to the priest in the tribunal of penance."[82]

Utica's diocesan director, determined to preserve the role of the priest and protect the social workers from moral contamination, insisted that though diocesan charities needed the services of female professionals, some cases must always be reserved for pastors. Prominent among these cases were "unmarried mother problems" which should be immediately "turned over to the priest for handling and solution."[83] Female workers must always be on guard lest the sinful world in which they were immersed take its toll on their own good character. Rev. Joseph LeBuffe, the Jesuit director of the School of Social Service at Fordham, knew that social work was regarded by Catholics as "morally dirty work" which was "not suited to a good Catholic girl." But LeBuffe was consoled that only a small percentage of social workers must "deal with morally distressing problems" and that there were many branches of the work "into which the sex delinquent does not come." And he argued that even in the case of the sex delinquent of "the worst type," the Catholic social worker with the right motives and the right training could be saved from contamination. "If we do it for the love of God, we can handle the filth and not be tainted by it," he promised.[84]

These local efforts to confine female social workers to the tasks of material relief and to protect them from the dangers of their new profession gradually yielded to more inclusive approaches. Conceding that Catholic social workers were inevitably going to enter the traditional pastoral precincts of marriage and the family, employers and Catholic social work educators became determined to indoctrinate the workers to properly manage their "religious case work." Because Catholic social workers also entered the public arena as representatives of the church in community councils and public agencies, the clergy of charity meant to train them as apologists for a Catholic social outlook.

The indoctrination consisted of philosophical and theological training that would equip them to give a reasoned account of "the Catholic position" on social and moral issues.[85] It also included spiritual direction. Social workers were instructed to avail themselves of the sacramental resources of their religion and to seek the guidance of confessors and spiritual directors on a regular basis in order to navigate the rough waters of their vocation. Not all Catholic social workers complied with these directives, of course, but most of the women who sought Catholic training and positions in Catholic agencies accepted clerical guidance in the classroom and the confessional—although they were not indiscriminate in choosing their mentors. They believed that the sacramental resources of religion strengthened them and that those same resources were of great importance to the poor with whom they worked. Their attitude in this matter lent a degree of parity to their relationships with their clients, and it reinforced the role of the clergy in the lives of both clients and workers.

Ironically, as Catholic social work education developed in the 1920s, it drew heavily on the foundation developed in the Protestant charity organization societies before World War I and particularly on the work of Mary Richmond. In her 1917 classic, *Social Diagnosis*, Richmond distilled two decades in private charity experience into an authoritative account of the "science of social evidence." The language of the law and of legal practice gave her presentation the quality of logic and scientific objectivity. The book featured techniques for investigating the background and circumstances of persons applying for aid—a standing practice of both private charity organization societies and public relief agencies. Her prescriptions for the proper investigation of cases were followed by recommendations for "diagnosis" and "treatment." Here her use of the language of the medical profession added credibility to the fledgling enterprise of social work. The entire procedure stressed "differential diagnosis"—a commitment to avoid routine responses to human misery, to treat each human being as an individual, and to meet needs as far as possible in a personalized way.

Instructors in Catholic schools of social work made Richmond's ideas the basis of their casework classes, and Catholic graduates carried her principles back to the diocesan staffs. NCCC secretary John O'Grady borrowed heavily from her when he set out to write his own textbooks on social work.[86] Her contention that "environment" was the crucial factor in diagnosing and remedying the problems of the poor resonated strongly with Catholic clergy and lay workers. Richmond's views accorded with their own conviction that "environment" played a dominant part in creating the social abuses and injustices that fostered poverty. Catholic social workers agreed that the deprivation they encountered among immigrants and industrial workers was as likely to result from conditions created by the weak will and poor planning of the well-to-do as from the heredity and character of the poor. Catholic social work educators simply adapted Richmond's basic approach to create a "Catholic case work," grafting the theological doctrines of sin and grace and the sacramental practices of the church onto her social diagnosis.

Although this modified Richmond approach remained the centerpiece of Catholic training and practice, the ink on *Social Diagnosis* was hardly dry before Richmond's authority was eclipsed among secular social work leaders. Her environmentalism rapidly lost ground during the 1920s to the new interest in psychology and psychiatry and to the rising tide of therapeutic casework. Although the landmark 1929 Milford Conference report on the state of the profe sion confirmed "the paramount importance of generic [environmental] social case work," it also recognized that social investigation was being heavily challenged by those who believed that the therapeutic relationship between caseworker and client was a much more significant approach to "unadjusted individuals."[87] Diocesan pastors, charities directors, and Catholic social workers all reacted guardedly to this development, which carried threats of many sorts beyond Freud. Psychiatric social work challenged both the traditional role of the confessor and the standing of the salaried workers who lacked necessary psychiatric training.[88] But psychiatric practices were embraced by juvenile courts and private agencies, and Catholic charities tentatively began to incorporate the approach in their new child-guidance clinics.

The development of a distinctive casework practice reinforced the claim of Catholic charities agencies to a special place in the distribution of public resources. In an extension of the argument used in nineteenth-century New York, Catholic charities agencies demanded that the religious background of Catholic dependents and delinquents should be considered in plans for their care. Diocesan charities, they argued, were best able to supply the necessary intervention for Catholics whose difficulties went beyond temporary insolvency. Catholic agencies argued that they deserved the financial support of the community and the state to meet the social and religious needs of these persons. These claims anchored Catholic participation in most community chests and in state relief programs during the New Deal.

As the country ground its way through the Depression and attempted to absorb the programs of the New Deal, Catholic willingness to accept psychiatric social work increased. The "relief" function of social work agencies was being rapidly absorbed by the government, and private agencies scrambled to find new rationales for existence. In their search for a new role, Catholic charities quietly began to accept social work's growing investment in individual and family counseling. Reigning professional voices declared that each person was unique and that casework should be tailored to meet the needs of individual clients. Catholic social work educators agreed and, in spite of their reservations about psychiatric social work, urged their students to accept "all valid findings for the enrichment of individualized service to our fellow men." As New York casework instructor Margaret Norman put it: "Candor should compel us to acknowledge our debt to those who have opened new vistas of knowledge."[89] Catholics remained attached to Mary Richmond's environmental method but salted it now with a concern to nurture the personal growth and development of their clients in the changing climate of state welfare provision during the 1930s.

Catholic leaders both lay and clerical, however, continued to promote the idea that their casework offered an important difference from mainstream professional practice. In the face of what they took to be growing cultural relativism, they championed an outlook derived from the ongoing revival of Thomistic philosophy. Although social work educators admitted that "the Thomas Aquinas of Catholic social case work has not yet appeared," they welcomed the objectively ordered universe of the Thomistic revival and used it to bolster their conviction that the new social work goal of personality adjustment was meaningless without an objective standard. "How can anybody be maladjusted except in relation to some norm outside the individual himself?" as one reviewer put it simply.[90] The strong doses of scholastic philosophy, dogmatic and moral theology, and canon law in their social work curricula testified to the Catholic determination to adhere to standards of objective truth in the face of growing relativism and to defend those standards in public forums. This commitment, which underwrote their spiritual and material assistance to the poor, became the hallmark of Catholic social casework.[91] It made Catholic social workers especially important in public battles over signature issues like birth control, abortion, sterilization, and divorce. The thought that birth control might become an accepted form of social provision in private and public agencies, for example, drove Catholic leaders to especially strenuous efforts to address it in the training of their own social workers. Along with extensive instruction in the church's view of the inviolability of marriage, the "Catholic philosophy of social work" stressed the social workers' obligation to oppose the use of artificial birth control by clients.[92]

As church leaders worked to provide a distinctive kind of social work training for their coreligionists, Catholic social workers began to demonstrate their ability to influence both Catholic and public social provision. Rose McHugh is a leading example. McHugh graduated from the University of Chicago in 1904 and spent ten years as a social worker for the (non-Catholic) United Charities of Chicago, where she served as the secretary of the original mothers' pension organization in the country, the Chicago Funds to Parents Committee.[93] After World War I, McHugh left public welfare work and joined the National Catholic Welfare Conference as assistant director for the NCWC's Social Action Department office in Chicago. A decade later she returned to the public arena as a member of the Advisory Committee of the Children's Bureau, an Assistant State Commissioner of Welfare in New York, chief of the Division of Surveys of the Social Security Administration, and a consultant to the Social Security Administration's Bureau of Public Assistance under Jane Hoey.

Rose McHugh gave special time and energy to the effort to improve conditions for Catholic social workers. During her years with the NCWC, she became a leading source of information on Catholic charities as a result of her survey research on diocesan organizations and institutions in the East and Midwest. McHugh consistently promoted the importance of family casework and the benefits of professional training. Although her efforts led her to offer unflinching criticism of Catholic standards and practices, she remained committed to Catholic teachings on marriage, family, and reproduction. Her convictions about the importance of Catholic influence in the wider society were unwavering and even quietly militant.

In her efforts to improve Catholic social services, McHugh ran into strong opposition from diocesan directors and male charities leaders. In 1926, for example, she was asked by the NCCC's conference of diocesan directors to evaluate Catholic family casework in diocesan agencies. McHugh organized a committee to survey five diocesan family agencies and produced a report for the directors.[94] A central aspect of the report was quickly suppressed by the clergy's representative on her committee. Rev. Edwin L. Leonard, director of Baltimore Catholic Charities, took strong exception to the contention that professional social workers should begin to replace diocesan priests as executives of the diocesan bureaus. He was infuriated at the suggestion that the tasks of administering an agency constituted a distraction to the priests and prevented them from discharging their proper spiritual duties.[95] Leonard dismissed the members of McHugh's survey team as prejudiced and inexperienced and altered the conclusions of the report. Eliminating what he labeled the "interpretations" of the committee, he claimed that the survey data supported the conclusion that a priest must always be the executive director of diocesan charities. The rest of the diocesan directors responded to Leonard's angry reaction by burying the report in committee. Robert Keegan of New York agreed to chair an ad hoc Committee on Standards in Family Social Work, where the report was received and its contentions about the clergy formally discarded.[96]

Undeterred by these responses, Rose McHugh continued to champion the cause of Catholic social workers. In 1933 she began to lobby for the creation of a permanent section on professional social work in the NCCC. The importance of the NCCC was increasing as it took an active role in shaping New Deal social provision, and, in an effort to give social workers a more prominent role in those developments, McHugh volunteered to survey the status of the professional worker in Catholic agencies. Her preliminary report underscored the fact that, in spite of the need for better-educated staff, professional development for Catholic social work had been very slow.[97]

In response to McHugh's prodding, the NCCC leadership agreed to create a permanent Topic Committee within the Conference as a forum for all the issues related to "the status of the professional social worker." The Conference executive committee also approved a Committee on Professional Education for Social Work. McHugh chaired the committee and produced its 1935 study of personnel practices in Catholic agencies.[98] Adapting the family agency questionnaires developed for the Russell Sage Foundation by Ralph Hurlin, McHugh's committee surveyed twenty-seven diocesan organizations employing 426 workers in 1934.[99] On the basis of those results, the NCCC's Executive Committee asked McHugh to prepare a fuller survey and report for the 1935 annual meeting in Peoria.

The 1935 report declared that its work had been undertaken in order to help diocesan directors recognize the "problems of the profession-ally trained social worker in the Catholic agency." It claimed to have "brought forcibly" the question of "whether the concept of professional training for service in Catholic agencies has been accepted by the direc-tors of agencies." Sixty central offices and forty branch offices were asked to participate in the study, which attempted to determine levels of pro-fessional education, salaries, and policies regarding staff in these Catholic agencies. Fifty-nine agencies with twenty-three branch offices responded to the survey (representing thirty-three archdioceses and dioceses). The information provided by them covered 621 professional staff and 373 clerical employees. On the one hand, women accounted for 532 of the 621 professionals. Men, on the other hand, held sixty-two of seventy-two executive director positions. Only twenty-seven men were employed in other capacities in the fifty-nine agencies.

The report highlighted "the discrepancies in standards of salaries for the same position in the Catholic and non-Catholic agency when both share in funds from Community Chest or from other forms of joint financing." Noting the resistance of agencies to releasing salary figures, the report insisted that "figures should be available" to allow Catholic college graduates to weigh the cost of professional education for social work against the salaries available in Catholic agencies. "Catholic agen-cies, especially those sharing in community funds, should be aware of desirable standards of salaries for professional workers. They should be interested in seeing that their staff workers receive salaries comparable to those paid workers in non-Catholic agencies for the same type of work."[100]

The 1935 report documented the slow progress of professional social work in Catholic agencies. Diocesan organizations still clearly relied more heavily on experience than professional credentials in choosing their employees. At least 26 percent of the caseworkers included in the survey had no formal training in social work. The McHugh report suggested diplomatically that some seasoned workers had experience that fit them for the work "far better than the mere formal course." The real problem arose, however, when staff members with social work degrees were blocked out of supervisory and executive jobs by workers who, as the report put it, were less able to "comply with present standards of formal education."[101]

The survey revealed that most of the agencies required a five-and-a-half-day work week and offered two or three weeks of paid vacation only after two full years' service. Sick leave policies seemed adequate in most agencies, but the report found that forty-four agencies reported no regular provision for salary increases. Thirty-one agencies had established criteria for promotion for their workers, but only one agency routinely invited staff participation in setting agency policy. The report noted that the agencies generally supported the idea of comprehensive health insurance but could not afford to provide it to their employees. Only five offered group life insurance, and only eleven made provision for medical care.

Rose McHugh's committed efforts to insure a larger role at the NCCC to address the needs of social workers were unsuccessful. The conclusions of the 1935 study were not included in the *Proceedings* of the Conference, and although NCCC Executive Secretary John O'Grady did present the committee's report to diocesan directors, the one-sentence announcement in the *Proceedings* gives no indication of any response from the priests.[102] During the annual business meeting, the Committee on Reorganization of Topic Committees, chaired by Bryan McEntegart of New York Catholic Charities, ignored the request for a permanent section on professional development and turned instead to the pressing questions of the New Deal's impact on Catholic agencies and to their efforts to develop a new school of social work at Catholic University of America.

John O'Grady was the leading figure behind the agenda of a Catholic University school of social work. O'Grady was a relentless critic of the efforts of the National Council of Catholic Women to run an independent school in Washington. His longtime antagonism toward the NCSSS was well-known to insiders in Catholic social work circles. The office of Catholic Charities of Washington, which O'Grady directed, should have been a primary source of desperately needed placement opportunities for NCSSS field work. Instead NCSSS students were placed in non-Catholic private and public agencies in the District and in Baltimore, because John O'Grady was fundamentally convinced that neither the women of the NCCW nor the Board of Managers of the NCSSS should be entrusted with social work education for Catholics. He made no secret of his long-range goal, telling NCSSS director William Kerby bluntly: "I believe that the School should be taken over by the Catholic University."[103]

When James Hugh Ryan became the new rector of the university in 1928 and began a major campaign to bring the university into line with American academic practices, O'Grady sensed that the time was right to pursue his own program of professional education in social work.[104] His initial concern was to improve social work training for the clergy. Between 1920 and 1928 CUA's Department of Sociology had tried to provide student-priests with a rudimentary social work curriculum to prepare them for assignments in diocesan charities. As social work training programs developed more demanding standards, this approach became increasingly inadequate, but the university leadership during the 1920s remained unresponsive to O'Grady's demands for a full-fledged program. University leaders also feared that the education of priests for social work would invite an unacceptable departure from precedent by requiring the use of female faculty on the campus and enlarging the presence of females in the student body.[105]

John O'Grady looked for support from the new diocesan directors of charities, who were beginning to demand professional training for younger priests on their staffs and were even willing to send their men to non-Catholic programs: "It became an accepted principle in the more forward-looking Catholic agencies," O'Grady remembered, "that a priest who needed training in social work should attend the New York School of Social Service."[106] He used the needs of key dioceses like New York and Baltimore to push for a professional school at CUA and persuaded the diocesan directors to form a "school committee" to provide financial support for the proposal. He also insisted that CUA's Department of Sociology was no longer an appropriate venue for social work education, and warned that as a member of the Sociology Department he would refuse to certify its diocesan student-priests for membership in the American Association of Social Workers.

O'Grady's pressure worked. In the spring of 1934, he was named dean of the new Catholic University of America School of Social Work, and at that point his ambitions expanded considerably.[107] Laywomen constituted the major market for social work education, and O'Grady was eager to recruit them to fill his seats. His plans targeted the women at the National Catholic School of Social Service, but he faced serious constraints in openly challenging NCSSS for priority in the matter of recruiting and educating female social workers in Washington. There was strong resistance from conservative clergy to the presence of women on CUA's campus and to proposals for educating women and priests in the same social work courses. NCSSS supporters also wielded considerable influence at Catholic University. NCWC general secretary John Burke still chaired the board of NCSSS and made his home at the school.[108] Members of the Catholic University faculty who taught at NCSSS also rushed to protect its interests. John A. Ryan, Thomas Verner Moore, and the ailing William Kerby joined Burke in defending the territory of the NCSSS. O'Grady received a pointed admonition from university chancellor Archbishop Michael J. Curley, who warned him "not to take any step that might be interpreted as an act of vengeance or ruthlessness against the Catholic School of Social Service" and admonished him to "go slowly, quietly and gently, otherwise, I am afraid you are going to undo the foundation already laid for the work of our Social School in the Catholic University."[109] And although CUA rector James Hugh Ryan supported the School of Social Work initiative, he too resisted O'Grady's demands that the school recruit laywomen.[110]

James Ryan's caution was well-warranted, because the battle over social work education for women soon became implicated in his ouster from the CUA rectorship. The urbane Ryan was abruptly sent to Nebraska as the new bishop of Omaha in 1935. Philadelphia priest Joseph Corrigan replaced Ryan as rector and responded to pressures to reverse Ryan's curricular initiatives and restore the study of neo-Thomistic philosophy to the leading place in CUA's educational efforts.[111] Among Corrigan's plans was a scheme to absorb the School of Social Work into a new School of Social Science that would stress the theoretical aspects of Catholic social teaching and de-emphasize the practical dimensions of training for social work.

In the ensuing struggle to save the school, John O'Grady enlisted the support of the dean of the School of Social Administration at the University of Chicago. The indomitable Edith Abbott had devoted her career to the cause of professional social work education and was most distressed by the rumor that one of the schools in the network was about to be "enlarged" into a School of Social Science by ecclesiastical fiat. Her letter rehearsed the point of view of the professional accrediting agency, the American Association of Schools of Social Work, which under Abbott's leadership took the position that social work was fundamentally different from the social sciences. Abbott explained that social workers assume the great responsibility of caring directly for human beings; social scientists do not. "Our Social Science friends do not understand our point of view," she pointed out. "They complain that we spend so much time on our 'cases.'" Abbott acknowledged, "And of course we do and must. The men in the departments of Social Science in Chicago are good friends and colleagues, but they are not interested in taking care of Mrs. Jones and her children."[112]

Edith Abbott's concern for the future of the CUA School of Social Work was heightened by her conviction that Catholics must be included in the ranks of professional social workers. "[E]veryone who is working to put the Social Services of the country on a scientific basis knows that we must have members of your church among those who have had this training," she wrote. "Your church has great influence in the public Social Services in this country and there is great need of men and women who have had the best possible training who represent your religious group." Abbott reminded O'Grady that the University of Chicago had provided "a good many scholarships" to Catholics because "we thought that was one way to help the profession. To have your own group demote our profession from its proper status will be a blow to all of us."[113] The weight of Edith Abbott's letter reinforced the threat of loss of accreditation, and Joseph Corrigan did an abrupt about-face in the fall of 1937. When classes opened in the first week in October, there were two schools at CUA—a nominal school of social science headed by Rev. Francis Haas and the School of Social Work.

The School of Social Work survived the takeover attempt, but John O'Grady was not spared the humiliation of being ousted as its dean.[114] Over his strenuous protests, including appeal to the Vatican, O'Grady was removed from the deanship, and although he retained his position as secretary to the National Conference of Catholic Charities, the loss of the dean's post marked the end of O'Grady's active leadership in social work education. Meanwhile John Burke's death on October 31, 1936, saved him from further involvement in the school wars. After O'Grady's dismissal plans to incorporate the NCSSS into the Catholic University school went slowly forward. The new dean of the CUA school, Richmond priest Thomas Mitchell, worked to arrange a full exchange of students and faculty between the schools by 1939. The university delayed absorbing the NCSSS officially until after World War II, when its last defender, Agnes Regan, was dead and its faithful NCCW supporters finally resigned themselves to the inevitable.

CHAPTER THREE

Inside the Institutions:
Foundlings, Orphans, Delinquents

While diocesan bureaus and professional social workers expanded their influence and public role, child-care remained the anchor of Catholic charities. The service and sacrifice of the religious congregations initially enabled Catholic charities to "put children first."[1] From 1729, when the Ursuline sisters established the first orphanage in New Orleans, Catholics built infant asylums, orphanages, protectories, and reformatories in a massive work of succor and salvation for the children of Catholic immigrants. By 1910, when the National Conference of Catholic Charities was organized, thousands of religious, primarily women, staffed and administered institutions caring for 88,860 dependent or delinquent children.[2] By the end of the Children's Year of 1919, the Sisters of Charity and the Daughters of Charity alone operated sixty-two maternity hospitals and infant homes and orphanages and cared for 10,653 infants and children.[3]

Increasingly these institutions faced the challenge of the "home first" principle accepted by secular professionals and Catholic leaders at the 1909 White House Conference on the Care of Dependent Children. Who should and how best to care for the child remained hotly contested questions, with the New York charities investigation of 1916 providing only the most dramatic example of an ongoing debate. Throughout the 1920s, the sisters, like their counterparts in the Protestant Florence Crittenton homes and Jewish orphanages, struggled to meet standards set by professional social work organizations, public welfare agencies, and the federal Children's Bureau.

Ironically the major challenge to the work of the sisters came from within the church. Fund-raising by the sisters and their lay auxiliaries was curtailed as bishops moved to one or two charity drives annually.[4]

Bishops appointed businessmen to institutional boards of directors to monitor operations and finances. Although the directors of diocesan bureaus of charity secured community chest funds for the institutions, their aid came at a price. A new Code of Canon Law promulgated by the Vatican in 1917 further extended the authority of the bishops and restricted the sisters' actions.[5] Then, at the bishops' request, the NCWC and NCCC dispatched teams of social workers to survey their agencies and institutions. It was the reports of the NCCC social workers and the diocesan bureaus that interpreted the sisters' labors to church and community. The sisters were clearly not credentialed professionals in the sense insisted on by the social workers. Essentially they learned on the job, trained by older sisters in what "worked" in the institution. NCWC field secretary Rose McHugh sensitively summarized the pain and poignance when "an old institution which has for many years regarded itself as an agency doing important work for the community at genuine sacrifice suddenly finds itself an object of distrust by its old friends."[6]

The Catholic institutional landscape under such scrutiny was vast and immensely varied. At the beginning of the twentieth century, more than 50,000 religious women staffed parochial schools, hospitals, orphanages, infant asylums, protectories, and homes for the aged. By 1920 their numbers increased to 90,558, spread across 224 orders and congregations. Their members provided an ethnic microcosm of American Catholicism. American foundations such as convert Elizabeth Bayley Seton's Sisters of Charity and the African-American Oblate Sisters of Providence were joined by the Irish congregation of the Sisters of Mercy, the German School Sisters of Notre Dame, the Polish Felician sisters, Mother Cabrini's Italian Missionaries of the Sacred Heart of Jesus, and the Czech Sisters of Notre Dame in Cleveland. European congregations had responded to exhortations from Rome to send their sisters to missions in America; bishops traveled to France, Germany, and Ireland to plead with provincials and mothers general for sisters for their dioceses. Established congregations such as the Sisters of Charity aided new arrivals like Mother Cabrini until they could find housing and support. In each diocese the sisters found first and second generation Irish, and then German, Polish, and Italian-American girls and women ready to serve the needs of new immigrants.[7]

The Catholic women who entered religious life were choosing a vocation, accepting a "call from God." Their moral example, their commitment to save children and women in distress, and their dedication to a life of service were shared by many Protestant and Jewish women caregivers, but their vows of poverty, chastity, and, particularly, obedience set them apart. Housed in convents, the sisters, bonded in communities of single women, were the church's auxiliaries. "Loyal soldiers" sent by superiors and bishops, they served where needed, generally on the front lines.[8] More than 80 percent of them taught in parochial schools, where they provided a steady stream of vocations of young women moved by their example. Less than 5 percent chose social service.[9]

Each of the religious congregations had its special charisma, or collective personality, based on its founders, constitutions, and history. Young postulants and novices, who frequently entered the community in their early teens, learned the life and heard the congregations' stories of heroic and dramatic events: the Ursulines' flight from the fires set by a Charlestown mob in 1834, Mother Pariseau of the Sisters of Providence begging for donations in western mining camps, and the charismatic Sister Blandina Segale of the Sisters of Charity of Cincinnati facing angry Apaches. Each congregation could point to moments of imminent disaster, perils overcome, and work sustained by the power of prayer.[10] Surviving early crises, the sisters built, managed, generally financed, and staffed a wide network of institutions. Their teaching, nursing, and social ministries were traditional women's work; their unusual opportunities and challenges in administering institutions and resources were clearly untraditional and expanded "the vocational spaces" of women. Working and praying together, these "deceptively meek ladies with downcast eyes" determinedly labored to find the means to respond to the will of God and the needs of the poor.[11]

The sisters served and administered in a hierarchical church governed by men who not only shared the stereotypes of their contemporaries on women's place but had views on the role of religious women with roots in the Middle Ages. The familiar phrase "the good sisters" frequently had the ring of a paternalistic pat on the head. For their life of labor, the sisters' annual salaries from parish or diocese might range from zero to two hundred or three hundred dollars, but always their compensation was well below that of the male congregations. Bishop Hubert LeBlond explained: "We may think that we are unfair to our Sisterhoods . . . when we do not ask for more to pay them for their services . . . but I think our Sisters would be the very first that would resent our trying, to commercialize the wonderful sacrifice they are making by even suggesting that they can be compensated for the work that they do."[12] More important, however, than the question of financial support was the essential issue of control. How much authority could the sisters exercise in their own house?[13]

Confronting challenges within and without, the sisters resisted, defended their work, and eventually adapted. During the survey of New York's Catholic charities in 1919, one frustrated social worker reported that the mother superior of the French Hospital of St. Vincent de Paul met her at the entrance and (in full habit) announced that it was a Protestant hospital. The sisters claimed they had no notice of any survey from the archbishop. Even if they had, they would not allow their institution to be inspected.[14] Such bold recalcitrance was the exception, however, not the rule. A more productive response of the sisters was to organize. Stung by harsh assessments of their institutions in the surveys, 139 religious women responded to John O'Grady's invitation to attend a special Conference of Religious held at the Catholic University of America in 1920 in conjunction with the meeting of the National Conference of Catholic Charities. On the one hand, it was obviously O'Grady's intent to bring them to the conference for instruction in professional trends and standards. On the other hand, it was an opportunity to have their own forum. When a social worker leveled a sharp attack on the sisters' institutional work, Sister Miriam Regina Walsh, a Sister of Charity, tall, weighing over two hundred pounds, and a veteran of the New York City charities investigation, rose to denounce the charges and to demand a public apology. The assembled religious had found their champion.[15] Working with John O'Grady, they formed the Sisters' Conference, later the Conference of Religious, as a standing committee of the NCCC. Sister Miriam Regina was elected chair, a post she held until her death in 1935.[16]

The task of saving the child began with the cradle. The most famous and largest Catholic institution for infants, the New York Foundling Asylum, bore the brunt of the waves of immigrants in the cycles of depressions in the 1870s and 1890s and was the only institution in the city taking in infants with no questions asked. Desperate mothers left their babies in a reception crib outside the building. Not infrequently, the mother left a note. One wrote in anguish after she left her four-week-old boy:

> Necessity compels me to part with my darling boy. I leave him, hoping and trusting that you will take good care of him . . . will you try to find some kindhearted lady to adopt him and love him as her own while he is young that he may never know but what she is his own mother? It would break my heart to have him grow up without a mother to love and care for him. God only knows the bitter anguish of my heart in parting with this little dear; still if it costs me my life I am obliged to give him up.[17]

When a baby was left at a church, the parish priest knew he could take it to the Foundling Asylum. Reporter Jacob Riis observed how rapidly the crib filled as "babies took to coming in little squads instead of in single file."[18] Facing strained resources in the depression of 1873, the sisters moved the crib inside. When one mother brought her infant and threatened suicide if the sisters did not allow her to stay with the child, she was admitted and asked to nurse her child and another baby. Persuaded of the need, the sisters rapidly expanded their work to maternity care. When the state legislature passed the Children's Law in 1875, the Foundling Asylum had five hundred infants in the institution with another one thousand being cared for in the homes of wet nurses under contract with the asylum. Ten years later, when Josephine Shaw Lowell visited the imposing six-story Foundling Asylum, she reported 2,747 infants supported by $248,711 of city funds. A staunch opponent of public support for private institutions, she nevertheless noted that "the personal influence of the devoted Sisters is apparent everywhere, and the healthy, happy, natural appearance of the children in the institution is most satisfactory." The infants kept coming. Four years later a new infant discovered in the crib received the number 20,715.[19]

Between 1870 and 1930, thirty-five Catholic infant and maternity homes and hospitals were established in the larger dioceses.[20] Haunted by the question, "To whom will these children turn if we abandon them?," the sisters opened their doors to all who came.[21] They fiercely protected the identity of mothers, determined to return them physically and spiritually healthy to a community that remained ignorant of their past.[22] The Catholic tradition was to hate the sin and love the sinner. Robert Keegan of New York's Catholic Charities somewhat floridly summarized the Catholic practice, with his emphasis clearly on the child, not the mother: "to accept in secret in her foundling hospitals the little stray waif of a sinful world, to give to him every care that loving kindness could prompt, to place him out with families where his origin could never rise to disturb the placid equilibrium of his later existence."[23] In more professional language, he insisted at a 1920 conference sponsored by the federal Children's Bureau that if the mother assumed responsibility for raising the child and needed state aid, she should have access to mothers' pension funds. Keegan insisted that the rights of the child always stood "paramount."[24]

The challenge of caring for both mother and child seemed unrelenting. In 1919 more than three hundred religious cared for 5,869 children in maternity hospitals and infant homes.[25] Celebrating its golden jubilee that year, the New York Foundling Hospital reported 23,301 children returned to their parents or guardians, 24,658 placed in foster homes, and another 3,200 legally adopted. Seventeen thousand mothers had been sheltered.[26] But the challenge was also changing. Regional conferences in New York City and Chicago, sponsored by the Children's Bureau in 1920, recommended that all illegitimate births should be reported to a public child-welfare agency and that the state should license and supervise private maternity hospitals and infant asylums. A committee of the National Conference of Commissioners on Uniform State laws drafted a uniform illegitimacy act in 1921, calling for effective state supervision.[27] NCCC's John O'Grady was almost as wary at the extension of state supervision as the sisters, complaining that a Minnesota law requiring that private agencies send complete records of unmarried mothers to the Offices of the State Board of Control was "carrying matters entirely too far."[28]

Catholic social worker Mary C. Tinney, the general inspector of the Department of Public Welfare in New York City, discussed the implications of new laws and recommendations at the 1920 Sisters' Conference. Reviewing changing attitudes, she urged a treatment plan "based directly on our own religious training—that we are all sinners. . . . We are not so far removed morally from these sisters of ours, and who knows how red our sins may be." When "we do treat these women as fellow-sinners, . . . we are on the way to a real constructive solution to the problem." She added a grim warning (though never mentioning the word) on abortion.[29] Practically every other girl who came to her office for help reported an attempt to prevent the birth of her child. Social workers in public and private New York agencies had been asking, where are the babies? Unless the problem of illegitimacy was effectively dealt with, Catholic girls were "going to be educated along lines which we would shudder to contemplate." John O'Grady was more direct, asserting that the statistical decline in illegitimate births might mean that "in addition to one mortal sin, the abominable crime of murder is being added." With Catholics comprising 78 percent of the 2,311 cases of unmarried mothers accepted as public charges by Tinney's department, there was a clear imperative to provide help for the mother and to save her child.[30]

The sisters provided remarkable institutional resources. But they continued to face, as did the administrators of the Crittenton homes, the criticism of the social workers that they lacked professional training and were deficient in the crucial areas of admissions, health care, and aftercare.[31] The central recommendations for improvement were consistent: add professionals to the staffs of the maternity hospitals and foundling homes and cooperate with the diocesan bureaus of Catholic charities.

The 1919 NCWC Pittsburgh survey reports on the Roselia Foundling Asylum and Maternity Hospital and St. Rita's Home for Infants provide clear examples of the social work critiques.[32] On loan from New York Catholic Charities, Mary Anne Kennedy investigated Roselia. Established in 1891 by the Sisters of Charity of Western Pennsylvania, Roselia's Maternity Hospital attracted a private clientele of "respectable married women" who chose to have their babies in the attractive nearby old mansion that was the main building. Others, "not the poorer class in any sense," came for "protection in their misfortune" and paid eighteen dollars a week for a single room. Those fees augmented the $9,000 received from the State of Pennsylvania, support from the community chest, and the donation of more than $10,000 raised by their ladies' auxiliary.[33]

Roselia's charity was for a "different class of girl." These mothers and infants were housed in a separate section. In four large, well-lighted, and ventilated dormitories, seven to ten mothers slept next to their infants' cribs. Roselia insisted that each mother nurse her child, optimally for a year but at least four weeks. She could remain at Roselia up to one year, earning room and board and two dollars a week in helping in the laundry and housekeeping. Some chose to work outside the institution, paying board for their infants. One nursery, during Kennedy's visit, had forty-four infants, two to a crib. Although the two or three sisters in the nursery had long experience, the social worker noted that there should be at least six for that number, particularly when so many were bottle fed. Babies were delivered by either the two interns from Mercy Hospital who lived at Roselia or by the visiting staff of nine physicians. In spite of these generally good conditions, of the 508 children cared for in 1919, 113 died. Eighty of those were bottle fed. Yet Kennedy concluded that, given the physical condition of the mothers and of many of the children received, a 25 percent mortality rate was "certainly very low." Although Roselia's rate was double that of Pittsburgh, the Children's Bureau statistics indicated that the mortality rates for illegitimate babies were frequently double or triple those for legitimate babies.[34]

Roselia, Kennedy concluded, was "doing much good work." Each case was dealt with individually. The sisters generally tried to help the mother secure a job to enable her to keep the child or to have relatives either adopt or board it. Only about 8 percent of the children were placed for adoption. In accord with the consistent conclusion of social workers in the 1920s, Kennedy suggested that when the Conference of Catholic Charities developed a "well managed" children's division, Roselia might have the preliminary and after-care investigation carried out by the social workers of the Conference.[35]

In contrast the social worker who visited St. Rita's Home for Infants in the same Pittsburgh survey found few of the healthy conditions of Roselia. Of 409 children, from one day to five years of age, received in the past year, 116 died. One sister had charge of up to 43 infants under two years. The children were "not put on the floor to creep or get dirty as children should when they try to develop their muscles. . . These tiny tots are tied in rocking chairs and rock like old women in their second childhood." *"Institution,"* she concluded, "seems stamped upon everything under this roof."[36]

Another survey was commissioned in 1926 by Cincinnati's new archbishop, John T. McNicholas, O.P. He asked the NCCC to dispatch a team to review his diocesan bureau of charities and institutions to see how they "measured up to the best modern standards." O'Grady sent Alice Padgett from his Washington Bureau of Catholic Charities to organize the effort. Most of the Catholic institutions, she discovered, had "gone ahead with their programs without any regard for the Bureau." Indeed, the initiatives of the Bureau of Catholic Charities were seen as not only intrusive but as a reflection on the institutions and their staffs, who felt "fully qualified to take care of their own affairs without any outside interference." More distressing, Padgett found that "the heads of our institutions seem always to have been under the impression that the more children for whom they cared, the more souls they were saving, and parents who wanted to rid themselves of the obligation of caring for their children seem to have been past masters of the art of appealing to the sensibilities" of the sisters.[37] Nowhere was the problem of standards more alarming to Padgett than at St. Joseph's Maternity and Infant Hospital. Founded in 1873 by the Sisters of Charity of Cincinnati, St. Joseph's accepted Protestants or Catholics from anywhere in the country (at the time of the Padgett team's visit only 34 percent had come from Cincinnati), provided it was their "first offense" and that they carried no infectious diseases.[38] Yet the sisters, concluded Padgett, had no way of knowing if either was the case. They carried out no background investigation because they was committed to protecting the reputation of the mother. There was no preliminary medical examination and no routine physical examination either before admission or during the period between admission and childbirth. There was no prenatal program. Once her baby was born, the mother could arrange never to see it, if she paid an agreed-upon sum to have the sisters care for the child for a year. The sisters did not "try very hard," according to Padgett, to persuade mothers to nurse their babies. The mothers' failure to breast-feed their babies was the cause "more than anything else that the institution has such an abnormally high infant mortality rate."

During Padgett's visit, St. Joseph's had fifty bottle-fed babies in the nursery under the charge of one sister, a trained nurse. With little sympathy for the exhaustion and staggering burden of the sisters, Padgett observed that in the best-regulated institutions there were ten babies for every nurse. She concluded, "With its present personnel St. Joseph's cannot discharge its responsibilities toward the seventy children under one year who have been committed to its keeping. It cannot absolve itself for the abnormally high mortality rate among the children under its care."

Padgett found the recordkeeping on these deaths both deceptive and illegal. To protect the reputation of the mothers, the sisters accepted assumed names; they also registered new births under these fictitious names, a clear violation of Ohio law. On checking the births and deaths reported by St. Joseph's to the Vital Statistics Bureau in Cincinnati for 1925, Padgett's colleague, Florence L. Sullivan, finally computed the death rate for illegitimate babies at 457.8 per thousand. Most of the infants who died at St. Joseph's before reaching six months of age expired at around three months. Feeding problems and a high proportion of "nutritional deaths" underscored the need for insistence on breast-feeding and at the very least more personnel in the nursery to assist in feeding.[39] Conceding that there might be inaccuracies because the record-keeping and reporting by the institution were so garbled, Padgett insisted that the question of feeding had to be addressed.[40]

The Sisters of Charity immediately appointed a new superior. Florence L. Sullivan wrote with some concern to John O'Grady: "It seems too bad for a new Superior to be permitted to get her start without any guidance, when she has such a poor background to start with, and if she has to find her own way from the start." She urged O'Grady to come to Cincinnati. If that weren't possible, Sullivan was ready to meet with the new superior. With the authority of her position with the Division of Charities of the Ohio Department of Public Welfare, she added: "I do not see how I can recommend a 'certificate of approval' in the light of the findings on this study—until definite changes are made in the policy."[41] Six months later another new superior was named. A social worker was added to the staff in 1926, buildings were modernized, and the kindergarten was improved.[42] The changes clearly continued. By April 1935 *Catholic Charities Review* noted that the St. Joseph's superior was giving a training session to representatives of the child-caring agencies of Ohio.

As the Cincinnati survey was completed, Inspector Irene M. Killip of the New York State Board of Charities forwarded a highly critical report on Our Lady of Victory Women's and Children's Hospital and Our Lady of Victory Infant Home of Lackawanna in the Buffalo diocese to John O'Grady. She included excerpts from the monthly magazine, *The Victorian*, sponsored by the "Association of Our Blessed Lady of Victory," which described "A National Work of Charity . . . saving from loss and destruction the newly born and illegitimate babe, housing and protecting the unmarried mother in her maternity needs and affording hospital care for the sick, poor and homeless dependents." The magazine reported that more than 1,345 "unfortunate mothers" from fourteen states had been "cared for and restored as far as possible to the standing which they have lost through their misfortune." Five thousand infants had been received and cared for.

These records were not easily traced, Killip reported. Infants born at Our Lady of Victory and surrendered by their mothers and others brought to the institution were accepted "without inquiry as to the desirability or necessity" of the surrender. In some cases "a friend of the family" arrived at the door with a child, gave whatever information she chose, and the sisters accepted it, frequently without a prior physical examination. This left the institution in October 1925 with thirty-six "unplaceable children" who had a variety of physical and mental handicaps.

For those children well enough to be placed in families, the record was so poor when placement was taken over by the Buffalo Catholic Charities that removals were immediately instituted. In one instance the Catholic Charities social worker found a child placed in a home where the foster parents were not married; in another case the foster parents separated, each charging infidelity. Adoption was abrogated by the courts in another placement due to the tuberculosis of the mother, the financial dependence of the family, and its religious instability. In another case the child placed by Our Lady of Victory had been living in one room with foster parents and a dog; it was returned to the infant home after the Board of Health reported the child had come to a dispensary "with a dent in head."

When they became aware that the social workers wanted complete histories of the children before placing them, the sisters of Our Lady of Victory refused to work with the Buffalo Catholic Charities Child Placing Department. Determined to shield the mother's and the child's background, the superior directed that no records be made available to the diocesan workers. Equally determined, the Bureau refused to accept children from Our Lady of Victory for placement. As at St. Joseph's in Cincinnati, the state interest could threaten licensing. And also as at St. Joseph's, at issue was the institution's desire to be as accessible as possible to the woman and child in need and the insistence by social workers at the diocesan and state level that the mother and child would be better served by the admissions and placement standards set by professionals.[43]

Also in 1926, Catholic Charities of the Archdiocese of New York asked NCWC's Rose McHugh to assemble a team and undertake a survey and develop social service programs for its three institutions caring for unmarried mothers and their children. The team was to determine as far as possible the extent of illegitimacy "particularly among our own people" and how agencies dealt with it.

At the New York Foundling Hospital much had changed, but much remained the same. Sister Anna Michella, the superintendent, reported at the 1923 annual NCCC meeting: "It has always been our policy to keep the mother and baby together, for the baby's health and for the mother's morals." In most cases the mothers stayed through the weaning period. The Foundling Hospital set no specified time requirement for leaving or boarding out because the sisters knew "that when her maternal instinct is aroused she will not desire to be separated from her baby." The 17,749 mothers sent back to the world, the sisters reported, were "well fortified spiritually to commence life anew, and like the sinful woman ever ready to obey the admonition of the Master, 'Go and sin no more.'"[44] McHugh's report to the archdiocese traced a changing institutional profile. In 1926 only seven unmarried mothers were admitted on a monthly average. There was a similar sharp decline in the number of illegitimate children admitted, although the Foundling Hospital still had several thousand children under care either in the institution or in foster or boarding homes. McHugh made several recommendations to meet both the changes in clientele and the standards of the profession. Most were in the area of placement and boarding-out.[45] She wrote with frustration and some passion that considering "the sacrifices voluntarily undertaken by these women in entering a religious order for the service of others and the zeal with which they perform their duties, it is deplorable that their opportunities for moulding human character are so dwarfed by the use of unsound methods."[46] Her conclusion, given the proud history of the Foundling Hospital, was radical and sweeping: "Until Sisters can be trained as social workers, it is essential that the work . . . be carried on by lay workers who have the necessary training and experience."[47]

The sisters were making changes. They added social workers to their staffs, and a small number enrolled in programs of social work.[48] At their 1924 meeting, the Conference of Religious agreed to appoint its own committee to formulate standards for Catholic maternity homes.[49] During that meeting, three religious superintendents spoke to an invited gathering of seventy on their work with unmarried mothers and children. (Bryan McEntegart of New York had suggested a limited audience as discussions on the topic usually resulted "in a circus for the morbid-minded.")[50] Emphasizing medical care, Sister Lidwina of Misericordia Hospital in Chicago asserted that "our twentieth century infant caring homes must be a scientific gateway to life," adding: "This is the birthright of babies and we may no longer defend ourselves behind the old fallacy that God sets the death rates." She astutely observed: "In our work with these mothers we are coping with conditions rather than causes. Who are these mothers of the many children born out of wedlock each year?

With what heritage are these children endowed? What are the possibilities of care for these mothers and to what extent do we help them? All these questions are involved in the formulation of our social program and we must not be satisfied with the mere queries but we must answer them."[51]

In the discussions on standards and practices at the NCCC meetings, there was almost no discussion of race. In an otherwise sensitive article on the "Ethical Aspects of Illegitimacy" in the January 1927 issue of *Catholic Charities Review,* John O'Grady asserted: "Some races take illegitimacy as a matter of course. They do not make any particular effort to conceal illegitimate births. They are willing that the mothers should take the children into their own homes with the full knowledge of the community." "How far," he asked, "should we foster the peculiar attitudes of these races toward illegitimacy?" His answer was clear: "Social case work cannot afford to foster low standards of family life in any race." He ended with the question, "In view of the higher ideals we have set before ourselves for the elevation of the general standards of family life, how can we continue to foster low standards in sex relationships?"

Although the trend in caring for the unwed mother was increasingly toward foster care, Catholics still maintained forty-nine maternity hospitals and infant asylums in 1939. In that year the NCCC Committee on Children presented a 1939 state-of-the-art panel on the "Differential Approach to the Problem of the Unmarried Mother and Her Child." Social workers from Catholic bureaus in St. Louis, Los Angeles, and Minneapolis spoke on the care of unmarried mothers in foster homes and on mothers who relinquished and those who kept their children, but the major speaker was Sister Annette of St. Ann's Hospital in Cleveland on the care of the unmarried mother in the Maternity Home.[52] St. Ann's history offers a microcosm of changes in Catholic maternity homes and infant asylums. Cited by both Rose McHugh and Florence Sullivan as a model institution, St. Ann's had been founded in 1873 by the Sisters of Charity of St. Augustine to protect Catholic women from the "vigorous proselytizing" of the Retreat, founded by the Cleveland Woman's Christian Association. New Deal social insurance, relief payments, and probably birth control practices had so reduced the numbers using maternity homes that its old rival, the Retreat, had been forced to close. In surviving St. Ann's had clearly changed with the times. Primarily a maternity hospital for private patients in 1939, it maintained a sixty-bed capacity in Loretto House, a special department for unmarried mothers. This was funded partly by the community chest of Cuyohoga County and the Catholic Charities bureau because unwed mothers on public assistance could receive only outpatient services. Sister Annette spoke of a "new social attitude . . . expressed not in sentimentality, but in an earnest effort to understand the difficulties of the unmarried mother and to assist her to reestablish herself socially, economically and morally." But she also articulated the old mission: "The real work is in that invisible world of human souls where only God Himself can estimate its value." The imperative to care for one's own also remained, but the responsibility was now broadly shared by sisters, social workers, diocesan bureaus, and communities.[53]

The haven for most Catholic dependent or neglected children was the orphan asylum.[54] Of the seventy-seven private asylums founded for children by 1850, twenty-one were Catholic, usually staffed by the Sisters of Charity.[55] As wave after wave of immigrants flooded New York, Boston, Baltimore, and midwestern cities, Catholics and Jews built orphanages to care for their own and to preserve faith and culture. Fifty-six orphanages served New York's needy children by 1895, a 180 percent increase since the passage of the Children's Law in 1875.[56] Ethnic groups, particularly German and Polish Catholics, struggled to take care of their own. Faced with staggering numbers, dioceses and congregations generally built large congregate institutions. Jewish orphanages, with the exception of the Hebrew Orphan Asylum of New York, were usually smaller than Catholic institutions and generally seen by contemporaries as more progressive. In both Catholic and Jewish orphanages, "half orphans" were almost always in the majority.[57] The institutions provided a safety net for families temporarily unable (and sometimes unwilling) to care for their children.[58] Responding to the gospel imperative, "Suffer the little children to come unto me," the sisters, as they had in their maternity hospitals and foundling homes, essentially had an open-door policy.[59] Also, as in their maternity hospitals and foundling homes, they faced the criticism of Catholic social workers and the determination of the diocesan bureaus of Catholic Charities to extend their control.

The 1919 Pittsburgh survey team found all of the ills attributed to institutional life glaringly evident in St. Paul's Roman Catholic Orphan Asylum. When the Sisters of Mercy opened St. Paul's in 1846, they cared for thirty children. At the time of the visit of social worker Mary Anne Kennedy, St. Paul's housed almost nine hundred boys and girls in a congregate institution. The priest superintendent and the religious superior supervised a staff that included the school principal, nine teaching sisters, ten sisters who took care of the dormitories, nursery, hospital, and detention room, and seven "house" sisters who were in charge of laundry, kitchen, and the sewing room. The only paid staff were the prefect, two engineers, a baker, a gardener, and two women employees who patrolled the halls at night. Resident boys worked in squads on the thirty-six acres that produced all of the vegetables for St. Paul's and, when necessary, brought in lumps of coal from the mine located on the property. "Industrial" boys and girls did most of the cleaning and scrubbing indoors. In 1918 St. Paul's receipts totaled $225,713.17. More than $155,000 was raised from the Christmas and orphans' week collections in the parish churches. Relatives of "inmates" paid $22,832.92. There was no state support of this diocesan facility.[60] Expenditures in 1918 totaled $93,435.02, or only 41 percent of receipts, perhaps due to the superintendent's efforts to amass enough capital to construct a new school building. Based on an average number of children in residence during the year, Kennedy estimated the annual per capita expense per child at $86, concluding: "it would seem . . . too little."[61]

Admissions and discharge records were so poorly kept that it was difficult for Kennedy to get an accurate census. Usually a child was sent to the institution with a letter from a priest; the priest superintendent interviewed the parent or relative and determined whether to admit and the rate of payment. Kennedy gave two examples. In one instance in July 1918 a fairly well-to-do Italian couple decided to separate and to place their three children in St. Paul's. Their pastor provided a letter for the superintendent, who admitted the children and asked for $20 a month board for all three. The father, who owned two homes and a business, thought this was too low a figure but agreed. Three months later when he removed his children he complained that $20 was too much considering that the children's heads and bodies were covered with sores. In the other case, two boys were admitted and discharged within a week. The mother explained that she took them to St. Paul's because her husband was cross. When he promised to do better, she took them out. Kennedy observed: "Some investigation of the case and study of the people, would probably have obviated the necessity of these children ever going to the Asylum."[62]

Discharge policies were, if anything, more haphazard. Again Kennedy gave an example. At Christmas 1918, the uncle of two orphaned Italian children, Frances and Nicholas, asked that they be discharged to him. He was presented with a bill for $1,448 and told that when the bill was paid the children would be given up. Kennedy observed: "Despite the overcrowded condition of the Asylum and the impossibility of providing adequate facilities for the large number of children being cared for, these two children were to be held until their uncle who had never made any agreement to pay for them," paid more than a thousand dollars. He refused. Four months later Nicholas ran away. No one informed the uncle, but Nicholas wrote and pleaded to come home. He had been with the uncle ever since. Although twelve girls and twenty-five boys ran away during 1918, Kennedy could find no evidence that St. Paul's staff "took the slightest interest" or "realized a responsibility for the care of a child whom it had accepted and thereby classed as an orphan, whether a physical or a moral one."[63]

For those remaining or returning to St. Paul's, institutional life seemed to hold few pleasures. Food, clothing, hygiene, recreation, and medical care all received severe criticism from Kennedy. At mealtime each child found his plate, bowl, and utensils in place and fairly generous portions of food before him. No napkins were provided, nor did the children wash before coming to the dining room. After grace was said, a whistle blew and eating began. Kennedy found "no semblance of homelikeness"; more seriously she saw no milk being served. While fifty gallons of milk reportedly were consumed each day, and the little children were served milk between meals in their playroom, Kennedy noted that the quantity available did not allow even one-half pint per child per day.

During Kennedy's visit clothing was not marked for individual use. The girls wore a uniform blue dress and apron; the boys wore blue shirts and corduroy trousers. Three young girls, only at St. Paul's a month before being discharged to their mother, complained to a visiting social worker that they were not allowed to wear their own clothes. They claimed when visitors arrived they would have to wait a half hour while the children were "cleaned up."[64] The general impression of the young children and of the boys, Kennedy found, was "decidedly untidy."

The bathing, toilet, and lavatory facilities Kennedy found deplorable. With twenty tubs for the boys and twenty tubs for girls, children took their baths in assembly-line fashion. Older children helped with the washing and drying of those younger and were supposed to scrub out the tubs between washings. The same brush was used on one child after another. Babies were bathed by a sister in large zinc tubs, each provided with "large pieces of strong yellow soap." Boys' and girls' washrooms close to the dormitories had twenty old-fashioned toilets in which the water for flushing flowed about once an hour. Two of these dormitories had more than two hundred children.[65]

The hospital building adjacent to the main building of St. Paul's was well-equipped. Children were quarantined on arrival and kept segregated if contagious. The sister in charge was a graduate nurse and a qualified assistant pharmacist. Two undergraduate nurses from Mercy Hospital assisted her. On the day Kennedy visited the hospital, seventy-three children were patients. Considering that twenty-two reportedly had over-eaten and had upset stomachs, Kennedy noted "too large a number." Five children had skin and eye trouble.[66]

The most troubling case noted by Kennedy involved a young Italian boy, Gregory. His brother, who lived in St. Joseph's Protectory, visited

Gregory and was alarmed when the boy couldn't raise his arm to his head or use it for eating. He "stole" his brother away to West Penn Hospital, where an x-ray revealed a neglected fracture and a bone pushed through the socket. Physicians recommended an operation. Meanwhile the prefect of St. Paul's tracked down the runaway and returned him to the orphanage. Gregory's parish priest had himself appointed his guardian and, accompanied by the police, arrived at St. Paul's, took Gregory, and arranged for treatment. Gregory reported that after his arm had been broken, a sister had bandaged it. The following morning a doctor said the "cask" was all right. When the bandage was removed, however, and Gregory could not straighten his arm, the doctor advised him to carry an iron around to "weigh it down." His medical report of June 10, 1919, was marked "O.K." though at the time he could neither straighten his arm nor lift it. Kennedy concluded her report: "The boy's condition seems to have worried no one except his older brother, who finally stole him away so that he might go to the hospital where another younger brother had already been treated for skin disease."[67]

Kennedy found "No excuse . . . adequate" that an institution that saved $105,000 from its 1918 revenues should not spend it on children. She added: "The authorities have never displayed the slightest appreciation of their responsibility. The mere housing and mass feeding and clothing of children has been considered all that was necessary." She noted, however, that when the superintendent had gone abroad, he placed his prize ferns in the care of an expert gardener, observing that he wouldn't "think of allowing the plants to 'just grow.'" Kennedy exclaimed: "And yet, the children in the institution have not even been allowed to just grow. They have been needlessly exposed to vile contagion and have not been given the cleanliness and food that any plant would obtain."[68]

Next to the horrendous conditions in health and hygiene, Kennedy rated the situation in education and recreation as merely poor to inadequate.[69] Boys' indoor play space consisted of a large room with benches; "absolutely no games, toys, nor apparatus of any kind are provided." The girls' social rooms were also bare except for benches. When the children played outdoors, they found little equipment. Outdoors the younger boys walked around aimlessly and seemed "too listless to be troublesome." Again she compared the children's environment with that of the superintendent, observing: "In his own study, he shows a commendable appreciation of what a homelike room should be; books, pictures and some fine plants are strongly in evidence. And yet, not in one place throughout the building, has there been any attempt made to provide a homelike atmosphere for the children."[70]

Change was swift and effective. In his summary report of the survey of the Catholic institutions to Bishop Regis Canevin, John O'Grady noted that there had already been a great deal of citizen criticism of St. Paul's, but "there was every reason to believe that . . . the institution was taking steps to remedy the conditions. . ." The bishop, however, was taking no chances. He immediately relieved the superintendent who had served since 1897 and assigned him as pastor to a city parish. The mother superior of the Sisters of Mercy assigned a new superior, Sister M. de Lellis McNamara, who immediately began acting on Kennedy's criticisms. The sister infirmarian was soon replaced, pre-admission physical examinations were insisted upon, and an energetic and eventually successful campaign addressed the skin and eye diseases. A new school building was completed in 1920; a new model dormitory for boys that could be adapted to the group plan followed. Pre-admission casework reduced the number of children in the institution. Outplacement was handled by a social worker who worked with the Catholic Daughters of America's Home Finding Bureau. By 1925 John A. Lapp, a member of the survey team and then director of the Social Action Department of the NCWC, described St. Paul's as "quite a model institution." The response of the Sisters of Mercy in Pittsburgh proved typical throughout the decade. Redress of criticism was as swift as resources would permit.[71]

Determined to speak for themselves, the Conference of Religious appointed its own standards committee in 1921. Headed by Rev. Bryan J. McEntegart, the committee included Rev. Karl J. Alter, director of the Toledo Bureau of Catholic Charities, Sister M. Lucia, Sister Katherine, and Sister M. Celestine. The sisters were in the majority, but the chair was the powerful New York director of the Children's Division, a representative of the Bureau of Catholic Charities and the professional lay social workers. Still it was a good mix and a good opportunity to bring together the sisters' on-the-ground experience with that of the bureau professionals.

It was also good timing. In Washington a Children's Bureau committee was designing a handbook of standards for child-caring institutions. The Sisters' Committee's slender twenty-two-page document, *A Program for Catholic Childcaring Homes,* was published in June 1923, a few months before Children's Bureau Publication No. 170, a heftier handbook of 119 pages, went to press.[72] On most standards there was clear consensus. Both reports reaffirmed that the best place for the child was in its own home; both insisted that a thorough effort should be made to improve the economic or social conditions of the home before even considering the removal of the child. Both agreed that the child-caring institution was at its best a temporary substitute for home, until the child could be returned to her own family or placed in a foster care home. Both reports emphasized the benefits of the cottage over the congregate system.

The major differences were in approach and audience. The NCCC report had the more difficult task. It had to convince religious, who dedicated every waking hour of their lives to the children in their care, that they could do better. The report began with an affirmation: "the care of needy children is the noblest work undertaken by our religious orders." The sisters' calling demanded that, like true mothers, they give to each child the best they possessed. The NCCC report posed three essential challenges. Because home was the best environment for the child, the sisters were strenuously urged to review their almost open-door policy and to exercise more judgment and professional screening in their admissions. Recognizing that most of their child-caring institutions were built on the congregate model, the report suggested ways that current buildings could be remodeled to set up a small group system. Finally the report stressed improvements in after-care because in the past that was the area "responsible for most of the sad occurrences which have helped to give a false impression of the value of institutional care."[73]

Commenting on the major recommendations of the report at the 1923 NCCC conference, Mary Godley of Catholic Charities of New York suggested that it would probably be of greatest value to the sisters who rarely had an opportunity to visit other homes. She added an olive branch, noting that "the visitors who come to them are often willing and eager to give adverse criticism, but almost never offer constructive suggestions."[74] Rev. C. H. LeBlond, Director of Catholic Charities of Cleveland, came to a quite different conclusion and emphasized: "the necessity of central diocesan control, direction, and supervision of every child-caring agency that the diocese possesses, so that they may be correlated, unified, systematized, and standardized, to prevent the waste and weakness that comes from duplication, disagreement and competition."[75] Centralization was crucial in the area of child-care. Because 90 to 92 percent of all children in Catholic and sectarian orphanages had one or two parents living, each child represented a family problem. Because no orphanage was properly equipped to "do adequate family work," the diocesan family division should handle all admissions and discharges. In the ensuing discussion, the Director of Catholic Charities of Boston agreed that unprofessional work and duplication must be stopped but conceded that "the autonomy of some of the institutions is at times very difficult to break."[76]

Frictions between sisters and social workers continued. A brief article in *Catholic Charities Review* reviewed the status of sister–social worker relations in 1927. Conceding that "many of our religious communities have a distinct impression that lay workers fail to appreciate or sympathize with them" and admitting that "religious communities irritate us when they appear to oppose our social work standards," the author, probably Alice Padgett, cited the "lack of a complete understanding between the religious and lay workers." Social workers had not yet learned that religious communities "cannot be dictated to" nor realized that their autonomy might prove important in upholding "the principle of free initiative in Catholic social work." Though the sisters were "naturally slow about taking on new methods until it has been demonstrated that they can work more effectively than the old," Padgett believed that their resistance would eventually be overcome.[77]

Sister Miriam Regina made the case for the sisters in her 1927 NCCC paper, "Recent Progress in Catholic Child-Care." A successful superior of orphanages in Brooklyn and Nanuet, New York, she had once startled a tailor at Nanuet by stating, "I want my boys to look perfect," and insisting that he measure each of her four hundred boys for a new suit (rather than sending the usual generic small, medium, and large).[78] All of the standards recommended in NCCC's *Program for Catholic Child-caring Homes,* she asserted, were in place. No child was admitted before a thorough investigation determined that there was no way to keep the child in her home. Institutional care was the last resource. Physical examinations, quarantines, regular attendance by doctors and dentists, skilled dietitians, and well-planned menus meant that "no trouble" was spared in providing for the physical well-being of each child. Schools within each institution met the city and state and diocesan standards. The prescribed course of study was "vivified by the personnel of the teaching staff. Religious, consecrated to their work by vow, [were] . . . not guided by any worldly or mercenary motives."[79] Homes had established the group system. Before discharge the state or city and Catholic charities professionals examined the home situation or found a suitable boarding house. Social workers made follow-up visits. Good records were maintained from admission through after-care. Sister Miriam Regina concluded: "The overwhelming pressure following upon the introduction of these new methods should not mean the sacrifice of personal interest . . . in our zeal for advancement let us never forget that the heart of each little child is craving for that natural, human affection which adverse circumstances have snatched from her grasp."[80] The first question posed to Sister Miriam Regina in the general discussion was whether the conditions described were real or ideal.

Less than ideal was the Catholic record in providing orphanages for African-American children. A survey commissioned by the bishops in 1928 listed a total of only 203,986 Catholic African-Americans. Almost half were in Louisiana. Twenty-two thousand were in Baltimore, home of the African-American Oblate Sisters of Providence. Nationwide there were only twelve orphanages and only eighty-six sisters caring for African-American dependent or delinquent children. St. Elizabeth's in Baltimore, staffed by sixteen white Franciscan sisters, sheltered 200 boys and girls. It was an institutional neighbor to the parish church of the diocesan director of Catholic Charities, Edwin Leonard. Leonard's unneighborly reluctance to seat six "colored" converts at Sunday mass at St. Bernard's received a stinging rebuke from Archbishop Curley. The colored came "in some numbers," Curley pointed out, to the Cathedral. No one objected. If they had, he would certainly have ignored them, for "when all is said and done, they have souls and they are children of Jesus Christ just as much as you and I." Curley's own bias, however, emerged in his subsequent order to Leonard to remove any black children he had placed in foster homes and to send them to the Mission Helpers who needed "a goodly number to train" and to help them carry on the work of their laundry. He concluded: "Colored children are infinitely better off, I repeat, with the Mission Helpers than they would be in any colored home."[81]

The most comprehensive study of Catholic child-caring institutions of the 1920s was *Children's Institutions*. Appointed by the NCCC Committee on Children and financed by a $16,500 grant from the Commonwealth Fund, John M. Cooper of Catholic University assembled a team of Catholic social workers and studied more than eighty Catholic institutions for dependent children.[82] Highly sensitive to the need to reassure the religious, Cooper and his team stressed that they were undertaking a *study* not a survey. They were visiting the orphanages to learn what worked well, not to tabulate wash basins or to check lighting. "The main thing," he concluded, was "to gather detailed information on the experience and successes of our Catholic institutions and of the Sisters and others who are giving their lives, their thoughts and self-sacrificing devotion to the care of God's children. . . . Our single purpose has been to gather together these policies, methods and devices and put at the disposal of all our institutions the good things which each has."[83] A first draft was sent to all motherhouses, superintendents, and superiors of Catholic child-caring institutions, to all diocesan directors of charity, and to other Catholic and non-Catholic professionals for review. Enlivened by hundreds of examples, *Children's Institutions* was a masterful blend of accepted theory and standards, studded with the detailed advice from the sisters on what worked.[84]

The first section on religious care and training introduced Cooper's theory-practice-example approach. Recognizing the profoundly religious atmosphere of the institutions, Cooper warned that "the institution's most subtle and deadly foe, routine, is not easily vanquished, and in no field is routine more subtle and deadly than in that of . . . religious education." Mass should be offered as late as possible, and it should be short. "Long services, especially before breakfast, kill the best of good intentions. . ." for "very few souls are saved after the first twenty minutes." If benediction or novenas were "tacked on," it could lead to "a psychic strain that is apt to build distaste in many."[85] The children, Cooper gently reminded his readers, were not members of religious congregations.

Turning to moral education, the Cooper study examined how to cultivate good habits and cure bad ones. Religious and their lay staffworkers should blend the new methods with the Catholic tradition, while always keeping their emphasis on "the supreme importance of supernatural motives and of Divine Grace." The underlying causes and not just the symptoms of bad habits had to be treated. Aware that some psychiatrists at child-guidance clinics might give recommendations "not in harmony" with Catholic principles, Catholic child-caring institutions could find Catholic psychiatrists and clinics through the help of local Catholic social workers. "For the great bulk of Catholics," Cooper concluded, "the best and surest road toward keeping morally straight and, when things have gone awry, toward getting morally straight again is the practice of regular and frequent Confession and Communion. In nine cases out of ten, it gets the results aimed at."[86]

Children's Institutions stressed the general rule that the fewer the penalties and punishments, the better. Children should not be reprimanded publicly and never punished by being sent to the chapel and made to say their prayers. Corporal punishment was only to be used as a last resort and never administered in anger. So many of the children, one superior reported, had "had so much corporal punishment at home that it has little effect when administered in the institution." Sisters should work to encourage a habit of obeying from "the inner motive of religious love or duty."[87]

Self-reliance was encouraged by asking the children to help with chores in the institutions, but Cooper warned that the chores should not be too onerous and should not erode the recommended two to three hours of free time. Vary the routine, vary the chores, and allow some breathing space. One superior cautioned against overburdening the older girls with the care of young ones, adding: "Youth passes too quickly. As mothers their lives will be spent in caring for their own. Some girls are not fond of children; after years of this duty in their youth, will they want a family of their own when they grow up?"[88]

Cooper and the superiors who contributed to this enlightened study were especially concerned that the child not become institutionalized. One institution that allowed older girls to go shopping with a sister encouraged them to choose clothes that were stylish but conservative, "but if any girl sets her heart upon a dress not entirely approved by the sister she will ordinarily be permitted to purchase it, and if it proves too ultra the girl will thus learn by her own mistakes."[89] Children should be provided with lockers to keep their clothing, toys, and "junk." They should, in brief, be allowed space and privacy, particularly the older girls and boys for "nobody envies the goldfish." Never should they be told how grateful they should be to the institution.

Cooper and the superiors were most prescriptive in the section on medical care. Detailed descriptions of medical programs showed a trend away from volunteer physicians and dentists; the ideal was obviously to contract for a full-time supervising physician. Fresh air, sunlight, and recreation were all-important to physical and mental health. Play, asserted Cooper, was a school of self-mastery, obedience, justice, and charity; competitive play "puts to rout flabbiness, dawdling, infirmity of purpose and volitional mollycoddleism." Spontaneous play could offset the restrictions and routine of the institution. Play should be adapted by age and gender. Boxing was "not for girls," but basketball, particularly if played by boys' rules, could provide the same values for the girls as the boys.

The majority of the institutions responding to Cooper's survey offered instruction through the first eight grades. One-fourth had kindergartens. About three-fourths of their residents attended high school outside the institution. One-third had flourishing bands or orchestras. Most put on plays and had handicrafts and nature study included in their curricula.[90]

The final sections of *Children's Institutions* dealt with social policies, administration, and finance. Reasserting the church's emphasis on the primacy of the family and the central principle that the child's place is in his own home, Cooper emphasized that intervention by social agencies in the affairs of the family and separation of a child from parents was only to be undertaken as a last resort. Better case methods and investigations by a social worker, optimally one employed by the child-caring institution, but usually from the Bureau of Catholic Charities, reduced admissions. Parents or relatives should be responsible for much of the costs of keeping the child, but because studies showed that up to one-half of the children in Catholic child-caring institutions were kept with no family remuneration, it was important that bureaus of Catholic Charities work to obtain community chest support and state per capita payments. After discharge the institution should continue its interest in follow-up care just as a parent for a child who had left home.[91]

Acknowledging the importance of lay governing boards for their support and advice to the institutions, Cooper urged the sisters to work for representation from middle- and lower-income groups in their communities, observing that "one of the gravest hazards today to our American social work, Catholic and other, is its marked tendency to come under the control of the upper income groups."[92] While boards helped to finance the institution, the other major funding sources were special diocesan collections and parish assessments and community chest funds. The institutions surveyed were almost unanimous in their support of community chest plans.[93]

The most earnest advice in *Children's Institutions* was reserved for the superior. She must insure that the religious and lay members of the staff were well-trained and not overburdened. (Cooper recommended one staff member to a maximum of five children and noted one-fourth of the institutions surveyed met this ratio.) Good quarters and reasonable time off, at least a few hours daily, were essential. The superior should have a college education and professional social work training; each member of the staff should have a good general knowledge of child welfare work and rudimentary knowledge of practices in religious education, character building, child health, hygiene, recreation, and domestic science. Cooper ended with the obvious. This work was not for the decrepit, and he warned superiors or provincials against sending religious who had failed in hospital or school work to child-caring institutions.[94]

Summarizing the study at the 1929 NCCC meeting, Cooper concluded that generally the institutions were "decidedly healthy." He found "a wholesome *unrest*" and "steady and measured progress each year." His study had brought sisters, lay social work professionals, and diocesan directors together in a genuine cooperative enterprise. Yet Cooper acknowledged that their differences were by no means completely eradicated. The field was still "honeycombed with conflicting views, surmises and antisurmises."[95] Old methods were hard to change. The discussions would continue, for in 1929 at the onset of the Depression, sisters still staffed more than 350 orphanages and cared for 54,350 dependent children, the highest total in the century. The funding provided by Aid to Dependent Children and the trend to place children in foster homes rather than institutions dropped the number to 33,206 by 1940.[96] Those institutions that remained increasingly cared not for the poor, but for children with physical, mental, or emotional needs.

The challenge of finding Catholic homes for children was severe. More Catholic children than from any other denomination needed placement from institutions, the courts, city agencies, and bureaus of Catholic Charities. The New York experience graphically underscored the dimensions of the problem. The Foundling Asylum worked with pastors to find local Catholic placements, but faced with placing sometimes five hundred children a year, it also sought Catholic homes in other states. The Asylum's orphan trains or "baby specials" went as far west as Arizona; a sister or agent accompanied the children and visited the homes arranged for by the local pastor. Ironically, driven to a practice that seemed to mirror Charles Loring Brace's removals to the West, the Foundling Asylum clearly had better follow-up. No adoptions were allowed for three years and until the sisters' or their agents' visits confirmed that the child was in a satisfactory home.[97]

By 1903 the Catholic Home Bureau of New York became the outplacement agency for twenty-two institutions. Thomas Mulry described its early experience: "As the way to place out seemed to be to place out, we began with the simple proposition of accepting every home and taking every child offered. . . . Experience taught us that not every householder looking for a child was actuated by charity, and that many who were charitable were not wise, or discreet, or careful, or possessed of those qualities which the protector of a child should have."[98]

In the wake of the New York charities investigation of 1916, Cardinal John Farley wrote to his pastors of their responsibility to "search out good Catholic homes for Catholic dependents." Bryan McEntegart of Catholic Charities' Children's Division insisted that a Catholic agency with Catholic investigators and supervisors reporting to a Catholic superintendent and board was the best medium for finding and supervising Catholic foster homes.[99] In New York Catholic Charities lobbyists succeeded in adding language to laws on dependent children; in all possible cases, when a child was committed by the state to a private agency, it must be to an agency of the same religious faith as the child. More important was the provision that the child should only be placed or boarded out with families of the same religious faith.[100] In New York the city did not board out children directly, but supervised, inspected, and, as in the case of orphanages, paid religious and private agencies to provide the care.[101]

The experience of the New York Catholic Home Bureau for Dependent Children provided thousands of instances of what did and did not work. Social worker Mary Tinney, in 1916 an investigator for the New York Department of Public Charities, reviewed the Bureau's record in 3,000 placements at the annual NCCC meeting.[102] More than sixty-five percent remained in the first placement, although there was a horrendous example of one girl placed in thirteen different families. Failed placements arose when foster parents became ill, suffered financial reverses, or sometimes requested a change when "child had light hair" or "child seemed Japanese."[103]

The Catholic Home Bureau found no ideal profile of the right home for the child. Occupations of those requesting children ranged from the driver of a delivery wagon to a wealthy contractor. One-half of the requests for boys came from farmers who obviously wanted someone to help with the chores. If the farm were not too far from church and school, and the chores and wages suitable, the placement might be made under tight supervision. Most important in their placements, however, was the requirement that the foster parents be practicing Catholics. The parish priest was the sole criterion of the placing-out agency on this matter.

Although Boston's Catholic charities reported an ample list of Catholic foster homes, this seemed the exception rather than the rule.[104] Participants at the 1921 NCCC meeting shared strategies of varying success in finding good Catholic free or boarding homes. In some dioceses the bishop designated one Sunday a year as Charity Sunday. A letter read from the pulpit in each parish appealed for homes.[105] In Hartford, Connecticut, a social worker from Catholic charities visited a different parish every Sunday and asked that families interested in taking a child apply for one the following Sunday when she would arrive with three or four children. It was effective as a placement method for many children; however, it was brutal "if a little girl, perhaps, did not happen to have blue eyes and light, curly hair," and was rejected Sunday after Sunday. Hartford also adopted an economic approach. The diocesan director of the Bureau of Catholic Charities went to several churches to report that his institutions were "filled to overflowing with placeable children." He warned if more foster homes were not found for these children, additions would have to be built for these orphanages. This would be expensive for the diocese. It would obviously be to the advantage of Catholics to meet the challenge of economics as well as of "love of neighbor" and take in these dependent children. Parents who came forward after these appeals were interviewed by the diocesan director and then visited in their homes by a social worker, a questionnaire was completed, references given and checked, and placements made. In 1921 using these methods, Hartford reported 1,475 children in foster homes and 123 children in boarding homes.[106]

Advertising in Catholic newspapers was tried by several agencies and bureaus of Catholic charities. However, Edmund Butler of New York warned that sometimes advertising brought applications from families from slum districts or areas where the child's welfare could not be protected. In Baltimore the St. Vincent de Paul Society evaluated the stationery, handwriting, and composition of letters responding to its ads in the *Baltimore Catholic Review*. Butler found it more productive to send a trained agent into the neighborhoods. The agent did not look for the homes of the wealthy or the highly educated or those who were too old. What she sought was the normal home for the normal child. The best advertisement in any community, Butler concluded, was a good placement.[107]

Occasionally bureaus of Catholic Charities found exhibits at Catholic conventions or state fairs useful. Father Joseph Kroha of Milwaukee argued that exhibits were also effective as Catholic apologetics, showing "what the Church is doing for the unfortunates. We take, only too often, the attitude that we are strangers in our own country."[108]

When the NCWC team reviewed the placement records of the Pittsburgh Catholic Child Saving Bureau in 1919, they found that foster parents widely varied by age and ethnicity but generally not by class.[109] Overwhelmingly working-class families accepted the dependent or neglected child whether for companionship, board, or adoption. The ethnic and class bias of the social workers appears in their reports: "the child looks like American child though has Polish name," "like many Italian homes, it has the appearance of being overcrowded," "mostly foreign element, Italians, Slavs, and Croations," "properly managed home of man of 'millworker class' . . . satisfied to be always in the 'working people' class."

The foster homes visited by the survey team were about half boarding and half free. Boarding homes were generally more economically hard pressed. One widow, a sixty-year-old Irishwoman who already had her daughter, son-in-law, and a boarder living with her, responded to an ad in the Catholic newspaper and took in three Italian children under six years of age. Their own mother was "hopelessly insane"; their father contributed nine dollars a week, which the foster mother found inadequate. Because he didn't furnish many clothes, the children "stay in a lot."[110] Visiting another placement where a child had been placed with a Croatian family whose mother had six children of her own, the social worker cited the mother's appearance as "impossible"; she was nervous, indifferent, decidedly *not* a good housekeeper, and "delicate looking. No wonder!" The foster father used to drink but was "better now." The child's father contributed to her upkeep and took care of her in the evenings, but, concluded the visitor, for the child this was merely "sheltering arms," not a home. The survey team concluded that the Bureau did "not seem to realize that proper placement means more than finding homes and finding children for them."[111] By the mid-1920s, the trend in foster care was clearly toward boarding homes. Catholics, warned Rev. J.F.R. Corcoran, director of the Conference of Catholic Charities of Pittsburgh, had to disabuse themselves of their "curious prejudice" that the mother who accepted board for taking in a child had "commercialized her mother love." The standards for boarding homes, he insisted, were no lower than the standards for free homes. John O'Grady warned

Bryan J. McEntegart that if Catholic organizations failed to develop boarding home work, they would be left behind professionally and economically. He cited the appropriation of $60,000 by Cook County, Illinois, to pay for children in boarding homes.[112] In 1926 the New York Catholic Home Bureau began for the first time to place children in boarding as well as free foster homes.[113]

The survey of the New York Foundling Hospital's Placing Out and Boarding Out Departments by Rose McHugh in 1927 demonstrated again both the magnitude of the task and the need for professional standards. The Placing Out Department had 1,900 children under the care of Sister Cyrilla and seven agents with no training in social work. (This was a figure well down from the 3,538 boys and girls reported by the Foundling Hospital in free foster homes in a 1923 Bureau of the Census report.)[114] Sister Cyrilla had begun her work in 1888 as a nurse; she had been in the first graduating class at the School of Social Service of Fordham University. McHugh observed that the sister, while remarkably capable, was laboring "under a superhuman task." She not only managed the department but supervised the unwed mothers and gave them religious instruction. McHugh exclaimed, "How one person can carry such diversified responsibilities is almost incomprehensible to the lay mind." Sister Cyrilla, she believed, was probably too old and set in her ways to reorganize the department "according to modern social work ideals."[115] The agents seemed unaware that "the behavior of a child is a matter of delicate adjustment" between himself and his caregivers. The lack of a "modern psychiatric attitude toward the individual child," she found most distressing.

McHugh was also disturbed that the word of the foster parent was always accepted over the child's. She cited the example of an Italian boy's foster father reporting he couldn't get the child to go to school. Sister Cyrilla sent agent O'Hara, who doubled as the Foundling Hospital chauffeur, to give him "a good talking to." O'Hara, devoid of training and "wholly devoid of personality," had no understanding of the problems of children. When a fifteen-year-old girl was brought to the office having left her foster home, Sister Cyrilla remarked to a social worker on the McHugh team, "Look at this big girl that just walked out of her home. Don't you think she ought to be ashamed of herself after all the trouble we've had with her." The girl had no chance to tell her side of the story. In another instance a child of three was returned from her second foster home, and Sister Cyrilla wrote on her card, "I have given the child two chances and feel she will not make good." McHugh concluded: "It is a strange reversal of the order of things when a child of three is expected to 'make good' instead of the adults charged with her care."[116]

In her comments on the foster homes selected by the Foundling Hospital, McHugh found it surprising that a number of houses were in crowded sections, even with addresses on Mott Street and Sullivan Street. Children in such a congested tenement area would be forced to the streets for companionship and would be exposed to "untold moral dangers." She was particularly unhappy about a placement with an African-American family, wondering "by what standards a two-room house in the rear of a store in New York City is considered a satisfactory home for a child." The race of the family troubled her because it was not clear that the child's parentage was black or mixed. McHugh strongly recommended that the sisters end their integrated care of white and black children awaiting placement. It was an area where the sisters' standards were clearly more progressive than the social worker's.

McHugh's report highlights the major trends in Catholic foster care in the 1920s: the increasing professionalization of the work, the centralization of responsibility in the children's divisions of the diocesan bureaus, and the continuing shift away from institutional to foster boarding care. Diocesan directors of Catholic Charities worked with legislators, city councils, and community chests for funding and supervisory rights. Catholic lay social workers rather than the sisters worked with the boarding mothers in placing and protecting the Catholic child.[117]

While Catholic religious maintained orphanages as temporary havens for dependent children, they were simultaneously establishing protectories, industrial schools, and, most notably, the houses of the Good Shepherd to save their delinquents. Catholics comprised 50 percent to 64 percent of the children and young adults appearing in the juvenile courts in New York, Chicago, Boston, Philadelphia, Pittsburgh, and Cleveland.[118] Psychologist William I. Thomas noted in his 1923 study of the unadjusted girl that most of the children in the juvenile court were "naturally, the children of the poor"; they were, more precisely, "lower-class, ghetto-dwelling, Catholic immigrants with minimal educations."[119]

The predominance of Catholic delinquents guaranteed Catholic involvement. The first chief probation officer of the pioneering Chicago juvenile court was Timothy Hurley of the Catholic Visitation and Aid Society, a lawyer who had helped draft the original court bill in 1899. Catholic volunteers served as probation officers; Catholic professionals joined the national discussions on the factors leading to delinquency and appropriate treatment. When the court determined that Catholic delinquents should be institutionalized for their rehabilitation, Catholic religious provided institutions. For the errant boys, the massive New York Protectory; St. Mary's Industrial School in Baltimore, with its famous resident Babe Ruth; and Father Flanagan's BoysTown were among the most well-known, but most large urban dioceses provided industrial schools.[120] Catholic delinquent girls committed to institutions by the juvenile courts were generally sent to the House of the Good Shepherd.[121] There they came under the specialized care of an order of cloistered nuns with centuries-old experience in saving "fallen" women and girls. The French order of the Sisters of the Good Shepherd established their first American house in Louisville in 1842. By 1938 they had 340 houses in the United States, staffed by 10,000 religious, caring for 80,000 women and girls. Like the orphan asylums, the houses of the Good Shepherd generally were large congregate and, from the outside, somewhat forbidding institutions.[122]

The Good Shepherd sister's vocation was to return the lost and strayed to the world morally and spiritually healed. The work of their seventeenth-century French founder, St. John Eudes, was expanded by Mother Mary of St. Euphrasia, who won papal approval in 1835 to organize a generalate and to establish refuges not only in France but in the "universe." Sisters dispatched to establish houses in the United States were armed with her remarkable instructions for their difficult work.[123]

The Good Shepherd sister, sustained by prayer, was instructed to be firm. Mother Euphrasia emphasized that authority was rooted in "a certain air, a certain ascendance which commands respect and obedience." Once authority was accepted, the sister must be amiable. She advised: "Endeavor with kindness and gentleness to sustain the bruised reed. . . We should, like the fig tree, keep what is bitter for ourselves and give the sweet to others."[124]

The past of a young girl in their charge was never discussed. The sister working with her knew her background; only the mother superior knew her name.[125] Though sensitive to the dangers and temptations that the girl committed to their care might have faced, the Good Shepherd sisters believed that the sin was the result of a rational and voluntary act.[126] Rehabilitation in the House of the Good Shepherd centered on molding character and strengthening the will.

A regular life of work, study, and prayer was prescribed. Young women were taught domestic skills such as plain sewing, mending, and housekeeping. Mother Euphrasia believed that they "should not get ideas beyond their position in life, but should be taught how to fulfill that position in the most perfect manner possible." "As a life of labor is the allotted portion of our children, they should be early accustomed to habits of industry, thrift, and economy." The end of education was to form "our children with a view to their eternal salvation."[127] A realist, Euphrasia warned her sisters to provide for the temporal needs before speaking of the spiritual, adding: "do not imagine that allowing them to suffer helps to convert them."[128]

Sisters of the Good Shepherd were instructed never to strike a child nor to raise their voice. Kindness, piety, and love would win the soul in the end. A superior should not be feared.[129] Punishment was a last resort. The most serious infractions might result in time alone in a room. A young rule-breaker might be made to stand with an apron on her head or to wear her dress inside out.[130]

In the 1920s the average stay in a House of the Good Shepherd was a year to eighteen months. Some sisters and staff social workers believed three years or more was the optimum time for character building. One social worker reported the Good Shepherd success rate in rehabilitation with good after-care sometimes was 85 to 90 percent.[131]

Mother Euphrasia had instructed her sisters to be open to change and to learn how things were done elsewhere. Apparently that particular instruction was not always followed. Catholic social worker Leslie Foy of the Public Charities Association of Pennsylvania wrote to John O'Grady of some institutional intransigence: "I suppose the Houses of the Good Shepherd could not even be touched without an explosion. . ."[132] Yet, as they accepted commitments and remuneration from the juvenile court system, the sisters had to meet standards of care and after-care set by probation officers and social workers. They were particularly scrutinized and advised by survey teams of NCCC and visitors from the protective divisions of diocesan bureaus of Catholic Charities.

In the 1919 NCWC Pittsburgh survey, the House of the Good Shepherd at Troy Hill, a large congregate institution, was visited by social worker Mary Anne Kennedy. Eleven sisters, she reported, cared for one hundred and thirty-six girls and women. They were divided into three groups: the Inebriate, the Reformatory, and the Protectory. There was also a group of older women, the consecrates, who elected to remain in the convent and worked with the sisters to rehabilitate new arrivals. Some chose to enter the order of Magdalenes, founded by Mother Euphrasia, to live a life of expiation through prayer and manual labor.[133] Kennedy, noting the sisters' belief that many of the consecrates would not be able to take care of themselves in the world, urged them to carry out mental testing before encouraging their charges to renounce the world. Gratuitously she suggested that they try to "strengthen, rather than weaken, the will of the girls." A questionnaire completed during Kennedy's visit showed that ninety-two respondents did not wish to remain in the convent, whereas twenty-six did. Eighteen were either undecided or ignored the question.[134]

These responses to the questionnaire provide a remarkable profile of the girls and women at Troy Hill. There were eleven questions surveying age, family background, length of stay, previous schooling and work, and what each expected to do on leaving. The majority reported they had been assigned by the juvenile court. Most had not completed the sixth grade. Though one listed her father as an architect, all of the others were clearly from the working class. Those in their twenties generally had little schooling; the handwriting, spelling, and quality of the responses generally suggested that this group was poorly equipped to enter the workforce.

As usual the visiting social worker found that recordkeeping needed improvement. More serious was her criticism of the education and work schedule. Of the eighty-two girls and women not in class, nineteen reported that they had not completed more than the first three grades in school; another forty-three had finished the sixth grade. Many had been put back a grade in the Good Shepherd classroom, reflecting possibly a previous high degree of truancy or learning disability. For those taking classes, the morning was spent in domestic science, which meant helping in the kitchen or dining room. In the afternoon they took classes in speech, penmanship, reading, spelling, geography or history, hygiene or language, and arithmetic, interrupted by a brief session of calisthenics. Classes were also offered in needlework, cooking, and typewriting. Friday was set aside for review. For the girls committed for "immorality," a truncated schedule began with writing at 7:30 A.M. and concluded with grammar at 10:00 A.M. Nine girls were enrolled in a commercial course of bookkeeping, shorthand, and typewriting. All of the women and girls worked in the well-equipped modern commercial laundry at least four hours each day, frequently going back after supper to complete the orders for the Troy Hill Laundry. Kennedy noted that none of the girls indicated they would chose laundry work on leaving the House of the Good Shepherd. Most listed housework or remaining at home. In 1919 Troy Hill fell somewhat short of Mother Euphrasia's determination that girls with the sisters of the Good Shepherd should be as well-educated as those in public schools.[135]

In the 1920s the trend in rehabilitation was clearly away from congregate institutions "with four brick walls to shut in the sinners."[136] Yet inside the walls the sisters were increasingly open to new casework methods. In the spring of 1925, the *Catholic Charities Review* published a series of three articles featuring their houses in Cleveland, Cincinnati, Duluth, and St. Louis. Each house insisted on physical examinations, including Wasserman tests, and provided well-staffed infirmaries and ongoing medical and dental care. All who came through the juvenile courts were given intelligence tests; all others were tested at admission for classification. All of the institutions provided recreation. One social worker cited the power of baseball, gardening, or caring for animals "to transfer morbid and sinful tastes into wholesome instincts, and [to] help to soften the ground in which grace is finding its foothold." Campfire leaders, drama coaches, musicians, and volunteers from the Catholic Collegiate Association visited the institutions. At each of the Good Shepherd houses surveyed, all girls under eighteen were in classes, from elementary through a commercial course. The curriculum was the same as offered in parochial schools; the sisters were trained for their teaching. There was also heavy emphasis on vocational training in sewing, laundry work, and ironing. All still worked in the commercial industries of the houses.[137] At the release of each woman or girl, the social worker presented a discharge plan to the court. Those going to a wage home were supplied with dresses, accessories, and enough pin money to last until payday. Supervision by the social worker continued until the girl reached twenty-one. In monthly meetings the social worker assessed the girl's progress in her spiritual life. Big Sisters and a Good Shepherd Auxiliary helped in the job hunt.[138]

While lay caseworkers emphasized the high standards and success rate of the Good Shepherd houses, the sisters provided a more nuanced account of their blend of social work and salvation. Sister Mary of St. Anthony Norris related the story of Francesca. Arrested on a charge of immorality, she had been committed to the Philadelphia House of the Good Shepherd. She remained as a consecrate for seventeen years, eventually developing eye trouble "dated to her first misstep at nineteen." Although she could have been treated in the convent, the "tempter gave her glimpses of the world." She left, "married a bigot," and turned from the faith. A priest later alerted the sisters when Francesca was hospitalized in the last stages of tuberculosis. When two sisters visited and prayed with her, she held the crucifix and asked for a cup of the convent's boiled coffee. A Catholic nurse detained the husband during these visits. In "one more striking evidence of God's mercy," reported Sister Mary of St. Anthony, she died in the faith.[139]

Reflecting on the sisters' essential work of saving souls, Sister Mary of St. Anthony observed that they saw "so little fruit of their toil." She added: "Of course, from time to time there are marvelous conversions, beautiful deaths among the children; but of the large number who continually pass through our hands the actual result often seems painfully small. We use the word 'seems' advisedly for we firmly believe there are many lovely death scenes where the remembrance of a stay, long or short, in the House of the Good Shepherd proves to be the saving grace. . . . Those who go out and obliterate their sinful past by good behavior, like to forget their wrong doing and all connected with it."[140]

Although the Sisters of the Good Shepherd adapted to changing standards in rehabilitation, they needed help from the NCCC in the 1930s, not to survive the Depression but the New Deal.[141] Catholic leaders supported the sweeping reemployment/recovery provisions of the 1933 National Industrial Recovery Act (NRA), believing it closely paralleled Pope Pius XI's vision of cooperative economic organization. Yet NRA posed an unexpected practical problem for Catholic "employers" and "workers" in the houses of the Good Shepherd.[142] When sixty-four houses of the Good Shepherd did not meet the NRA Cotton Garment Code on wages and hours, anxious superiors appealed for advice and help to both the NCWC and the NCCC.[143] Manufacturers hesitated to place orders for their work fearing code violations; union executives were pressing them to meet the NRA wage and hour standards for their "employees." The sisters saw their exclusion from NRA as threatening the training and discipline their work programs provided for their charges; economically it also left many of their houses in severely straitened circumstances.

John O'Grady became their mediator and interpreter. He worked to win the exclusion of the work produced by sheltered workshops like the houses of the Good Shepherd and Goodwill Industries; he also won appointment to the National Sheltered Workshop Committee, which supervised institutional compliance. It proved more difficult to get information and compliance from the superiors of the Good Shepherds.

To qualify for sheltered workshop status and the privilege of displaying the Blue Eagle, superiors had to sign a Pledge of Fair Competition and fill out a lengthy questionnaire. Some of the sisters questioned why they should sign a pledge for something that "does not concern us." They were not in business but in rehabilitation. From Hot Springs, Arkansas, the Sisters of the House of the Good Shepherd wrote to O'Grady: "We are very poor, and have 100 children of various ages to support—only 6 of whom pay anything for their maintenance. Awaiting further instructions & hoping that our little Laundry is not worth mentioning to the N.R.A."[144] One lamented, "I do not know *how* to answer the questions"; others, who had had their questionnaires returned as "very incomplete," received explicit instructions from O'Grady. Some superiors sought his help in reassuring manufacturers that they could legally contract with them. As one explained, "since the loss of our sewing revenue it has been impossible to meet current expenses, and this is a source of considerable anxiety." T. A. Byrne, the Code Authority representative, visited houses of the Good Shepherd in the northeast and worked with manufacturers to obtain contracts at comparable rates and to spread the work so that the Good Shepherds' products did not significantly compete with union work.

O'Grady sought further help, suggesting to diocesan directors of charity that orphanages might use the garments produced in the houses of the Good Shepherd. At the same time, he offered the "splendid idea" to provincials of religious communities that they help one another by buying articles made in Catholic institutions. He had arranged with the McCosker Company of New York, a religious goods firm, to sell the muslin undergarments, underskirts, aprons, and nightgowns made in the sisters' institutions. The sisterhood was not buying. By what right, one asked, did the secretary of the National Conference of Catholic Charities issue such a letter? Yet the work of the houses of the Good Shepherd went on with the blessing of the NRA. Not surprisingly, the NCCC Executive Committee, in planning for its annual convention, determined that "every effort should be made to secure the attendance of the Sisters of the Good Shepherd."[145] The sisters who did attend the 1935 NCCC meeting found that other religious congregations were also confronting the impact of the New Deal, as the Aid to Dependent Children and Child Welfare provisions of Social Security extended federal welfare to America's children.

Outside the Institutions:
Pensions, Precaution, Prevention

Although Catholic child-caring institutions provided a safety net for thousands of children, they did so after 1909 in the context of the principle of "home first." At the White House Conference on the Care of Dependent Children in that year, the conference vice-chair, Thomas Mulry of the St. Vincent de Paul Society of New York, and the other Catholic representatives supported the declaration that "home life is the highest and finest product of civilization." Children should not be deprived of it except for urgent and compelling reasons, certainly not because of poverty. If worthy parents faced "temporary misfortune" or "deserving mothers" were "without the support of the normal breadwinner," aid, preferably from private charity, should be offered "to maintain suitable homes for the rearing of the children."[1] Both the principle and the practical reality were compelling. In the major cities of the Northeast and Midwest, Catholic families and children were those most clearly at risk and in need. The National Conference of Catholic Charities supported the state drives for mothers' pensions that built on the momentum of the White House Conference, and diocesan bureaus of charity expanded their networks of social services to support children and youth at home and in the community.[2] Though they could not guarantee the religious nurture provided by the sisters in the institutions, diocesan directors of charities, their social workers, and Catholic volunteers were nevertheless determined to be involved in caring for their own.

Between 1911 and 1913, a remarkable coalition of child/family savers secured legislation for mothers' pensions in twenty states. Juvenile court judges and the National Probation Association argued that enabling widows to remain at home would reduce delinquency and truancy. The National Consumers' League stressed that mothers' pensions would reduce the numbers of children forced to work. The early and powerful rationale advanced by maternalist reformers, particularly by the National Congress of Mothers, stressed the responsibilities and rights of motherhood. This position was ably supported by Catholic juvenile court judge William H. De Lacy at the fifth meeting of the NCCC: "We give the soldier a liberal pension, because the soldier protects the state. But if it were not for the mother, there would be no state to protect. So it is entirely a matter of justice more than a matter of charity when the state gives the dependent mother a pension."[3]

Although Catholic leaders gradually became part of this broad coalition, Catholic institutions were frequently the target of the scare tactics of the pension campaigners. Editors of the crusading *Delineator* emotionally argued that these laws would give the money to the mother rather than to the institution where "her children are *imprisoned.*" The January 1913 issue featured "Motherless Children of Living Mothers" and the story of a poverty-striken New York widow forced to commit her four children to a Catholic orphanage. Thomas Mulry rejected both the familiar attacks on the institutional child and the assumption that mothers' pensions would threaten Catholic orphanages. In this he was vigorously seconded by Rev. Hubert LeBlond, who supervised Catholic charitable institutions in Cleveland. When the Ohio law was passed, LeBlond's institutions quickly sent thirty-eight children home to their widowed, and now publicly supported, mothers. He reasoned: "If we feel that the mother can care for the child better than we can, then why should we keep it in an Institution? And we may be sure, there will never be a lack of children to enter our Institutions." If, he continued, "Mothers' Pension would make it possible for every child to remain with its relatives, and thus close our institutions, I think we should be the first to urge that law, and keep those children home." There would be "plenty of other work to do."[4]

By 1920 forty states had mothers' pension laws in place. The good news was that the state increasingly accepted the responsibility of providing funds for its children (if not their mothers); the bad news was that most of the early legislation was permissive rather than mandatory, that appropriations frequently did not follow legislation, and that funding rarely met full need and generally was predicated on the able-bodied widow working. When local or state money was provided, it came only to worthy mothers, generally widows, in suitable homes, and it came with the investigation and assistance of a social worker who determined need and developed a family budget.[5]

When Illinois passed the first state-level mothers' pension law in 1911, the Funds to Parents Act, the need was immediately and graphically demonstrated. The Chicago *Record-Herald,* again raising the specter of the dread institution, described the Widow Smith, faced with giving her children to the sisters, suddenly facing "a new and beautiful tomorrow." During the first week after the law went into effect in Cook County, "one Mrs. Smith after another, whose only crime has been to lose her husband and the natural provider for her children, [was] released from sentence of indefinite earthly banishment from her family through government pension." The president of the Board of County Commissioners reported women "flocking in" and predicted "we will be swamped within a short time."[6] Catholic probation officer Mary E. Shinnick of the Cook County juvenile court, which determined funding, reported on the first year of the Chicago experience to the NCCC. Rehearsing the familiar fears of critics that the pensions would be too costly, that they would ultimately pauperize recipients, or that they would be subject to political abuse, Shinnick slyly noted "the fear of maladministration has not abolished the pension paid to old soldiers." The direct funding of mothers would be less costly in the long run than institutional care. She echoed Judge De Lacy in insisting that the pensions were not alms but payments for ongoing service to the state, which had an obvious interest in seeing its citizens raised properly. Though some NCCC delegates feared that "the state may follow its funds [into the home,] and its agents may not care for Catholic teachings," they generally acknowledged that Catholic resources were "strained to the utmost" and that public financial aid was a growing necessity—and perhaps even a right.[7]

In Chicago Catholic social workers and volunteers were centrally involved in implementing the Funds to Parents Act. Rose McHugh was secretary of the Funds to Parents Committee, which advised the juvenile court on criteria and qualifications. Joining Jane Addams and Julia Lathrop on that executive committee were Lenora Z. Meder of the Chicago League of Catholic Women, James Kennedy of the St. Vincent de Paul Society, and Rev. C. J. Quille of Catholic Charities. Meder, who had originally been in the camp of those who argued that an adequate system of social insurance would obviate the need for mothers' pensions, was converted by her Chicago experience. But concerned over the intrusiveness of caseworkers, she cited the complaint of a Chicago widow: "[First] the dietitian comes around and tells me how I must diet, and fix food for the baby. Then an inspector comes and asks to see my supply of underwear and linen." Meder stressed the role of private agencies as intermediaries between the resources of the state and the distress of the poor.[8] When the Mothers' Pensions Department was subsequently established by the juvenile court, Emma Quinlan, Catholic social worker and graduate of the University of Chicago School of Civics, was its first director.

These Catholic administrators and advisers were clearly serving many Catholic pension recipients. The majority of Chicago's pension grants went to widows, frequently foreign-born, with two or three children. When Illinois passed a new Mothers' Aid law in 1913, specifying that only citizens and only widows or mothers whose husbands were permanently disabled were eligible for assistance, the impact was predictably severe. Seventy-eight percent of Chicago's population were first- or second-generation immigrants. Two years later the legislature again revised the law; this time it made the American-born children of foreign-born women eligible for assistance. In the first six months, the number of grants increased 58 percent.[9]

Pennsylvania's 1913 mothers' pension law was administered not by the juvenile court or departments of public welfare but through county commissioners appointed by the governor. Again Catholics were key administrators. The State Supervisor of the Mothers' Assistance Fund of the Pennsylvania Department of Welfare was Catholic social worker Mary F. Bogue.[10] In Allegheny County Teresa Molamphy of Pittsburgh was one of three Catholic women appointed to the seven-member board of commissioners. In its first eight months of operation, the Allegheny commission received sixteen hundred applications, and the women volunteers were determined to investigate each one. "I do not wish to cast any reflections on men," Molamphy chided, "but we do find at least in Pennsylvania, that when offices carry good emoluments with them, men fill those offices." Molamphy insisted that the commissioners ignored the religion of the applicants when they made their recommendations, but she did estimate that as many as fifty percent of the applications in Pittsburgh were from Catholic women.[11]

The struggle to pass a mothers' pension bill in New York was especially protracted. After the defeat of the first measure introduced in 1897, pension bills were hardy perennials; six were introduced and voted down in 1913 alone. It was clear that New York's children needed some assistance, but would the aid be better administered by public agencies or private organizations? It was also clear that the overwhelming number of children in need, as in Chicago and Pittsburgh, were Catholic. The New York Association for Improving the Condition of the Poor (AICP) reported in 1912 that 89 percent of the widows receiving "pensions" from the Association's funds were Catholic. Two years later an AICP social worker reported on the private aid provided to Mrs. Katherine M., "an American Catholic widow with eight children." The parish priest paid ten dollars a month for rent for six months, the St. Vincent de Paul Society provided two dollars a week for groceries. The church had referred the mother, ill with tuberculosis, to the AICP, which provided an additional thirty-seven dollars a month and a friendly visitor to monitor spending, budget, and progress. The Report of the Commission on Relief for Widowed Mothers, commissioned by frustrated pension proponents in the legislature in 1913, estimated that 2,716 children of widowed mothers were in institutions "at public expense" due to the poverty of the family. Robert Hebberd, secretary of the New York State Board of Charities and director of investigation for the Commission, blamed the New York "charities trust" and "people with large sums of money at command, the Russell Sage Foundation, for example," for creating the state's "exceedingly backward" attitude toward pensions.[12] Led by Edward Devine of the Charity Organization Society, private relief organizations issued their own committee report arguing that private relief was nearly meeting the need, and, more important, the private organizations had the expertise to provide both investigations and supervision. The solution, the committee argued, was not pensions but social insurance. One of the signatures on this committee report was Michael J. Scanlan, treasurer of the Superior Council of the Society of St. Vincent de Paul.[13] Thomas Mulry later ruefully admitted that not all of the resistance had come from Russell Sage and accepted his share of responsibility for killing the bill in the legislature in 1914. Like many of his colleagues from the Charity Organization Society and the National Conference of Charities and Corrections, Mulry preferred private initiative in social provision. He had become a convert to public money given the sheer inadequacy of the funds available through the Society of St. Vincent de Paul, explaining: "we were repeating the story of the dog in the manger. We could not do the work ourselves and we seemed not to wish that anyone else did it."[14] Mulry endorsed the conclusion of the state commission that private charities lacked the resources to meet the needs of New York's children.[15]

When the New York legislature finally passed the Hill bill and created mothers' pensions in 1915, the law contained two interesting provisions. The first, reflective of the legislative strength of both Catholics and the Russell Sage lobby and of the ongoing conflicts over funding and institutional care in New York City, limited the "allowances" paid to widows to the amount "necessary to pay to an institutional home for the care of such widow's child or children." The city was clearly not going to have a financial incentive to remove a child from a Catholic institution. At the same time, assistance would only be granted to children when it was clear that without it they would have to be cared for in an institution. New York was not going to allow the new Child Welfare Boards to be profligate with public money.[16]

The federal Children's Bureau monitored the implementation of the mothers' pensions. On the tenth anniversary of the enactment of the first Illinois law, the Bureau's Emma Lundberg reported on the trends in "Aid to Mothers with Dependent Children." More than 75 percent of the aid recipients were widows, but state laws and/or local administrators were gradually expanding eligibility to include mothers who were deserted, divorced, or whose husbands were totally incapacitated or imprisoned. Lundberg estimated that whereas 200,000 children were receiving aid, the need was probably closer to 400,000. The standard budgets developed by state and county agencies only provided approximately one- to two-thirds the amount they allocated for boarding children in foster family homes. Lundberg protested: "Mothers' pension administration offers perhaps the most obvious arguments as to the futility . . . of placing laws on the statute books but failing to make them practically effective through adequate appropriations and proper administration."[17] The NCCC reported on the Children's Bureau studies and also tracked the experience of Catholic professionals in administering the laws. Catholic supervisors and commissioners from public agencies reporting on Buffalo, Albany, Minnesota, and Pennsylvania universally echoed Lundberg on the need for larger allowances and broader inclusion.[18] Ada Burns of the Erie County Child's Welfare Board, observing that the $21.66 maximum monthly payment per child was not sufficient to meet the needs of a widow with two small children, hoped that New York would soon amend its law to grant an allowance to the mother as well as her children. Work and supplementary assistance from other agencies were usually necessary for survival. "True," she observed, "these widows have not been permitted to die of starvation," but "many gradually, often imperceptibly, landed in hospitals and institutions because of continued social neglect."[19]

Having backed the state campaigns for mothers' pensions, the NCCC also supported the federal legislative initiative, spearheaded by the Children's Bureau and their lobbying network of women's organizations for the Sheppard-Towner or Maternity and Infancy Act of 1921. In this effort the NCCC was joined by the National Council of Catholic Women, obviously with the blessing of the NCWC. The Children's Bureau studies of mortality rates for mother and child provided convincing and grim statistical evidence of the abysmal record of the United States compared with that of other western industrial nations. After extensive compromises in the face of the opposition of the American Medical Association, the Children's Bureau and women lobbyists won a modest federal-state program, administered by the Bureau, that provided a $5,000 federal grant to each state and, with legislative approval, a matching grant up to $5,000 with additional funding based on the state's population. The money provided workshops and clinics run by public health nurses, dentists, dietitians, and physicians; training for midwives; and education for mothers through exhibitions, public lectures, films, classes, and correspondence courses.[20] The *Catholic Charities Review* summarized the first official report from the Children's Bureau on Sheppard-Towner in 1924 and noted that most of the effort aided rural mothers and children because urban mothers, which included most Catholics, already had access to health facilities. Two years later, when the Children's Bureau and their network of lobbyists again faced the American Medical Association in an unsuccessful campaign to renew the legislation, Mrs. Francis E. Slattery, president of the League of Catholic Women of Boston, was dispatched by Cardinal William H. O'Connell of Boston to testify against federal intrusion and paternalism. Claiming, somewhat dubiously, to speak for 400,000 Catholic women, she asserted that Massachusetts had no need of federal money because the state provided for its mothers and children. Pressed to elaborate on these good state programs, she was nonplussed, admitting that she was unsure what the state offered because she was not a professional social worker. Neither the NCCC nor NCWC testified at these hearings, and the claim of "Catholic" opposition seems to rest primarily on the evidence of Mrs. Slattery's inept testimony.[21]

The Catholic position is clearer in the case of day nurseries. Though a few Catholic day nurseries, such as San Francisco's Children's Day Home, had been started in the late nineteenth century, the vast majority opened during World War I and the early 1920s when a combination of women working in new war jobs, fathers' low factory wages, or inadequate mothers' pensions left parents unable to meet health and shelter expenses for their children.[22] The U.S. Census of 1920 confirmed that one-quarter of married women were in the workplace, but this statistic did not include the widowed, divorced, or unmarried mothers of children. Three years later the Census reported 613 day nurseries caring for 22,822 children; 100 of the 218 nurseries operated by religious organizations were Catholic.[23] Ethyll M. Dooley, executive secretary of the Association of Catholic Day Nurseries, declared: "The day nursery is no longer an agency of doubtful value, but has taken its place in the field of child-welfare. So long as the mother is the support of the family in whole or in part, as found today in thousands of homes in New York, so long will day nurseries be necessary."[24] Catholic day nurseries, like orphanages and foundling asylums, were established not only to meet the urgent practical needs of Catholic children but to save them from the proselytizer and for the faith. At the first meeting of the NCCC in 1910 during a lively discussion on the competition for "the possession of our Catholic children," Mrs. Thomas Hughes Kelly of the Committee on Day Nurseries of the New York Association of Catholic Charities observed how "consoling" it was "to note how often the Catholic mother gladly and bravely chooses to take her children to a poor, bare, crowded little Catholic institution rather than to any other if only she can find one to go to." Mrs. Mary Gaynor Wilson of Chicago reported that a Protestant nursery established only two blocks from the Catholic institution was clearly "founded to take the Italians away from us," and because it was free, it was "a great temptation to the mothers to take their children there."[25]

As usual Catholic Charities of the Archdiocese of New York served the largest number of families and children. The 1922 annual report of CCNY listed twenty-four day nurseries with a capacity for 2,229 children. All but four of these were run by religious. By 1926 two more had been opened in the most economically distressed areas of the city, on Christie Street in the Village and in the East Bronx. When Archbishop Hayes was chided that Catholics were doing little to assist African-Americans, a day nursery was opened in Harlem. The Harlem nursery was one of only three Catholic nurseries for African-American children in the country.[26]

One Catholic charities' study profiling the population of a New York nursery in the center of the city reported that of 119 parents or guardians, seventy-nine had been born in Italy and nineteen in Ireland. Thirty-eight percent had not become citizens. Most of the fathers were laborers or mechanics with average wages of $28.33 a week. Forty-six percent of the working mothers were employed in factories; thirty-three percent were in domestic or household work. Their wages averaged $13.00 to $15.20. From their home visits, social workers estimated that more than one-third of the mothers were in poor or delicate health. Reviewing their religious practices, the visitors found that eighty-two were practical Catholics, meaning they attended Mass on Sunday and received the Sacraments once or twice a year.

Of the 193 children surveyed in the same study, 167 were born in the United States, whereas twenty-one had been born in Italy. Most were from small families of two or three children. All the Catholic children were baptized. Their homes were of the "old type of tenement building," set in the middle of a busy business district. Most were overcrowded, particularly in their sleeping quarters. Only one home had hot running water. In two homes there was no daylight at all. Twenty-five percent of the families had contacts with other social agencies, which the social workers interpreted as a healthy attempt by the parents to seek help. Whereas one-third of the children had come to the nursery through the recommendation of the parish priest, more than fifty percent of the parents had brought their children on their own, seeing the nursery as their neighborhood institution.[27] Support for the day nurseries came from a combination of payments from the parents, contributed services of the sisters, appropriations from Catholic Charities, contributions from the business community, and, in community chest cities, from the chest.

Staff visiting the children's homes were instructed to be sympathetic and sensitive to ethnic customs, traditions, and tastes. The sisters also brought mothers to the day nurseries. Because the families served and the sisters staffing the nurseries were primarily of one nationality, speakers at these sessions generally gave their health talks in the mothers' language. The frequent mothers' meetings were intended to "give the mother instruction that will help her to meet more effectively the everyday problems of living, to better her understanding of the great social forces which surround her and to quicken her sense of obligation to the community."[28] Close contact with other mothers could lead to friendships and a network of possible help in the community; close contact with the sisters and social workers would bring "the spiritual side of life" before the mothers.[29]

Sisters and social workers believed that it was the spiritual benefits of the day nursery that were the most important and long lasting. Ethyll Dooley declared that the Christ-like charity and devotion of the sisters had to make a deep impression "on the recipients of such service. . . . The teachings of the Church now appear to them in practical form and if of themselves they do not become more practical Catholics, they at least are well disposed to receive and heed the advice of Priest or Sister." "Truly," Dooley concluded, the day nursery was "an agency which is doing much for the upbuilding of the childhood of America."[30]

Yet there was a continuing philosophical discussion of the nursery's impact on the child and family. Was the day nursery enabling employers to continue paying fathers less than a family wage? Was the day nursery eroding the arguments for more realistic funds for mothers' pensions? Was the day nursery providing a means for mothers, who were driven to work not by necessity but by the many lures of a consumer culture, to shirk their responsibilities to their children? All of these questions were posed in three major sessions on the day nursery as a social agency at the 1923, 1924, and 1926 meetings of the NCCC and in a follow-up summary article in the *Catholic Charities Review*. All of these queries were accepted as valid cautions and as cause for renewed commitment to work for social justice in the long term. But in the short term, the day nursery was hailed as filling a real need for Catholic families and communities.

Catholic charities focused on the older child in need or trouble through the social service of their schools and clinics. John M. Cooper, author/editor of *Children's Institutions,* saw the schools as early warning devices and urged that the casework expertise of a visiting teacher be made available to Catholic schools.[31] But the number of parochial schools and the students to be reached was daunting. Boston had 113 parish schools, New York 118; Chicago's parochial school enrollments were as large as the entire public school system of Detroit. The dimensions of the challenge were even more evident at the classroom level. A Catholic social worker, visiting eight ethnic parochial schools in the 1919 Pittsburgh survey, reported overcrowding, inadequate equipment, poorly trained teachers, and parents who took their children out of school as soon as they were old enough to work.[32] School counselor Sara Laughlin, surveying predelinquents at Assumption School in Philadelphia, reported that the staff of seven sisters and a lay teacher faced enrollments of over eighty in each classroom through the fifth grade. Only in the eighth grade did the enrollment fall below thirty. When the NCCC's John O'Grady suggested that the sisters, "with all the prestige of school and church combined," consider designating two of their number for home visiting work, it might well have received less than an enthusiastic reception from the exhausted teachers. Though they might agree on the need, who could they spare?[33]

For the troubled young girl or boy who needed professional help, bureaus of Catholic Charities increasingly recommended and provided the child-guidance clinic.[34] Jane Hoey, assistant director of the Welfare Council of New York, described the child-guidance clinic as "the best social machinery yet devised for diagnosis of personality and behavior difficulties of children." Yet acceptance of the clinic's holistic approach, which brought the social worker, physician, psychiatrist, and sometimes priest to address the troubled child, was not achieved overnight. Terms such as "the mental hygiene of childhood" and "psychopathology" were not reassuring to clergy and laymen raised with a suspicion of psychologists and Freudian psychiatrists. Bishop Thomas Drumm observed at the NCCC meeting in 1926, the year the National Association of Psychiatric Social Workers was founded: "It will perhaps take many years to put over the idea of better mental study of children."[35] The director of the St. Vincent de Paul Mental Clinic in Detroit was confronted by the skepticism of James Fitzgerald, the executive director of the St. Vincent de Paul Society. He was not persuaded by the "assumption by the expert" that his conclusions were "demonstrably true" nor that ordinary people would be "so gullible to accept . . . the scanty proofs psychiatry is in the habit of giving." That is, if ordinary people could understand the experts' jargon.[36] Yet Catholic professionals increasingly adopted the therapeutic approach in their casework and joined the ranks of psychiatric social workers.[37]

When a Catholic child did get into trouble and ran afoul of the law, he faced the judgment of the juvenile court. First established in 1899 to deal with the overwhelming numbers of delinquent and dependent children of Chicago, the juvenile court experiment spread across the nation almost as rapidly as mothers' pensions (which they frequently administered). By 1919 every state except Wyoming and Maine had created juvenile courts. The court acted as *parens patria*.[38] Catholic social theorist Paul Hanly Furfey placed the work of the juvenile court squarely in the Catholic tradition of dealing with the offender/sinner. The judge's role, Furfey explained, was like the priest's in the confessional: "the essence of the process is to view the sinner as a whole, to get back from his acts to his motives. . . . The skilful confessor [and judge] is less interested in the guilt of the penitent than he is in helping [him] to avoid sin in the future."[39]

The state's embrace, though well-meaning, could be heavy. The intrusiveness and arbitrary actions of judges and probation officers, coupled with the predominance of delinquents with a Catholic background as the objects of the courts' concern, guaranteed Catholic involvement. Catholic delinquents comprised 50 to 64 percent of the children and young adults appearing in juvenile courts in New York, Chicago, Boston, Philadelphia, and Cleveland. In Buffalo 85 percent of the boys appearing in the court were Catholic.[40]

Most experts agreed that delinquency began in the home and was nurtured in poverty.[41] At the second NCCC meeting, Michael Doyle of the St. Vincent de Paul Society in Philadelphia raised a firestorm by asserting that it was a well-established fact that Catholics had larger families than Protestants, and that "the larger the family, the greater the strain upon the head of the family to support it, and the greater the responsibility and the duties upon the mother," and the greater probability of delinquency. Judge William De Lacy of the District of Columbia juvenile court challenged Doyle's assumption and then heatedly inveighed against social workers in his court who insisted: "Judge, she has too many children." He stormed: "How do they know that? It is true she may be the mother of from seven to ten children. It is true she is working from early morning to late night. Her work is never done." His social worker stereotype followed: "When a good woman, with no family connections and no present prospects of ever having family connections, who lives at a club, and wears tailor-made clothes, says to the court that the home is not in the apple pie order of her club apartments, I gently remind her that the poor mother's economic condition does not enable her to employ three or four servants."[42]

But the poverty–large family issue did not go away. In 1914, Rev.

Cassian Hartl, observing the children of immigrants in the Pittsburgh juvenile court, sympathetically cited the number of mouths to feed when parents had "neither the means nor the knowledge to look after their children." When both worked, the children were neglected and "the home appears untidy and repulsive." Immigrant working mothers tended to be ignorant not only of the customs of the country but the behavior of their children. Frequently the children of drunken and brutal fathers were "kicked up" rather than brought up.[43] These problems were only compounded when the children were sent out to work too early to dead-end or dangerous jobs.[44]

Communication with these parents and children in the courts could be difficult. One judge vented his frustration when the child before him could not speak Italian and the mother could not speak English. In his critical study of the first decades of the Milwaukee juvenile court, Steven Schlossman concluded that a working-class mother talked back to the judge at the peril of her child. He cited the 1920 case of Mrs. Gmiczyk, who had bailed out her son after only one night in detention and faced the wrath of the juvenile court judge, who fumed: "I don't like the idea if a boy steals, of you people running up and bailing him out of here. We want a little time to let him think it over upstairs. Let him stay here a week, it will do him good. This case is continued for an hour, until she makes up her mind, and if she doesn't do it, I will seriously consider sending this boy to Waukesha."[45] Mrs. Gmiczyk yielded. The court, Schlossman observed, "felled anyone who questioned its mission," especially if they were working class and had no lawyer.[46]

Catholics always emphasized the importance of religion in deterring delinquency. One priest marveled: "How our non-Catholic boys and girls remain as wholesome as they are is a mystery to me! They must have two guardian angels to our one—Divine Providence must watch over them or else. . ."[47] Thomas Quigley, on the board of the New York State Agricultural and Industrial School for Boys, reporting that almost half the 750 inmates were Polish and Italian Catholics under sixteen, insisted that only religious training and practice could prevent others following in their footsteps. Surveying the records of the Pittsburgh juvenile court, lawyer Charles Gillespie concluded that the young Catholic who attended church regularly and received the Sacraments rarely appeared before a judge.[48] In Brooklyn Catholic probation officer Patrick Mallon affirmed that few Catholic children who attended parochial school arrived in his court. Rev. C. J. Quille was even more emphatic, alleging that of the 90,000 children in the 183 Chicago parochial schools, only one case of immorality by a parochial school girl was brought before the juvenile court in six years![49]

The key to effective treatment and rehabilitation was the probation officer.[50] Preferably as in New York and Chicago, legislation mandated the assignment of a delinquent to a probation officer of the same faith. City by city and court by court, Catholic organizations and bureaus of Catholic Charities worked out arrangements for supervising Catholic delinquents.[51] The founder and first chief probation officer of the Chicago juvenile court was Timothy Hurley of the Catholic Visitation and Aid Society. The Catholic president of the Big Sisters of Chicago reported continued constructive relations with the court.[52] When the Pittsburgh juvenile court was established in 1903, the Civic Club appointed and paid the salaries of three women probation officers. Because none were Catholic, the Knights of Columbus secured the appointment and paid the salary of a Catholic woman officer who reported to them and the court on her supervision of Catholics.[53] In Cleveland the juvenile court provided a room for the Big Brother representative of the St. Vincent de Paul Society aided "by a capable young woman to look after the girls." In Kansas City the court generally assigned a Catholic for rehabilitation to a priest or someone suggested by a Catholic agency. In St. Paul there was a "mutually helpful" relationship between the juvenile court and the Bureau of Catholic Charities. Cincinnati's Bureau of Catholic Charities and Social Service maintained a representative at the juvenile court. She worked out plans for probation with the Catholic Big Brothers and Big Sisters. In New York City, where the Catholic Big Sisters had worked with the Children's Court since 1902, a "perfect spirit of harmony" reportedly existed between the volunteer workers and the probation staff of the court.[54]

Whether volunteer or paid official, the Catholic probation officer was dedicated to the spiritual well-being of her charge. Spiritual control was as important as social control. Volunteer Caroline E. Boone reported to her NCCC colleagues in 1914 that if she found her charge had not received his first communion, or rarely went to Mass, or said his prayers, that the parents would "learn the probation officer's point of view pretty clearly." Preparation for the Sacraments became part of her probation program.[55]

In the 1920s as the National Probation Association, state boards, and professional social workers lobbied for the appointment of trained professional probation officers, the "older school of supervision" yielded to the new emphasis on investigation and social treatment. Hans Weiss, probation officer of the Boston juvenile court, described his staff as "social physicians."[56] With their extensive volunteer service of Big Brothers and Big Sisters and the St. Vincent de Paul societies, Catholics faced the challenge of developing a cadre of trained professionals eligible for appointment to the civil service probation staffs. The 1920 NCCC meeting featured papers by Joseph P. Murphy and Bernard J. Fagan, the chief probation officers of the courts of Buffalo and New York City. Murphy, noting that the day of "mawkish sentimentality" was past, found the standards of Catholic workers were far below those maintained by other social workers. Formal education, specialized education, temperament, apprenticeship, and a sound religious training were essential if Catholic probation officers were to "remold character." One year later the quintessential professional, Rose McHugh, while crediting the enthusiasm, spirit of service, and liaison with the community that a volunteer could bring to the task, insisted that only the carefully selected, trained Catholic volunteer could be useful in probation work.[57]

Determined that Catholics provide an example of excellence, New York's Cardinal Hayes worked with Edwin J. Cooley, the Catholic chief probation officer of the Court of General Sessions, to establish a model probation bureau. Cooley secured legislative backing for a demonstration project in 1925, won the sponsorship of the judges of the court, and, of course, the financing from Catholic Charities. With such powerful backing, he organized the Catholic Charities Probation Bureau for the Court of General Sessions, gathering a staff of thirty trained probation officers—young college graduates to replace those of "the old type." Cooley reported his findings at Catholic and National Probation Association meetings and published his results in *Probation and Delinquency: The Study and Treatment of the Individual Delinquent* in 1927. His program, he claimed, met the best current standards, including the insistence on the relevance of religion, and produced an 85 percent success rate in rehabilitation. Reviewing the record, the New York State Probation Commission agreed: "It is no exaggeration to state that the best probation work for adult offenders to be found in the United States is done by this Bureau."[58]

Catholics dedicated to rescuing children and youth agreed that prevention was better than rehabilitation. The Knights of Columbus, Holy Name Societies, Ladies of Charity, and Big Sister and Big Brother organizations provided an army of middle-class volunteers to reach out to young Catholics adrift and vulnerable to the lures of fast money and the fast life of the American city. Determined to save their own, bishops, clergy, and lay volunteers erected alternatives to the YMCA and YWCA centers, formed Catholic troops of Boy and Girl Scouts, and, in the 1930s, created a national Catholic Youth Organization. As always, Catholic recreational leadership was directed at the salvation of souls. New York's CYO director, Rev. Edward Roberts Moore, stated it well: "for us Catholics, program without apostolate is a contradiction in terms. . . We must always keep first things first: neither more participants nor swelling biceps in themselves mean stronger character, better citizens or whiter souls!"[59]

In prevention and rehabilitation, the tasks were frequently determined by gender and, interestingly, by chronology. Saving the girl dominated in the Progressive decades and the 1920s; whereas the muscular Christianity of boyology was emphasized in the 1930s. As in Catholic work for dependent children, the pattern of "saving" was the same: volunteers and religious were challenged by professionals; lay leadership was superseded by clerical administration; parish responsibilities increasingly were augmented and directed by diocesan and national organizations.

Saving the girl was essential for the future of Catholic motherhood and the Catholic family. In his history of Catholic charities, John O'Grady places the chapter "Protective Care for Girls" immediately after his lengthy study of children's work.[60] Chicago Catholic Lenora Z. Meder, who chaired the National Committee on the Protection of Young Girls, observed: "The young girl in our country has asked for protection and has not received it. . . . In most instances, due to social, economic and moral evolution, she has been made helpless and dependent for her safety on the decency and sympathy of society. . . . Let the young girl of today be guarded wisely, and the country will find that the ounce of prevention is more economic than the pound of reformation."[61]

This Catholic preoccupation with the "girl problem" was broadly shared by Progressive reformers. The uprooted immigrant girl loose on the city streets, working in a garment factory, cannery, or, if lucky, at a department store for less than a living wage attracted the attention of reformers and charity organizations. Early purity crusades spawned vice commissions from Los Angeles to New York; settlement house residents reached out to "women adrift"; protective legislation guarded women in the workplace. Writing from her Hull House experience, Jane Addams asserted in 1910: "Never before in civilization have such numbers of young girls been suddenly released from the protection of the home and permitted to walk unattended upon city streets. . ." The modern city found only two uses for these thousands, by day, their labor, by night "pandering to their love of pleasure to get their 'petty wages' back."[62] Anxieties about the nurture and protection of American girls enormously expanded during World War I when thousands of young women joined the war effort in new jobs in new cities. Emphasizing the moral threats to the war effort from unsupervised girls, the federal Committee of Protective Work for Girls labored to shield soldiers from prostitutes and "uniform crazy girls."[63] In the 1920s working- and middle-class girls faced the lure of dance crazes, movies, illicit drink, and sex.

Catholics organized to save their *own* girls. Although boys outnumbered girls two or three to one in the juvenile courts, reformatories, and training schools, delinquent girls, who were almost always charged with immorality, seemed to pose the greater danger to themselves and to society. Mary W. Dewson, who spent her early career as a probation officer in Massachusetts, observed "the difficulty of their restoration was increased both by the degradation resulting from their experience and by the wide-spread intolerance of society toward delinquents of this class."[64]

At the initial meeting of the NCCC in 1910, Judge Michael F. Girten of the Chicago juvenile court reported that "one of the things that loomed up strongly in my experience is the wayward girl . . . she has run away from home or has been seduced or has been found in an improper place." At the founding meeting of the NCCW, Bishop Schrembs exhorted the members to address the "girl problem." Rev. Harold P. Chilcote, director of Catholic Charities of Toledo, reporting to the NCCC 1926 meeting on his survey of eighty-seven cases of girls dealt with by his Juvenile Guidance Department, announced that sixty-two cases were concerned with sex.[65] William I. Thomas's classic study of *The Unadjusted Girl* as well as his work on the Polish peasant had further relevance for Catholics in his observations on the disintegration of immigrant peasant culture in urban America and the young girls' longing for an affluent life and the tempting illegal and immoral means to achieve it.[66]

Saving the girls was complicated by the steadily increasing numbers of young women in the workforce, changing public attitudes toward "fallen women," and the emergence of the "new woman" and "new morals." In response professionals in recreation and rehabilitation developed new standards, programs, and therapies.[67] For John Cooper, attempting to coordinate the efforts of the NCWC Women's Committee at the end of the war, the first priority was to secure proper and affordable shelter for the thousands of young Catholic women working away from home. A 1919 "Girls Welfare" pamphlet from the Women's Committee of the NCWC was graphic: "Hermits no longer live in caves and woodland lean-tos. They live in cities—in but not of the community, unknown to the folks next door or in the apartment across the hall, unknown and unknowing. The hermit girls are legion. And the more populous the city, the more isolated they are. . . . They have passed through the net of the station or dock and are lost in the city's sea."[68]

A study of New York working girls in 1918 estimated that less than 5 percent of those living away from home were housed in organized boarding homes. The 120 boarding houses organized by Catholic sponsors had places for less than 8,000. All had waiting lists. Estimating that approximately 350,000 to 400,000 Catholic working women lived away from home, Cooper concluded that their Catholic religious and middle-class sisters were meeting the needs of only 2 percent; archbishops and bishops shared Cooper's sense of urgency. In Chicago Archbishop Mundelein built three new boarding homes, the St. Rita Club No. 1, No. 2, and No. 3 on the north, west, and south sides. On the drawing boards was a large downtown hotel, the Jeanne d'Arc. With these new residences, Chicago could house 10 percent of their Catholic girls working away from home. Although this left the problem of the other 90 percent, the Chicago hierarchy managed to "console themselves in the thought that Catholics in other cities are not caring for more than five percent of the Catholic women wage-earners who are adrift."[69] The Detroit League of Catholic Women established a dormitory at their St. Anne's Community House for young women factory workers and added Rowena House and Watson Club for those working in downtown stores and offices.[70]

The most dazzling housing success achieved by Catholic middle-class women was reported by Anna D. Polanek of the Catholic Women's Association of St. Louis at the NCCC meeting in 1924. In ten years the Association had established a downtown headquarters with reading rooms, a Catholic free library operating as a branch of the public library, and a cafeteria that served eight hundred patrons daily. They had bought a country club "since the Catholic self-supporting woman of limited means . . . had no place near the city where she might withdraw from her daily routine" and had just opened a hotel in which "every comfort and convenience have been provided so an atmosphere of cheerfulness and quiet elegance prevails." A weekly rate of $7.50 to $11.50 included breakfast and dinner daily and three meals on Sunday. Sewing and laundry rooms were available. The manager was a trained social worker. The Catholic Women's Association, Polanek noted, had accomplished all of this without launching a fund drive. Dues, a few donations, and good management had brought their assets to $100,000 in their first decade.

Polanek's presentation provoked a lively discussion on what kind of housing was best for the Catholic working girl. Social workers and women volunteers from New York and Omaha worried that girls who stayed too long in a working girls' home or hotel would become too used to the companionship and would not be well-prepared for the "future spells of lonesomeness in married life." Catholic managers should limit residence to no more than three years. They should find alternative housing for working girls with Catholic families and, when "loneliness drives them out," should provide Catholic centers so that the working girls would not be lured to the ever present dance halls.[71]

Archbishop Michael J. Curley wrote to his director of the Washington, D.C., Catholic Charities, John O'Grady, and to all of his parish priests to urge their cooperation with a Community House project of the Catholic Daughters of America. He wanted the house to be an alternative to the YWCA for Catholic government girls. He also encouraged support for the Catholic Daughters' efforts to establish a room registry.[72]

To John Cooper the room registry was the most practical solution. In Pittsburgh the Catholic Women's League joined with representatives from the YMCA, YWCA, the Associated Charities, the Council of Churches, and the Council of Jewish Women to develop a permanent room registry. Cooper used the New York Catholic Room Registry, conducted by the Catholic Women's League, to underscore the need. Whereas the Catholic registry placed about seventy-two women a month, the YWCA Central Branch registry placed 1,951 Catholics, 26 percent of their 1920 total. There were twenty other Catholic room registries across the country, but, Cooper insisted, there should be at least ten times that number.[73] The National Council of Catholic Women discussed the special insignia that should be placed on each Catholic home listed in the registry and urged that the initial "C" for Catholic be used in the insignia so that a stranger could find it easily in the phonebook.[74]

Another initiative Cooper supported was the subsidized boarding home, a commercial enterprise underwritten by an organization of Catholic women. This operation took away the stigma of "charity" that some young girls attached to the homes run by the sisters. The *in loco parentis* of the sister-managed homes could also be daunting. The director of St. Joseph's by the Sea in Point Pleasant, New Jersey, spoke of "the tenderness, kindness, and loving interest of a mother, the firmness and severity of a father" provided by the sisters to the working girls. She then expressed her concern about the modesty of some tenants, observing: "To be fashionable a girl thinks she must lose her self-respect. We must teach our Catholic girls to make the flesh over in the majesty and might of the spirit." It was a reminder of Cooper's insistence that there must be options in the housing offered because "girls and women are not like Fords."[75]

In November 1923 the National Directory of Catholic Boarding Homes and Room Registries for Girls and Women listed 26 room registries and 139 organized boarding homes, housing 9,000 girls and women. Although this seemed commendable progress, Cooper worried that many of the boarding homes were filled with more mature, better-paid working women. All the "urgencies of charity" cried out that those residents give way to the young and inexperienced girls who were grossly underpaid.[76]

Cooper pointed out that there would be no need to provide housing for Catholic working girls if they were paid a living wage. He questioned whether those working so strenuously to provide housing at rates below

commercial rates were contributing to the continued injustice of employers. Reports of the Women's Bureau of the Department of Labor and the
Consumers' League made it clear that a living wage for the single girl in
a major city was $14 or $15 a week in 1919. Half of the women workers
in one Philadelphia survey earned less than $10.30 a week; 20 percent
earned less than $8.00 a week, the weekly rent in many organized
boarding homes in New York or Chicago. Surveying these reports, Cooper concluded that 50 percent of women and girls in industry were not
receiving a living wage. What were Catholic organizations of women
doing to support minimum wage legislation in their states? The vast
majority were "nescient." He challenged: "How long shall we continue
straining out gnats and swallowing camels? How long shall we continue
tithing mint and anise and cummin and leaving the weightier things of
the law? How long shall we continue making clean the outside only of
the cup? *Can we build up charity on the ruins of justice?*"[77]

Reports on the activities of women's organizations in 1921 confirmed
Cooper's judgment. They were obviously doing much good meliora-
tive work, but reform was not on the agenda. The Cincinnati Catholic
Women's Association listed projects ranging from Americanization work,
sewing classes, the juvenile court committee, support for the Santa Maria
Institute, service on the civic and vocational league of public and parochial schools, and a better films campaign. Teresa O'Donohue of the
League of Catholic Women in New York reported a similar wide range
of good works: opening a temporary shelter for mothers and infants,
supporting a summer camp, providing scholarships, burying the dead,
and assisting at marriages. "Girls," she observed, "are coming to us from
churches, schools, parents, and welfare organizations."[78]

The lure of the city and the danger for the Catholic working girl were
consistent themes at NCCC meetings. At the founding meeting of the
NCCC in 1910, the largest attendance was on the session on the Protection of Young Girls. Three hundred and fifty women crowded an audi-
torium at Trinity College to hear Monsignor Mueller-Simonis of the
International Catholic Association for the Protection of Young Girls.
Mueller-Simonis' list of temptations was daunting: "premature contact
with the enticements of life, uncontrolled intercourse with boys and men,
amusements of all kinds, dances, moving picture shows, strolling at late
hours, unchaperoned outings." He graphically described how "led astray
from her intended route, many an innocent girl disappears, only to be
found again after many years in some hospital—a physical and moral
wreck!" Six years later Lenora Z. Meder, the chair of the National
Committee on the Protection of Young Girls, echoed Jane Addams, asserting, "Youth demands recreation and will have it one way or an-

other. . . . She seeks diversion and consolation, whether it be in the public dance-hall, the boat excursion where liquor is sold, the low theatre and movie," and to forbid her access without a positive alternative would be fruitless. Meder concluded, "It is easier to remove the poison from the child than the child from the poison."[79]

Even more disturbing was Teresa O'Donohue's report to the NCCC in 1920 on "The Disappearance of Young Girls in Our Large Cities." O'Donohue, using police reports, blamed the disappearance of 1,906 girls in New York on: "the unadjusted home; the spirit of adventure, augmented by moving pictures; the lure of the stage; the desire for the life of luxury followed by immorality and the impelment of sex, immoral dancing, and immoral mode of dressing."[80] The family, girls' clubs, recreational centers, playgrounds, and community centers all had a role to play. O'Donohue insisted that wholesome recreation should begin at home, even in the home of "the hard working classes too tired . . . to give any time to their children." They and middle-class parents pushed the child out of doors at their peril. To O'Donohue "the home that drives recreation from its doors is not a home but a hollow place . . . for love goes out of the window when one cannot recreate in one's own home." Lack of space was no excuse; storytelling, coloring of pictures, even dancing could take place in a two-by-two area. A more sympathetic and realistic assessment was made by Mrs. W. J. O'Toole of St. Paul who asked: "how much spare time has the mother of six children, who acts as seamstress, laundress and cook for her household, how much spare time has she to supervise the idle moments of her children?"[81]

The Jesuit editor of *The Queen's Work* chided Catholics for their old-fashioned belief that young people were taken care of at home. Catholic concepts of recreation, he charged, were mired in the eighteenth century, while Catholic children were determined to have fun "in the manner of the twentieth." Adrift in strange cities, young Catholics naturally mixed with the nearest group. Because they were "the future material of the Church," there was a "real and crying need for Catholic sociability," to encourage Catholic marriages and future Catholic homes. Catholic women had "the natural genius for solving such questions."[82] His suggestions, should this natural genius falter, included supporting Girl Scout troops, promoting parish and parochial school playgrounds, and developing clubs and recreational centers as alternatives to the YWCA.[83]

Some Catholics obviously needed to be converted to the benefits of scouting for girls. John Cooper asked "Girl Scouts or a National Catholic Organization?" in a 1922 *Catholic Charities Review* article. At the NCCC meeting the previous year, Mrs. Benjamin Carpenter, active in Scout work in Chicago, observed that some of the sisters and priests had objected to Scout work in the parishes because "it made the girls rough and mannish, and spoiled their interest in the home." Carpenter found no foundation in this argument because they "did not make a point of parading the girls." The girls of the South Chicago steel mills were "rough and noisy," she acknowledged, "but that wasn't the fault of scouting," and the leaders were doing all they could "to tone them down."[84]

Much more prominent in articles in the *Catholic Charities Review* and at the sessions of the NCCC were Catholics' strenuous resistance to the immoral fare purveyed in the movies of the 1920s. Writing in the *Catholic Charities Review* in 1921, Charles McMahon estimated that Catholics comprised one-fifth of the 130,000,000 weekly audience at the movies. They paid producers more than $200 million a year for sleaze. In a series of articles, he recited a litany of cinema evils: "unwholesome sex appeals, adultery, unfaithfulness, moral laxity, indecent dressing and undressing, crime, disrespect for law, for religion, and for plain morality." Catholic parents who allowed their children to go to the movies once or twice a week exposed them to "a diet of visual hodge-podge that may sicken the minds and dwarf the souls. . ."[85] Bernard Fagan, chief probation officer of the Children's Court of New York City, insisted that movies, more than any other entertainment, led to delinquency and demoralization. Films, particularly those shown in the cheaper houses, were "reeking with filth and sex," making "vile impressions on impressionable children."

Seeking its own data, the Women's Committee of the National Catholic War Council dispatched social worker Mary Hernan to survey the movie houses and dance halls of Philadelphia in 1919. Hernan went to forty-three theaters and reported on the quality of the films, facilities, and the audience. Her most frequent adjectives for the films were "cheap" and "sensational"; these were usually paired with descriptions of "audience excited." Her evaluation of the primarily working-class audiences was expressed in her notes on "poor class of people," "rough appearing people," "rough audience," "colored disorderly-conditions undesirable." Her descriptions, critical as they were, mirror the ethnic, working-class audiences Lizabeth Cohen described in Chicago in the 1920s. Although Hernan found "objectionable features," it clearly did not matter. The movies were the community's clear first choice of recreation throughout the 1920s.[86]

Catholics' chosen weapon in the war against movie immorality was the mobilized force of public opinion. The middle-class National Council of Catholic Women, joined by the National Council of Catholic Men, pledged twenty million Catholics to "an unrelenting fight against immoral and unwholesome motion pictures," promising to discourage attendance at objectionable films. At its 1927 convention, the NCCW passed a resolution "against those violations of womanly dignity known as beauty contests, against the moving pictures, the magazines, the books that lower the dignity of the Christian girl and the Christian mother." All Catholic women were urged to "work for the fuller restoration of the divine-given dignity" of womanhood. Six years later the American bishops established the Legion of Decency, which screened and rated films on sex and violence and promised boycotts of immoral fare. The pledge to follow the Legion was signed by eleven million Catholics. Hollywood promised self-policing by enforcing a Production Code (written by Catholic Martin J. Quigley with the help of Rev. Daniel Lord, S.J.) and appointing Catholic Joseph I. Breen (approved by the Catholic bishops) as head of the Production Code Authority.[87]

For many Catholic women's organizations (as well as Lutherans, Presbyterians, and Baptists), the dance hall was an even more immediate danger for the working girl. Crusades to clean up dance halls were a fixture throughout the Progressive era, but the dance craze, so elegantly highlighted by Vernon and Irene Castle, accelerated in the 1920s with the faster syncopation of jazz and the warmer rhythms of the blues.[88] Teresa O'Donohue charged: "Immoral dances of today do more harm to men and women than anyone realizes."[89] Cleveland Catholic settlement house worker Helen Phelan scored the "cheap dance hall with its jazz of the worst kind, the opportunity for pick-up acquaintances." The Women's Committee of the NCWC again dispatched Mary Hernan, this time to observe the behavior in Philadelphia dance halls. Though she found generally "tasteful dancing," particularly in the hall managed by a member of the Knights of Columbus who upheld "the Catholic point-of-view," her testimony was drowned out by a chorus of other concerned Catholics. Probation officer Bernard Fagan testified to the consequences of the dance hall, noting it led the list of the amusements of girls appearing before the Children's Court of New York City.[90]

Catholic women's organizations and Catholic social workers mounted a multifaceted attack to save young girls. (It is not clear whether their efforts were appreciated by the objects of their attention.) Social worker Sara Laughlin reported to the NCCC on her work for the Hygiene Board of Philadelphia "to safeguard the girl in her headlong rush to satisfy her natural desire for the companionship of youth." She and two other professional colleagues warned, took home, or sent to court the girls they found roaming the streets or generally misbehaving. In 1919 they had warned or arrested 386 girls, 228 of them for speaking to strange men. Almost a third had left school at age fourteen; almost half were factory workers. When asked what recreation they preferred, the movies, dance halls, and public parks were clear winners. Observing that the Catholic girls she warned had meager church-sponsored recreational opportunities, Laughlin concluded "it is small wonder that their childish understanding of the responsibility of religion gives way to the forces which surround them during their working and playing hours."[91]

Another Catholic social worker, A. Madorah Donahue, active in the postwar programs of the Interdepartmental Social Hygiene Board, pressed Catholics to join community efforts to provide both wholesome recreation and effective prevention. Organized groups of Catholic men and women should attend police courts and defend the clean-up efforts of police. They should work to pass city ordinances to control dance halls, work with management, and, when standards were not met, to demand enforcement by the police. Only constant vigilance and sympathetic response to the young would staunch the "army of steady marchers to the courts."[92]

The most organized yet personal response of Catholic women volunteers to the young girl at risk came from the Big Sisters. By the end of the decade, every urban diocese had an organization. New York's Big Sisters of the Ladies of Charity worked with more than 1,300 little sisters in 1920, most assigned by the Children's Court.[93] Writing of the Catholic Big Sisters of Cleveland, director Catherine McNamee described their work as "personal, individual, intensive, character developing work with the adolescent girl between the age of fourteen and twenty-one years." The big sister had to have "personality, understanding, and love . . . patience, insight, sympathy, resourcefulness and a religious spirit of consecration." It was not enough, asserted the president of the Philadelphia Catholic Women's Alliance, for a big sister to be kindhearted.[94] Sara Laughlin suggested that big sisters should have a "fairly normal girlhood of their own, in the not too far distant past," and should "still remember the amount of amusement which they craved and enjoyed in their girlhood." Whereas Laughlin urged training for big sisters involved in casework, Anna E. King argued that the big sister honed her skills on the job, developing "the technique of friendship," the "art of helping people," social psychiatry, and group leadership. The little sister was not "a case."[95]

Recruitment and training were issues throughout the 1920s. At the 1926 NCCC annual conference, Margaret Talty of the Washington Bureau of Catholic Charities reviewed her three-year effort to recruit and train big sisters and other volunteers in the Juvenile Division. First she arranged a series of informal but high-powered lectures in a private home; John O'Grady and Louise McGuire of the National Catholic Service School were followed by ten executives of the social agencies of

D.C. The second year, aided by a committee from the Sodality Union, she sponsored another intensive series of lectures at the National Catholic Community House, featuring William Kerby, John O'Grady, and John M. Cooper. At the end of thirty lecture sessions, Catholic Charities and the Sodality Union formed a new Volunteer Social Service Association of a "group of women from all walks in life to render personal service to the poor." Talty's long campaign garnered forty-eight volunteers.[96]

In their preventive work, the Big Sisters worked with the home and the schools. Teresa O'Donohue of New York emphasized that "unless we get right to the girl in the home our efforts will be of no avail."[97] The Big Sisters of Chicago had a more roundabout approach. Their strategy was to rehabilitate the home by providing scholarships to send some of their little sisters to boarding school, away from "their deteriorating environment." Chicago's organization had a map in the office with the parishes "properly pegged" to show the neighborhoods with the worst records for producing delinquent girls. They expanded their recruiting efforts for volunteers from these areas.

The Big Sisters reported a range of activities. They offered wholesome recreation through picnics, camping, and good movies; reading and education through courses in business skills; sewing; and advice on managing a budget and clothes for the job, which they might have found for the little sister. Many saw their most important work as encouraging their little sisters in practicing their faith. Yet the magnitude of the task was almost overwhelming for the volunteer force.[98] At the end of the decade, the National Conference of Catholic Charities commissioned a survey of the effectiveness of the work of the Big Brothers and Big Sisters by Frederick A. Moran, executive secretary to the Board of Managers of the New York Catholic Protectory and New York state Director of Probation. Moran visited organizations in eight cities and surveyed nine others through questionnaires. His final report was bleak. Writing to John O'Grady in June 1929 "in rather a perturbed state of mind," Moran concluded that "most of the work being done is simply rotten."[99]

After a quarter-century of social service, the Big Brothers and Big Sisters movement, he summarized, had failed to develop either standards of work or outstanding leadership. He found little time or thought had been given to either the needs of the underprivileged Catholic children or the best role that Big Brothers or Big Sisters might fill in a community social service program. They were only beginning to perceive the need for preventive work through coordinated efforts with schools and bureaus of Catholic charities. Only one organization of those he visited had carefully worked out plans on intake; others were assuming responsibilities they were unequipped to meet. Cases were assigned without complete investigations or a plan of treatment. When Catholic charities' children or family divisions gave good case summaries to the Big Brothers, they were ignored, possibly because of overwork or "lack of understanding. . ." There was a general lack of leadership. Executives tended to be trained in recreational leadership with only superficial training in casework. The selection of volunteers was poor; their training was superficial and sporadic. Their budgets clearly were not able to support an adequate staff unless funded by either the Community Chest or bureaus of Catholic charity. In spite of their emphasis on the religious aspects of their work, Moran found that "stereotyped and formal methods" were followed in the development of spiritual value. He added, "Is it heresy to suggest that it is high time that the methods employed in teaching spiritual and moral values be critically evaluated?" In the future Big Brother and Big Sister work had to be more than "a cheap method of supervising children or giving to some quasi-religious agency an objective for existence."[100]

Moran provided examples of both good and inept casework by the Big Sisters. The case of Angelina Lapella (fictitious name) of Cincinnati was a success story. Angelina's step-father, Italian-born Andy Capponi, was a junk dealer "rough in appearance and of common type" who was "a heavy drinker and very cruel to his family." The big sister suspected that he might be a bootlegger because a "great many colored people frequent his home." Seventeen-year-old Angelina's only clothes were dark blue overalls that she wore helping her father with the mechanical work of the junk shop. Her step-father allowed her no recreation and was "most cruel to her mother if she allowed Angeline [sic] to have any amusement." Angelina's retarded brother was mistreated and her two step-brothers were malnourished and fearful of their father. Angelina had threatened suicide "as her outlook on life was a hopeless one." Her teacher referred her case to the juvenile court, which found that the home "was not a fit one." A physical examination found Angelina "was intact." She had a mental age of ten and an I.Q. of 76; however, the results were suspect because Angelina spoke only Italian in the home. The court recommended that she be removed from home and school and be placed with a private family. The Catholic Big Sisters accepted supervision, placing Angelina as a maid in a home that was thoroughly investigated by a Bureau of Catholic Charities worker. The big sister reported that Angelina had difficulty understanding that she was to be a maid. At first "she insisted upon tuning in on the radio, playing the piano and dancing to the tunes of the victrola." When it came to setting the table, she insisted upon putting the pots and pans on the table as they did at home. Eventually she proved a competent maid and a good caregiver to the children in the house. Her big sister enrolled her in a cooking class at night school and encouraged her to start a bank account and contribute part of her wages to her mother. For recreation she took her to an amusement park, lunches, and shows. Angelina, her big sister reported, was enjoying good health, attended to her religious duties, and was a member of St. Clara's church.

Although Angelina's case was a good example of the cooperation of school, juvenile court, the Bureau of Catholic Charities, and the Big Sisters, Moran gave several examples of cases of the "hit or miss methods of case work" of Big Brother and Big Sister organizations. He was highly critical of one case accepted by the Big Sisters, quoting the report: "One dear little woman had chaos descend upon her without warning. One day her husband kissed her good-bye with a cheery word and departed for work. He failed to return at his accustomed hour and for six months thereafter was unheard of until he telephoned his wife to say that she had better forget him and not try to find him. . . . But how could she work away from home all day and leave her delicate little nine-year-old child alone, exposed to possible dangers and mishaps!" The Big Sisters took on the case and provided some scholarship assistance to send the child away to school. Moran was appalled. Why wasn't the case referred to a family agency? Why hadn't an effort been made to find the deserting husband? Why hadn't day nurseries been investigated?

His essential conclusion was that "Catholic Big Brother and Big Sister work is in a chaotic condition and should be given careful and serious consideration." Because the presence of the Big Brother and Big Sister organizations had "apparently been responsible for the failure of Catholic bureaus of charities to develop any real program of protective care," he called for much tighter coordination and, in a recommendation always present in the NCCC surveys of the 1920s, urged that any future organization of Big Brothers and Big Sisters should have the approval of the diocesan director of Catholic Charities.[101]

As in other Catholic volunteer organizations, the women were more numerous and more effectively organized than the men (with the exception of the St. Vincent de Paul Society). In all of the communities Moran visited, he found low standards in the casework of Big Brothers and comparatively higher standards in Big Sisters' work. Most Big Sister organizations had recreation programs. With the exception of summer camp programs, Big Brothers had not developed either recreational or spare-time programs. One of the outstanding weaknesses Moran found in the Big Brother organizations was their failure in the spiritual aspects of their work. However, he applauded the spiritual intrusiveness of the Big Sisters. Frequently, he reported, Big Sisters planned a Saturday shopping trip or movie to end in church with confession, the big sister going first and telling the confessor that her little sister would follow![102]

In 1929 Moran reported to the NCCC meeting as the chair of a new Committee on a Catholic Protective Program. His summary of recommendations included: "Serious consideration should be given to the need and desirability of diocesan bureaus of charities organizing divisions of protective care. The number of Catholic delinquents appearing before the courts or committed to correctional institutions indicates the need for study and research to discover the factors responsible for this condition and as a basis for establishing an intelligent and constructive program of protective care."[103]

Efforts to save the Catholic girl were the most publicized in the 1920s, yet the needs of Catholic boys were also addressed through "muscular Christianity."[104] The earliest nationwide Catholic youth work directed at boys was launched by the Boy Life Bureau of the Knights of Columbus in 1923. The Knights engaged Brother Barnabas, former director of the New York Protectory, as the Bureau's executive secretary and adopted scouting as their major program for twelve- to fifteen-year-olds. In his early forays into the dioceses, Brother Barnabas had a threefold mission: to convince skeptical Catholics that the Boy Scouts was not a Protestant institution; to inspire volunteers to lead parish troops; and, finally, to persuade Catholic laymen, pastors, and bishops that the work needed trained leadership. With his usual energy and public relations skills, Barnabas conducted "boyology institutes" and won thousands of Catholic volunteers to the new profession he labeled "boy guidance." By 1924 the Knights' support led to the establishment of a Department of Boy Guidance and a two-year Master of Arts program at the University of Notre Dame. By 1928 there was a small cadre of graduates, a thousand Catholic Boy Scout troops, and a Catholic Committee on Scouting under the honorary chairmanship of Cardinal Hayes of New York.[105]

New York again pioneered in this Catholic initiative. Victor F. Ridder, a Catholic member of the National Executive Board of the Boy Scouts of America, convinced New York's Archbishop Farley in 1912 that scouting was a nonsectarian movement that promoted clean living. In 1919, through the influence of Cardinal Gibbons of Baltimore, the Vatican issued a letter endorsing scouting. The Catholic Committee on Scouting, under the direction of New York's social action leader Rev. Edward Roberts Moore, developed a Plan of Cooperation with the Boy Scouts in 1932, setting out spheres of authority and responsibility.

Though scouting might be nonsectarian, Catholic leaders explored ways to "spiritualize" the Scout experience for their boys. A leader in Dubuque suggested that the Scout motto "Be Prepared" might be explained to the Catholic Scout as meaning that he should be always ready to explain and defend his religion. He added: "In its fullest sense the motto can be made to mean that the boy should order his life so as to 'Be Prepared' to meet his God at any time."[106] The most serious challenge to the Plan of Cooperation was posed by the emphasis on and interpretation of the Twelfth Scout Law, "A Scout is Reverent." The Archdiocese of Los Angeles devised an award and merit badge for reverence, called the Ad Altare Dei Cross. A bronze cross with "Ad Altare Dei" [To the altar of God, a phrase from the Catholic Mass] inscribed on it was inset in a Boy Scout first-class badge. The dispute over the badges was not resolved until 1939 when the Catholic chaplains suggested awards for the Twelfth Scout Law be made by church groups on a national basis, and the Scouts' executive board unanimously concurred.[107]

Catholic scouting spread with the force of a prairie fire throughout the 1930s. Nowhere was the growth more extraordinary and, indeed, flamboyant than in Chicago under the leadership of Auxiliary Bishop Bernard Sheil. Founded in June 1930, the Chicago Catholic Boy Scout organizations expanded in five years to 200 troops and 8,500 Scouts. At one gigantic religious rally in October 1933, 5,000 Scouts carrying flags, banners, and standards filed in review before Cardinal Mundelein, Bishop Sheil, the mayor, and other clergy and civic leaders gathered on the steps of the Cathedral of the Holy Name. Each boy, before he was accepted as a Scout, was required to join the Junior Holy Name Society. Every month the members of the troop, dressed in uniforms, received communion in a body with the Holy Name Society, providing "an inspiration to hundreds of other boys," and "a source of pleasure and comfort" to older members of the congregation "who cannot but marvel at so fine an exhibition of discipline, well mannered and well groomed Catholic boys."[108]

Bishop Sheil was vice-chair of the national Catholic Committee on Scouting. Described as a cross between the Hollywood priest images of Bing Crosby and Spencer Tracy, Sheil was a master organizer, showman, and publicizer. A decorated veteran, former chaplain at Joliet prison, accomplished athlete and pianist, quintessential man's man, and the "boys' bishop," Sheil was known for his statement: "Youth has plenty of problems, but for anyone who loves youth, there is no youth problem."[109] As outgoing as Cardinal Mundelein was reserved, Sheil initiated a wide network of boy-saving activities at the end of the 1920s and expanded them through the Depression and New Deal. The Catholic Youth Organization (CYO), founded in 1930, was his centerpiece.

Sheil recognized that youth had to be won and that Catholic "leakage," the loss of its young men, had to be curtailed. For boys the winning was accomplished through athletics. A marveling counterpart, Rev. Edward R. Moore, CYO director of New York, reported that to be a CYO boy in Chicago was like being on the Notre Dame football team. CYO events made the sports pages of the major dailies. The Chicago CYO boxing tournament regularly filled Wrigley Field with 30,000 fans. When Moore's New York CYO boxing champions were challenged to take on Chicago's finest at Wrigley Field, Sheil met the team at the train station with a brass band playing the national anthem. The mayor of Chicago presented the keys to the city. Limousines were waiting with a motorcycle escort to take them to the South Shore Country Club for breakfast. In the evening police estimated a crowd of 50,000 attended a "Pageant of Youth" featuring bands, fireworks, and speeches at Jackson Park. The bouts were broadcast on a nationwide radio hook-up. Gene Tunney shook hands with Joe Louis at ringside. The governor of Illinois and the mayor were present. Thousands unable to get tickets milled around outside. Winners received medals designed by the personal sculptor of Pius XI, commissioned by Mundelein. "It was *something!*" Moore exclaimed. He decided against a rematch in New York, for "we didn't think we would survive it."[110]

At the grassroots, Chicago's CYO activities were less dramatic, but the record was impressive. Sheil, speaking to the meetings of the NCCC in 1935, 1936, and 1937, reeled off the accomplishments. He reported that in five years of CYO work, delinquency among boys had dropped 50 percent. He gave credit to the Holy Name men engaged in Big Brother work (perhaps reformed following Moran's scathing attacks). He then detailed a staggering array of services: CYO homes and hotels for 2,000 transients; unemployment retreats for 5,000 young men; a Working Boys Home, fully equipped with a modern printing plant and a central commissary where jobs were found and training provided. The CYO financed scholarships through the profits of the Chicago Catholic Salvage Bureau from scrap collected and reconditioned with the aid of students at the Lewis Holy Name Technical Training School at Lockport, another CYO endeavor. Thirty-four vacation schools enrolled 30,000 students. In addition to the boxing program, 12,000 played basketball, 4,000 baseball. A total of 30,400 athletes participated in CYO activities in 1936. The 2,000 entrants in the boxing tournament of 1935, in addition to their stringent physical tests, had undergone a rigorous spiritual examination and all, reported Sheil, were now attending Mass.[111]

Sheil was always the dervish at the center. New York's Moore spent a week with the peripatetic bishop, who, in addition to running the CYO, was also a pastor and vicar general of the archdiocese. Each night Sheil toured CYO club houses and centers. On the South Side, he quietly began playing the piano to cheer up the "boys of the road" at a back-of-the-yards house; he watched boxers put on a show. At the girls' hostel, Moore reported, "for once he disappointed me." He just walked his visitor through the house with a pleasant word or two. On the way home (in a scenario Horatio Alger could have created), they stopped to check on Joey the Little Italian newsboy, bought all of his papers, and drove him home in the bishop's limousine.[112]

To Sheil, who worried about the lure of Communist-sponsored athletic programs and appeals to youthful idealism, "the fight for the hearts and minds of youth is so keen and so bitter that we will do well to bind to our cause every available agency and organization and service."[113] The vacation schools had full access to Chicago's public playgrounds and parks and the "counsel and personal services" of the recreation department staff. When the National Youth Administration (NYA) was created in 1935, CYO counsel William J. Campbell was appointed the NYA Illinois state director. Chicago's CYO had more than 300 NYA personnel assisting in parish recreational programs, helping to run vacation schools, and mending broken toys brought in by the Catholic Salvage Bureau. The NYA was also generous in supplying tools, cloth, and leather scraps for children's leisure activities. Sheil's efforts also garnered Works Project Administration (WPA) equipment and support for CYO recreational and cultural programs. One hundred and fifty workers helped with athletic events, supervised playground recreation, and led tours of museums and the zoo. Chicago agencies, with Sheil's approval of the arrangements, found little to fear "about the traditional bugaboo" of government interference or control.[114] Sheil had also won a powerful friend in the White House when he "publicly raked [Roosevelt-critic Fr. Charles] Coughlin over the coals for Cardinal Mundelein." Roosevelt sent a telegram to a testimonial celebration in Chicago to join in honoring him as "the Apostle of Youth."[115]

Sheil's success and the publicity he gained for the Chicago CYO spurred diocesan imitation and a national movement. Cincinnati's Archbishop John T. McNicholas issued a three-page pastoral letter in March 1935 to be read from all of the parish pulpits announcing that the Chicago experience "makes it apparent that one of the most important duties resting on those of us who have the responsibility of souls is to promote a similar organization in the Archdiocese of Cincinnati."[116] Also in March the new Youth Committee of the NCCC had its first meeting in St. Louis to plan for the annual conference and for a needs assessment. They had a report from O'Grady on his visits to youth leaders in New York, Chicago, Gary, and Cleveland. With federal funding for relief diverted to youth through NYA programs, the NCCC executive secretary clearly sought to take stock. He wrote to diocesan directors in October 1935 asking them to identify who was directing youth work in their bureaus. Students from the Catholic University School of Social Work developed questionnaires and fanned out on their Christmas vacation to visit youth programs. In 1936 the NCCC discussed contracting with Edward R. Moore for a comprehensive study of Catholic youth work. Moore's price tag was $50,000, and the study apparently remained at the discussion stage.

Meanwhile Bishop John F. Noll of Fort Wayne, secretary of the Administrative Committee of the NCWC and chair of its Committee on Lay Organizations, sponsored a conference at the University of Notre Dame to enable clergy directing CYO programs to exchange ideas and to develop a plan to coordinate youth activity at the parish, diocesan, and national levels. Three years later the Administrative Board of the NCWC named the Bishops' Committee on Youth.[117] Clearly the two national organizations had mobilized for Catholic youth. It was equally clear that they were still sorting out who would speak most definitively "for the Church" to youth and to the nation.

CHAPTER FIVE

Catholic Charities, the Great Depression, and the New Deal

As the legislative torrent of the New Deal's first hundred days began to transform the American way of welfare, the National Conference of Catholic Charities gathered in New York for its 1933 convention. In a remarkable four days, a cross section of leaders from government, church, and profession discussed issues of social justice and programs for social action. The dazzling array of speakers from the government included President Roosevelt, Frances Perkins, Harry L. Hopkins, James Farley, Senator Robert F. Wagner, and former Governor Al Smith; from the church and Catholic charities came Apostolic Delegate Amelto Cicognani, William J. Kerby, John A. Ryan, John O'Grady, and Mary L. Gibbons; participants from private social work included William Hodson, Linton B. Swift, and Mary K. Simkhovitch. There was pomp—when the Conference opened October first with a solemn Pontifical Mass at St. Patrick's Cathedral, forty-two archbishops and bishops and a congregation of six thousand celebrated the one hundredth anniversary of the St. Vincent de Paul Society. And there was circumstance—when the Conference ended with dinner in the ballroom of the Waldorf-Astoria with an address by the President of the United States broadcast nationwide by 127 radio stations. Monsignor Robert Keegan, president of the NCCC and director of Catholic Charities of New York, was well aware of what the Conference signified. It had fixed "the place of Catholic Charities in the realm of human welfare as an agency of extraordinary force."[1]

Unmistakably the New York connections of the Roosevelt administration and the growing importance of Catholic voters to the Democratic Party had secured the New Deal administrators for the Conference. Once there Perkins, Hopkins, and Wagner used the NCCC platform to extol their federal relief and recovery initiatives. Catholic speakers, in turn, suggested the influence of the 1931 papal encyclical, *Quadragesimo anno,* on the New Deal. The president of Fordham University not only insisted that "the great encyclical was known and studied by the leaders of the new movement," but that Catholic writing on social justice was aiding in "the ready acceptance" of the New Deal by Americans.[2] Although there was general agreement on principles of social justice by NCCC and administration speakers, the challenge lay in policy and practice.

In their separate meeting at the convention, the diocesan directors crafted "A Charter of Catholic Charities" to clarify roles and responsibilities. Although "government has a fundamental duty to prevent human suffering, . . . the relief of distress has ever been an essential part of the mission of the Church. We can, therefore, never think of turning over our entire responsibility to the state or to any other agency." As the New Deal struggled to provide relief, to promote recovery, and, finally, to enact reform, Catholic charities claimed a role. With more agencies and institutions committed to charity than any other private organization, Catholic charities were vitally concerned with the spirit and substance of the emerging American welfare state.

Leaders of Catholic charities waged three distinct and sequential campaigns during the Depression and New Deal to defend their central work with children and the family. First, admitting that their own resources were hopelessly inadequate to deal with the immensity of the economic disaster, they joined with other agencies and called for public local, state, and federal funding to meet the emergency. Their major campaign in the early New Deal years was to continue a role in providing essential relief for Catholics, even as the responsibility for funding relief was shifting to government and public agencies. Here Catholic charities confronted the dicta of Harry Hopkins and the Federal Emergency Relief Administration that public funds should be distributed by public agencies. The second campaign, launched in 1935, brought Catholic charities into the crucial debates over Social Security, particularly the provisions for Aid to Dependent Children and Child Welfare Services. As the fragile federal safety net for children was created, they fought to limit its extension to protect the religion of Catholic children and to maintain a role in child-care, albeit modified, under the new dispensation. Finally, as the "welfare state" assumed the major responsibility for the material needs of the poor in the last years of the 1930s, Catholic charities worked to organize Catholic voters to lobby local, state, and eventually federal agencies and legislatures to insure a continuing role in the care of Catholic children and families and to insist, more broadly, that the rights of all Americans to an adequate subsistence were protected.

When the Great Depression struck the United States, contemporaries compared the gathering devastation to war, hurricane, tidal wave, and avalanche. Hoover's Secretary of the Interior Lyman Wilbur succinctly described the disaster as a "forest fire which kills many trees and scars them all." The impact was both vast and personal. By 1932 more than thirteen million, at least one-fifth of the workforce, was unemployed. Only one-fourth of them were receiving assistance of any kind.[3] At the beginning politicians, social workers, and church leaders all accepted the truism that charity begins at home. When food and shelter were needed, wrote Gertrude Springer in *Survey*, "it is the community organization that holds the bag, the community that must measure its problem and muster its resources to deal with it."[4] Yet no community was prepared for the onslaught of thousands of unemployed. Many cities had no Department of Public Welfare; most were only legally able to provide public relief funds through institutional care.[5] During the first winter of 1930, private agencies across the nation strained to provide emergency relief for the millions of new unemployed. By the winter of 1932, 80 percent of relief was provided from city, state, and, finally, federal funds.[6] Vital early debates over private and public agencies and the responsibility of private citizen and government were moot.[7] The magnitude of the human need was patently obvious from the shouts of hunger marchers and the testimony of beleaguered social workers, labor leaders, and governors in congressional hearings.

Catholic charities, which had confronted the waves of new immigrants, now faced the cries for help from the thousands of their sons and daughters, the "new poor" of the middle and working class. Catholic Charities of the Archdiocese of New York (CCNY) estimated that 50 percent of those aided by city work projects were Catholic. In the emergency diocesan bureaus around the country reached out to pastors, conferences of the Society of St. Vincent de Paul, the Ladies of Charity, Big Brother and Big Sister organizations, and the Catholic Daughters of America. They increased their professional staffs and brought in volunteers, mostly women, in a herculean attempt to coordinate material, psychological, and spiritual assistance. Through their membership on councils of social agencies and community chest boards, through the placement of Catholic social workers in public agencies, and through lobbying in city councils, state legislatures, and eventually Congress, the diocesan leaders of Catholic charities and the national leaders of the NCCC and the NCWC fought for resources. Most of these early on accepted the need for public funds and insisted on the responsibility of the government to provide relief for its citizens. New York's Cardinal Hayes observed that in a great earthquake, fire, or other catastrophe,

Americans look to the government to care for the needy and the suffering.[8] This crisis was no different.

In New York City, the crisis and response had long-range significance. It had the greatest concentration of wealth, the greatest concentration of unemployed (567,000 by early 1931), and the greatest concentration of professional social and philanthropic organizations. At least sixteen leaders of the New York social work community eventually brought the experience and ideas tested in the city to Franklin D. Roosevelt's New Deal. They faced tremendous challenges in resources and coordination. Because New York was not a community chest city, each of the private agencies had its own campaign. Catholic Charities of the Archdiocese of New York had 209 agencies and institutions and 370 parishes to serve 1,273,291 Catholics, but clearly its annual charity drive could not raise the funds needed in the expanding economic disaster. They had to garner more private and public resources.[9]

Catholic charities professionals were well-placed for the effort. As the Depression began, Catholic Bernard Fagan was president of the city's Conference of Social Workers. Jane Hoey was assistant director of the New York City Welfare Council. Rev. John C. Carr, director of Catholic Charities of Buffalo, served as president of the New York State Conference on Social Work, and veteran social worker Rose McHugh was appointed assistant commissioner of the New York state Department of Social Welfare.[10]

Work, and failing that, work relief, were the primary goals of the social agencies, including Catholic Charities. "Jobs! Jobs! Jobs!" was the cry of three out of four who applied for help. These new applicants were different. They were, the 1930 archdiocesan annual report observed, "unemployed through no fault of their own" and "ashamed of their plight." Many were skilled; most had never applied for charity. Some, ironically, had been contributors to Catholic Charities. These were workers who were worthy of their hire. Using all of the emergency resources available to it, Catholic Charities found 1,176 full-time positions.[11] It was a major achievement, but tens of thousands remained unemployed and at the end of their resources.

A campaign to fund work relief was launched in the summer of 1930. William Matthews of the Association for the Improvement of the Condition of the Poor and the leaders of the Charity Organization Society approached Seward Prosser, chair of the Bankers Trust Company, to head a six-million-dollar campaign. Worried that the Prosser campaign would make it impossible to launch an effective Catholic campaign, Robert Keegan insisted that Catholic Charities and Jewish Social Service be included as full partners in the enterprise. With all of the family welfare agencies signed on, the drive raised $8.2 million. Financed by the Prosser funds, Matthews had an Emergency Work Bureau (EWB) in operation by October. Catholic Charities set up an EWB branch at its central office and placed 6,119 on projects. Pastors and superintendents of Catholic institutions identified work that needed to be done and conferences of St. Vincent de Paul located unemployed heads of families in the parishes and connected them with the EWB. The pay was $5 a day for three days a week to stretch out one job for two people. It was obviously tide-over or "staggering on" pay, but it did enable those hired to maintain some self-respect. More than $800,000 in wages were paid for work on Catholic projects. Parishioners had tangible evidence that the church came through, pastors had added respect for Catholic Charities' ability to deliver, those helped were drawn closer to the church, and finally, Catholic Charities improved relations with organizations like AICP "where friendliness did not exist before." By the end of the year, the EWB carried 20,540 on its payroll. A conservative estimate set the jobless total in the city at 300,000.[12]

To meet the immediate needs of families for food, shelter, and medical care, Catholic Charities spent $806,725 with funds from the Prosser Committee, the parishes, and donations to provide direct relief to 15,084 families with a total of 45,252 children.[13] The bureau recognized that it was providing only minimum subsistence. Meanwhile its staff tried to help eligible Catholics gain access to mothers' pensions and the funds raised by the city's 1 percent tax on the paychecks of some city employees.

The year 1931 brought more misery and a changed welfare environment. While private agencies remained active in planning for work projects and direct relief and a Citizens Family Welfare Committee continued the fund-raising and distribution system of the Prosser Committee, the major source of new funds was from city and state government. As dire necessity led Catholic charities to turn to the state, they were buttressed philosophically by the principle of "subsidiarity" set forth by Pope Pius XI in his 1931 encyclical, *Quadragesimo anno*. An organic theory of social structure, subsidiarity posited that "nothing should be done by a higher and larger institution that cannot be done as well by a smaller and lower one." It also favored maximum participation in decision making. Translated into the relief crisis of 1931, subsidiarity meant that assistance should first be given by local voluntary agencies. Should they be unable to meet their responsibilities, then government should provide the assistance needed. If local organizations or government could not cope with the emergency, then help could come from a higher level. But the pope cautioned against indiscriminately turning over *all* responsibility to the government (giving up the right to and need for voluntary association), and he warned that it "would be a grave evil and a disturbance of right order for a larger and higher organization to arrogate to itself functions which can be performed efficiently by smaller and lower bodies."[14] In 1931 subsidiarity provided both a theoretical basis for Catholics to seek aid from the government and an argument for a Catholic role in determining policy.

In the fall the New York legislature passed a State Emergency Relief bill providing twenty million dollars for state aid, and Governor Roosevelt established the Temporary Emergency Relief Administration. Now aided by state funds and enabling legislation, the city established the Home Relief Bureau headed by Mary Gibbons, on loan from the Family Welfare Division of CCNY. In a whirlwind of activity in its first twelve weeks, the Bureau organized seventy-nine districts, trained several thousand new workers, many of them from the ranks of the unemployed, and aided 100,000 families.[15] As the unemployed besieged the Home Relief Bureau offices, observers struggled to describe the magnitude of the enterprise; Belgian War Relief was one analogy. Catholic Charities described the Home Relief Bureau as a "godsend to the family relief agencies," admitting in its annual report that it had "about reached the end of its resources, not only in money . . . but in energy of its workers."[16] They now had a public agency, directed by one of their own.

As more businesses failed and more people joined the ranks of the unemployed in 1932, private funding in the city dropped by 50 percent. Forced to reduce its caseload by 550 families, CCNY sent them to the Home Relief Bureau. When the City Work Commission cut its workforce by 50 percent, CCNY estimated that another 7,500 Catholics had to turn to the Home Relief Bureau. City and state resources were obviously failing to meet the desperate needs. In May, when the 72nd Congress considered proposals for federal relief, William Hodson of the New York Welfare Council and newly elected president of the National Conference of Social Work declared "federal relief is respectable. The time has come." Catholic Charities of New York had reached the same conclusion five months earlier. At its January 27, 1933, meeting, the Board of Trustees asserted that federal assistance was clearly necessary.[17]

The New York experience was replicated with variations in communities across the nation. In each the emergency worsened from 1929 through 1932; in each there was an initial effort to meet the crisis locally, followed by a call for state funds, and the final realization that federal money was necessary. Each bureau of Catholic Charities first struggled for the resources to meet the immediate material needs of Catholic families and, beyond that, to continue to provide service and religious casework.

Cincinnati faced the Depression with a community chest organization, a council of social agencies, a public welfare department able to provide relief to families in their homes, and a history of hard-won cooperation between private and public agencies.[18] Catholic Charities director Monsignor Marcellus Wagner, like Robert Keegan in New York, brought more than a decade of experience to the emergency. The crisis was not long in coming. In 1929 the caseload of Catholic Charities tripled. A city appropriation provided work relief through the public welfare department. The pay was thirty cents an hour for three days a week. If New York's $15 work relief wage was staggering-on money, Cincinnati's wage of $7.20 was not even family subsistence. The community chest provided additional relief funds to private agencies. Reporting in the *Catholic Charities Review*, Luella Sauer of the Family Welfare Division of Catholic Charities observed that with this cooperative policy, Cincinnati had no demonstrations of the unemployed and, "as much as was humanly possible," was meeting essential needs.[19]

But in 1931 Cincinnati faced a gathering crisis. In his appeal for support of the community chest, Archbishop McNicholas exhorted Catholics "to share their superfluous possessions with the needy." The chest's budgetary allowance for the Bureau of Catholic Charities for 1931 was almost $95,000; Catholic institutions and the St. Vincent de Paul Society received an additional $200,000. This was augmented by $250,000 from a special chest fund for the private agencies to distribute to the unemployed. Again it was clearly not enough. In February 1932, 90,000 families were carried on the relief lists of social agencies; another 1,000 families were being added each month. Archbishop McNicholas, in issuing his 1932 appeal for the chest, warned that unless there was "a speedy reconstruction of the social order," the nation would "face great social disorder." Marcellus Wagner broadened the call to arms. As in war, he declared at a community chest rally, it was the duty of citizens to sacrifice and finally of governments to confront the distress of the country.[20]

Several hundred miles from Cincinnati, in Pittsburgh, where Catholics comprised 35 percent of the population, private agencies strained to meet massive relief needs. Public relief, when available, was riddled with corruption.[21] As the emergency deepened, Pittsburgh business leaders created the Allegheny County Emergency Association to raise $2,300,000 for work relief programs. In 1930, when Bishop Hugh Boyle allowed each pastor to use 3 percent of his gross receipts for relief, the pastor of St. Peter's parish on the South Side reported paying $5,000 to unemployed parishioners for work in the church and cemetery. Other rectories and convents provided free meals; Mercy Hospital averaged more than 300 meals a day. Social activist priests, outraged at the slowness of the city politicians' response, organized a Catholic Radical Alliance "for the purpose of DOING something about the present social and economic mess."[22] At St. Patrick's parish, Rev. James Cox established a hospitality house feeding more than 800 a day, offering medical care through a clinic, and providing shelter for 300 each night. Overall, in the period from January to June 1931, the diocese disbursed an estimated $120,000 in relief. The Conference of Catholic Charities' staff, faced with more than a thousand people seeking help each day, expanded to ninety-two paid workers and sixty volunteers.[23]

With his charity funds depleted and aware that it was no time to launch a major campaign, Bishop Boyle agreed with the board of Catholic Charities that it was finally time to apply for admission to the community fund.[24]

The first check arrived in January 1932. In the next six months, Catholic Charities disbursed $399,726.59. The Allegheny County Emergency Association provided $379,197.92 of that total and the Welfare Fund the rest. But the *Pittsburgh Catholic* reported worsening conditions. In a wave of bank closings, two casualties, the Diamond National and Duquesne National, held the deposits of "an exceptionally large number" of parishes. Boyle's appeal for the Christmas orphans collection claimed the sisters were having difficulty providing food and clothing for the children. Bills had to be held over. Convinced that neither city nor state resources could meet the needs of the Catholics in Pittsburgh, Boyle later concluded, "the federal government will have to put up the money, or—well, God help us all."[25]

In Denver the new bishop, Urban Vehr, reported being "besieged by beggars" in 1931. "We couldn't get our work done. Someone was running to answer the door every few minutes."[26] By the summer of 1932, an estimated 65,000 were unemployed, one-sixth of the workforce. In early 1933 the unemployed staged a mass march for unemployment insurance and a moratorium on the payment of debts.[27] To respond to the disaster, Denver's Bureau of Catholic Charities had neither the resources nor the clout of its eastern counterparts. Its director, Rev. John Mulroy, a transplanted New Yorker, described opening a small two-room office in 1927 "with six months paid rent, a borrowed social worker, a secretary paid . . . if we had the money, a volunteer Vincentian, some old clothes, some meal and lodging tickets."[28] The St. Vincent de Paul Society and the Denver Council of Catholic Women, which worked extensively with the migrant Mexican sugar beet workers, underwrote the Bureau's modest salary and equipment costs. The Knights of Columbus helped through a benefit minstrel show.[29] In 1929 Mulroy had applied for the admission of his fledgling Bureau to the community chest. The chest, although it aided Catholic orphanages, "did not see its way clear" to accept the diocesan Bureau for membership nor to allocate money to it until 1930. The remainder of its support continued to come from parishes and the Knights of Columbus. Clearly Catholic Charities lacked the funds to provide adequate relief to the large numbers applying for aid.

Just as clearly the Department of Social Welfare of the City and County of Denver saw relief as its responsibility. In 1931 the Social Welfare Department distributed more than $100,000 to the needy, whereas the community chest provided about $40,000 for family relief. Catholic Charities had an arrangement with the Department of Social Welfare whereby the Bureau would work with Catholic families who came to either agency for one month. If they could not resolve the case during that time, the families would be turned over to Social Welfare for assistance. By October 1931 that policy was in jeopardy. The director of the city agency now informed Mulroy that Catholic Charities had to refer cases to her department within forty-eight hours if the Bureau did not intend to carry them permanently. Writing for advice to John O'Grady of NCCC, Mulroy explained that the St. Vincent de Paul Society wanted to work with families at least a month to "discover any spiritual problems . . . and perhaps settle them." The director of Social Welfare, however, complained that the SVPS budget for the families was higher than her department could afford to give. Mulroy argued that the higher Vincentian funding was "a real blessing to the poor." But Mulroy was more annoyed than alarmed. During the year Catholic Charities, with an expenditure of $5,106.89, had handled 2,289 cases, only turning over one hundred cases to the city. Obviously their assistance was in the form of service not relief. Still Mulroy looked forward in his 1931 annual report to the time when Catholic Charities would be "sufficiently supported through generous and benevolent people" and be better able to respond to Catholics in need.[30]

Meanwhile Mulroy and Catholic Charities did cooperate with other social agencies to establish a Citizen's Unemployment Committee to coordinate relief and employment efforts. With the state facing its worst crisis in the winter of 1932, Mulroy chaired the Denver Council of Relief agencies and the State Board of Visitors to Welfare institutions. He worked to have a member of the Catholic Charities Board named president of the community chest and later chair of the State Board of Public Welfare. When the New Deal began, Mulroy and Catholic Charities were well-placed on the Emergency Relief Committee distributing federal relief funds.[31]

Baltimore faced the onset of the Depression with a strong tradition of private giving. Unlike Denver, there was no city Department of Public

Welfare, nor would there be one until 1937. Relief was provided primarily through the private agencies. The Bureau of Catholic Charities defended that tradition in a city and a state with a strong Catholic presence. Baltimore's nearly 190,000 Catholics were led by the aggressive, and sometimes pugnacious, Archbishop Michael J. Curley. The City Council was dominated by Catholics and the Democratic political boss, Irish-Catholic William Curran. Like Pittsburgh, it was a city of strong ethnic neighborhoods; almost one-third of Baltimoreans had at least one foreign-born parent. With a diversified economic base in industry, commerce, and shipping, Baltimore was slow to experience the full impact of the Depression. In late 1930 the Baltimore Association of Commerce still bravely declared that "industry as a whole is in good shape." Archbishop Curley, Mayor Howard W. Jackson, and the perennial incumbent, Governor Albert C. Ritchie, shared a "preference for local prerogative and state sovereignty." Only in the desperate conditions of 1932 did they finally accept public responsibility for relief and only after much intergovernmental wrangling.[32]

Baltimore's Catholic Charities did not join the Community Fund. Its Catholic base of support and city and state appropriations for the care of orphans and delinquents allowed Archbishop Curley to remain independent. Curley not only feared that one fund drive would not meet the needs of the Catholic, Protestant, and Jewish charities but also worried about "cold lifeless charity." Each year the archbishop hosted a banquet for prominent Catholic businessmen to publicize the work of Catholic Charities and to gain their pledges of support. Working with his director of the Bureau of Catholic Charities, Rev. Edwin L. Leonard, Curley sought more parish conferences of the St. Vincent de Paul Society and branches of the Ladies of Charity. By the end of the 1920s, however, less than half of the fifty-seven parishes had a conference; only eight parishes were organized by the Ladies of Charity. Yet in 1929 Curley reported that Baltimore Catholic Charities and its institutions had spent nearly one million dollars to meet the needs of Catholic children, families, and the aged.[33] What he did not report was that much of the funding came from public sources.

By January 1931 Baltimore had nineteen breadlines in operation; at year's end unemployment reached 19 percent. The largest private social agency, the Family Welfare Association, needed emergency funds from the Community Fund to continue operations. Its relief costs had skyrocketed from $173,496 in 1930 to $614,354 in 1931. The Jewish Social Service Bureau, which had formed an Emergency Employment Bureau, faced a 1930 deficit of more than $133,000. In March 1931, police, who counted the numbers of unemployed in their districts and gave tide-over aid in food and clothing, were forced to discontinue their relief efforts. Ethnic groups held dances and bazaars to take care of their own, as did African-Americans who faced a 50 percent unemployment rate. In this crisis only the Bureau of Catholic Charities, while spending $17,000 a month, continued to report it could meet the needs of those who sought assistance.[34]

A Citizens Emergency Relief Committee, organized by business leaders in 1931, surveyed relief needs and launched a drive for $350,000, although its chair observed ruefully that $600,000 was probably needed. The funds were disbursed through the private social agencies. Mayor Jackson, vehemently denouncing the dole, refused the Community Fund's request for emergency city funding. Only in March 1932, when the Family Welfare Association began closing its offices and announced that 27,000 families would have to find other means of survival, did Jackson use city funds for relief.

Nearly 70 percent of families receiving the city relief money worked for it. The private agencies investigated the clients and disbursed the funds. Catholic Charities, working with the parishes and the St. Vincent de Paul conferences, supervised its clients and visited families each week. Wages were paid through the parish priest. Meanwhile the parishes and the SVPS continued to offer what relief they could. Sometimes the Catholic clients shopped for a better deal. Archbishop Curley wrote to Edwin Leonard of the appeal of one pastor for money and bags of flour for the poor of his parish. He forwarded the pastor's lament that the "Italians have absolutely deserted him . . . they have transferred their allegiance to the parishes where they are getting more" than the $2 to $3 a week he offered.[35]

Although the source of the money had changed, the Baltimore system of private agencies remained. In 1932 five hundred SVPS volunteers disbursed $215,694 for relief, the largest amount in eighty years. A little less than half of the total came from city money; the remainder from the archbishop's funds.[36] As the New Deal was launched in the spring of 1933, Leonard spoke to the leaders of Baltimore's social agencies in support of the continued role of private agencies for unemployment relief. Yet Catholics also joined in urging the legislature to enact statewide employment insurance, and Archbishop Curley, in the *Catholic Review* in January 1933, though not yet calling for federal aid, called for a restoration of social justice and, using the phrase of president-elect Roosevelt, a new deal.[37]

As bishops and diocesan directors of Catholic Charities worked with local communities and state governments to meet the needs of their citizens, John O'Grady, representing their interests as executive secretary of the NCCC, pressed for federal action. Throughout 1931 at meetings of the Family Welfare Association, the National Conference of Social Work, and the American Association for Labor Legislation, he spoke out for public works programs. "What we are interested in," he asserted, "is a program that provides work for the unemployed this winter, not five years from now."[38] At the September meeting of the NCCC in Wilkes-Barre, prompted by O'Grady, the diocesan directors supported a federal works program and resolved: "There is work to be done and the Federal Government has the necessary resources within its reach. . . . We look to our state and national government for prompt and constructive action."[39] Two months later at their annual meeting, the bishops, while warning that "federal aid, since it eventually means Federal control and domination, must be limited as far as possible," agreed "that in the present emergency Federal measures that would relieve the immediate distress and suffering should be supported."[40]

To move the reluctant Hoover administration, advocates of congressional action needed ammunition, evidence that suffering was not being alleviated through traditional means. Stung by the embarrassment of not knowing how many were unemployed, Congress directed the Secretary of Labor in 1930 to gather statistics and to estimate the number of unemployed each month. The Children's Bureau, the Association of Community Chests and Councils, the Russell Sage Foundation, and the NCCC also documented the grim reality. John O'Grady's assistant, Alice Padgett, compiled an NCCC monthly registration of family relief figures from the diocesan bureaus of Catholic Charities and conferences of St. Vincent de Paul societies. In the November 1931 *Catholic Charities Review,* she summarized the responses from fifty-two central diocesan agencies, sixteen St. Vincent de Paul societies, and seven other lay organizations, putting the Catholic effort in the national context by including figures from the Children's Bureau and the Russell Sage Foundation. Catholic Charities of New York, Rochester, and Pittsburgh, and the St. Vincent de Paul societies of Philadelphia and St. Louis led in the distribution of funds. Five bureaus of Catholic Charities had increased their volunteer staffs by 300 percent. Padgett worried about the changing nature of the work. Family agencies were "forced to do more and more economic case work and to give less and less medical, psychological and religious services."[41] In the January 1932 *Catholic Charities Review,* Padgett reported that forty-five Catholic agencies in forty-five cities had distributed $1,952,273.24 in direct aid to families in 1931. Fourteen of the forty-five agencies responding were from New York state, six from Connecticut, and six from Southern California. She had no response from Chicago, Boston, San Francisco, Baltimore, and Cincinnati.[42] Although this was the best survey of Catholic Charities available, Padgett's report, like those of the Children's Bureau, the Russell Sage Foundation, the Association of Community Chests and Councils, and even the Bureau of the Census, was woefully incomplete. What they did reveal was that the situation was worsening, and resources in many areas were nearing exhaustion.[43]

John O'Grady joined the stream of social workers testifying for a public works program at the hearing of Senator LaFollette's Subcommittee of the Committee on Manufactures in December 1931. He emphasized the need for speed. Perhaps the funds would not be administered with the highest standards of efficiency and accountability, but, he argued, "You have to take some chances with it." O'Grady then advanced the two essential strategies of Catholic Charities in dealing with public measures of social provision. First he recommended "a very elastic plan." Second he urged the utilization of existing agencies (including Catholic Charities) rather than setting up an entirely new structure.[44] The NCWC was decidedly more wary of federal action. William Montavon, director of the NCWC Legal Department, testified immediately after O'Grady. The Catholic bishops, he reported, did support federal aid in the present emergency, but it should be limited "since it eventually means federal control and domination."[45]

When Hoover finally approved a compromise Emergency Relief and Construction Act in the summer of 1932, an O'Grady editorial in the *Catholic Charities Review* hailed "Federal Relief at Last," but he railed against an administration that "set its face against any acceleration of Federal public work." The legislation proved too little, and for the Hoover administration, too late. The Bonus Expeditionary Force was encamped on Anacostia Flats and lobbying Congress for the veterans' bonus; the Farmers' Holiday Association was blocking roads on the Great Plains. From Mississippi Senator Bilbo warned, "Folks are getting a little pink down here."[46] The November elections brought a resounding repudiation of the "old order" and swept in the Democrats, Franklin D. Roosevelt, and a New Deal.

During his campaign Roosevelt had emphasized that Americans wanted action and action now. Between March and June of 1933, the New Deal delivered. Fifteen major pieces of legislation established new agencies from the Agricultural Adjustment Administration through the innovative Tennessee Valley Authority. For Catholic Charities the most immediately significant initiative was the Federal Emergency Relief Administration (FERA). When FERA was created, four million families were on relief. Only $130 million of the available $300 million had been disbursed through the Hoover federal "loans" program to the states.

Crisis had followed crisis as the Reconstruction Finance Corporation refused to approve funds for more than a month or two in advance. Generally states and communities continued to provide relief through the structures and cooperative arrangements already in place. All of that changed with FERA.[47]

Congress appropriated $500 million in federal grants to the states through FERA. Half was distributed on the basis of matching funds (one federal dollar to three state dollars) to a state emergency relief agency that had submitted a plan for federal approval. Like TERA in New York, FERA state administrations were created as temporary agencies separate from state boards of public welfare. Also like TERA, FERA had teeth. Administrator Harry Hopkins, brought by Roosevelt from TERA, could insist that states set up relief organizations staffed with professionals and complying with federal standards. The relief machinery was tripartite: the federal government supplied the money and set regulations; the states executed the federally approved plan and supervised the local government agencies, which investigated cases, determined need, disbursed funds, and also recommended work projects. If a state government balked at providing matching funds, Hopkins could refuse to release federal money. As he had at TERA, Hopkins chafed at both needs tests and payment of relief in kind. Although FERA provided funds to meet urgent and immediate needs for food and shelter, Hopkins always encouraged work relief and payment in cash. Increasingly he used FERA discretionary funds for relief.[48]

One month after FERA was up and running, John O'Grady reviewed the trends in the distribution of relief funds. He reported a drift toward public agencies administering relief but found that in cities where there had been no, or poorly administered, public relief, there was a tendency, "quite pronounced," "to use existing relief structures." In St. Louis and Kansas City, all public relief was administered by private agencies. In Chicago relief was administered by public and private agencies. O'Grady contended that where public administration predominated, it was both more expensive and riddled with politics. In some cities the experience and "inspiration that comes from private charity" had been lost. Not surprisingly O'Grady argued that private agencies (like Catholic Charities) should administer relief to families that needed specialized casework.[49]

Harry Hopkins determined otherwise. In June and July, he issued significant new directives, Rule 1 and Rule 3. After August 1, 1933, FERA money must be spent only by public agencies. If the public agency continued to use skilled private social workers on loan from private agencies, it had to add them to public payrolls. If the public agency disbursed funds through a private agency, that private agency now had to be identified as a branch of the public agency. FERA's policies "established once and for all a clean-cut principle and a broad philosophy of governmental responsibility for relief."[50] O'Grady saw the FERA policies as "a very decided revolution of public welfare administration in the United States." The new rules would essentially end Catholic Charities' role in federal emergency relief. He insisted that the "policy obviously must be interpreted on a realistic basis in the various parts of the United States."[51]

From Washington O'Grady vigorously supported the efforts of the diocesan directors of Catholic Charities to remain partners in relief. He pressed Hopkins to appoint a Catholic assistant, someone who understood the local situations of Catholic Charities, especially because "the administration is interested in keeping out of trouble in these matters." His own recommendations for the post included Mary Gibbons and Rose J. McHugh, and he asked Robert Keegan to use his New York connections.[52] When no Catholic appointment was forthcoming, O'Grady secured the next best thing—direct access to Harry Hopkins. He found him "very reasonable about the whole situation." Although Hopkins was "anxious to have the public departments developed," O'Grady believed that he was also "in hearty accord with having the private agencies continue to make their proper contribution." It would prove a matter of interpretation.[53]

As the diocesan bureaus sought a "proper contribution" in the face of Rules 1 and 3, their major success stories came from the cities where Catholic Charities was well-established and politically well-connected. In 1931 Chicago's Catholic Charities had been approved by the Illinois Emergency Relief Commission (IERC) to administer public relief funds to Catholic clients among the city's more than half million unemployed. A rising storm of protest rose from Chicago's Council of Social Agencies (exclusive of the Catholic representative, no doubt), when Catholic Charities was made an agent of the Emergency Welfare Fund of Cook County and received $1,000,000 to disburse to Catholic families. Social work professionals from the Council of Social Agencies and the American Public Welfare Association were not only angry at this preferential treatment but concerned over the high number of volunteers in the Catholic agency and the violation of the principle that public funds should be administered by public agencies.[54]

With a new Democratic governor and a new Democratic president assuming office in 1933, the controversial Catholic Charities arrangement in Cook County continued. It survived the continued opposition of social work professionals, the criticism of the IERC, and the FERA determination that public money only be disbursed through public agencies. Chicago's Cardinal Mundelein had been a powerful early supporter of Franklin Roosevelt. When FERA announced that after August 1 all public funds must be administered by public agencies, representatives from Chicago's Catholic Charities met with Hopkins in Washington and, working later with the FERA field agent in Chicago, won the (continued) designation of Catholic Charities as a public agency. Catholic Charities workers became public employees. The volunteers on the Catholic staff would now be paid by federal funds; moreover they could only be dismissed after consultation with the supervisor of Catholic Charities. Professionals on the IERC staff seethed as these "untrained and unskilled" Catholic volunteers dispensed public relief funds. A year later, when a FERA official initiated a study of the federal program in Chicago, he telegraphed Harry Hopkins suggesting that he terminate this special understanding. Hopkins' reply simply ordered the agent: "make no changes regarding Catholic Charities until further discussion with me."[55] Chicago's Catholic leadership and the machine of Mayor Edward J. Kelly remained staunch New Deal supporters; the support was reciprocated.

In Pittsburgh Catholic Charities also remained a partner in relief. Luella Sauer of the Conference of Catholic Charities served on the Advisory Committee of the new Allegheny County Emergency Relief Board (ACERB). ACERB handled the simple unemployment cases and employed some of the Catholic Charities caseworkers in its relief units. Pittsburgh Catholic Charities decided which "complicated" cases it wanted to carry. Relief orders issued by the emergency relief agency were sent to Catholic Charities, which distributed funds and provided service.[56]

In Baltimore the Bureau of Catholic Charities and the St. Vincent de Paul conferences comprised one of four units of the Baltimore Emergency Relief Committee (BERC). Catholic Charities added six new workers to supervise the work of the SVPS investigators. Bureau personnel and Vincentian volunteers became temporary agents of the public relief effort. Speaking at a Knights of Columbus communion breakfast in December, diocesan director Edwin Leonard reported that although he originally had "some grave doubts" about FERA, they had "been dispelled." Indeed he found it an inspiration to work with some of the BERC guests at the breakfast. It would be particularly easy to work with one of the district supervisors, Elizabeth Mulholland, who was also the president of the Catholic Ladies of Charity. Not surprisingly FERA field investigators reported that Baltimore had not appreciably changed its tradition of private relief. The connection between public assistance and the private agency remained a "serious matter in Baltimore where racial and church alignments in relief work are pronounced." FERA field representatives urged the BERC to end its arrangements with the private agencies with their policies of unhealthy paternalism and pressured the city to emphasize work relief projects. City administrators were unmoved.[57]

As in Baltimore, Pittsburgh, and Chicago, Catholic Charities staff and volunteers in St. Louis were integrated into the public emergency relief efforts. The central office of the St. Vincent de Paul Society temporarily became a public agency. Its director, John Butler, became assistant director of the Citizens' Committee on Relief and Employment. John O'Grady wrote Butler approvingly, "You got a better bargain from the Federal Relief Administration than any other city so far."[58]

From cities where the Catholic presence was less substantial and where Catholic Charities was not so well-positioned, the reports of the diocesan directors ranged from troubled to frantic. By far the greatest hue and cry came from John Mulroy of Denver. FERA regional director Pierce Williams announced that he would enforce Rules 1 and 3 to the letter and instructed the Denver City–County Relief Committee to decide immediately which key individuals of the private agencies would be "taken over" as public welfare officials and paid by FERA funds. Door signs and stationery had to display the title of the Relief Committee and not the private agency. Although these arrangements had been accepted by diocesan directors in Chicago and Pittsburgh, an exercised Mulroy wired John O'Grady: "Private agencies given ultimatum by Williams. Rule laid down by him requires our supervisor become public welfare official, paid by local federal committee, all new cases to be assigned our agency thru city charities. . . . Shall we accept above humiliating terms, or step out? Please wire advice." Complaining to Williams that his directives were more rigid than arrangements in St. Louis, Chicago, or Baltimore, O'Grady added, "too rigid arrangements will make it appear that you are pressing us to wall." Meanwhile he advised Mulroy to comply. In December Mulroy again contacted O'Grady, announcing: "The war is on again . . . the private agencies of the Chest distributing Federal relief are battling again for a place in the picture." It was an emergency situation. Hopkins was cutting off federal funds because the Colorado legislature had failed to approve its matching state funds for relief. Mulroy reported that City Charities was pressing the mayor to take over relief in the crisis and "forget the private agencies." At the same time, Pierce Williams' replacement was initiating a survey of private agencies that Mulroy believed would target the relief work (supported by public funds) of Catholic Charities. Again asking for O'Grady's support, he stressed the "very critical situation for us all as far as family case work is concerned."[59]

In spite of Mulroy's vigorous outcry, O'Grady found the most serious confrontation with FERA in Tulsa, Oklahoma, where there was "a movement on foot to eliminate the private agencies completely." Diocesan director Bart A. Murtaugh reported a crisis complicated by politics and, he believed, bigotry. The Tulsa County Supervisor had announced that only the FERA agency was needed in the county; by September the United Family Relief, which had been created by the public and private agencies to distribute federal relief funds, would no longer function. Although its social workers might be employed by the Tulsa FERA relief organization, Murtaugh found that when he applied only women workers were being added. Adding further insult, according to Murtaugh, FERA was bringing in thirty new staff members from outside the area because a "better job will be done if case worker does not know client." When Murtaugh asked Bishop R. C. Kelley to intercede with the governor, he was told that the whole affair was "enmeshed hopelessly in politics." Bishop Kelley believed, to Murtaugh's dismay, that Catholic Charities should leave family relief to the secular agencies and confine its work to the diocesan orphanage and the delinquents in the House of the Good Shepherd. Writing to Marcellus Wagner in October, Murtaugh enclosed a report from a Catholic Charities visitor, then on the staff of the FERA organization, that her supervisor "had been given orders to refer no cases whatsoever to the Catholic Charities."[60]

As these FERA rulings were implemented, John O'Grady held a meeting in St. Louis with diocesan directors from Chicago, St. Louis, Denver, Peoria, Springfield, and Cincinnati. Writing to Robert Keegan of New York afterward, he explained, "I felt if I did not do something they might feel that I had neglected my duty." One disgruntled director seemed to believe that "by some magic wand I could pull all his chestnuts out of the fire." Defensively he insisted he had been as active as anyone representing a national organization. Deputized by the directors to draft a statement on Catholic Charities and federal relief to be presented to Harry Hopkins, O'Grady did so reluctantly. Taking the protest to the national level might bring on a fight in Congress, and, he cautioned, "In such a fight we would stand to lose. Harry Hopkins has pointed this out to me a number of times. Washington is very different from the big Catholic centers."[61]

O'Grady's subsequent dutiful one-page statement reviewed the service of the private agencies in the first three years of the Depression. Accepting the government's right to insist on efficiency and standards, O'Grady argued that it should not insist on one pattern of organization in states and communities, especially when that meant "the practical wrecking of many of the best private organizations." Catholic agencies were "ready and willing to deal with unemployment relief" and would do it more economically than public agencies. More important, they were better able to "deal with the fundamental difficulties of family life." In his most salient passage, O'Grady concluded: "Catholic agencies believe that the material cannot be separated from the spiritual in family life. They believe that any type of care that fails to reckon with the spiritual problems of human life is doomed to failure."[62]

In the spring of 1934, as the massive but short-lived work relief programs of the Civil Works Administration were terminated, FERA reviewed its programs, reorganized its administrative structure, and strengthened its regional offices and oversight of policies at the state and local level.[63] Denver again became a storm center. John Mulroy wired O'Grady that Bishop Vehr wanted Catholic Charities "to fight it out" over FERA's rejection of any relief role for private agencies. When Vehr's wires to Colorado's senators and congressmen proved unavailing, Mulroy wired O'Grady that Benjamin Glassberg, "federal relief dictator," was cutting off public funds to private agencies April 1. While O'Grady advised Denver to keep up the pressure, he urged Glassberg to be flexible and to allow the public agency to use private agencies for specialized services for problem families. In Washington he argued for three hours with FERA's Aubrey Williams, who "felt I had not made any impression on him nor had he made any impression on me." Reporting to Mulroy, O'Grady wrote defensively that he had done all that he could, but in Washington it "is largely a matter of tactics." Believing that they "should not go into a losing fight," O'Grady decided against orchestrating a protest from the diocesan directors. The Denver setback, he insisted to Mulroy, was "about the first serious reverse" in dealing with FERA administrators. Mulroy moved to his fallback position and worked for the appointment of a sympathetic director of the Denver Public Welfare Department.[64]

Throughout the spring and summer months of 1934, O'Grady urged the diocesan directors to continue to work for inclusion in the emergency relief efforts.[65] When Peoria's diocesan director Rev. Edward M. Farrell worried that the Family Welfare Association survey would recommend ending relief requisitions to Catholic Charities and the Salvation Army, O'Grady urged him to "hold fast" for if "they get you out of the picture they will want to get Springfield and Chicago eventually." Catholic Charities "should not surrender without offering resistance."[66] From Cincinnati an irritated Marcellus Wagner complained of high-handed actions by the State Relief Commission. New orders arrived each day. The situation was "becoming so distasteful" that he was inclined to withdraw except for the principle involved and the impact on other cities.[67]

When the NCCC met in Cincinnati in the fall for its 1934 meeting,

Wagner and O'Grady seemed ready to accept the inevitable. Public agencies would assume the major responsibility for material relief. In his presidential address, Wagner quoted Pope Pius XI on subsidiarity, the "duty of the public authority to supply for the insufficient forces of individual effort, [and to act for] the maintenance of the family." In a remarkably sanguine passage given his complaints about public intervention, he concluded that the government relief efforts could emancipate private social work from the "drudgery of relief giving" and be a "veritable deliverance from bondage." Private social work could direct its energies and resources to meet "the cultural needs of man." Like Wagner, O'Grady saw the future mission of Catholic agencies and institutions as service and specialization. Catholic professionals could provide spiritual and educational assistance. The private agency could give to families "the guidance and inspiration which alone can lift them up. It can bring to them something that is the product of Christian charity, of Christian thinking and living."[68] The leaders of Catholic charity, however, would continue as advocates for the poor (which encompassed large numbers of Catholics) and for relief programs that provided adequate subsistence.

Such advocacy was clearly in order as Roosevelt made the startling announcement in his December 1934 State of the Union Address that the federal government would launch a massive new federal works program, the Works Projects Administration, and then turn "this business of relief" back to the states and communities.[69] Though the diocesan directors of Catholic Charities supported federal work relief, they shared the fears of social workers in private and public agencies that there would be severe dislocation and suffering as FERA was phased out. Insisting that the federal withdrawal must be "conditioned by the ability of the state, municipal, and private charities" to take on new burdens, they cautioned that private charities would be of little assistance because the "tremendous governmental expenditures have definitely closed the doors of many sources of income to organized private charity."[70] As relief and welfare responsibilities returned to the states and communities, Catholic Charities worked to continue or renew the contracts and subsidies from local governments that enabled them to provide services for Catholic children and families. At the same time, the NCCC and bureaus of Catholic Charities took up the challenge of securing, where it was still possible, inclusion in other New Deal initiatives.

Bolstered by sweeping Democratic victories in the congressional and state elections of 1934, Roosevelt set an ambitious recovery and reform agenda for 1935 that culminated in the Social Security Act, the anchor of the American welfare state. Only the cataclysm of the Great Depression, the persistence of pressure groups, and, finally, the leadership of the

Roosevelt administration secured its passage. Elderly Americans in need and their guilty and desperate children backed the revolving pension scheme of Dr. Francis Townsend and bombarded their congressmen with more than 1,500 letters a day to demand old-age assistance. The American Association for Labor Legislation urgently pressed its arguments for unemployment insurance. The Children's Bureau resurrected aspects of the Sheppard-Towner maternity and child health plan and, in the face of faltering state mothers' pension programs, called for federal aid for dependent children. Harry Hopkins insisted on a commitment to federal work programs and a Department of Public Works to administer them. Roosevelt wanted comprehensive health care. What emerged, not surprisingly, was the loosely cobbled together insurance and welfare package of Social Security.[71]

Roosevelt began the process in June 1934 by creating a cabinet-level Committee on Economic Security (CES) chaired by Secretary of Labor Frances Perkins. Serving as the executive director of CES, Edwin Witte oversaw the drafting of the Social Security bill and coordinated the work of a blue-ribbon citizen Advisory Council and a Technical Board of experts. When no Catholics were named to the Advisory Council, John Burke of the NCWC immediately protested to the president. Not about to rouse such potent antagonists at this early stage, Roosevelt and Witte accepted nominations from the NCWC bishops. Witte named John A. Ryan of the NCWC Social Action Department to the Council, only to find to his chagrin that Ryan was not one of the nominees. He then added one of the bishops' choices, Elizabeth Morrissy, an economist from the College of Notre Dame of Maryland, for a final Council roster of twenty-three.[72]

Witte and the CES met Roosevelt's tight deadline and had a bill ready in December for his State of the Union message. Congress held hearings in January and February and through the spring heatedly debated the issues of highest administration priority—unemployment insurance, old-age insurance, and a health program, which fell early victim to the determined opposition of the American Medical Association. Although the report of the Committee on Economic Security intoned that "the core of any social plan must be the child," this was not where the congressional action was. But for Catholic leaders, the child welfare proposals *were* the core. "Catholic" support for Social Security was contingent on the provisions for the child. The NCWC and NCCC each actively lobbied, although they did not always manage to speak with "one voice." The NCWC used its access to Roosevelt, whereas the NCCC worked with its contacts in Congress and the Children's Bureau. On this issue the NCCC clearly played the dominant role.[73]

The responsibility for drafting the child welfare provisions of the Social Security bill naturally fell to the Children's Bureau, specifically its new chief, Katharine Lenroot; the assistant chief, Martha Eliot; and outgoing leader Grace Abbott.[74] After the grim Hoover years when they had struggled to maintain the Bureau's initiatives, they now had an opportunity to create a comprehensive federal program dealing not just with health, as had the Sheppard-Towner legislation of the 1920s, but with "the whole child." Lenroot, Eliot, and Abbott immediately appointed a subcommittee of public health experts and social workers to work with them. Chaired by veteran Homer Folks, it included Bryan McEntegart, the NCCC's almost official liaison with the Children's Bureau.

The report that the Children's Bureau sent to the CES emphasized "the necessity of developing coordinated public-health and social welfare programs covering all types of need, with definite provision for participation of the Federal Government, the States, and local communities."[75] Like the Social Security bill, however, the proposals proved more a package than a comprehensive program. The recommendations were for categorical assistance; their targets were areas of critical need. Aid to Dependent Children (ADC) added a federal partner to the mothers' pension programs already in existence in forty-five states. The Child Welfare Services proposal provided modest funding and professional support to encourage states to expand services for children in rural, underserved areas. Maternal and Child-Health Services, which included aid for crippled children, essentially resurrected and expanded the Sheppard-Towner programs. In her testimony before the House Ways and Means Committee, Lenroot emphasized that these provisions for children's security did "not set up any new or untried methods of procedure, but build upon experience. . ." They followed the federal, state, and local pattern of cooperation of Sheppard-Towner and, indeed, FERA. The funding request, she added, was "very conservative."[76] The NCCC was instantly alert to the possible implications for Catholic Charities both in the Aid to Dependent Children and Child Welfare Services.

In support of its proposal for ADC, the Children's Bureau reported that although forty-five states had mothers' aid programs, only an estimated one-third of eligible mothers and children were actually receiving funds and only an estimated one-half of the public agencies were actually authorizing grants. The availability of federal matching funds for relief through FERA had proven an attractive alternative to beleaguered state welfare departments. In 1934 approximately 358,000 families headed by women were aided by FERA, and an estimated 109,000 were receiving mothers' pensions. To the Children's Bureau, mothers' pensions were a long-term commitment, involving both financial assistance and social casework.[77] Emergency relief was no substitute. ADC would create a federal–state-mandated mothers' pension plan. The federal appropriation would start at twenty-five million dollars and increase to match augmented state funding of forty million dollars. States would control the funds and create plans to administer the program. As in the state mothers' pension programs, ADC targeted assistance for "fatherless" families. The funds were "not primarily aids to mothers but defense measures for children," protecting their entitlement to economic security in childhood. Also retained from the earlier mothers' aid programs was the provision for social casework.[78]

Catholic Charities leaders had no quarrel with either the philosophy or substance of Aid to Dependent Children as proposed by the Children's Bureau. But that was not the proposal sent to Congress. In the final mark-up of the Social Security bill, the CES made two critical changes. To the dismay of the Children's Bureau, CES recommended that FERA administer ADC. To the distress of Catholic Charities, FERA's language defining dependent children was substituted for the Bureau's more limited and traditional "fatherless" dependent child. FERA's dependent children were those "under the age of sixteen in their own homes, in which there is not an adult person, other than one needed to care for the child or children, who is able to work and provide the family with a reasonable subsistence compatible with decency and health." "Able to work" was the key phrase. FERA's Josephine Brown believed that broadly interpreted, "able to work" might include all those who could not find jobs and thus were "unemployable." Aid to Dependent Children, as conceived by FERA, she explained, meant "general relief or assistance on a family basis to all families having children under sixteen." The potential impact of ADC on Catholic child-caring institutions and agencies was obvious. Clearly state and local governments providing per capita payments to the institutions would have a significant financial incentive to move the children to families where they would be supported by ADC. The FERA umbrella could also cover children in foster care supervised by Catholic bureaus. Catholic Charities was concerned in both instances about placements—who would make them and provide supervision. How would the religion of these children be safeguarded?[79]

The Children's Bureau proposal for Child Welfare Services also seriously alarmed Catholic leaders. The Bureau recommended funding (1.5 million dollars) and services to states and communities to aid in developing programs to address the needs of the estimated 250,000 dependent and neglected children who were receiving care away from their homes. The Bureau's proposal particularly emphasized the need for social services in isolated rural areas, pointing out that only one-fourth of the states had county welfare boards. Federal money and state grants-in-aid could utilize the equalization principle (already used for education in some states) to improve standards of care in these underserved areas.[80] *Mandated* state participation in the financing of child-care programs would jeopardize the local funding of Catholic Charities in key states such as Pennsylvania, where the constitution prohibited the allocation of state funds to private institutions. Catholic agencies in Philadelphia and elsewhere in the state might lose $500,000 in local subsidies annually. New York's Catholic Charities would face a similar disaster.[81] The diocesan directors wanted the federal government "as a matter of policy [to] leave Child Welfare" to the states. Their backup position was that if the federal government "enter[ed] the field of caring for children away from their own homes, it should be on an experimental and demonstration basis only" and in "remote areas that are not being covered by existing public or private agencies."[82] More broadly, the diocesan directors feared that the administration of the Child Welfare Services by the Children's Bureau might eventually mean that the entire child welfare program of each state had to be approved by the Bureau. "In reality this would mean surrendering Child Welfare entirely to the supervision of the U.S. Children's Bureau." "It would," they concluded, "affect the whole Catholic program of Child Care in the United States."[83]

The NCCC and NCWC met in Washington in January 1935 to review the Social Security bill as the House Ways and Means and the Senate Finance committees began their hearings. Neither sent representatives to testify, although each forwarded a statement to be placed in the record.[84] First they tried to thrash out a position. An NCWC-proposed amendment sent for consideration to the NCCC clearly aimed at an end-run around the prohibition of state funds for private institutions. It stated: "No grants of money shall be made under provision of this Title to any non-governmental agency, except that nothing in this Title should be interpreted as prohibiting a State from payment of compensation for specific services to individual children, to any private agency or agencies recognized as standard by the State," if these payments were explicitly authorized in state plans approved by the Children's Bureau. If the NCCC approved this draft, the NCWC was prepared to inform the Roosevelt administration that with this amendment, "the Catholic group" would support Social Security. The diocesan directors were not buying. Their agencies and institutions would face double jeopardy. First they would have to secure explicit authorization in the state plans, and then these plans had to be approved by the Children's Bureau.[85]

Rejecting the NCWC language, the NCCC drafted two amendments and urged the NCWC to support them. For ADC (Title II, Section 203) they essentially recommended a return to the Children's Bureau's "fatherless" child definition, adding language to limit ADC funding to children living with a parent or relative within the second degree of kinship (with the greater possibility of a Catholic child cared for by a Catholic relative). Otherwise, they insisted, the federal government would essentially be entering the field of foster care. Because "the care of the dependent child away from his own home has been the great appeal of private social work," this federal initiative would "rob private social work of its most powerful appeal."[86] Turning to the Child Welfare Services (Title V, Section 703), the NCCC diocesan directors supported the emphasis on funding for rural areas but wanted federal money and services to be allocated for demonstration or experimental programs only. Ironically, although the core of their opposition was mandated state funding, they did not include this in the proposed amendment, apparently preferring to lobby behind the scenes. Still hoping for Catholic unity, Marcellus Wagner instructed the directors to wait for a progress report from an NCCC committee that was meeting with NCWC representatives and for the bishops' approval before lobbying Congress.[87]

During the first weeks of February, John O'Grady and members of a directors' subcommittee rallied their forces. Rev. John Butler, diocesan director of Catholic Charities of St. Louis, met with Perkins and her legal counsel, Thomas Eliot. O'Grady, Butler, and O'Dwyer of Los Angeles met with the bill's cosponsors, Senator Wagner and Representative David Lewis of Maryland, and conferred with other congressmen. O'Grady urged the other diocesan directors *immediately* to telegraph members of Congress and to organize a campaign for amendments to Sections 203 and 703. Senator Wagner's staff faced a blitz of letters from New York clergy.[88]

Claiming that "everybody seemed to be sympathetic," to the NCCC's positions, O'Grady then met with Edwin Witte and members of the technical advisory staff of the CES. At O'Grady's request, Witte subsequently set up the key meeting with Katharine Lenroot and Martha Eliot for Marcellus Wagner, Butler, and O'Grady. The lengthy session was, Witte attested, "one of the most successful" conferences "during the entire period of the development of the Social Security Act." The NCCC leadership immediately pressed for restricting the child welfare services primarily to rural areas (where the numbers of Catholics were lowest). Because the Children's Bureau had already emphasized the needs of rural counties and small towns where services were "extremely limited or non-existent," agreement on this point was not difficult.[89] The Catholic leaders failed to convince Lenroot and Eliot to institute the new programs on "an experimental and demonstration basis." But they won their most fundamental point. The Children's Bureau recommendation of mandated state grants-in-aid was dropped. Federal grants-in-aid were retained, but these posed no threat to Catholic Charities' local arrangements. Reporting that he had not understood the implications for Catholic services, Witte persuaded Lenroot to yield. In exchange Witte had O'Grady's promise that the NCCC would not oppose other sections of the bill and would actively work for its passage.[90]

The NCCC was simultaneously campaigning to revise the ADC definition of dependent children. The goal again was to limit the scope, to protect the carefully built up state/local support for Catholic services, and to safeguard the religion of the children. Bryan McEntegart estimated that if the federal government entered the field of foster care, it would "reduce by one-half the volume of Catholic child care in the country." Robert Keegan of Catholic Charities of New York wrote to Frances Perkins asking that children in foster homes be specifically exempted from coverage under Social Security.[91] The follow-up blitz of diocesan directors' letters to Senator Wagner argued that extending federal aid to children in homes other than those of their parents or close relatives was really foster care. Aid should be limited to those dependent children living with their parents or relatives within the second degree of kinship.[92]

Specifically the NCCC proposed that ADC should enable states to provide financial assistance to dependent children "in their own homes . . . who have been deprived of normal parental support and care by reason of the death, absence or physical or mental incapacity of a parent." They also suggested new language for Section 406 (which replaced Section 203), defining *dependent child* as one "under the age of sixteen who is living with his father, mother, grandfather, grandmother, brother, sister, stepfather, stepmother, stepbrother, stepsister, uncle, or aunt in a residence maintained by one or more of such relatives as his or their own home and in which home there is no adult person other than one needed to care for the child or children who is able to work and provide the family with a reasonable subsistence compatible with decency and health." It was an interesting blend of FERA and Children's Bureau language, anchored by a kinship provision that attempted to insure that a Catholic child deprived of her parents would be supported in the home of a Catholic relative. A notation scribbled on the minutes of the meeting by John Butler of St. Louis suggested that "Senator [David I.] Walsh will make every effort to have this included and Tom Eliot will help him."[93]

Winning on these essential points, the NCCC opted out of the administrative infighting over which agency would administer ADC. John Butler of New York had particularly warned the diocesan directors to "steer clear of any entangling alliances" given the "strong feeling among different groups of the administration forces in regard to this bill."[94] The CES recommended FERA rather than the Children's Bureau, but the House Ways and Means Committee, after some significant skirmishes over turf, amended the proposal and established a Social Security Board to administer both Aid to Dependent Children and Old Age Assistance. The Senate Finance Committee gave ADC to the Children's Bureau. The conference committee made the final determination, creating the Social Security Board with a Bureau of Public Assistance administering the categorical assistance programs. Writing to Marcellus Wagner, O'Grady observed that he personally "would have liked to have gone much farther," and taken a position, but he feared he "might lose everything for which we had struggled."[95]

The Social Security Act signed into law on August 14, 1935, had the full support of the NCCC. Congressman John McCormack of Massachusetts, after meetings with O'Grady, Butler, and O'Dwyer, made their recommended changes in the executive sessions of the Ways and Means Committee. Seventeen of the twenty-five members of the committee agreed to support amendments to the ADC and Child Welfare Services sections. In the Senate Senator Gerry added language to insure that the bill did not extend either state or federal control over private charitable institutions.[96] Writing to John Mulroy of Denver, who had asked if it wouldn't be better "for the time being to attempt to block the passage of any legislation cooperating with the Federal Government in such a proposed child care program," O'Grady reassured him, particularly on ADC: "We've made the child security provision in the bill 'sufficiently innocuous. . .'"[97] NCCC president Marcellus Wagner agreed that the diocesan directors should be pleased. Writing to Bryan McEntegart, he concluded, "If we believe in the Bill I think we should make every effort to see that the Bill is passed and put into operation."[98] Edwin Witte testified that the Catholic support promised to Lenroot had indeed been forthcoming. John O'Grady was "in close touch with many members of Congress and proved one of the most valuable supporters of the bill." He added: "he influenced a great many members of Congress to support the bill who otherwise would have opposed it."[99]

The final provisions of Aid to Dependent Children did supply a new, though inadequate, safety net for dependent children. By 1939 an estimated 700,000 children were receiving benefits.[100] Although benefits varied widely from state to state, the average monthly payment in 1939 was $32.13. But ADC was seriously flawed. Instead of setting the federal share at one-half of the state appropriation, Congress legislated only one-third. The federal maximum monthly payment was $18 for the first child and $12 for each additional child; there was no provision for the mother.[101] Southern congressmen used their power as chairs of committees to delete the clause that benefits would provide "reasonable subsistence compatible with decency and health," which they saw as threatening the racial caste system of the South. The newly created Social Security Board and its Bureau of Public Assistance lacked the experience and record of advocacy of the Children's Bureau in dealing with single mothers and children. ADC also retained the weaknesses of mothers' pensions. In addition to the consistently low benefit levels, middle-class behavioral norms were imposed. More than half of the states enacted a form of the "fitness" requirement suggested by the American Public Welfare Association that children should live "in a suitable family home meeting the standards of care and health." Discriminatory administration along racial lines was commonplace. Means and morals tests became part of the state programs. Catholic social worker Jane Hoey, the director of the Bureau of Public Assistance, cited lingering "opinion and attitude," which denied aid to children "because their parent's behavior does not conform to a certain pattern." ADC, like mothers' pensions, was frequently granted "on a basis of promoting the nice families." The 1939 amendments to Social Security setting up the Old Age Survivors Insurance (OASI) provided benefits to widows and surviving children of the male "breadwinner" and emphasized further the difference between "worthy" widows with "nice families" under OASI and the dependent, deserted, or never-married single mothers assisted by ADC.[102]

The Social Security Act created an American welfare system of contributory-insurance programs for unemployment and old age along with benefits and assistance for dependent and crippled children and the blind. Linda Gordon and others have argued that it led to a two-track system and the "gendering" of American welfare. Essentially the male breadwinner contributed to unemployment and old-age insurance and thus had a "right" to his payments. However, dependent children and their mothers received assistance based not on rights but on needs. On this two-track or needs/rights system, women and children were indeed last.[103]

Catholic leaders argued for social justice and a living wage in terms of the male breadwinner, and Catholic social workers did adopt the needs/rights language of the profession in conference papers. But their arguments were essentially grounded in class not gender. At the 1938 NCCC conference, chair of the Social Security Board Arthur J. Altmeyer's paper, "Benefits Based on Rights Under the Social Security Act," was followed by Mary Gibbons' presentation, "Benefits Based on Needs. . . ." Gibbons, now First Deputy Commissioner of the New York state Department of Social Welfare, noted that states were slow to develop their programs for ADC and wondered whether it was because ADC covered "not only the responsible and . . . respectable widow and her children but many other classes of children who should be kept in their own home." "Undoubtedly," she concluded, "this category has met resistance."[104]

At the NCCC convention one year later, Rose McHugh made a powerful argument that the needs/rights distinction was not part of the Catholic tradition. McHugh, chief of the Administrative Surveys Division of the Bureau of Public Assistance, asserted as basic Catholic principles that "rights are not established by governmental agencies; that man by his nature has inalienable rights; and that rights cannot be exercised unless known." Needs create rights. Reviewing the contributory and assistance programs of Social Security, she emphasized: "As part of our [American] inheritance from the English Poor Laws the idea still persists that contributory programs are based upon individual rights and that non-contributory programs, such as public assistance, are not. You are aware that this has never been the Catholic position. The right to subsistence is a primary natural right from which the right to a living wage is deduced." Building her case, she quoted the early church fathers, Thomas Aquinas, the popes, and John A. Ryan's position in *A Living Wage* (1906) that "every human being has not only a claim in charity, but a strict right to as much of the wealth of the community as is necessary to maintain his life." Now, she asserted, the challenge to Catholic Charities was "to make known the Catholic teaching on the right to subsistence and the right to a living wage." The Social Security Act's passage made this task easier because it "breaks completely with the Elizabethan laws of poor relief in the protection to individual integrity which it gives to applicants and recipients"—particularly in their right to appeal and to have a fair hearing on their appeal for assistance. Obviously much of the public would need to be convinced of this interpretation. It was up to "Catholics particularly to see that this doctrine of rights which is so completely their own becomes a living reality." Catholics should "bear witness to the rights of disadvantaged groups, to their sufferings which result from inequitable administration of assistance." The task ahead was to study, research, and lobby "to promote the development of sound social policy."[105]

Although the Social Security Act provided the federal funding and established the bureaucracy for an American welfare system, regulations and policies still had to be devised, state programs developed, and decisions made on standards and supervision. With considerable legislative success behind them, the NCCC and its diocesan directors now faced the daunting challenge of influencing state policy and the implementation of ADC and Child Welfare Services. John O'Grady and the diocesan professionals increasingly turned to Catholic volunteers and voters to support their efforts to gain influence and inclusion as the states developed their programs. At issue was both the ability of Catholic Charities to continue to serve Catholic children in need and to safeguard the religion of Catholic children aided by *f* merican welfare.

As the Children's Bureau established its Child Welfare Services division, Katharine Lenroot assured the NCCC that the state programs would be "developed with due regard to state and local relationship, and in cooperation with public and private groups engaged in promoting public health and social welfare." The child welfare services were primarily for rural areas and areas in special need "outside the reach of public and private services that have been available mainly in the larger cities." These services would not relieve private agencies of any of their current responsibilities.[106]

A more hardnosed version of the federal initiative was presented in the October issue of *Survey* by Mary Irene Atkinson, the newly appointed director of the Child Welfare Services division. A Catholic with experience in private, state, and federal agencies, Atkinson warned any private agencies that expected a return to pre-1929 conditions would "find themselves waiting in the wings for a cue which will never come." She fully supported the principle established by FERA that public money should be spent by public agencies. Private agencies that "rid themselves of certain outworn traditions and sentimentality," however, would find many opportunities to develop special programs and experiment with new techniques. In the long run, success in the Social Security programs would depend on whether those in children's work chose, "like Agamemnon, to sulk in their tents," or to bring "their rich experience and their powers of interpretation into the new and swift social current whose fountain head is government."[107]

On issues of child welfare, Catholics were, of course, well out of their tents. When Bryan McEntegart was appointed to an advisory committee for Atkinson's Child Welfare Services division, he urged John O'Grady to insist on fuller Catholic participation. Lenroot proved accommodating and added Marcellus Wagner and Dr. Alice Leahy of Catholic University.[108] McEntegart's influence on the committee was obvious in the position it took on the religious and social development of the children and its assertion that the cost of maintaining children in institutions or foster homes should be met by state or local funds and not by federal funds earmarked for the Bureau's child welfare services (and based on the principle of public funds to public agencies and institutions). The committee further urged state agencies to help local units in developing policies "to assure the employment of persons of proven ability in family and child welfare work and utilizing community resources for children."[109]

Diocesan bureaus of Catholic Charities were not alone in their anxiety over the child welfare services. When Lenroot suggested calling a conference in 1937 of representatives from public and private child welfare agencies, Atkinson was enthusiastic, given the "feeling among private agencies that public agencies may be trying to supplant them." C. C. Carstens of the Child Welfare League agreed that it might be helpful because "some private agencies are almost hysterical." But McEntegart was more cautious. The topics might be wide-ranging, and he reminded Lenroot that the new welfare services were to supplement services and not to reform policies dealing with state and local and public and private relationships. Retreating somewhat, Lenroot decided on a smaller gathering and appointed McEntegart to a committee to set an agenda. He obviously approved two statements prepared for discussion: "Private agencies should have the fullest opportunity for development so long as they operate under approved standards," and "The development of good public service depends on good private service." The conference agenda contained the statement: "The public structure needs to be braced with a continued good private program," although, it continued, "certain private agencies and institutions need to change their programs. . . ."[110]

Having helped to frame the discussion, McEntegart urged that John O'Grady and ten other NCCC leaders be invited to the conference, which would be held concurrently with the twenty-fifth anniversary celebration of the Children's Bureau. Diplomatically he suggested that it might be advisable to invite Monsignor Michael Ready of the NCWC. In accepting Lenroot's invitation, O'Grady ungraciously wrote of the "very definite impression abroad that the child welfare services, instead of playing a supplementary role. . ., are working toward the changing of the patterns of child-care that have grown up in the various local communities." He particularly criticized the social worker who charged into a community and developed programs "without bringing the different groups along" and who gave "the impression that she wants to change the local programs over night." Frequently, he complained, child welfare workers had a "purely negative" attitude toward institutional programs as an "antiquated system of child care."[111]

About seventy professionals from public and private agencies arrived in Washington in April 1937 for a two-day meeting. Atkinson's report to the Advisory Committee on the first fourteen months of operation of the Child Welfare Services division had been impressive. The division had disbursed $895,878 to programs in forty-two states and the District of Columbia. Emphasizing flexible planning that started "where the States were," Atkinson stressed that federal funds should only be expended for services that would not otherwise have been provided.[112] Reviewing the record, the conference participants supported a position on public and private relationships that could easily be endorsed by O'Grady, McEntegart, and the Catholics present: "In every State there should be a comprehensive program of child welfare. Extension of both public and private services is necessary in many areas where adequate resources for case work and foster care do not now exist. Private agencies operating under approved standards should have the fullest opportunity for development. Good public service should be fostered by good private service."

McEntegart was on the committee that summarized the conference discussions and edited the final report. Although it cited the need for state leadership and supervision to assure professional standards and the need for skilled casework, it also emphasized the need for cooperation between public and private agencies, especially in a decision to transfer a child to a foster home or an institution. Public funds paid to private agencies should be authorized on a per capita per diem basis for services to individual children. Finally the report emphasized the responsibility of both private and public agencies to secure the child's rights to the "closest possible approximation of normal home life, to religious and moral training, to understanding and guarding of her personality, and to opportunities for health protection, education and recreation."[113] Catholic participants were clearly pleased. In the April 1937 *Catholic Charities Review,* an O'Grady editorial hailed the fine cooperative spirit engendered at the meeting by the Children's Bureau and concluded: "No private agency in the field of child care can complain about the work and the spirit of the U.S. Children's Bureau." (O'Grady remained on guard, however, against further expansion of the child welfare services and was highly critical of the Children's Bureau in testimony at hearings on the 1950 Social Security amendments.)[114]

Although the NCCC had significant experience and connections with the Children's Bureau, they had to create a relationship with the new Bureau of Public Assistance (BPA) and its director, Jane Hoey.[115] Like Atkinson, Hoey was a Catholic who brought a wealth of experience in public and private agencies. A close friend and former colleague of Harry Hopkins, who had lobbied to win her the BPA post, Hoey was also devoted to Monsignor William Kerby, founder of the NCCC and her former teacher at Trinity College. Hoey knew the Catholic social work network and added Catholic professionals to the BPA staff, taking special pleasure in helping to secure the appointment of her old friend Rose McHugh as chief of the Division of Administrative Surveys of the Social Security Board.[116] That the two administrators most responsible for dispensing federal money and approving state plans for ADC and Child Welfare Services were Catholic was obviously not the result of intense NCCC or NCWC lobbying. But it must have given their leadership hope that these women might prove both understanding and helpful to the work of Catholic Charities. Although they were understanding and tireless in their efforts to aid children and families in need, Hoey and Atkinson were also firm supporters of the policy that public money should be administered by public agencies.[117]

The NCCC diocesan directors early dispatched a committee of John Butler of St. Louis, Thomas O'Dwyer of Los Angeles, and M. F. McEvoy of Milwaukee to pay a courtesy call on Hoey and Frank Bane, the executive director of the Social Security Board. John O'Grady and Edwin Leonard of Baltimore then met and posed the central question to Hoey. Could local private agencies be utilized to care for dependent children living with relatives under the ADC provisions? Hoey was "very much opposed" and stated that the Board "would not approve it."[118] Would all of the cases of dependent children currently supervised by private charities or the St. Vincent de Paul Society have to be transferred to a public agency to be eligible for federal funds as Hoey insisted? Would this create the danger of a loss of faith to the children?

Hoey's response triggered action on two fronts by the NCCC Continuing Committee, created in 1934 to monitor federal policies. Because the requirement that public agencies administer ADC funds was not in the law but only a Social Security Board ruling, diocesan directors were urged to lobby their senators and representatives to pressure the Board to change the policy. The Continuing Committee also surveyed the eighty directors to gauge Social Security's impact on their programs.[119] In March 1936 eighty diocesan directors were asked how aid to dependent children would affect Catholic children who were public charges.[120] Thirty-two respondents described more a range of expectations than the impact of programs. Most of their state legislatures had not acted, or their plans were not yet approved by the BPA. This was the case in New York, New Jersey, Connecticut, Massachusetts, and Pennsylvania. Bryan McEntegart expected little change in New York City, although the legislation proposed would extend coverage to illegitimate children and children of divorced mothers. As usual Catholic Charities of New York had asked for a clause in the statute protecting the religious faith of the children aided. Diocesan directors in Pittsburgh and Boston anticipated no change because Pennsylvania and Massachusetts law already prohibited allocating state money to private agencies. Though Colorado did not have an approved plan, John Mulroy observed that the social workers who were "setting up the program in all probability have no intention whatsoever of making use of private agencies and workers as their representatives in supervising dependent children. That would cut down the number of professional jobs so why do this." Mulroy's assessment was echoed by John Gallagher of the St. Vincent de Paul Society of Seattle. State and local officials, he observed, were guided "by the professional social service worker who is primarily interested in more and better paid jobs for professional social service workers. It is a racket."

In the West, although most of the diocesan directors anticipated little change, some worried that the juvenile courts, which had administered mothers' pensions, would no longer be able to work with Catholic Charities in placements. Rev. William Flanagan of the Little Children's Aid agency in San Francisco reported that his county provided $108,000 in assistance to 363 children living in their own homes or with relatives in 1935. Supervision of these children had been assigned by the juvenile court, an arrangement challenged now by the Social Security Board. Flanagan noted that the State Department of Social Welfare had ordered the court to transfer these cases to the County Welfare Department, although he cited a ruling by the Attorney General of the United States that "our set-up is legal." Ready to fight, Flanagan asserted that "persons of high political standing in San Francisco have bombarded Washington from every side in our behalf. . . . If other communities did the same Washington would move more slowly. This is election year so why not take advantage of it." O'Grady urged Flanagan to alert Senator Johnson, William McAdoo, and representatives Lee, Kahn, and Welsh.[121]

Reviewing the diocesan responses, the Continuing Committee found that consistently the diocesan directors feared the "danger of neglect of religious care" when Catholic children were supervised by a public agency. E. C. McQueeney of Akron saw this as not merely a danger "but a positive menace to the faith and morals of the children."[122] John Mulroy expressed his alarm at an NCCC meeting, placing the current crisis squarely in the context of the New York charities wars of 1916. Warming to his task, he asked: "Shall we permit non-Catholics to board our problem children in whatever type of home they please? Shall we stand idly by while millions are distributed in material aid to dependent children under the Security Act in a manner that deprives tens or even hundreds of thousands of their spiritual heritage? Shall non-Catholic social workers determine what is the proper Catholic home for a Catholic child?" To Mulroy the answer was obviously a resounding no.[123]

The NCCC Continuing Committee, charged with monitoring legislation, developed position statements and suggested a range of tactics to the diocesan directors. Essentially the committee urged the diocesan directors to work for flexibility, inclusion, and participation. (The same positions were advocated by NCCC with FERA.) Because the Social Security Act gave considerable latitude to states, the committee recommended that state departments of public welfare be pressed to allow communities to use existing private resources in aid to dependent children. In mothers' aid cases where religious problems were involved, the supplementary service of Catholic workers should be made available. Directors were alerted to the New York example of insuring by statute that the welfare department should "see that the religious faith of the children is preserved and protected." Where possible, as in Baltimore, directors should arrange with public agencies for Catholic supervisors to be assigned to Catholic cases, or at least Catholic workers be appointed in proportion to the number of Catholic cases. If all else failed, the diocesan directors should ask for a list of Catholic dependent children supervised by the public agencies and try to follow up. Finally, after reiterating the need for flexibility, the Continuing Committee, in a warning obviously intended more for public administrators than diocesan directors, concluded that "the evils of remote control may well tend to arouse criticism and opposition to the Security measures which are so worthwhile in other ways."[124] The final draft of a position statement sent by the Continuing Committee to the diocesan directors emphasized the importance of carefully working out federal-state relations that respected "the traditions that have been woven into the fabric of American life." As county boards took over the administration of aid to dependent children, foster care would increasingly replace institutional child-care. Catholics, organized in the dioceses, would have to be ready to exert pressure to have Catholic children placed in Catholic homes.[125] Having rallied the diocesan directors, the Continuing Committee set up a conference for a subcommittee to discuss with Jane Hoey and Frank Bane the effects of the social security program on their agencies and possible amendments to the Act.[126]

In 1937 the Continuing Committee continued to express its concerns over safeguarding the religion of Catholic children under the new dispensation of ADC and Child Welfare Services. In the past juvenile court judges and other officials had referred children for Catholic supervision. Under ADC county agencies were using federal and state funds to support children in their homes or in the homes of relatives. The Continuing Committee worried about casework in these home placements, fearing that "without proper Catholic guidance many of the local public agencies will not exercise proper care in the placement of Catholic children." Indeed there was "evidence on all sides that the new public agencies are inclined to adopt very unethical practices in dealing with Catholic families." One committee memorandum ended with the sober warning that unless the diocesan directors made a systematic effort to reach the entire area of their diocese, emphasizing the rural areas, they would "find themselves without influence in large sections of the country. Children who heretofore were sent to diocesan institutions or referred to diocesan agencies will be cared for in their own counties. There will be no Catholic influence in the work of most of the local public welfare boards."[127]

John O'Grady joined in these exhortations to the diocesan directors to work with legislators but complained that "reading the public welfare laws passed by the various state legislatures during the past year one would not think there were any private agencies . . . or that they had any responsibility for public welfare."[128] Commending particularly the wording of the Maryland statute, "A child should be placed in a suitable home where the child's religious faith shall be fostered and protected," O'Grady noted that only Maryland, Delaware, New York, and North Dakota had succeeded in adding a religious clause in the legislation establishing the state plan for ADC.[129]

In the midst of these efforts on the state level, the NCCC leadership was also alert to the amendments being suggested to the federal social security programs. They were astonished at a request from the NCWC in 1937 to consider a proposal to extend federal aid to the aged in Catholic institutions and to children in foster care and Catholic institutions. Some NCCC leaders had complained that NCWC had "interfered disastrously" in 1935 when Social Security was passed. Obviously the NCWC still didn't get it. O'Grady tried again. Although it was understandable that dioceses not receiving state funds should explore federal possibilities, he pointed out that federal funding that required state participation would threaten the whole structure of Catholic child-care in New York, Philadelphia, Chicago, and San Francisco. States that had never provided public funding for children in private institutions would certainly not be eager to share an infusion of federal funds with private agencies. At their December meeting, the directors unanimously opposed any amendment to extend Title IV to foster care.[130] However the NCCC did join the Children's Bureau and other professional groups in supporting amendments to Title IV, increasing the federal share of payments to ADC from one-third to one-half dependent and removing the limit on maximum grants. Committee members also supported the authorization for the federal government to defray fifty percent of the cost of administering ADC within the states.[131]

Clearly the landscape of charity and child-care had radically changed. Catholic Charities shared with every other private social agency the challenge of mission. Although institutions, religious, professionals, volunteers, diocesan bureaus, and the NCCC and NCWC all faced the new realities, work with the child and the family remained central. A year after Social Security was enacted, the diocesan directors reiterated: "One of the major interests of Catholic Charities in the United States has always been the welfare of the child through the entire period from infancy to maturity. To the welfare of the child, Catholic Charities has given its largest efforts and has made its greatest sacrifices." The new NCCC president, John Butler of St. Louis, emphasized: "Child welfare will continue as the most absorbing interest of Catholic Charities in the future." But he added: "It is quite clear that the private social work of the future will not follow the same pattern. . . . We must be ready for changes and be prepared to face them courageously." Citing the care of Catholic Charities for 60,000 children away from their own homes, he suggested that increasingly efforts should be directed to children needing special care and training in their own homes.[132] Questions of selectivity ranged from what "kind of" families should Catholic Charities "take in" to what services should be offered by the religious in institutions they had established to shelter children. Issues of the *Catholic Charities Review* carried articles such as "Institutions Change with Changing Times," "Another Institution Redirects Its Program," and "New Institutions for Old" describing the shift of service from the economically dependent to the physically, mentally, or emotionally troubled child. Religious extended their spiritual casework to home visits through their work in the Confraternity of Christian Doctrine. Diocesan bureaus developed new child-guidance clinics to serve the still expanding parochial school systems. With a growing Catholic middle class, the CYO and other recreation programs reached out to the "over-privileged" as well as the underprivileged. Expanding opportunities for service in the "aging of America" were taken up. In one of the more optimistic assessments of new opportunities for Catholic Charities, Thomas O'Dwyer of Los Angeles stressed the "constant opportunity [for agencies and laity] to encourage the tendency of . . . governments to delegate to adaptable private agencies those functions involved in the more intimate and profound objectives of social welfare, and to make monetary grants to private agencies in the fields of family and child welfare, medical social welfare, and character-building."[133]

The NCCC chose a top-down/bottom-up strategy in confronting its hard choices. Grappling with mission, Catholic Charities focused on selectivity and worked to coordinate and expand resources. There was a measure of déjà vu as Catholic Charities turned to the St. Vincent de Paul conferences and the Ladies of Charity in the parishes. Volunteer values, once consigned by some agencies to "the attic of oblivion" were "like overstuffed furniture" on the way back.[134] In an editorial in the March 1937 issue of *Catholic Charities Review,* O'Grady called for concerted

Catholic action. Some had asked, he observed in a rare show of defensiveness, "why not think first about the welfare of the child?" "This," he insisted, "is precisely what we are endeavoring to do." He rallied the Catholic laity to the cause: "Will our St. Vincent de Paul men stand by while Catholic children are being placed in unsuitable homes, while workers are using public assistance for the teaching of birth control, and while the poor are not receiving the kind of assistance to which they are entitled?" Catholics did not like to see their children taken out of institutions to be placed in homes where there was a divorce or common law marriage or placed with relatives "whose lives do not measure up to proper moral standards." Whereas some workers in public child-care seemed prepared to accept what Catholic leaders considered a lack of moral standards in home life, more dangerous to O'Grady were those "schooled in the old liberalism" who wanted to change the state programs that had been using private agencies. In a call to arms, he warned that "the time is coming when we may have to fight hard to conserve the religious welfare of our children." O'Grady's brief apologia for the "higher good," protecting the spiritual welfare of Catholic children, skirted the tacit implication of his argument. The Catholic position could limit the. number of children eligible for public assistance.

Catholic Charities increasingly turned to the laity for support. The new public welfare program, O'Grady noted, provided a "rich field for study clubs and aggressive Catholic action." Monsignor Vincent Ryan, director of the Catholic Welfare Bureau of Fargo, North Dakota, shared his plan to use lay Catholics to push public thinking "in right channels." In Fargo three women volunteers in each parish met to study Catholic social principles, assisted in locating suitable Catholic homes for Catholic children, and then worked with public agencies to safeguard the religious interests of Catholic children. Organized by Catholic Charities into county units, this force of women and their pastors, Ryan believed, would "provide a potent influence in the State."[135]

At the 1937 NCCC meeting, the presidential address of Monsignor Thomas O'Dwyer was part eulogy for New York's "Cardinal of Charity" Patrick Hayes, who had died in September, and part call to action. Hayes and his Catholic Charities of the Archdiocese of New York "had assumed a leadership in all worthwhile movements designed to aid the underprivileged in this country." O'Dwyer called on his audience to do no less.[136] Catholic workers should bring "a new sense of their duty to assist other organizations serving on a community-wide basis." Bishop Hubert Le-Blond also invoked New York as an exemplar. Remembering Thomas Mulry's role at the 1909 White House Conference and his support for mothers' aid, he concluded: "When the Social Security Act makes aid available for the care of children in such [suitable] homes it is therefore following Catholic teaching and practice." Like O'Dwyer, LeBlond urged cooperation with public agencies and also stressed the need for statewide Catholic influence to enable Catholic Charities to continue to meet the religious problems of families aided by public agencies.[137]

The major conference session featured Mary Gibbons, now the First Deputy Commissioner for New York City's Department of Social Welfare. In her professional career, Gibbons offered a model of the cooperation with public agencies now promoted by the NCCC. She had directed New York's Emergency Home Relief Bureau while on loan from Catholic Charities, returning in 1934 to that bureau to head the Division of Families. She had also served as vice president of the National Conference of Social Work. Elected at the Richmond conference as the first woman president of NCCC, Gibbons was hailed by Harry Hopkins at the conference's closing banquet as "that fine girl we all love and admire."[138] Her paper, "Benefits Based on Needs Under the Social Security Act," exhorted lay Catholics to organize at the grassroots level. Conferences of the St. Vincent de Paul Society, the Ladies of Charity, and other parish groups should form a Committee on Cooperation with the Public Welfare Department. This Catholic group action, complemented, of course, by the diocesan bureaus, could achieve better understanding and cooperation from public officials and continue the mission of Catholic charity.[139]

Mary Gibbons particularly emphasized the role of women volunteers, the traditional backbone of Catholic charity. At an institute for four hundred women at the 1938 NCCC meeting, Gibbons discovered a wide range of activities in relief and service. The women raised money by almost every means "short of stealing," but the card party remained the most popular and profitable source of revenue. Relief was almost all in emergency aid: milk for a family, temporary shelter, clothes for school or church occasions. In their service the volunteers emphasized the spiritual rewards, reporting their effort to "try to decide what Christ would do in similar circumstances," and "to use [the] situation as a means of sanctification." Children remained the major focus of their volunteer work.[140]

Gibbons had some specific recommendations for volunteer action in her 1939 NCCC presidential address. Volunteers could help Catholics in need by demanding that they "benefit to the fullest from public services to which we all must contribute" and, reiterating her earlier advice, that they form citizen pressure groups guided by a central diocesan agency to support diocesan policy.[141] Diocesan bureaus, in turn, should use the power of the press to swell the voice of both the diocesan bureaus and the energized laity.[142]

To invigorate and integrate the work of women volunteers, the NCCC commissioned a survey directed by Rev. Edward Swanstrom of Brooklyn. Sixty-four diocesan directors reported they had discovered organizations working in dioceses for years "whose names we have never heard." It was a mixed picture. In some dioceses the Ladies of Charity, the Legion of Mary, and the Council of Catholic Women were effective partners. Several respondents, asking that their names not be used, reported little cooperation, much less coordination, from their women's organizations. Cleveland's diocesan director noted ruefully that he had roused deep suspicions when he asked about income and had to reassure his "touchy" women's auxiliaries that no one was going "to gobble them up." More revealing, perhaps, was the lament of the Duluth director who found it difficult to get "some of our lodges to shift from Lady Bountiful charity" to support planned diocesan programs. He did confess that the bureau had not been aggressively pressing for cooperation because "we cannot figure where they will fit." Another director observed that part of the problem was that his bureau tended to ignore the organizations or take them for granted. There was little sensitivity that both the bureaucracy and professionalization of the diocesan organization might be a barrier.[143]

While NCCC and diocesan leaders struggled to regain the confidence and the help of the volunteers, they were aware that the expanding numbers of Catholic professionals on the staffs of local, state, and federal agencies could prove another source of influence. A report from Rose McHugh to Jane Hoey on the administration of Aid to Dependent Children in Massachusetts makes it clear that, although these two Catholic professional women served at the administrative top of the Bureau of Public Assistance, there were substantial Catholic troops in the state trenches. Four of the eleven state workers whose credentials and caseloads were investigated by McHugh and her team had come to the state from Catholic agencies and organizations. Three were graduates of the Social Service program at Boston College; one had had coursework at the Young Men's Catholic Association.[144] In New York the decision of Catholic social workers to work for public agencies was actively encouraged. Cardinal Hayes' policy was "to train properly qualified persons and encourage them to accept positions in Public Welfare Departments." Thirty-one professionals in New York had left Catholic Charities and were "holding key positions in public departments."[145]

Diocesan directors clearly wanted Catholic social workers involved in the social provision of the emergent welfare state, but it was equally clear that the public agency offered incentives of opportunity, responsibility, and salary. There was literally no room at the top in the diocesan agencies. Although Luella Sauer in Pittsburgh and Marguerite Boylan essentially ran their bureaus, they were anomalies. Priest-directors were still the order of the day. Although Mary Gibbons finally served as president of the NCCC in 1939, the powerful Continuing Committee was all clerical. There were no women professionals included in their strategy sessions.

On the national level, John O'Grady worked to coordinate the efforts of the diocesan directors. Representatives of diocesan organizations from Illinois, Wisconsin, Minnesota, Iowa, Nebraska, and Missouri gathered in Chicago in early 1939 to discuss diocesan child-care and developments in public programs.[146] O'Grady pressed the directors. What machinery had they developed to contact the legislators? How did they keep informed on bills? Was there a unified approach on issues of Catholic interest, hospitals, welfare, education? What interdiocesan organization had they developed? Surveying the record, he admitted: "In most of the states we have not as yet even made a beginning in assuming any leadership program. We still depend on the old methods of approaching politicians to kill some measures that we consider inimical to us." Undeterred, he stressed the need to review the NCCC's relationship with the NCWC and initiatives in dealing with Congress.[147]

The White House Conference on Children in a Democracy in 1939 and 1940 provides a good measure of the position of Catholic Charities in the emergent welfare state of the New Deal. There were significant echoes of the 1909 White House Conference on the Care of Dependent Children. Homer Folks, so prominent in 1909, was one of the seven vice-chairs of the 1939–1940 meetings. Reminiscent of Mulry's chairmanship of 1909 and the importance of New York Catholic Charities was the selection of Monsignor Robert F. Keegan to offer the opening address. He rephrased the central principle of child-care professionals articulated in 1909: "Home life is the highest and finest product of civilization. The home is in fact the very cornerstone of society and the child is the capstone of the home. Any program for children must preserve and strengthen home life."[148]

But obviously much had changed since 1909. Katharine F. Lenroot was careful to consult with Bryan McEntegart on appointments to key committees. His thirty-five suggestions reveal recent Catholic professional choices; twenty-two held responsible public welfare positions, thirteen served with Catholic charities agencies or were on the faculty of Catholic universities.[149] McEntegart accepted a post on the Report Committee, chaired by Homer Folks. John O'Grady of the NCCC, Michael Ready of the NCWC, Agnes Regan of the NCCW, and George Johnson of the National Catholic Education Association all served on the Planning Committee, as did Jane Hoey of the Bureau of Public Assistance. As in

1909, Catholics participated both as organizational representatives and as respected professionals in public service. Yet the importance of the positions held by Jane Hoey and Mary Irene Atkinson would have been unimaginable for Catholic women three decades earlier. And just as in 1909, Catholics could not be ignored; in 1939 they had a national "voice," and their sense of inclusion in the New Deal had considerably blurred the them-us dichotomy.

The conference's final report and recommendations underscore this Catholic presence. The report on religion (a topic not emphasized in 1909) was essentially drafted by Bryan McEntegart. He powerfully asserted the importance of safeguarding the religion of the child. "The child," he wrote, "whether in the family, the school, the church, or engaged in leisure-time activities, needs to have personal appreciation of the higher spiritual values. Any program of child development that falls short of this level not only is superficial from an educational point of view but is not consonant with the ideals of democracy."[150] Five recommendations affirmed the "fundamental place of religion" and the importance of religious resources in counseling and educating children.

The report and recommendations on social services for children recognized the obligation of both public and private agencies to develop adequate standards and resources. If a child in foster care needed service, the public welfare department and the private agency should have a formal agreement "as to which is to render such service." The final recommendation was all that might have been hoped for by the NCCC and NCWC: "Community, State, and Federal child-welfare services should be developed on the basis of careful planning participated in by health, educational, and social service agencies, public and private, and by representative citizens."[151] In decisions about the care of children and the allocation of resources, Catholic Charities had earned a significant voice in the development of American welfare.

Conclusion

The dramatic developments in Catholic charities and American welfare from 1870 through the New Deal were eloquently linked in the powerful peroration of Bishop Aloisius Muench of Fargo at the 1935 meeting of the NCCC: "The poor belong to us. We will not let them be taken from us!"[1] Decrying both the centralization of Catholic charities and the expansion of public social provision, Muench appealed for the charity that engendered the sanctification of client, volunteer, and diocesan worker. His plea resonated powerfully, but the dilemma only deepened. Five years later William O'Connor of Chicago's Catholic Charities stated it succinctly in *Catholic Charities Review*. "A diocesan bureau," he warned, "may unwittingly develop charitable activity on some other than a parish basis and suddenly find it has lost both the interest and the support of the clergy and the laity." It would "be a sad day when parish priests and their people cease to say 'our poor' and speak rather of 'your cases.'"[2]

Catholic charities had confronted the massive challenge of caring for the Catholic immigrant poor in the late nineteenth and early twentieth century. Thousands of religious women and men and lay volunteers responded to that challenge and tried to care for "their own." Together they built the largest private system of social provision in the United States. In the drive to centralize, coordinate, and respond to professional standards, bishops and clergy established more than eighty diocesan bureaus by the 1930s. Clerically led, these agencies coordinated family and children's services and expanded their oversight of religious in institutions. In the process they increasingly turned from volunteers to professionals for their work of charity. Ironically, in their own house, Catholic charities turned the principle of subsidiarity on its head and became top-down organizations. In the 1920s and 1930s, the executive secretaries and members of the powerful committees of the NCCC and NCWC were priests or monsignors; service as the diocesan director of charities became in many instances an accelerated path to episcopal rank bishopric. The clerical leadership continued. In the early 1960s, the twenty-one-man administrative staff of Catholic Charities of the Archdiocese of New York was entirely clergy. Lay social workers, who knew that they would not rise above the rank of casework supervisor, turned to public and nonsectarian agencies.[3]

Yet the gains were substantial. Organization and professionalism won the inclusion of diocesan bureaus and institutions in councils of social agencies and community chests. Cooperation augmented the private resources that Catholic Charities was able to give to the poor. Diocesan organizations secured and retained access to public funds in cities and some states through contracts for services and, in some instances, subsidies. During the 1920s and the crucial years of the New Deal, the NCCC provided a national voice for Catholic Charities. Skillful lobbying combined with the growing number of Catholic voters and their position in the emergent Democratic coalition enabled the NCCC to defend gains already won in cities and states. While losing battles over federal relief, they had a significant impact on the creation of the child welfare provisions of Social Security.

By the end of the New Deal, Catholics in financial need were assisted primarily through public agencies.[4] Catholics caring for the material needs of "their own" increasingly did so from the professional ranks in the public welfare departments. Indicative of a further sea change since the first decade of the century, one 1960s survey of Catholic, Jewish, and Protestant agencies found that Catholics were now the least worried that government intrusion would follow government money. Public agencies contracted with Catholic Charities for services, and, because children's institutions and services remained such an important part of the mission of Catholic Charities, their share of the tax dollar was significantly higher than that of Protestant or Jewish agencies. In 1994 government funds for contracted services provided 65 percent of an almost $2 billion budget for Catholic Charities, U.S.A. Almost half of those aided were living in poverty and receiving federal and/or state welfare assistance.[5]

Increasingly the poor were not "us." During World War II and after, many Catholics entered the expanding American middle class. They contributed to community chest drives and diocesan and parish charities, even as Catholic positions on birth control and abortion led Catholic Charities to confrontations with Planned Parenthood and, in some instances, withdrawal from community chest/united fund drives. As they migrated to the suburbs in the 1950s and 1960s, many Catholics, although "house poor," built and supported thousands of new churches and schools. Yet the financial charitable contributions of individual Catholics, which had been such a model of poor helping poor early in the century, began to lag behind that of Jewish or Protestant Americans. Although the small Catholic Worker movement, founded in the crises of the 1930s, still provides a remarkable model of personal service, the proportion of Catholics volunteering for any cause was also well below the percentage of Protestant and Jewish volunteers in 1990. In her 1995 study of Catholic philanthropy, Mary Oates contends that tight pocketbooks are certainly related to the professionalized, impersonal, and "distant" diocesan campaigns and "clerical dominance of leadership roles."[6]

Charges of impersonal and distant bureaucracies were more insistently leveled at the American welfare system after World War II by conservative politicians and restive taxpayers. Amendments expanding the occupations and populations covered by the insurance programs of Social Security in the 1950s led to the optimistic prediction that federal assistance programs would eventually be unnecessary and "wither away." The cost of ADC in 1960 was only $1 billion. It was a total that escalated rapidly. The "re-discovery" of poverty in the 1960s through best-sellers such as Michael Harrington's *The Other America*, the "discovery" of the intergenerational culture of poverty, and the claims of civil rights' advocates led to the ambitious programs of Presidents Kennedy and Johnson. The Social Security amendments of 1962, the War on Poverty, and Great Society legislation broadened coverage and increased federal benefits to millions while emphasizing opportunity, education, training, and work. With increasing numbers receiving assistance and a continuing shortage of social workers, federal regulations in 1969 strongly encouraged state welfare agencies to purchase services for ADC families from either public or private agencies such as Catholic Charities. Since the 1960s Catholic Charities has opened its doors to all in need, from all religions (and none).[7]

After the flurry of legislation and the urban unrest of the 1960s, the poor had a new visibility and a new face. The clients of Aid to Families with Dependent Children (AFDC) were now perceived as predominantly African-American single mothers and their children.[8] In the 1970s and 1980s, after the failure of Nixon's Family Assistance Program, campaign rhetoric waxed increasingly critical of the "welfare mess" and increasingly insistent on workfare. Reagan's allegations of welfare chiselers in the 1980s (a recurrent charge since the 1940s) and his dramatic assessment that "we fought a war on poverty and poverty won" were accompanied by taxpayer revolts and a growing demand from Republicans and

Democrats that absent fathers be made to support their children. As the income gap between rich and poor grew in the 1980s, critics pointed out that the public support for welfare mothers was just below the income of many of the families of the working poor.[9] In 1990 11 percent of American households were living in poverty. Census data showed the increasing feminization of poverty; 42 percent of single women who were divorced, separated, or widowed with children were below the poverty line. For never-married mothers, the rate was 44 percent. When presidential candidate Bill Clinton campaigned on a promise to "end welfare as we know it" in 1992, AFDC payments totaled $20 billion to assist fourteen million mothers and children. The poor comprised more than 14.5 percent of the population, the highest poverty rate since 1983. Academics and the press alarmed the public with accounts of a growing and intransigent "underclass."[10]

In 1994 the newly elected Republican Congress, alarmed at both welfare costs and children at risk, took dead aim at AFDC with its "new ideas." In a syndicated column in November, Ellen Goodman exclaimed in disbelief: "Try these for openers," "Charity and orphanages!" She followed with a one-liner: "Been there. Done that."

The Republican determination to end the existing welfare system and growing public support for some reform combined with the pressure on Clinton to deliver on his campaign pledge culminated in the passage of the Personal Responsibility and Work Opportunity Act in August 1996. Within two years the heads of most families on welfare would have to find work or face the loss of benefits. Single mothers who refused to identify fathers could lose at least 25 percent of their benefits. Unmarried teen mothers remained eligible for benefits only if they stayed at home and in school. States that did not reduce their welfare rolls by 20 percent by 1997 faced cuts in their federal block grants. An outraged Senator Daniel Patrick Moynihan charged: "the premise of this legislation is that the behavior of certain adults can be changed by making the lives of their children as wretched as possible."[11]

Three of the architects of Clinton's original plan, which contained funds for education and training, resigned on principle. One of them, Catholic Mary Jo Bane, assistant secretary of Health and Human Services, who would have had the responsibility for implementing the new legislation, provides a direct link back to her Catholic predecessor, Jane Hoey, the director of the Bureau of Public Assistance. Bane refused to preside over the reversal of sixty years of a federal assistance program that Hoey had worked so long to put in place.[12]

During these welfare debates of the 1990s, Catholic Charities remained a consistent and staunch advocate for the domestic, immigrant, and refugee poor. Its chief lobbyist, laywoman Sharon Daly, fighting against draconian cuts and new regulations that adversely affected mothers and children in need, argued from a position that the Sisters of Charity in the New York Foundling Asylum in the 1870s or Jane Hoey in the 1930s would have found familiar. "If you need help, you should get it, that it doesn't matter how you got there, that true compassion cannot be conditional." "It's reasonable," Daly observes, "for the government to have rules and expectations of those who get help. But we would not turn someone away because we disapprove of their behavior." Bishop Edward Conway of Chicago with a delegation of bishops meeting President Clinton linked the material and spiritual imperatives: "We all see creation as redeemable and with the possibility of conversion. It becomes easier for someone to understand God's presence when they have a sense of hope and renewal."[13]

Beyond Washington, Catholic charities' network of 1,400 social agencies and institutions and more than 200,000 volunteers assisted more than eleven million Americans through emergency service and social service programs. The majority of the clients of Catholic charities in refugee or emergency service in the 1990s have not been Catholic. In Baltimore, where Catholic Charities maintains a broad array of services for families, children, the aging, and the homeless or almost homeless, non-Catholics total more than 70 percent of those aided. As public funding has been cut, Catholic charities have tried once again to provide a safety net and emergency care for the urban homeless.[14] Yet leaders of Catholic charities know and face the reality they confronted in the 1870s—that private charity will not meet the needs of the millions. Only shared public and private responsibility, realistic public funding, and, in its broadest sense, an acceptance that the poor belong to all of us, will address the challenge of poverty in America.

From its beginnings, Catholic Charities in the United States has demonstrated both remarkable adaptability and consistency: adaptability in responding to the changing environment of American welfare and consistency in its advocacy for the poor. Part of the complexity in this historic development has been its resistance to the secularization of charity and its simultaneous and deliberate accommodation to the emergence of the modern welfare state. The complexity remains. The issues confronted in the 1870s persist: Children are still in peril and poverty still haunts the land. The challenge continues—to provide *Catholic charity* in the changing context of American welfare.

Sources

The following manuscript collections were used in this book:

Bureau of Public Assistance Papers, National Archives, Suitland, Maryland
John J. Burke Papers, Paulist Archives, Washington, D.C.
Catholic Women's League, Archives of the Archdiocese of Boston
Children's Bureau Papers, National Archives, Washington, D.C.
Conference of Catholic Charities Papers, Archives of the Diocese of Pittsburgh
Archbishop Michael Curley Papers, Archives of the Archdiocese of Baltimore
Paul Hanly Furfey Papers, Archives of the Catholic University of America (ACUA)
Cardinal James Gibbons Papers, Archives of the Archdiocese of Baltimore
Cardinal Patrick J. Hayes, Archives of the Archdiocese of New York, Yonkers, New York (AANY)
Jane Hoey Papers, Trinity College Archives, Washington, D.C.
William Kerby Papers, Archives of the Catholic University of America (ACUA)
Archbishop Joseph T. McNicholas Papers, Archives of the Archdiocese of Cincinnati
Minutes of the Board of Trustees, Catholic Charities of the Archdiocese of New York, New York City (CCANY)
National Catholic War Council, Archives of the Catholic University of America (NCWC, ACUA)
National Catholic Welfare Council, Archives of the Catholic University of America (NCWC, ACUA)
National Conference of Catholic Charities, Archives of the Catholic University of America (NCCC, ACUA)
John O'Grady Papers, Archives of the Catholic University of America (ACUA)
Oral History Collection, Columbia University Oral History Archives
Sisters of Charity Papers, Mt. St. Vincent College Archives, New York

Sisters of Charity of Cincinnati Papers, Mt. St. Joseph's Archives, St. Joseph, Ohio

Sisters of Mercy Papers, Carlow College, Pittsburgh

Social Security Board Papers, National Archives, Washington, D.C.

Richard J. Tierney—*America* Papers, Georgetown University Special Collections

Senator Robert F. Wagner Papers, Georgetown University Special Collections

Notes

Introduction

1. A.I.C.P. *Annual Reports,* cited in Jay Dolan, *The Immigrant Church: New York Irish and German Catholics, 1815–1865* (Baltimore: Johns Hopkins, 1975), 184, n. 25; and Philip M. Hosey, *The Challenge of Urban Poverty: Charity Reformers in New York City, 1835–1890* (New York: Arno Press, 1980), 85, 175, n. 67–68.
2. "Pastoral Letter," issued by the Second Plenary Council of Baltimore, 21 October 1866, in Hugh J. Nolan, ed., *Pastoral Letters of the Catholic Bishops of the United States,* 4 vols. (Washington: The National Conference of Catholic Bishops, 1984), I:199–200.
3. Margaret Tucker, "Cross Currents in Catholic Charities," *Catholic Charities Review,* 6 (March 1922): 73–80.
4. "Report of Juvenile Court Work [of the Knights of Columbus Juvenile Court Association of Pittsburgh], April 1, 1910 to July 1, 1910," and "Children Before the Juvenile Court, March 15, 1905 to June 30, 1910," in *Proceedings of the First National Conference of Catholic Charities* (Washington: National Capital Press, 1910), 261; and *Proceedings of the Second National Conference of Catholic Charities* (Washington: National Capital Press, 1912), 307–8.
5. M. Mercedes Murray, "The Child in the Reformatory," *Proceedings of the Fourth National Conference of Catholic Charities* (1916), 107–13; and Rev. James Donahoe, "Causes of Delinquency," *Proceedings of the Second National Conference of Catholic Charities* (1912), 318–21. Catholic workers were, however, often indignant at the charges leveled against poor children. "[O]ut of one hundred cases which I investigated in the children's court, the majority were so trivial as to arouse a sense of indignation. There were forty cases of shooting crap," reported Rev. Thomas J. Lynch of the Catholic Prison Society, and two "for selling chewing gum without a license." He

criticized the arresting officers' judgment and attributed the children's situation to poverty. Ibid. (1912), 325.

6. Katherine Dinan, "The Support of Dependent Mothers by Private Agencies," *Proceedings of the Third National Conference of Catholic Charities* (1914), 134–40; and Mary Tinney, "Remarks," *Proceedings of the Fourth National Conference of Catholic Charities* (1916), 141.

7. Anne Culligan, George P. O'Conor, Joseph Scully, and Herbert LeBlond, "How Far Should Catholics Care for Their Own Poor?" *Proceedings of the Eighth National Conference of Catholic Charities* (1922), 94–111.

8. The New York Foundling Asylum (later Hospital), for example, which was opened by the Sisters of Charity in 1869, sheltered 65,174 needy children and 10,230 maternity patients by 1915. Statistics were published in the annual reports of the institution and summarized by Rev. John T. McNicholas, "Sister Nurses of the United States," *Proceedings of the Fourth Annual Conference of Catholic Charities* (1916), 260–69.

9. See Maureen Fitzgerald, "Irish-Catholic Nuns and the Development of New York City's Welfare System, 1840–1900," Ph.D. dissertation, University of Wisconsin, 1992; Fitzgerald, " 'The Perils of Poverty and Passion': Women Religious and the Care of Single Women in New York City, 1845–1890," *U.S. Catholic Historian* 10 (1990); Mary Oates, "Organized Voluntarism: The Catholic Sisters in Massachusetts, 1870–1940," in Janet James, ed., *Women in American Religion* (University of Pennsylvania, 1980), 141–69; and Oates, " 'The Good Sisters': The Work and Position of Catholic Churchwomen in Boston, 1870–1940," in Robert E. Sullivan and James O'Toole, eds., *Catholic Boston: Studies in Religious Community, 1870–1970* (Boston: Roman Catholic Archbishop of Boston, 1985).

10. For a general review of the 1875 Children's Law and of the work of the New York State Board of Charities, see David Schneider and Albert Deutsch, *The History of Public Welfare in New York State, 1867–1940* (Chicago: University of Chicago, 1941).

11. See Elizabeth McKeown and Dorothy M. Brown, "Saving New York's Children," *U.S. Catholic Historian* 13 (summer 1995): 77–96; and Sister Margretta Shea, "Patrick Cardinal Hayes and the Catholic Charities in New York City," Ph.D. dissertation, New York University, 1966. Catholics also benefited from new public welfare measures, as Tammany representatives in the state legislature won a "market basket" of new welfare measures that, in the second decade of the century, anticipated the programs of the New Deal. See Joseph Huthmacher, "Charles Evans Hughes and Charles Francis Murphy: The Metamorphosis of Progressivism," *New York History* 46 (January 1965): 25–40.

12. See the analysis of national statistics from the Catholic Directory in Rev. James Sullivan, C.M., "The Institutional Care of Children," *Proceedings of the First National Conference of Catholic Charities* (1910), 285–92.

13. See, for example, William Kerby, "Problems in Charity," *Catholic World* 91 (September 1910): 790–800.

14. For a review of the issues surrounding the identity of professional social work in the early decades of the century, see Daniel J. Walkowitz, "The Making of a Feminine Professional Identity: Social Workers in the 1920s," *American Historical Review* 95 (October 1990): 1051–75. Walkowitz's article does not include Catholic workers.

15. Catholic response to the New Deal has received attention from Aaron I. Abell, *American Catholicism and Social Action* (Garden City, N.Y.: Hanover House 1960); Francis L. Broderick, *Right Reverend New Dealer* (New York: Macmillan, 1963); George Q. Flynn, *American Catholics and the Roosevelt Presidency, 1932–1936* (Lexington: University of Kentucky Press, 1968); and David J. O'Brien, *American Catholics and Social Reform: The New Deal Years* (New York: Oxford University Press, 1968).

16. *Responding to Changing Times: Catholic Charities U.S.A., 1994 Annual Survey* (Washington: The Urban Institute, November 1995).

17. Theda Skocpol, *Protecting Soldiers and Mothers: The Political Origins of Social Policy in the United States* (Cambridge: Harvard University Press, 1992).

18. There is, of course, a vast literature on maternalism, ranging from Seth Koven and Sonya Michel, eds., *Mothers of A New World: Maternalist Politics and the Origin of the Welfare State* (New York: Routledge, 1993) through the work of Eileen Boris and Kathryn Kish Sklar. See Eileen Boris, "Reconstructing the 'Family': Women, Progressive Reform and the Problem of Social Control," in Nora Lee Frankel and Nancy S. Dye, eds., *Gender, Class, Race, and Reform in the Progressive Era* (Lexington: The University Press of Kentucky, 1991). Paula Baker has summarized the leading point concisely: "In the Progressive era, social policy—formerly the province of women's voluntary work—became public policy." See Baker, "The Domestication of Politics: Women and American Political Society, 1780–1920," in Linda Gordon, ed., *Women, the State, and Welfare* (Madison: University of Wisconsin Press, 1990): 70. For an evaluation of the concept of maternalism in an international context, see the symposium on "Maternalism as a Paradigm," *Journal of Women's History* 5 (fall 1993): 96–131. Molly Ladd-Taylor's contribution to this collection, "Toward Defining Maternalism in U.S. History," is an especially useful review of the American context.

19. Gordon's work on the role of professional social workers in the evolution of the welfare state also carries an analysis of maternalism. See Gordon, *"Pitied But Not Entitled": Single Mothers and the History of Welfare, 1890–1935* (New York: Free Press, 1994): 55. See also the debate between Gordon and Theda Skocpol in *Contention* 2 (spring 1993): 157–87. For additional discussion of the arguments on gender and the welfare state, see Kathryn Kish Sklar, "The Historical Foundations of Women's Power in the Creation of the American Welfare State, 1830–1930," in Koven, Michel; Gwendolyn Mink, *The Wages of Motherhood: Inequality in the Welfare State, 1917–1942* (Ithaca: Cornell University Press, 1995); Alice Kessler-Harris, "Designing Women and Old Fools: The Construction of the Social

Security Amendments of 1939," in Linda K. Kerber, Alice Kessler-Harris, and Kathryn Kish Sklar, eds., *U.S. History As Women's History: New Feminist Essays* (Chapel Hill: University of North Carolina Press, 1995); and Blanche D. Coll, *Safety Net: Welfare and Social Security, 1929–1979* (New Brunswick: Rutgers University Press, 1995).

20. John O'Grady, *The Catholic Church and the Destitute* (New York: Macmillan, 1929), 3.

21. See, for example, Gordon, *"Pitied But Not Entitled,"* chap. 10.

22. See Peter Mandler, "Introduction," in Mandler, ed., *The Uses of Charity: The Poor on Relief in the Nineteenth-Century Metropolis* (Philadelphia: University of Pennsylvania Press, 1990); and Michael Katz, *Improving Poor People: The Welfare State, the "Underclass," and Urban Schools as History* (Princeton: Princeton University Press, 1995), 57.

23. See, for example, Edward Ross Dickinson, *The Politics of German Child Welfare from the Empire to the Federal Republic* (Cambridge: Harvard University Press, 1996). Dickinson's review of the development of public child welfare policy and the response of Protestant and Catholic child-caring agencies in modern Germany places special emphasis on relations between the Deutscher Caritasverband and the German state.

1. The New York System

1. William Oland Bourne, *History of the Public School Society of the City of New York* (1870), cited in George Paul Jacoby, *Catholic Child Care in Nineteenth Century New York* (Washington: The Catholic University of America, 1941), 32–33.

2. See the discussion of RCOA's public financing based on the Minutes of the Asylum's Board of Managers and on its annual reports, in Jacoby, 89–121.

3. Catherine J. Ross, "Society's Children: The Care of Indigent Youngsters in New York City, 1875–1903," Ph.D. dissertation, Yale University, 1977, supplies a detailed analysis of three New York child-caring institutions: the New York Catholic Protectory, the New York Juvenile Asylum, and the Colored Orphan Asylum. She estimates that by 1863, for example, Catholics constituted nearly half of the youngsters in the New York Juvenile Asylum (Ross, 100). New York Jews were also deeply involved in providing institutional care for Jewish children during the period. See, for example, Hymen Bogen, *The Luckiest Orphans: A History of the Hebrew Orphan Asylum of New York* (Urbana: University of Illinois Press, 1992).

4. The *Catholic World* openly charged the CAS of proselytizing with the support of public funds. See "Public Charities," *Catholic World* 27 (April 1873): 1–23.

5. See Charles Loring Brace, *The Dangerous Classes of New York and My Twenty Years' Work Among Them* (New York: Wynkoop and Hallenbeck, 1872).

6. Ibid., 137.

7. For an assessment of the Children's Aid Society in its early years, see Bruce Bellingham, "'Little Wanderers': A Socio-Historical Study of the Nineteenth Century Origins of Child Fostering and Adoption Reform, Based on the Early Records of the New York Children's Aid Society," Ph.D. dissertation, University of Pennsylvania, 1984; Bellingham, "Waifs and Strays: Child Abandonment, Foster Care and Families in Mid-Nineteenth Century New York," in Peter Mandler, ed., *The Uses of Charity: The Poor on Relief in the Nineteenth-Century Metropolis* (Philadelphia: University of Pennsylvania Press, 1990), 123–60; and Bellingham, "Institution and Family," *Social Problems* 33 (1986): 833–57.

8. Complaints also began to come back to the Catholic leadership of New York from Catholics living in "the West." A priest in Ohio complained when a train car full of Catholic children arrived in his town for distribution. The children had been brought from the public nurseries on Randall's Island and allegedly sold for ten dollars apiece to local residents. Archives of the Archdiocese of New York, Rev. Charles F. Schelhamer, St. Mary's Church, Greenville, Ohio, 20 August 1867, cited in Francis E. Lane, "American Charities and the Child of the Immigrant: A Study of Typical Child Caring Institutions in New York and Massachusetts Between the Years 1845 and 1880," Ph.D. dissertation, The Catholic University of America, 1932, 118.

9. Brace, 142–55. For Archbishop John Hughes' estimation of the plight of New York's Irish poor, see Jay P. Dolan, *The Immigrant Church* (Baltimore: Johns Hopkins University Press, 1975), 33–37. For general context, see Kerby Miller, *Emigrants and Exiles: Ireland and the Irish Exodus to North America* (New York: Oxford Press, 1985), 319–20, and Hasia Diner, *Erin's Daughters in America: Irish Immigrant Women in the Nineteenth Century* (Baltimore: Johns Hopkins University Press, 1983).

10. See Alexander B. Callow, Jr., *The Tweed Ring* (New York: Oxford Press, 1966); John Webb Pratt, *Religion, Politics and Diversity: The Church-State Theme in New York History* (Ithaca: Cornell University Press, 1967); and Pratt, "Boss Tweed's Public Welfare Program," *The New York Historical Society Quarterly* (October 1961): 396–411, for an extended account of Tweed's "social security plan." Frederick J. Zwierlein, *The Life and Letters of Bishop McQuaid,* 3 vols. (Rochester, N.Y.: Art Print Shop, 1926), III:35, makes it clear that the largess of the legislature in the Tweed years was also available to Catholics upstate. After Tweed and his allies lost control at both city and state levels in the elections of 1871, voters passed a measure limiting state aid in 1872. Henceforth the child-caring institutions depended on revenues from the city treasury rather than from the state. This Tammany tradition continued in various forms until the New Deal.

11. For a review of Kelly's role in the recovery of Tammany after the fall of the Tweed Ring, see Arthur Genen, "John Kelly: New York's First Irish Boss," Ph.D. dissertation, New York University, 1971. For a period eulogy, see J. Fairfax McLaughlin, *The Life and Times of John Kelly, Tribune of*

the People (New York: The American News Company, 1885), and for broadsides written in the heat of later political events, see Gustavus Myers, *The History of Tammany Hall* (New York: Boni and Liveright, 1903 and 1917), and M. R. Werner, *Tammany Hall* (New York: Doubleday, Doran & Company, 1928).

12. Biographer J. Fairfax McLaughlin, who had access to Kelly's letters and papers, indicates that he lectured "repeatedly in the North, South and West" and delivered over fifty thousand dollars to charity after paying his expenses out of his own pocket. McLaughlin, 269.

13. *New York Times,* 14 March 1869, and 13 April 1869.

14. For the history of the Sisters of Charity, see Sister Marie de Lourdes Walsh, *The Sisters of Charity of New York, 1809–1959,* 3 vols. (New York: Fordham University Press, 1960).

15. Mary Hutchins [*sic*] to Sister Irene Fitzgibbon, 23 November 1869, and Mrs. Richard Connolly to Sister Irene Fitzgibbon, 8 December 1869, cited in Walsh, III:71–72.

16. The state legislature passed the 1870 enabling legislation empowering the city to grant the asylum a building site and to appropriate money for the building fund. Mrs. Connolly personally raised $27,560 to help match the city grant. The state legislature later approved a city per capita payment of thirty-eight cents a day for the Foundling Asylum. The 1871 city tax levy bill contained the stipulation that "the excise moneys derived from licenses for the sale of intoxicating liquors since the organization of the present Board of Excise Commissioners, and the moneys hereafter received for such licenses, may be appropriated for charitable purposes by the Board of Apportionment herein provided for, as they may determine from time to time." Mrs. Connolly also tapped this resource for "her" charities. See accounts in "Death of Mrs. Richard Connolly," *New York Times,* 14 March 1879; "Mrs. R. B. Connolly's Funeral," *New York Times,* 13 April 1879; and "Sister Mary Irene Dead," *New York Times,* 15 August 1896. Hasia Diner also notes Mrs. Connolly's contribution to the Foundling Asylum (137).

17. The building committee included Joseph J. O'Donohue, a new resident of the city in 1870. He had come across the East River from the Williamsburg section of Brooklyn, where he developed his extensive business interests and rose to become chair of the Democratic Central Committee of Brooklyn. He and his wife and daughters would remain faithful supporters of New York Catholic charities until the death of daughter Teresa in 1932. Joseph O'Donohue would soon be drafted by fellow Catholic and next Tammany boss, John Kelly, to help rebuild the Wigwam after the fall of the Tweed Ring. Also on the Committee were Paul Thebaud, whose wife headed the women's auxiliary for the Foundling Asylum, long-time charity worker and Tammany insider John D. Crimmins, and Tammany prosecutor Charles O'Conor. See Walsh, III:72–75. For discussion of the role of women in funding Catholic charities in nineteenth-century New York, see Mary J.

Oates, *The Catholic Philanthropic Tradition in America* (Bloomington: University of Indiana Press, 1995), and Colleen McDannell, "Going to the Ladies' Fair: Irish Catholics in New York City, 1870–1900," in Ronald H. Bayor and Timothy J. Meagher, eds., *The New York Irish* (Baltimore: Johns Hopkins University Press, 1996), 234–51.

18. Jacoby, 89–122. By an act of the state legislature in 1852, a board of male managers was given corporate control of the institution. The men were responsible for admissions, finances, and building maintenance; the Sisters of Charity retained control of internal operations.

19. Jacoby, 111. The RCOA did benefit from Board of Education appropriations as well as from excise funds. Investigator John Hassard calculated that the RCOA received $298,196.54 in public funds between the years 1844 and 1875. John Rose Green Hassard, "Private Charities and Public Money," *Catholic World* 29 (1879): 264.

20. Jacoby, 123–57.

21. From 1863 to 1875, the Protectory provided care and training for 9,712 children. John Hassard gives a figure of $2,030,454.47 in gross receipts from city and state to 1879, including the original $50,000 for the building fund. By comparison the non-Catholic reformatory, the Juvenile Asylum (1853), received $122.50 a year for each child. Hassard calculated that the Juvenile Asylum had received $1,442,292.87 in public funds by 1879 but housed far fewer children than did the Protectory (Hassard, 275).

22. The original trustees of the corporation included Dr. Levi Silliman Ives, Dr. Henry J. Anderson, Tammany attorney Charles O'Conor, and State Board of Charities Commissioner Henry L. Hoguet. The first two presidents of the Protectory's Society for the Protection of Destitute Roman Catholic Children were both converts to Catholicism. Dr. Levi Silliman Ives was a former Episcopalian bishop, and his successor in 1867 was Columbia University professor Henry James Anderson. See John O'Grady, *Levi Silliman Ives: Pioneer Leader in Catholic Charities* (New York: P. J. Kenedy & Sons, 1932).

23. Both girls and boys were paid a small wage for their industrial work and were encouraged to keep savings accounts. As the children grew older, they were expected to pay for their own clothes out of these accounts. See William Pryor Letchworth, *Homes of Homeless Children: A Report on Orphan Asylums and Other Institutions for the Care of Children, 1903* from *Annual Report of the New York State Board of Charities* (1876), 264–75.

24. Clarence C. Cook, "The New Catholic Cathedral in New York," *Atlantic Monthly* 43 (February 1879): 173–77.

25. Correspondence between the two men was published in the *Atlantic Monthly.* Clarence Chatham Cook to John Rose Green Hassard, New York, 27 January 1879; and Hassard to Cook, New York, 28 January 1879, in *Atlantic Monthly* 43 (March 1879): 415–16. Hassard, "Private Charities and Public Lands," *Catholic World,* 29 (1879): 127–40; and Hassard,

"Private Charities and Public Money," 255–83. Hassard used the records of the comptroller's office to review the grants and leases of land to private charities.

26. Hassard calculated that on the Protectory alone, Catholics had raised and spent more than a million dollars over and above the public money it had received (Hassard, "Public Money," 259).

27. Hassard, "Public Money," 283.

28. See David Schneider and Albert Deutsch, *The History of Public Welfare in New York State, 1867–1940,* chaps. 2 and 4 (Chicago: University of Chicago, 1941). The board was first called the Board of State Commissioners of Public Charities and later, the State Board of Charities. After World War I, it became the New York State Board of Social Welfare. There was a consistent Catholic presence on the Board as city and state politics began to reflect growing Catholic strength. Nineteenth-century members included Henry Hoguet and Terence Donnelly. In the first two decades of the twentieth century, Thomas M. Mulry, Theodore Ridder and his son Vincent, Charles Gillespie, and New York social worker Mary Gibbons all served.

29. The first Letchworth report was appended to the *Eighth Annual Report of the State Board of Charities* (1876). The other two appeared with the *Ninth Report* (1877). Subsequently all three reports were compiled and published by the State Board of Charities as *Homes for Homeless Children.* For an extended discussion of Letchworth's labors and of the Children's Law, see Schneider and Deutsch, chap. 4; and Ross, chap. 1. The clause was removed in 1876 and restored in 1878. For the Catholic role in restoring the religion clause, see Maureen Fitzgerald, "Irish-Catholic Nuns and the Development of New York City's Welfare System, 1840–1900," Ph.D. dissertation, University of Wisconsin, 1992: 492–93.

30. Although the New York Vincentian membership was heavily Irish, prominent French and German Catholic names like Coudert, Hoguet, and Metz were included in the Society's leadership, and the Vincentians who served as the first presidents of the New York Catholic Protectory were both Anglo-Americans.

31. J. W. Helmes, "Thomas M. Mulry: A Volunteer's Contribution to Social Work," Ph.D. dissertation, The Catholic University of America, 1938, reviews Mulry's correspondence and his articles and addresses on charity and welfare. The correspondence is no longer extant, so we rely on Helmes' scholarship here.

32. See Lilian Brandt, *The Charity Organization Society of the City of New York, 1882–1907: The History and Account of Present Activities, the Twenty-Fifth Annual Report* (New York: United Charities, 1907) for details of the activities of this umbrella organization of New York charities. Brandt's membership lists show the presence of other Catholics, including the wife and daughter of Tammany leader Joseph J. O'Donohue. The daughter, Teresa, was a member of the Fourth District Committee in 1907, and she and her mother were life members of the COS.

33. Josephine Shaw Lowell, *Public Relief and Private Charity* (New York: Putnam and Sons, 1884), 85. For Lowell's role in child-saving, see Elizabeth Kennedy Hartley, "Social Work and Social Reform: Selected Women Social Workers and Child Welfare Reforms, 1877–1932," Ph.D. dissertation, University of Pennsylvania, 1985.

34. See "Teresa O'Donohue, Charities Worker," *New York Times*, Wednesday, 18 August 1937, 19. For O'Donohue's own accounts of the work of New York Catholic female volunteers, see "The Association of Catholic Charities," *Catholic Charities Review* 2 (June 1918): 215–17; Ibid. 3 (October 1919): 244–49; Ibid. 4 (November 1919): 274–76; "Ladies of Charity of the Catholic Charities of the Archdiocese of New York," ibid. 5 (November 1921): 38; Special Meeting of Leagues of Catholic Women and Ladies of Charity, *Proceedings of the Sixth Biennial Meeting of the National Conference of Catholic Charities* (1920), 373.

35. Teresa O'Donohue to John O'Grady, 7 August 1923, Papers of the National Conference of Catholic Charities, Archives of the Catholic University of America. Hereafter NCCC, ACUA.

36. Corrigan scholar R. Emmett Curran offers a somber assessment of the Corrigan administration: "The fear that he and his advisors experienced about the threats they saw to their authority or the well-being of the Church led them to misuse their power and corrupt the very authority they were trying to preserve. They . . . thought that the higher ends could legitimize sleazy means. Corrigan . . . was not driven from office by his excesses, but they diminished him and left a record of intrigue that does not form one of the brighter pages of American Catholic history." See Curran's prefatory remarks in Robert Emmett Curran, *Michael Augustine Corrigan and the Shaping of Conservative Catholicism in America, 1878–1902* (New York: Arno Press, 1978).

37. John Talbot Smith, *The Catholic Church in New York,* 2 vols. (New York: Hall & Locke, 1905), II:415.

38. William V. Shannon, *The American Irish* (New York: Macmillan, 1966), 116.

39. Interview for the *New York Tribune,* 26 November 1886, cited in Curran, 208–9.

40. Zwierlein, III:6–7. See also Curran, 197.

41. In the bitter aftermath of the 1886 campaign, McGlynn refused to submit himself to the wishes of his ecclesiastical superiors, and Corrigan finally excommunicated him. He remained barred from exercising his priesthood until 1892, when he was reinstated after agreeing to remain silent on issues of religion and politics.

42. Curran, 197.

43. For a review of Boss Tweed's interest in parochial schools, see Pratt, 196–98. Public funds were used to educate children in the sectarian child-caring institutions. In 1882 the state legislature gave sixteen orphanages access to public school funds; only two were Catholic. The New York

Catholic Protectory petitioned the state for inclusion in school funding in 1889, but Evangelical Alliance successfully blocked the proposal. By 1893 the cost to the city of per capita payments to institutions equaled almost one-half of the city's Board of Education budget. See Ross, 99–101, 154.

44. Pratt, 229–30. Pratt makes a careful distinction between NLPAI and the notoriously anti-Catholic American Protective Association, arguing that the latter was not a significant factor in the New York controversy of 1894 (Pratt, 237–38). Catholic reviewer Humphrey J. Desmond indicates, however, that public appropriations for charitable institutions continued to be a factor in the political activities of the APA during the 1896 presidential campaign. See Desmond, *The A.P.A. Movement* (Washington: New Century Press, 1912 [1902]), 88–100.

45. Catholics bore a large share of the responsibility for renewed anxiety over schools when a heated internal debate over the school question flared up among Catholic leaders. The account of Catholic differences on the school question is given in detail in Curran. It is also given extended treatment in Edward M. Connors, "Church-State Relationships in Education in the State of New York," Ph.D. dissertation, The Catholic University of America, 1951.

46. A review of the events surrounding the constitutional debate is available in Pratt, chap. 4. For an analysis of Republican leadership and fortunes in New York State in the period, see Richard L. McCormick, *From Realignment to Reform: Political Change in New York State, 1893–1910* (Ithaca: Cornell University Press, 1981).

47. The formula empowering the SBC read: "all institutions, whether state, county, municipal, incorporated or not incorporated, which are of a charitable, eleemosynary, correctional or reformatory character" (Schneider and Deutsch, 131). The State Charities Law of 1896 subsequently established the composition of the State Board and detailed its powers and responsibilities.

48. There were actually three distinct sources of external authority in Catholic institutions after 1896, including the State Board of Charities, the City Commissioners of Charity, and the Society for the Prevention of Cruelty to Children. As the SBC launched a new round of inspections in the wake of the constitutional amendment, Board president William Rhinelander Stewart claimed that the most seriously inadequate institutions were "with surprising predictability those institutions tended to be run by Catholic clergy." See Ross, 176–79.

49. In his capacity as secretary of the State Charities Aid Association, Homer Folks controlled access to employment for charities inspectors on the state level by composing and administering the state's fledgling civil service exam. For a sample of the anti-institutional quality of his exam questions, see Fitzgerald, 594.

50. Accounts of the New York Society for the Prevention of Cruelty to Children are contained in Homer Folks, *The Care of Destitute, Neglected, and*

Delinquent Children (New York: Macmillan, 1902), 170–78, Schneider and Deutsch, 79–83, Jacoby, 75–79, and Peter Romanofsky, ed., *Social Service Organizations,* Greenwood Encyclopedia of American Institutions, 2 vols. (Westport, Conn.: Greenwood Press, 1978), 628–35.

51. State Board of Charities president William Rhinelander Stewart was a longtime participant in New York's welfare reform circle and a particularly devoted friend of Lowell. He published a memorial to her work after her death. See Stewart, ed., *The Philanthropic Work of Josephine Shaw Lowell* (New York: Macmillan Company, 1911). See Josephine Shaw Lowell, "Report Upon the Care of Dependent Children in the City of New York and Elsewhere," *Twenty-third Annual Report of the State Board of Charities* (December 10, 1889) in Stewart, 276–83. See also Folks, 176–77.

52. Morgan J. O'Brien was Corporation Counsel of the City of New York under Mayor Abram Hewitt in 1887 when he was elected a justice of the Supreme Court. He was a member of Cleveland's gubernatorial platform committee and a supporter of civil service reform. He became presiding judge of the Appellate Division of the Court in 1905. Justice O'Brien's brother-in-law was Tammany leader and prominent Catholic charities supporter John D. Crimmins, and his brother Miles O'Brien was chair of the School Committee of New York City.

53. The Court also issued a ruling on the status of private charitable institutions, finding that the 1894 Constitution intended to place under state supervision only those private institutions in receipt of public monies. See Schneider and Deutsch, 134. Josephine Lowell angrily insisted that the Court ignored the intent of the State Constitution and that the decision undermined respect for the majority of the judges on the Court. Her colleague State Board president William Rhinelander Stewart summarized the immediate impact of the decision: the Board had to relinquish over 660 of the 1,080 private agencies and institutions formerly under its supervision. See Josephine Shaw Lowell, "Inspection of Private Charities," *Charities* (January 27, 1900) collected in Stewart, 462–66; and William Rhinelander Stewart, "State Inspection of Private Charitable Institutions, Societies or Associations," *Thirty-fourth Annual Report of the State Board of Charities* (1900) cited in Schneider and Deutsch, 137.

54. "Comptroller Bird S. Coler," *New York Times,* 27 August 1899. See the extended discussion of the formation of Greater New York in David Hammack, *Power and Society: Greater New York at the Turn of the Century* (New York: Russell Sage Foundation, 1982). For Tammany affiliation, see E. Vale Blake, *History of the Tammany Society From Its Organization to the Present Time* (New York: Souvenir Publishing Company, 1901).

55. Bird Coler insisted that under the Stranahan law the comptroller was authorized to pay "the sum appropriated to each institution upon its appearing to his satisfaction, in such manner as he shall prescribe, that the expenditure thereof by the institution is lawful and proper." Bird S. Coler, "Municipal Subsidies to Private Charities, a Report to the Board of Esti-

mate and Apportionment, September 1, 1899," *St. Vincent de Paul Quarterly* 4 (1899): 319.

56. See Bird S. Coler, "Charities Regulated," in *Municipal Government As Illustrated by the Charter, Finances, and Public Charities of New York* (New York: Appleton and Company, 1901), 50–109, for his extended review of these issues.

57. Coler, "Municipal Subsidies to Private Charities," 309. Coler did target specific forms of private charity in New York, especially for using city funds to pay salaries. His example was the Children's Aid Society, whose 1898 report showed salaries at $106,265 of a total budget of $309,394. The CAS had received $100,764 from the city in 1898 (*Municipal Government*, 27–49).

58. Folks' supporters included Josephine Shaw Lowell, SCAA president Gertrude Rice, Jacob Riis, and Robert de Forest. When it was rumored that Mayor Low wanted to appoint a Catholic as Commissioner of Charities, Lowell sought support for Folks from a list of prominent Catholics that included Archbishop Michael Corrigan. See Ross, 195–96.

59. See the discussion in Ross, 199–203.

60. See Peter Romanofsky, "Saving the Lives of the City's Foundlings: The Joint Committee and New York City Child Care Methods, 1860–1907," *New York Historical Society Quarterly* 61 (January–April 1977): 49–68; and Schneider and Deutsch, chap. 10.

61. Comptroller Herman Metz to Commissioner Robert W. Hebberd, 7 January 1907, in Romanofsky, "Saving the Lives of the City's Foundlings," 66.

62. Daniel C. Potter, Chief Examiner of Accounts of Institutions, Finance Department, New York City, Statement in Response to Mrs. Don C. Seitz, *St. Vincent de Paul Quarterly* 9 (May 1904): 159.

63. Potter, 160–61.

64. In 1899, when Folks was NCCC secretary, Mulry chaired the Committee on the Care of Destitute and Neglected Children. At that time the Vincentian confided to Folks, "I feel drawn to you more closely than ever—There was a time when I did not have this feeling but I consider you one of my dearest friends." Mulry to Folks, 9 November 1899, quoted in Ross, 196.

65. Walter Trattner, *Homer Folks: Pioneer in Social Welfare* (New York: Columbia University Press, 1968), 57. According to Trattner, Folks thought that the state was a more intelligent, resourceful, impartial, and efficient administrative unit than local political divisions, that it commanded a better grade of talent, had more ample resources, and was less subject to partisanship (Trattner, 45).

66. William L. Riordon, *Plunkitt of Tammany Hall* (New York: E. P. Dutton, 1963 [1905]), 38. Plunkitt gives a pungent review of the state GOP designs on the City of New York in "New York City is Pie for the Hayseeds" (Riordon, 21–24).

67. Trattner, 57.

68. Folks *(The Care of Destitute, Neglected, and Delinquent Children)* indi-

cates his willingness to arrive at a compromise between institutionalization and placing-out. His approach to the city's public charities was tempered by the political realities of New York, and during his tenure as Charities Commissioner (1902–1903), he was unable to successfully exercise control over the private welfare institutions of the city as the New York system continued to flourish under the Fusion government of Seth Low.

69. Thomas M. Mulry, "The Care of Destitute and Neglected Children," *Proceedings of the National Conference of Charities and Corrections*, Twenty-sixth Annual Session, Cincinnati, Ohio, 17–23 May 1899, 166–70.

70. Thomas M. Mulry, "Care of Dependent Children," Paper read before the National Conference of Charities and Correction, Twenty-fifth Annual Session, New York City, May 1898, in *St. Vincent de Paul Quarterly* 3 (October 1898): 197–201.

71. Ibid., 198.

72. Ibid., 199.

73. Mitchel, whose father and uncle had both been prominent in New York Democracy, interned in private law practice in the offices of Eugene A. Philbin, a Catholic and a Republican, before joining the second McClellan administration in 1906. Ahern assumed McClellan would protect him, but McClellan, eager to be free from Tammany and the control of boss Charles Francis Murphy, supported Mitchel's work. For Mitchel's biography, see Edwin R. Lewinson, *John Purroy Mitchel: The Boy Mayor of New York* (New York: Astra Books, 1965).

74. The episode is reviewed in Neil Andrew Kelly, " 'Orphans and Pigs Fed from the Same Bowl': Catholics and the New York Charities Controversy of 1916," M.A. thesis, St. Joseph's Seminary, Yonkers, New York, 1991. Kelly's access to the archives of the Archdiocese of New York at Dunwoodie (AANY) makes his review valuable to the present study. He reproduces extensive passages of many of the documents relevant to this discussion. For McMahon's plan to provide Potter with a five-thousand-dollar purse as a "testimonial," see AANY, Charities Investigation, D. J. McMahon to Dear Father, 29 June 1910, in Kelly, 11. Kelly also indicates that McMahon eventually gave Potter $500. The Kelly manuscript was supplied by Monsignor James J. Murray, executive director of Catholic Charities of the Archdiocese of New York.

75. See the account in V. T. [Bishop Patrick J. Hayes], "The New York Charities Controversy," *Catholic Charities Review* 1 (January 1917): 16–23.

76. Formed in 1907 with the bequest of railroad and banking tycoon Russell Sage, the Foundation carved for itself a prominent position at the head of the emerging fields of social work, public administration, and urban affairs research. Its wealth, board membership, and New York location allowed it to set the tone for much of the debate over the development of social provision in state and national welfare.

77. Sister St. Neri, S.S.J., to Rev. Dr. James J. Higgins, Brooklyn, 6 March 1916, Tierney-*America* Papers, Georgetown University.

78. The three largest Catholic institutions, the Foundling Hospital, the Protectory, and the Roman Catholic Orphan Asylum, were not cited for deficiencies in the Kingsbury report. Because these institutions had the highest admissions rate in the city, their exemption raises questions about the scope of the investigation. Were these institutions simply above reproach, or did they also have powerful patrons who could protect them from outside evaluation and censure?

79. William Doherty, "A Study of the Results of Institutional Care. A Paper Read Before the National Conference of Charities and Corrections" (New York: Russell Sage Foundation, 1915), Tierney-*America* Papers, Georgetown University. See also Kelly, 16–19.

80. Doherty, 18.

81. The Strong Commission was appointed under the terms of the Moreland Act of 1899. The legislation gave the new commission investigatory and subpoena powers but did not bind investigators to follow proper courtroom procedures. Counsel was limited to the attorney for the State Board, John Bowers, and the attorney for the Commissioner of Public Charities, Robert Hotchkiss. Hotchkiss initiated all inquiries, individual witnesses were not able to confront and challenge accusers, and Charles Strong was both judge and jury.

82. The most lurid descriptions of institutional misdeeds came from press accounts of the testimony given at the Strong hearings in January and February 1916. Because the hearings did not observe the usual rules of evidence and cross-examination, there was no check on the utterances of witnesses. Testimony was further sensationalized by the New York press. For official assessments of the condition of the institutions, see the *Annual Report of the Department of Public Charities of the City of New York for 1914* [issued November 1915]: 15, 47–56. There is additional material in the *Annual Report for the Department of Public Charities of the City of New York for 1915* [issued December 1915]; and in William A. Prendergast, Comptroller, "Report Upon the Cost to the City of New York of Its Contributions for Charitable Purposes and Upon the Distribution and Growth of Such Contributions During the Ten-Year Period Ended December 31, 1913," Bureau of Municipal Investigation and Statistics, March 1915; and the *Annual Report of the State Board of Charities for 1915* [issued in March 1916], Tierney-*America* Papers, Georgetown University. Defenders, sponsors, and staffs of the institutions all appeared before the Strong Commission. See William H. Hotchkiss, "Brief on Behalf of the Commissioner of Public Charities of the City of New York," 15, Tierney-*America* Papers, Georgetown University.

83. Robert W. Hebbard had been Secretary of the New York State Board of Charities for sixteen years. Prior to that he had served as a New York Commissioner of Charities for four years.

84. The Richard H. Tierney-*America* Papers at Georgetown University contain a collection of materials generated by the controversy, including "Newspaper Comment on Governor Whitman's Charities Investigation, Conducted

by Charles H. Strong, Commissioner Appointed Under the Moreland Act" [referred to as "the Moree pamphlet"], "A Campaign of Calumny, The New York Charities Investigation" (New York: America Press, 1916), and a reprint of an article from the August 1916 *Extension Magazine* by Msgr. John J. Dunn, "What's Behind It All?" Kelly, chaps. 6 and 7, provides a spirited, detailed account of the charges, countercharges, and conclusions. See also Florence D. Cohalan, *A Popular History of the Archdiocese of New York* (Yonkers: The United States Catholic Historical Society, 1983), 201–7.

85. William B. Farrell, "A Public Scandal: The Strong Commission Investigating the Charges of Charity Commissioner John A. Kingsbury Against the State Board of Charities and the Charitable Institutions," privately printed, New York, 18 February 1916, Tierney-*America* Papers, Georgetown University.

86. Daniel Potter was tagged a "marplot" by Jesuit editor John J. Wynne, who defended the work of Commissioner Charles Strong. See John J. Wynne, S.J., to Richard H. Tierney, S.J., New York City, 4 May 1916. Tierney-*America* Papers, Georgetown University; and Wynne to Tierney, 22 May 1916, Tierney-*America* Papers, Georgetown University.

87. Moree pamphlet, 21 February 1916, Tierney-*America* Papers, Georgetown University.

88. Robert W. Hebberd, "The Charities Investigation: Its Inspiration"; James J. Higgins, "The Charities Investigation: The Hearings"; Richard H. Tierney, S.J., "The Charities Investigation: The Testimony"; Paul L. Blakely, "Mount Loretto: An Oliver Twist School," "Dominicans and Bichlorides at Blauvelt," and "St. Joseph's Home: A School for Drudges"; and Richard H. Tierney, "A Mayor, a Church, a Conspiracy," in *A Campaign of Calumny: The New York Charities Investigation* (New York: The America Press, 1916).

89. "How the Strong Commission Has Discredited Itself: An Open Letter to the Friends of Dependent Children," and "Priest-Baiting in 1916, the Strong Commission Now an Oligarchy" (c. 16 March 1916), Tierney-*America* Papers, Georgetown University. Bishop Patrick J. Hayes reported to his colleague Bishop Thomas Cusack of Albany, 31 March 1916: "I have reliable information that our phones have been tapped by this gang of pirates of which the chief is Mitchel. How Catholic New York stands for that man, why, I know not. Be careful of your own wire in Albany. . . . We are thinking of getting out another pamphlet containing the excellent editorials from the Brooklyn papers, without comment." Reel 0–2, Patrick J. Hayes Papers, AANY, St. Joseph's Seminary, Yonkers, New York.

90. Typed transcript of the address of John A. Kingsbury to the International Child Welfare League, Plaza Hotel, 25 March 1916. Tierney-*America* Papers, Georgetown University.

91. William B. Farrell, "Priest-Baiting in 1916: The Strong Commission Now an Oligarchy," Tierney-*America* Papers, Georgetown University.

92. The New York newspapers, especially the *New York Times,* carried the

sensational details of the Thompson hearings in May 1916. Monsignor John Dunn reported to Bishop Patrick Hayes that at the Thompson hearings, John Mitchel "broke out in a tirade against the G-D bunch on Madison Avenue [i.e., the residence of the Archbishop of New York], the greatest criminals in the city. The rest of his remarks were beyond belief, mixed with oaths and obscenity. He cried out that he would put before the public the crookedness of the whole machine." AANY, 0–2, Dunn to Hayes, 20 May 1916, quoted in Kelly, 99.

93. Report of Charles H. Strong, Commissioner to Examine into Management and Affairs of the State Board of Charities, the Fiscal Supervisor and Certain Related Boards and Commissions to Governor Whitman. Issued in New York City, 27 October 1916.

94. The State Board subsequently issued its own report on the proceedings. Counsel for the Board, John M. Bowers, challenged the findings of the Strong Report and advised that the State Board knew better than Commissioner Strong and the Mitchel administration how to get compliance from the institutions. The Answer of the State Board of Charities, Unanimously Adopted, New York City, 13 December 1916, to the Report of Commissioner Charles H. Strong (Albany: J. B. Lyon Company, Printers, 1916). Tierney-*America* Papers, Georgetown University.

95. See Kenneth S. Chern, "The Politics of Patriotism: War, Ethnicity, and the New York Mayoral Campaign, 1917," *New York State Historical Society Quarterly* 63 (October 1979): 291–313.

2. The Larger Landscape

1. See discussions of this point in Jay Dolan, *The American Catholic Experience: A History from Colonial Times to the Present* (New York: Doubleday and Company, 1985), 349–62; James Henessey, *American Catholics: A History of the Roman Catholic Community in the United States* (New York: Oxford, 1981), 234–43; Paula Kane, *Separatism and Subculture: Boston Catholicism, 1900–1920* (Chapel Hill: University of North Carolina Press, 1994), 128–31; and Edward R. Kantowicz, *Corporation Sole: Cardinal Mundelein and Chicago Catholicism* (Notre Dame: University of Notre Dame Press, 1983), chaps. 2 and 3.

2. Marguerite T. Boylan, *Social Welfare in the Catholic Church: Organization and Planning Through Diocesan Bureaus* (New York: Columbia University Press, 1941), 48–49. This volume is based on Boylan's doctoral dissertation at Columbia and offers a carefully researched analysis of four separate phases of diocesan charities' organization.

3. For an extended review of this pattern, including the cross-class assessment of voluntary participation, see Mary J. Oates, *The Catholic Philanthropic Tradition in America*. Barry D. Karl poses the values of the volunteer against the new culture of contract professionalism in "Lo, the Poor Volunteer: An Essay on the Relation between History and Myth," *Social Service Review* 58 (December 1984): 493–521.

4. See Christopher J. Kauffman, *Ministry and Meaning: A Religious History of Catholic Health Care in the United States* (New York: Crossroads, 1995) for a textured review of Catholic investment in hospitals and health care.

5. The archdiocese included the counties of Manhattan, Bronx, Richmond, Westchester, Putnam, Dutchess, Ulster, Orange, Rockland, and Sullivan. Four of these counties, Manhattan, Bronx, Richmond, and Brooklyn, were consolidated as Greater New York in 1898. The Diocese of Brooklyn remained a separate ecclesiastical entity that included Long Island.

6. Social surveying was developed in the late nineteenth century by London reformer Charles Booth, who documented the circumstances of poor people in order to create a supply of social facts that would lend scientific support to reform proposals. See Martin Blumer, Kevin Bales, and Kathryn Kish Sklar, eds., *The Social Survey in Historical Perspective, 1880–1940* (New York: Cambridge University, 1991).

7. Sociologist Philip J. Murnion has provided a very useful study of the diocesan priests of New York during the 1920s in *The Catholic Priest and the Changing Structure of Pastoral Ministry, New York, 1920–1970* (New York: Arno Press, 1978).

8. The archbishop had six divisional reports and a general report that, though highlighting the "immense amount of excellent work" accomplished, noted three major weaknesses: a lack of coordination, a lack of sufficient funds in "a great many places," and "great uncovered areas" where Catholic charitable works were needed. See Robert F. Keegan, "Survey of Catholic Charities," *Proceedings of the Sixth National Conference of Catholic Charities* (1920), 30–36. There is a printed summary of the findings of the survey in NCCC, ACUA, but researchers have been unable to locate the original six-volume report in the New York archdiocesan archives.

9. The spring 1918 New York Catholic war drive received extensive coverage from the press. City papers provided daily reports of the canvass as it approached the 3.5-million-dollar mark. Generous contributions from the city's Protestant and Jewish communities were highlighted; for example, "Jews Give $15,350 to Catholic Fund," *New York Times*, 16 March 1918, 8. "Not one of the Jews who were invited . . . yesterday to the rally at the Waldorf-Astoria in behalf of the Catholic Fund left without subscribing," the paper noted.

10. Keegan, 30–36.

11. At the time of Hayes' death in 1938, the *New York Times* estimated that the central bureau of Catholic Charities of New York had spent a total of twenty-one million dollars in the eighteen years of its existence, and the 212 individual agencies spent 110 million dollars. See Mary Margretta Shea, "Patrick Cardinal Hayes and the Catholic Charities of New York City," Ph.D. dissertation, New York University, 1966: 303. The success of the consolidated fund-raising of New York Catholic Charities in the 1920s and 1930s, together with its state revenues, allowed the organization to stay out of New York movements for a community chest drive until after Hayes' death. The city could not launch a successful combined drive with-

out Catholic participation, and so its first chest drive waited until 1939. [Cardinal Spellman's biographer also notes that Hayes left the archdiocese twenty-eight million dollars in debt. See Robert I. Gannon, S.J., *The Cardinal Spellman Story* (New York: Doubleday & Company, 1962), 265–66.]

12. Historians have claimed that the survey had "surpassing influence" on the course of social research in America. Clarke A. Chambers, *Paul U. Kellogg and the Survey: Voices for Social Welfare and Social Justice* (Minneapolis: University of Minnesota Press, 1971), 36–39. See also Steven R. Cohen, "The Pittsburgh Survey and the Social Survey Movement: A Sociological Road Not Taken," in Blumer et. al., 245–68.

13. Investigators were given a fourteen-point outline to cover in their reports on child-caring institutions ranging from equipment, health care, admission and discharge, income and expenditures, education, recreation, recordkeeping, and relation to state and local authorities as to supervision and inspection. *Pittsburgh Social Survey*, 34:1, NCWC, ACUA.

14. Introduction to the Pittsburgh Social Survey, 33; *Pittsburgh Social Survey*, 33:12, 2.

15. *Pittsburgh Social Survey*, 33:12.

16. Edward J. Misklow to Hugh J. Boyle, 9 October 1921, Papers of the Conference of Catholic Charities, Archives of the Diocese of Pittsburgh. Misklow's concerns about the church's welfare in Pittsburgh paid personal dividends when Bishop Boyle named him to the position of chancellor of the diocese in 1922.

17. For an extended discussion of Boston's Catholic charities, see Susan S. Walton, "To Preserve the Faith: Catholic Charities in Boston, 1870–1930," in Robert Sullivan and Joseph O'Toole, eds., *Catholic Boston: Studies in Religion and Community, 1870–1970* (Boston: Roman Catholic Archbishop of Boston, 1985), 67–119. The quotes are cited in Walton, 110. A firsthand account of the reorganization is available in William Henry O'Connell, *Recollections of Seventy Years* (Boston: Houghton Mifflin Company, 1934). For O'Connell's consolidation efforts, see Walton, 96–98, and Oates, 88.

18. Anne Culligan, George P. O'Conor, Joseph Scully, and Herbert LeBlond, "How Far Should Catholics Care for Their Own Poor?" *Proceedings of the Eighth National Conference of Catholic Charities* (1922), 94–111.

19. Ibid.

20. For a cultural analysis of the complexities of assimilation in Boston, see Kane's argument in *Separatism and Subculture*.

21. The task was made easier by the unusual legal character of the Archdiocese of Chicago. Mundelein was a "corporation sole." In contrast to the "corporation aggregate" characteristic of most dioceses, including New York, all of the property of the archdiocese of Chicago was incorporated in the name of the ordinary or bishop. As archbishop, Mundelein literally owned the assets of the archdiocese in his own name. See Kantowicz, *Corporation Sole*, chap. 3; and James Gollin, *Worldly Goods* (New York: Random

House, 1971) for an extended analysis of this aspect of the Chicago archdiocesan situation.

22. The "kiddies" quotation is cited in Kantowicz, 128. See Kantowicz, chap. 9, for an extended review of Mundelein's charities reorganization; and for the comment on independent orphanages, see Kantowicz, 139–40. A detailed report of Chicago Catholic work at the beginning of Mundelein's reign is compiled in "Women and Children First" (Chicago: The Associated Catholic Charities of Chicago, 1918), in NCCC, ACUA.

23. See Kantowicz, 143–49, and Gene D. L. Jones, "The Chicago Catholic Charities, the Great Depression and Public Money," *Illinois Historical Journal* 83 (spring 1990): 13–30. Chapter 5 of this text rehearses the Chicago situation in detail.

24. See Kantowicz, 22–24, and Hennesey, 241. Hennesey details Mundelein's instructions to Speaker of the Illinois House David Shanahan in March, when "bills adverse to Catholic orphanages were introduced in the legislature in Springfield" in 1917. Mundelein told the Speaker to "bury those bills in the wastebasket or in a committee where they cannot be resurrected."

25. Christopher J. Kauffman, *Faith and Fraternalism: The History of the Knights of Columbus*, rev. ed. (New York: Simon and Schuster, 1992) provides the context for the local work of the Knights. See especially his accounts of the work of the Knights on the Mexican border in 1916 and in the war camps during World War I.

26. Thomas Mulry had lamented a falling-off of participation in the parish work of the SVPS in the first decade of the century, and SVPS historian Daniel McColgan noted the erosion of Vincentian special works and city-wide works after 1920. See Daniel McColgan, *A Century of Charity: The First One Hundred Years of the Society of St. Vincent de Paul in the United States*, 2 vols. (Milwaukee: Bruce Publishing Company, 1962), I:383–84.

27. See Thomas W. Spalding, *The Premier See: A History of the Archdiocese of Baltimore, 1789–1989* (Baltimore: Johns Hopkins University Press, 1989), 335–37, for a positive assessment of Curley's diocesan reorganization.

28. Report of the Particular Council of Baltimore for the Year Ending December 31, 1907 (Baltimore: J. H. Furst Co., 1908): 5. See also Mark O. Shriver, *A Brief History of the Particular Council of Baltimore, Maryland, Society of St. Vincent de Paul* (Baltimore: Society of St. Vincent de Paul, 1931).

29. Robert A. Biggs to Rt. Rev. Michael J. Curley, Baltimore, 20 April 1923, Curley Papers, Archives of the Archdiocese of Baltimore (AAB). The remainder of the extended correspondence between the two men is also in this archive. For a defense of Biggs' Catholic practice by a leading figure in Catholic charities, see William J. Kerby to Michael J. Curley, Washington, 8 March 1932, Curley Papers, AAB. For a later summary of the matter that favors Curley, see Shriver, *A Brief History of the Particular Council of Baltimore*, in the archdiocesan charities office. And see Spalding, 335–37.

30. See Hubert LeBlond, "Catholic Organizations and Community Chests,"

[Rev.] Francis A. Gressle, "The Advantages of Participation in the Community Chest," [Rev.] J. C. Carr, "The Case Against Participation of Catholic Organizations in Community Chests," [Rev.] Edwin L. Leonard, "Community Chests, the Case Against Participation," and Discussion, [Rev.] John J. Butler [St. Louis], John J. Sheehan [Kansas City], and James Fitzgerald [Detroit], *Tenth National Conference of Catholic Charities* (1924), 188–212; E. C. McQueeney [Akron], "Report of Secretary for the Month of April 1924," NCCC, ACUA, Mitchell.

31. James E. Hagerty, "The Relation of Diocesan Charitable and Social Activities to Community Organizations," and Discussion, *Proceedings of the Sixth National Conference of Catholic Charities* (1920), 82–88.

32. John M. Cooper, "Is Class-Control Hobbling Charity?" *Catholic Charities Review* 11 (February 1927): 43–46.

33. Alice Padgett, "Death in Life," *Catholic Charities Review* 14 (November 1930): 228–30; "Chests and Relief Funds," ibid., 233–34; and "Editorial Comment," ibid., 16 (February 1932): 45.

34. McColgan notes that when Vincentians tried to meet the need for citywide programs by organizing central bureaus of Catholic Charities, they were aware of their own handicaps and limitations. They had "no influence over the various institutions of the diocese or the lay organizations of Catholic women" (McColgan, II:357).

35. See Proceedings of the White House Conference on the Care of Dependent Children, 25–26 January 1909 (Washington, D.C.: Government Printing Office, 1909), which includes a list of all delegates and recommendations. For Thomas Mulry's leadership role, see the account in Helmes, "Thomas M. Mulry," 93–99. For further comment on Vincentian participation in the White House Conference, see McColgan, II:299. An institutional history of the National Conference of Catholic Charities is contained in Donald Gavin's golden anniversary review, *The National Conference of Catholic Charities, 1910–1960* (Milwaukee: Catholic Life Publications, Bruce Press, 1962).

36. See *Proceedings of the First National Conference of Catholic Charities* (1910), 50–71. Massachusetts State Board of Charities member David F. Tilley also provided a review of the policies of each of the states with regard to financing and inspecting private institutions. "The State and Private Institutions," ibid., 72–79.

37. Vincentian James F. Kennedy reported that Chicago particularly had a "great demand for women volunteers, particularly among girls and women detained in police stations" (Ibid.). Mary Ritter Beard provides a contemporary review of the growing role of women in corrections work and in the juvenile court movement. Beard, *Women's Work in Municipalities* (New York: D. Appleton and Co., 1915), 220–86.

38. Kerby chaired the Department of Sociology at Catholic University and after its founding in 1902 also taught sociology to the women at nearby Trinity College. He wrote extensively for professional periodicals and journals of

opinion, both Catholic and secular, and undertook a series of editorial duties for the *St. Vincent de Paul Quarterly* and the *Ecclesiastical Review.* See Timothy Michael Dolan, "Prophet of a Better Hope: The Life and Work of William Joseph Kerby," Ph.D. dissertation, The Catholic University of America, 1981; and Bruce Lescher, "Kerby, Ryan and Furfey," Ph.D. dissertation, Graduate Theological Union, Berkeley, 1988.

39. Kerby urged his colleagues in social work to champion a "social constitution," based on a clear understanding of the demands of justice and a strong sense of local responsibility and volunteer engagement in public life. He hoped that the National Conference of Catholic Charities would become "the attorney for the Poor in Modern Society . . . toward the day when social justice may secure to them their rights." William Kerby, "An Interpretation," *Proceedings of the First National Conference of Catholic Charities* (1910), 411–20. See also William Kerby, *The Social Mission of Charity* (New York: Macmillan, 1921), 54–70.

40. O'Grady dictated his memoirs in 1950–1951 in preparation for what was to have been a biography called *Come Now, Monsignor* by Saul Alinsky. Alinsky produced a manuscript for Putnam in 1953 based on O'Grady's transcripts and heavily inflected by his own interests and convictions, but the book was never published. See Sanford Horwitt, *Let Them Call Me Rebel: Saul Alinsky—His Life and Legacy* (New York: Alfred A. Knopf, 1989), 262. There is also a manuscript version of O'Grady's public contributions written by his devoted coworker, Alice Padgett. These three manuscripts are located in NCCC, ACUA. For a scholarly account of O'Grady's legislative activities from the New Deal through the late 1950s, see Thomas W. Tifft, "Toward a More Humane Social Policy: The Work and Influence of Monsignor John O'Grady," Ph.D. dissertation, Catholic University of America, 1979.

41. Elizabeth Mandell to Kerby, Forest Hills, New York, 18 Sept. 1920, Kerby Papers, ACUA. Mandell told Kerby that his withdrawal "came as a *shocking* surprise" and wondered if "the initial purpose of the Conference, the exploitation of the laity in Catholic Charities, still exists."

42. John O'Grady to Madorah Donahue, 14 August 1919, NCWC, Committee on Reconstruction 4:8, ACUA.

43. See "Robert Fulton Keegan," *New Catholic Encyclopedia* 8 (1967): 142–43; Edward Roberts Moore, *Roman Collar* (New York: Macmillan, 1950); and his obituary, *New York Times,* 5 November 1947, 27.

44. James Fitzgerald, "At the Head of the List," *Catholic Charities Review* 12 (November 1928): 332–33.

45. For extended analysis of Burke's role, see John J. Sheerin, *The Career and Concerns of John J. Burke* (New York: Paulist Press, 1975); and Elizabeth McKeown, *War and Welfare: American Catholics and World War I* (New York: Garland Press, 1988). Kerby clearly influenced Burke's thinking on the matter. For the context of the Kerby-Burke relationship, see Douglas J. Slawson, *The Foundation and First Decade of the National*

Catholic Welfare Council (Washington: Catholic University of America, 1992), chap. 1.

46. The historian of the Clifton school and the National Catholic School of Social Service is Loretto Lawler, who writes with an intimate knowledge of the principal characters and events surrounding the school's history. It is evident that she had access to War and Welfare Council minutes, memoranda, and correspondence. Her book is designed as a tribute to John Burke and was written when the school was absorbed by Catholic University after Burke's death. See Loretto Lawler, *Full Circle: A Story of the National Catholic School of Social Service* (Washington, D.C.: Catholic University of America Press, 1951).

47. See the Reports of the Committee on Women's Activities, April 1918 to February 1919, National Catholic War Council, Committee on Special War Activities, Chairman's File Burke 24:2, ACUA. Hereafter, NCWC-Women's Committee. See also the extended summaries of the work of the Visitors' Houses, 29 May 1920, ibid., 24:8; and similar report on Community Houses, July 1920, in ibid., 24:9.

48. See Marguerite T. Boylan, *They Shall Live Again: The Story of the National Catholic War Council Overseas After World War I* (New York: Cosmopolitan Science & Art Service Co., Inc., 1945); and Marguerite T. Boylan, "The Social Work of Catholic Women in Europe," *Proceedings of the Sixth National Conference of Catholic Charities* (1920), 355–63.

49. Margaret Long to William Kerby, 25 April 1918, NCWC, CSWA, WC, 6:1, ACUA.

50. Long frequently reported to Cooper on the lack of "trained workers" and her difficulties in filling requests. Margaret Long to John Cooper, Chicago, 28 December 1919, NCWC-Women's Committee, 10:16.

51. For an example of episcopal objection to settlement, see "What We Are Doing in Settlement Work," *Proceedings of the Third National Conference of Catholic Charities* (1914), 213–20, 220–24, 231–33.

52. The latter was established to aid the Italians in Cincinnati and to save them from "the Presbyterian proselytizers." In settlement work as well as orphan asylums, this defensive action to meet the challenge of the proselytizer endured into the 1920s. See Papers of the Santa Maria Institute, Archives of the Sisters of Charity, Mt. St. Joseph's, Ohio; and McNichols Papers, Drawer 15, Files 4–5, Archives of the Archdiocese of Cincinnati. For a review of Catholic settlements, see Margaret M. McGuiness, "Body and Soul: Immigration and Catholic Social Settlements," *U.S. Catholic Historian* 3 (summer 1995): 63–76. Information on specific settlement efforts is contained in Walton (Boston) and Tentler (Detroit).

53. Margaret Long, Report to the NCWC Committee on Women's Activities on the National Catholic Community House, 18 August 1920, Cincinnati, Ohio, and Resume Report, 11 Dec. 1919–1 July 1920, NCWC-Women's Committee.

54. Report of Elizabeth Kelley, 26 Oct. to 1 Nov. 1919, and 16 Nov. to 23

Nov. 1919, NCWC-Women's Committee, 24:18; Elizabeth Kelley to John
M. Cooper, 29 Nov. 1919, NCWC-Women's Committee, 25:9. On Mary
Louise Rohr, see NCWC-Women's Committee, 25:10.

55. "Girls' Welfare," November 1919, CSWA-Women's Committee (NCWC-
USSC, ACUA), 25.

56. Field Secretary Camille Detert, reporting on the Baltimore Community
House and Day Nursery, 1 June 1920, noted that the Polish pastors agreed
that the day nursery could be an opening wedge for gaining the confidence of the Polish people, noting that "the Polish people are going to be
hard to handle. The words 'Americanization' and 'Citizenship' are hated
by them and are absolutely taboo." Report on Baltimore Community
Houses, NCWC-Women's Committee.

57. The name of the permanent organization from 1919 until 1922 was the
National Catholic Welfare Council. The canon law implications in the term
"Council" caused a shift to "Conference" in 1922. In 1967 the NCWC
became the National Conference of Catholic Bishops and its public policy
arm, the United States Catholic Conference.

58. For an extended account of the NCWC, see Douglas J. Slawson, *The
Foundation and First Decade of the National Catholic Welfare Council*
(Washington, D.C.: The Catholic University of America Press, 1992). Internal correspondence relating to the threatened suppression is reproduced
in William Kennedy, "The Work of Father John J. Burke, CSP, During the
Early Years of the National Catholic Welfare Council, 1917–1922," M.A.
thesis, St. Paul's College, Washington, D.C., April 1951.

59. Gertrude Hill Gavin was the daughter of Great Northern railroad developer
James J. Hill. She was born in St. Paul and attended the Spence School there
before coming to New York with her husband, a real estate attorney and
investment broker. See Gavin's obituary, *New York Times*, 12 January
1961, 29:3. Michael P. Malone, *James J. Hill: Empire Builder of the
Northwest* (Norman, Oklahoma: University of Oklahoma Press, 1996),
offers family context. For Regan, see Dorothy A. Mohler, "Agnes Regan,"
in E. Catherine Dunn and Dorothy Mohler, eds., *Pioneering Women at the
Catholic University of America* (Hyattsville, Md.: International Graphics,
1990).

60. See, for example, Lenora Z. Meder (Chicago juvenile worker), "The Care
of Young Girls in America," *Proceedings of the Fourth National Conference
of Catholic Charities* (1916), 336–42; (Miss) Margaret H. Robbins (Philadelphia probation officer), "The Delinquent Girl" and discussion, ibid.,
343–53; (Rev.) Edward Garesche, S.J., "The Catholic Young Woman: Her
Needs and Some Remedies," ibid., 353–65; and Paul Mueller-Simonis,
"The Protection of Young Girls in Modern Cities," *Proceedings of the First
National Conference of Catholic Charities* (1910), 242–50.

61. Already alerted to an attack on their institutions by city reformers, the
archdiocese responded with horror and heavy-fisted condemnation. Their
response to Sanger, however, served to fuel the issue rather than to defeat

it, and the high-profile skirmishes between Sanger and the Archdiocese of New York became emblems of the battle over birth control in the United States. See for example, Sanger's recollection of Mitchel's troubles with the church in Margaret Sanger, "Catholics and Birth Control," Letters to the Editor, *New Republic 56* (October 31, 1928): 302–3. See Ellen Chesler, *Woman of Valor: Margaret Sanger and the Birth Control Movement in America* (New York: Simon and Schuster, 1992), 297. For a note on John Kingsbury's role in the birth control crusade and for information on Charles Strong, see "Birth Control Facts for Mothers on Relief Are Demanded by Clergy at Mass Meeting," *New York Times,* 3 December 1935, 1. For further discussion of Sanger's relations to the Catholic church, see David Kennedy, *Birth Control in America: The Career of Margaret Sanger* (New Haven: Yale University Press, 1970), chap. 6; Linda Gordon, *Woman's Body, Woman's Right: A Social History of Birth Control in America* (New York: Viking Press, 1976), chap. 11; Chesler, passim; David J. Garrow, *Liberty and Sexuality: The Right to Privacy and the Making of Roe v. Wade* (New York: Macmillan Publishing Company, 1994), esp. chap. 1; and Carole R. McCann, *Birth Control Politics in the United States, 1916–1945* (Ithaca: Cornell University Press, 1994).

62. Recognizing that the supporters of birth control had better resources, both human and financial, than did the NCWC, Burke urged the American bishops to place more "trained, capable men and particularly *women* at our command," and in a plea for further funding, he argued: "The birth control advocates have money. They can afford to pay the expenses for attending a hearing to bring the specialists here. We can do nothing of this kind." John J. Burke to Rt. Rev. Joseph Rummel, 21 February 1931, with enclosure, Burke to Rt. Rev. John F. Noll, Re: Opposition Hearing Against the Gillett Birth Control Bill [n.d.], James Hugh Ryan Papers, Archives of the Archdiocese of Omaha.

63. See Margaret Sanger, *The Pivot of Civilization* (New York: Brentano's, 1922), chap. 9.

64. Agnes Regan's accounts of her efforts are contained in her annual reports. See Reports of the Executive Secretary, Papers of the National Council of Catholic Women, ACUA. The NCCW also supported Sheppard-Towner, the child labor amendment, mothers' pensions, and the welfare of working women. See stenographers' reports of the annual "Proceedings" in Papers of the National Council of Catholic Women, ACUA; and Slawson, *The Foundation.*

65. See Lawler for details. Gertrude Gavin, NCCW president from 1920 to 1924, provided most of the financing for the school in its first five years. Her donations totaled $110,000. John Burke to Mrs. Michael Gavin, 29 April 1921; Gertrude Hill Gavin to John J. Burke, 24 January 1922; John Burke to Gertrude Gavin, 25 January 1922; Gertrude Hill Gavin, Note of Agreement, 9 February [1923], John Burke Papers, Box 3, Archives of St. Paul's College. The NCSSS began to receive yearly grants from the Laura

Spelman Rockefeller Foundation in 1924, after conforming to a requirement of the Foundation that the school be reincorporated under the control
of the Board of Managers. The school received a total of $45,000 from the
Foundation.

66. Moral theologian John A. Ryan also lived at the school from the time of
his retirement from Catholic University in 1941 until his death in 1945.

67. See Rose Marie Moorman's accounts, including "The First Annual Convention of the National Council of Catholic Women," *Catholic Charities
Review* 5 (November 1921): 302–3; Ibid. 6 (December 1922): 362–64; Ibid.
9 (December 1925): 397–98; Ibid. 11 (November 1927): 349; and Ibid. 12
(December 1928): 334.

68. Note NCSSS Day Books and Kerby, Burke, Neill, Nicholson correspondence.

69. Most of the students who attended the NCSSS required scholarship support, and the school could not count on tuition to help it meet its own
administrative and capital expenses. It hovered on the brink of financial
collapse through most of its quarter-century of independent history.

70. *Fourteenth Annual Meeting of the Advisory Board of Trinity* [College], 10
June 1914; and *Dean's Report,* Trinity College, Washington, D.C., 10 June
1915. Archives of Trinity College, Washington, D.C.

71. Marguerite Boylan provides details in "The Diocesan Bureau of Social
Welfare," *Proceedings of the Twenty-third National Conference of Catholic
Charities* (1937), 129–40; and in *Social Welfare in the Catholic Church,*
201–28. She also notes the inauguration in 1934 of a School of Social
Service at Xavier of New Orleans for African-American Catholics in the
diocese of New Orleans. The founders were Katherine Drexel's Sisters of
the Blessed Sacrament for Indians and Colored People. For Xavier University, see Cyprian Davis, O.S.B., *The History of Black Catholics in the United
States* (New York: Crossroads, 1990), 254.

72. See "Reports from Directors of Courses of Instruction in Social Work,
Given in 1913–1914," *Proceedings of the Third National Conference of
Catholic Charities* (1914), 61–78; Frederic Siedenburg, S.J., "A Standard
Course in Relief Work," *Proceedings of the Fourth National Conference of
Catholic Charities* (1916), 309–14; Teresa Molamphy, ibid., 372–73; and
Mrs. P. J. Toomey, "Schools for Social Study," *Proceedings of the First
National Conference of Catholic Charities* (1910), 385–93.

73. The New York School of Philanthropy opened under the aegis of the
Charity Organization Society in 1898 and became the New York School of
Social Work, affiliated with Columbia University, in 1918. Its sponsors and
instructors eventually included the leading professional social workers of
the day. Volunteers such as Thomas M. Mulry offered courses in the
original night school. See Elizabeth G. Meier, *A History of the New York
School of Social Work* (New York: Columbia University Press, 1954).

74. Rev. John Fenlon, S.S., "Grappling With Our Charity Problems," *The
Ecclesiastical Review* 52 (March 1915): 264.

75. ACUA, Rector's File, Meeting of Monsignor Joseph M. Corrigan and the Advisory Committee of the School of Social Work, 30 June 1936.

76. John O'Connor, Jr., "Men Wanted!" *Catholic Charities Review* 3 (December 1919): 290.

77. Rev. Francis X. Wastl, Chaplain, Philadelphia Hospital for the Sick and Insane at Blockley, "Social Service by Hospitals," *Proceedings of the Third National Conference of Catholic Charities* (1914), 186–97. There was also a strong whiff of class-consciousness in the antagonism of Catholics toward "other" social workers.

78. Editorial Comment, "Social Work and Social Reform," *Catholic Charities Review* 13 (April 1929): 122–23; Editorial Comment, "Save the Men!" ibid. (June 1929): 192. By 1930 the U.S. Census confirmed that close to 80 percent of all social workers were women. For a summary of developments in the field, see Sydnor H. Walker, "Privately Supported Social Work," *Recent Social Trends in the United States,* vol. 2 (New York: McGraw-Hill, 1933), 1168–1223. For a reading of the role of gender in professional social work, see Daniel J. Walkowitz, "The Making of a Feminine Professional Identity: Social Workers in the 1920s," *American Historical Review* 95 (October 1990): 1051–75.

79. Their professional training qualified them for membership in the American Association of Social Workers (AASW), and female social workers soon began to receive complaints from the priests in diocesan charities whose seminary training was often judged inadequate for membership in the AASW. One prominent Catholic social worker expressed her impatience with these protests: "In regard to the Priests and the AASW, I hope they will assume an adult and not a childish attitude. . . They do not get into local chapters and make their influence felt effectively so that they inspire confidence. They are usually a law unto themselves and wait until some controversial issue arises to stake their position. Because they have not been working along in non-controversial areas, they have not given people on the inside a chance to know them thoroughly and thereby respect their judgment. It *is* a threat to them to have a little inexperienced college girl accepted without question." Mabel Mattingly, Director of Field Work, Fordham University School of Social Service, to John O'Grady, 7 February 1934, NCCC, ACUA.

80. "The Priest and the Social Worker," *Catholic Charities Review* 5 (November 1921): 3. By 1921 John A. Ryan was the contributing editor, and John O'Grady had become the editor of the CCR. O'Grady's voice dominates the editorial tone of the magazine through the 1920s and 1930s. By 1926 he had hired an "assistant-to-the-editor," Alice Padgett, who gradually began to publish under her own name and who was a lifelong colleague and close friend of O'Grady's.

81. James F. Borer, Director, Catholic Charities, Omaha, "What Part Should Religion Play in Family Case Work?" *Proceedings of the Fourteenth National Conference of Catholic Charities* (1928), 112–19.

82. Editorial Comment, "To the Confessional," *Catholic Charities Review* 15 (May 1931): 256.
83. Joseph L. May, "Catholic Charities, Utica, New York," *Proceedings of the Fourteenth National Conference of Catholic Charities* (1928), 195–97.
84. Remarks of Rev. Francis P. LeBuffe, S.J., in response to Rose McHugh, "Education for Social Work: Present Standards," in *Proceedings of the Eleventh National Conference of Catholic Charities* (1925), 273.
85. See Rev. Walter McGuinn, S.J., "The Task Confronting the Catholic School of Social Work in Meeting the Demands of the Catholic Agency," in *Proceedings of the Twenty-fifth National Conference of Catholic Charities* (1939), 413–20. See also, Walter McGuinn, *The Professional Secret in Social Work* (Boston: Boston College School of Social Work, 1938).
86. John O'Grady, *An Introduction to Social Work* (1928); James Hagerty, *Social Work Education* (1930); and Louise McGuire's lecture notes for her class in "generic social work" and the National Catholic School of Social Service all reflect the influence of Mary Richmond. McGuire's lecture notes covering the late 1920s and early 1930s were made available by Dorothy Abts Mohler of the Catholic University School of Social Work, who was a student at the school during those years.
87. *Social Case Work, Generic and Specific: A Report of the Milford Conference* (New York: American Association of Social Workers, Studies in the Practice of Social Work, no. 2, 1929), 11. The report noted that social casework "has all of the aspects of the beginnings of a science in its practice and it has conscious professional standards for its practitioners. The various separate designations (children's case worker, family case worker, probation officer, visiting teacher, psychiatric social worker, medical social worker) . . . have relatively less significance . . . in comparison with the generic term 'social case work.'" The challenge of psychiatric social work was given compelling expression by Virginia Robinson, *A Changing Psychology in Social Case Work* (Chapel Hill: University of North Carolina Press, 1930). In the new therapeutic approaches, "[v]erification of a fact in the old sense is seldom called for," Robinson noted. "The case worker's major interest now is in the individual's dynamic, propelling attitudes and the use these make of objects, people and situations—in other words, in the individual's own reality" (Robinson, 98).
88. See, for example, the views of NCSSS director Rev. Francis J. Haas: "The rapid increase of psychiatric clinics raises several issues about which Catholics can not be indifferent. Suppose it is the policy of a clinic to prescribe sexual promiscuity as a means of 'getting rid of a complex.' To an influential school of psychiatry this is accepted practice. To Catholics it is a grave sin. Quite clearly parents, priests and sisters cannot deliver nervous and subnormal children over to such practitioners. The only adequate solution is to train psychiatrists and psychiatric social workers in Catholic schools." Haas, "Social Service: A Field of Catholic Action," *Catholic Action* (July 1932): 24–25.

89. Margaret C. Norman, "The Application of Catholic Philosophy to the Practice of Social Case Work," *Proceedings of the Twenty-third National Conference of Catholic Charities* (1937), 59–72. At the time she wrote this thoughtful appraisal of Catholic philosophy and social work, Norman was a faculty member at the struggling School of Social Work at Catholic University.

90. Edward S. Pouthier, S.J., Dean, School of Social Service, Fordham University, "The Philosophy of Catholic Social Case Work," *Proceedings of the Twenty-third National Conference of Catholic Charities* (1937), 49–59; "A Changing Psychology of Social Case Work" (Book Review), *Catholic Charities Review* 14 (March 1931): 219. In 1948 one of William Kerby's students from Trinity College undertook the task of providing Catholic social casework with a proper Thomistic foundation. See Mary J. McCormick, *Thomistic Philosophy in Social Casework* (New York: Columbia University Press, 1948).

91. Catholic social work leaders remained determined to save souls as well as bodies. See, for example, Jesuit Felix Biestek of Loyola University School of Social Work (Chicago), who argued that students of social work must learn to assist individuals in their present environment as a prologue to "the ultimate objective of helping clients save their immortal souls." Felix J. Biestek, "Objectives of A Catholic School of Social Work," *Catholic Charities Review* 36 (November 1952): 210.

92. Social workers were suspected of being carriers of the "birth control plague." "If you could only hear the Catholic . . . trained social workers, who tell you that they really feel in their souls that they must support movements like birth control, bills for sterilization, and all that kind of thing, because there seems to be no other way to make decent families, and there seems to be no other way to make homes again, to bring back to us what we seem to have lost, homes and mothers and fathers, it would surprise you." Anne Doyle, U.S. Federal Health Service, "The Trained Worker in Social Service," *Proceedings of the First Annual Convention of the National Council of Catholic Women,* 12–14 October 1921. But the American Association of Social Workers did not endorse the practice and the National Conference of Social Work, with its substantial Catholic representation, did not allow the American Birth Control League (ABCL) standing as a "kindred" or affiliated group until 1929. Even then it did not openly support the ABCL agenda. Fears of Catholic and public opposition and their own conservatism in the matter kept Children's Bureau leaders from endorsing the movement until Katharine Lenroot finally yielded after 1940. To the extent that social workers were "carriers," their work was low-key and agency-specific.

93. Rose McHugh was born in 1881 in Marshall, Michigan, and graduated from the University of Chicago in 1904. She joined United Charities of Chicago in 1905, and was named secretary of the Funds to Parents Committee after the Illinois mothers' pension law passed in 1911. *New York Times,* 13 December 1952.

94. The Social Action Department Quarterly Report, September 1926, noted that McHugh prepared the outline of the study, directed the field work, and wrote the complete reports for Akron, Baltimore, Pittsburgh, and New York, as well as the general report summarizing the findings of the entire study. She was assisted by Louise McGuire of NCSSS, Florence Mason of the Children's Bureau of Cleveland, and Gertrude Marron of Catholic Charities of D.C. The dioceses surveyed included New York, Baltimore, Buffalo, Pittsburgh, and Akron. In addition to McHugh, the other members of the NCCC committee were veterans Helen Montegriffo and Marguerite Boylan and John O'Grady. Records of the Social Action Department-56P, National Catholic War Council-Committee on Special War Activities, ACUA.

95. See Edwin L. Leonard, "Report on a Study of the Family Division in Five Diocesan Catholic Charities," *Proceedings of the Twelfth National Conference of Catholic Charities* (1926), 455–69; and Edwin L. Leonard, "Case Work and Religion From the Standpoint of Our Catholic Agencies," *Proceedings of the Thirteenth National Conference of Catholic Charities* (1927), 93–101.

96. John O'Grady refused McHugh's repeated requests to publish the results of the family survey in the *Catholic Charities Review.* "There is such a thing as rubbing it in too much," he reminded her. John O'Grady to Rose McHugh, 30 August 1926, 18 September 1926, 30 October 1926, and 31 March 1927, NCCC-S, ACUA. Instead the *Catholic Charities Review* ran an editorial sympathetic to Leonard's view: "Trained Leadership in Catholic Work," *Catholic Charities Review* 10 (February 1926): 5.

97. By 1933 Catholic graduate programs in social work had been in existence for eighteen years, and, during that time, only 271 students had received degrees. One hundred and thirty of these were employed in Catholic agencies as the New Deal began, whereas 141 worked in nonsectarian welfare organizations. Put another way, fifty-four diocesan agencies of Catholic charities, operating almost a hundred separate offices, employed between five and six hundred persons as social workers. Less than a quarter of those were graduates of Catholic professional schools. McHugh pointed out that non-Catholic agencies continued to be more attractive to many graduates of Catholic professional schools because, as she carefully put it, "the place of Catholic professional graduate is not [secured] as advantageously in Catholic agency as in non-sectarian one." Round Table Meeting of Committee on Families, "Professional Education for Social Work," *Proceedings of the Nineteenth National Conference of Catholic Charities* (1933), 169–73. Rose McHugh was concurrently serving as a member of the Committee on Training Courses of the American Association of Social Workers.

98. New York priest Patrick A. O'Boyle acted as secretary of the committee. In 1935 O'Boyle was assistant director of the Division of Children in New York Catholic Charities and a personal assistant to Robert Keegan. O'Boyle eventually moved from New York to become the first bishop of the newly created Archdiocese of Washington.

99. [Rose McHugh], A Report of a Study of the Committee on Professional Education for Social Work, National Conference of Catholic Charities, September 1936, NCCC, ACUA. The committee chose the strategy of comparing their 1934 preliminary results with those of Ralph Hurlin's 1934 study of fourteen private family agencies in New York, acknowledging that there were great differences between conditions in New York and the widely scattered diocesan agencies. The Hurlin study involved 398 New York professional staff members, 76 percent of whom were college graduates and 47 percent of whom had "some" graduate training. Only 46 percent of the 426 workers in the Catholic sample had undergraduate degrees, and only 10 percent had a two-year graduate degree in social work. Of the 242 Catholic college graduates, 207 worked in Catholic agencies at a rank below that of executive or administrator.

100. Ibid. Salary ranges at the executive level in Catholic agencies reflected the fact that many of the priests were paid only a nominal salary for their services. Sixteen received less than $100 a month, or about as much as the workers-in-training. (Clergy generally had board and room at the parish and were often paid a salary for parish work as well.) Excluding those sixteen priests, the executive salaries began at $1,296 a year and went as high as $2,580. The report noted much more uniformity among the salaries of the caseworkers, for whom the median salary fell between $1,260 and $1,536, depending on experience, whereas the median for supervisors was $1,872 a year. When considered in the total pool of 621, only 21 percent of the professional staff received salaries of $150 a month or more.

101. Ibid. Two hundred of the 621 persons included in the report claimed to hold executive positions. (At least six of the agencies in the survey had only one staff member, and several others had fewer than ten.) Of these 201 persons, only 40 percent were college graduates, although some of the priests may have considered their seminary training a separate category from the college degree and failed to report it on this schedule. Fifty percent of the pool of 201 "executives" were members of AASW, whereas only 16 percent (63) of the 280 caseworkers were members. Six percent (23) had membership pending.

102. "Report on Meetings of Diocesan Directors of Catholic Charities," *Proceedings of the Twenty-first National Conference of Catholic Charities* (1935), 297.

103. John O'Grady to William Kerby, 26 February 1927, NCCC, ACUA. After James H. Ryan's appointment as CUA rector in 1928, O'Grady sent a copy of this letter to him. See Papers of James H. Ryan, Kerby File, Archives of the Archdiocese of Omaha. In the letter O'Grady insisted that it would be "exceedingly difficult to develop a satisfactory working arrangement between a school controlled by the National Council of Catholic Women and our local Catholic Charities" and implied that his views were shared by Baltimore Archbishop and Catholic University chancellor Michael Curley and the knowledgeable diocesan directors of charity.

104. James Ryan received his graduate education in Rome and had returned to the diocese of Indianapolis to teach at St. Mary's of the Woods College in Terre Haute from 1911 to 1920. Like John A. Ryan, John Cooper, and John O'Grady before him, James Ryan found a place in the NCWC as secretary of the Education Department from 1920 to 1928. For the Ryan years at Catholic University, see H. Warren Willis, "The Reorganization of the Catholic University of America During the Rectorship of James H. Ryan, 1928–1935," Ph.D. dissertation, The Catholic University of America, 1971.

105. Marguerite Boylan of Catholic Charities of Brooklyn cautiously noted that although it was gratifying to see the increase in the number of young priests receiving professional training for social work, "it is perhaps a cause for some concern to see them, in certain instances, become executives overnight, so to speak, before they have had an opportunity to become seasoned through experience in the ranks." Boylan, *Social Welfare in the Catholic Church,* 214.

106. John O'Grady to Joseph Corrigan, 25 July 1935, with enclosure: "Memorandum for the Rector of the Catholic University of America Regarding the School of Social Work, Its Objectives, Needed Improvements, and Desirability of a School of Social Science," Rector's Office, File on School of Social Work, ACUA.

107. For a full-length treatment of the university, see C. Joseph Nuesse, *The Catholic University of America: A Centennial History* (Washington: Catholic University of America Press, 1990).

108. The NCSSS director from 1929 to 1933 was bishop of Toledo by 1934, and his metropolitan was Archbishop John T. McNicholas of Cincinnati, a leading member of CUA's board of trustees and leading opponent of the James Hugh Ryan administration. Upon hearing of the trustees'·decision to approve the CUA School of Social Work, Bishop Alter immediately enlisted the aid of McNicholas to try to insure that the CUA school would be prohibited from admitting laywomen. Alter also hoped that the CUA curriculum would be limited to social legislation and property and labor economics.

109. Michael J. Curley to John O'Grady, 22 June 1934, Curley Papers, Archives of the Archdiocese of Baltimore. Curley shared O'Grady's dislike of the NCSSS and had encouraged plans to open the school at CUA. His opposition to the school was a part of his long-running battle with the NCWC and its National Council of Catholic Women.

110. James Ryan seems to have accepted a written agreement drawn up by Karl Alter during his term as director of NCSSS, stating that CUA would not poach on the territory of the women's school. See Karl J. Alter to John J. Burke, 23 July 1935, enclosing James H. Ryan to Karl J. Alter, 12 July 1935, Alter to Ryan, 17 July 1935, and Ryan to Alter, 20 July 1935; John J. Burke to Karl J. Alter, 10 August 1935, James H. Ryan Papers, ACUA. In the first public announcement of the opening of the school, John

O'Grady in fact claimed that women would be admitted to the school. The rector was furious at this tactic and made O'Grady "repudiate his statement." James Ryan to Karl J. Alter, 12 July 1935, James Hugh Ryan Papers, ACUA.

111. Joseph Moran Corrigan was rector from 1936 until his death in 1942. For accounts of the transition, see Roy J. Deferrari, *Memoirs of the Catholic University of America* (Boston: St. Paul's Daughters, 1962), 419; John Tracy Ellis, *Catholic Bishops, A Memoir* (Wilmington: Michael Glazier, Inc., 1983), 30; and Nuesse, 290.

112. Edith Abbott to John O'Grady, 24 September 1937; and John O'Grady to Joseph Corrigan, 28 September 1937, Rector's File, ACUA.

113. Ibid. It is highly likely that the source of Abbott's information on the CUA situation was John O'Grady himself. After hearing Corrigan's plans, O'Grady immediately began to inform the professional network of the proposal and to orchestrate opposition to it. And he did not need Abbott's reminder about the University of Chicago's generosity to Catholics. His assistant and colleague, Alice Padgett, was one of the beneficiaries. Padgett received her M.A. from the School of Social Administration in 1934, writing a thesis on the origins of the Children's Bureau, and began teaching social casework at Catholic University in 1935.

114. In a private memorandum to the apostolic delegate, Monsignor Amleto Cicognani, Joseph Corrigan attributed O'Grady's attitude toward the NCSSS directly to "a rupture in the relations between [himself] and Monsignor Burke." Corrigan also reviewed O'Grady's relationship with William Kerby: "When Monsignor O'Grady began to work in the [NCCC] under Monsignor Kerby, his tactics were such that Monsignor Kerby, who was a great lover of peace, finally gave up the work and left it to Monsignor O'Grady. . . . I had it from the lips of Monsignor Kerby that he felt it was better to get out of the work because he found Monsignor O'Grady impossible to deal with." Joseph Corrigan, Memorandum #2, 27 August 1937, Rector's Files, ACUA.

3. Inside the Institutions: Foundlings, Orphans, Delinquents

1. Mary Ewens, *The Role of the Nun in Nineteenth Century America* (New York: Arno Press, 1978), 252. Linda Gordon, "Putting Children First: Women, Maternalism, and Welfare in the Early Twentieth Century," in *U.S. History as Women's History: New Feminist Essays,* ed. Linda K. Kerber, Alice Kessler-Harris, and Kathryn Kish Sklar (Chapel Hill: University of North Carolina Press, 1995), 63.

2. Specifically the *Catholic Directory* listed 284 Catholic asylums caring for 53,475 of the 123,000 children in orphanages. Additionally 38 infant asylums or foundling homes received 14,570 babies. One hundred and twenty-three industrial schools trained 20,815 boys and girls [John O'Grady, *Catholic Charities in the United States* (New York: Arno Press, 1971),

148–56]. Fifty-nine congregations established new foundations in the United States between 1870 and 1890 (Ewens, 252). Rev. James Sullivan, C.M., analyzed the *Catholic Directory* statistics at the first annual meeting of the NCCC, *Proceedings of the First National Conference of Catholic Charities* (1910), 285–90. See Peter Romanofsky, "Saving the Lives of the City's Foundlings: The Joint Committee and New York City Child Care Methods, 1860–1907," *New York Historical Society Quarterly* 61 (January–April 1977): 49–68.

3. Sisters in more than forty other congregations cared for another 41,000. Fourteen hundred and twenty-six Sisters of the Good Shepherd cared for 7,036 delinquent and neglected girls in their fifty-eight institutions. Seven orphanages sheltered 973 African-American orphans. The Brothers cared for another 4,900 in their protectories, industrial schools, and orphanages. NCWC Women's Committee 1919 survey of Catholic child-caring institutions in thirteen archdioceses and seventy-seven dioceses, NCWC-USCC, ACUA. The numbers in Catholic orphanages are almost the same in this survey as in the *Official Catholic Directory* of 1919, but the statistics in the *Directory* cannot always be relied upon for accuracy.

4. Mary Oates, "'The Good Sisters': The Work and Position of Catholic Churchwomen in Boston, 1870–1940," in Robert E. Sullivan and James O'Toole, eds., *Catholic Boston: Studies in Religious Community, 1870–1970* (Boston: Roman Catholic Archbishop of Boston, 1985), 191. On the other hand, Archbishop McNicholas tried to protect his institutions from the local solicitations and gambling ordinances. See Joseph Albers to John A. Dempsey, 25 July 1933, Drawer 20, McNicholas Papers, Archives of the Archdiocese of Cincinnati.

5. Canon 500 was the most sweeping in restricting their authority. George C. Stewart, Jr., *Marvels of Charity: History of American Sisters and Nuns* (Huntington, Ind.: Our Sunday Visitor, 1994), 276–77. Ewens traces the application of Canon Law to religious congregations from the Middle Ages and details the difficulties of congregations adapting European constitutions to American conditions and the lines of authority to motherhouse and bishop (Ewens, 14–21, 132–33, 286–88). Mary J. Oates notes the restrictions in *The Catholic Philanthropic Tradition in America* (Bloomington: Indiana University Press, 1995), 87, and details the struggles of sisters in Boston with Cardinal O'Connell over mission in "The Good Sisters," 171–95.

6. Rose J. McHugh, "Some Conclusions from a Series of Studies by the National Catholic Welfare Conference," *Proceedings of the Fifty-sixth National Conference of Social Work* (1929), 128.

7. Stewart provides an overview of the charism, founding, and growth of the religious congregations and orders in America. See also Sister Marie de Lourdes Walsh, *The Sisters of Charity of New York: 1809–1959,* 3 vols. (New York: Fordham University Press, 1960), I:9–11.

8. Jo Ann Kay McNamara, *Sisters in Arms: Catholic Nuns Through Two*

Millennia (Cambridge: Harvard University Press, 1996), 574. For Protestant-Catholic comparison of child-savers, see Maureen Fitzgerald, "Charity, Poverty, and Child Welfare," *Harvard Divinity Bulletin* 25, no. 4 (1996): 12–17.

9. Sr. Mary Brigid Fitzpatrick, C.S.J., "The Sister Social Worker: An Integration of Two Professional Roles," Ph.D. dissertation, University of Notre Dame, 1962, 41. See Ralph C. Hurlin, "Results of an Occupational Census of the Sisterhood in the United States," *Proceedings of the Twentieth National Conference of Catholic Charities* (1934), 369–75.

10. Stewart, 174–80; Christopher J. Kauffman, *Ministry and Meaning: A Religious History of Catholic Health Care in the United States* (New York: Crossroads, 1995), 96–126; McNamara, 577–90.

11. McNamara, 574.

12. Ewens, 14–15. See LeBlond's comment in discussion of James E. Hagerty, "The Relation of Diocesan Charitable and Social Activities to Community Organizations," *Proceedings of the Sixth National Conference of Catholic Charities* (1920), 82–88.

13. Oates, "The Good Sisters," 177, 191. Oates provides a class-ethnic analysis of the women in congregations of Boston. See also her "Organized Voluntarism: The Catholic Sisters in Massachusetts, 1870–1940," in Janet Wilson James, ed., *Women in American Religion* (Philadelphia: University of Pennsylvania Press, 1980). See also Walsh, vol. I, and Mary Ewens, "The Leadership of Nuns in Immigrant Catholicism," in *The American Catholic Religious Life,* ed. Joseph M. White (New York: Garland, 1988), 14–20.

14. Robert Keegan to Hayes, 15 Nov. 1919, Reel 0–2, Patrick J. Hayes Papers, Archives of the Archdiocese of New York, St. Joseph's Seminary, Yonkers, New York (AANY).

15. "Mother Miriam Regina Walsh, 1874–1935," unpublished biography, Archives, Sisters of Charity, Mt. St. Vincent-on-Hudson, Bronx, New York, 619–21.

16. *History of the Conference of Religious of the National Conference of Catholic Charities* (Washington, D.C.: NCCC, 1957), 2–4. Mother Miriam Regina became superior general of the Sisters of Charity of New York in 1932. See biographical file, Archives, Sisters of Charity Center, Mt. St. Vincent-on-Hudson, Bronx, New York. A full profile is in Walsh, II:264–67.

17. Cited by Lisa Lipkin, "The Child I've Left Behind," *New York Times Magazine,* May 19, 1996, 44.

18. Riis' description could be applied to the foundling homes managed by the Catholic laywomen and the Daughters of Charity in Paris in the sixteenth and seventeenth centuries. See Kristin Elizabeth Gager, *Blood Ties and Fictive Ties: Adoption and Family Life in Early Modern France* (Princeton: Princeton University Press, 1996).

19. Walsh, III:71–89. Lipkin, 44–45. Josephine Shaw Lowell, "Report on the Institutions for the Care of Destitute Children of the City of New York," printed from *New York State Board of Charities Annual Report for 1885,*

203. Romanofsky notes the Foundling Asylum received ninety percent of its revenue from New York City (53–59, 68). A glowing account of the Foundling Asylum and Sister Irene in the 1890s is provided in Helen Campbell, *Lights and Shadows of New York Life: A Woman's Story of Gospel, Temperance, Mission, and Rescue Work* (Hartford: A. D. Worthington & Co, 1892), 381–92. See also Maureen Fitzgerald, "'The Perils of Poverty and Passion': Women Religious and the Care of Single Women in New York City, 1845–1890," *U.S. Catholic Historian* 10 (1990): 52–54.

20. O'Grady, 144.

21. Walsh, III:3, 25. For Cleveland see Marian J. Morton, "Fallen Women, Federated Charities, and Maternity Homes, 1913–1973," *Social Service Review* 62 (March 1988): 63.

22. St. Joseph Maternity Home history, RG 107, File 1, Archives of the Sisters of Charity, Mt. St. Joseph, Ohio. Their counterparts in the Florence Crittenton homes and rescue houses were equally protective of the identities of the women they aided. See Regina G. Kunzel, *Fallen Women, Problem Girls: Unmarried Mothers and the Professionalization of Social Work, 1890–1945* (New Haven: Yale University Press, 1993), and Peggy Pascoe, *Relations of Rescue: The Search for Female Moral Authority in the American West, 1874–1939* (New York: Oxford University Press, 1990), 85–110.

23. Robert F. Keegan, "The Problem of Illegitimacy," *Catholic Charities Review* 2 (Nov. 1918): 266–68. Maternalist reformers were also shifting their emphasis from the mother to the child by the 1920s. See Linda Gordon, *"Pitied But Not Entitled": Single Mothers and the History of Welfare, 1890–1935* (New York: Free Press, 1994), 39.

24. Robert F. Keegan, "The Practicable Ideal of Protection and Care for Children Born Out of Wedlock," *Catholic Charities Review* 4 (April 1920): 99–102.

25. Survey by the Women's Committee of the National Catholic War Council in 1919 of child-caring institutions in thirteen archdioceses and seventy-seven dioceses, NCWC, ACUA. The Children's Bureau estimated in 1919 that 32,000 white illegitimate children were born annually.

26. Walsh, III:82, 92. In the New York charities fight, the Foundling Hospital's counsel, Bayard L. Peck, sent a blistering letter to Charles H. Strong detailing the relatively low mortality rate of the institutions. Peck to Strong, 27 Feb. 1917, Tierney-*America* Papers, Georgetown University.

27. Katharine F. Lenroot, "Social Responsibility for the Protection of Children Handicapped by Illegitimate Birth," *Annals of the American Academy of Political and Social Science* 108 (Nov. 1921): 126–28. See Susan Tiffin, *In Whose Best Interest? Child Welfare Reform in the Progressive Era* (Westport, Conn.: Greenwood Press, 1982), 173–83.

28. O'Grady to Archbishop Michael Curley, 15 March 1924, Curley Papers, Archives of the Archdiocese of Baltimore.

29. See Mary C. Tinney, "Illegitimacy," *Proceedings of the Sixth National Conference of Catholic Charities* (1920), 99–110, and M. Madorah Dona-

hue, "A Study of Maternity Homes," *Proceedings of the Tenth National Conference of Catholic Charities* (1924), 357–71. Pascoe provides a comparison on attitudes of Protestant rescuers and their charges (103–10). See also Ruth Reed, *The Illegitimate Family in New York City: Its Treatment by Social and Health Agencies* (New York: Columbia University Press, 1934); Emma O. Lundberg and Katharine F. Lenroot, "Illegitimacy as a Child Welfare Problem, Part I: A Brief Treatment of the Prevalence and Significance of Birth Out of Wedlock, the Child's Status, and the State's Responsibility for Care and Protection," Children's Bureau Publication No. 66 (Washington, D.C.: Government Printing Office, 1920). Kriste A. Lindenmeyer-Dick in " 'A Right to Childhood': A History of the United States Children's Bureau, 1912–1938," Ph.D. dissertation, University of Cincinnati, 1991, provides a fine analysis of the Children's Bureau work in this area and the sensitivity of Julia Lathrop, Grace Abbott, and Katharine Lenroot on the Catholic church's position on birth control.

30. Tinney, "Illegitimacy," 99–110. Tinney, "What Are We Doing with the Unmarried Mother?" *Proceedings of the Ninth National Conference of Catholic Charities* (1923), 284.

31. Pascoe, 166–92.

32. Roselia's had been the target of the "Report of the Joint Commission Appointed to Investigate Certain Conditions alleged to Exist in Charitable Institutions in Western Pennsylvania," no. 5 (March 1, 1915). The legislature dismissed the criticism as unfounded. Tierney-*America* Papers, Georgetown University. See also Sister Daniel Hennefin, C.C., *Daughters of the Church: A Popular History of the Daughters of Charity in the United States, 1809–1987* (Brooklyn: New City Press, 1989), and Barbara Misner, *"Highly Respectable and Accomplished Ladies": Catholic Women Religious in America, 1790–1850* (New York: Garland, 1988).

33. *Pittsburgh Social Survey,* NCWC, ACUA. Roselia's small state appropriation was challenged several times in the 1920s on the question of whether its work was sectarian. Not until 1931 did the Pennsylvania Supreme Court determine that it was a sectarian institution. Until 1930 the city of Pittsburgh paid for the foundling babies and children it sent to Roselia. Roselia did share in the community chest funds. *Mother Seton's Sisters of Charity in Western Pennsylvania,* 139–41.

34. The infant mortality rate in Pittsburgh was 114 per thousand births. Glenn Steele, "Infant Mortality in Pittsburgh," Children's Bureau Publication No. 86 (Washington, D.C.: Government Printing Office, 1921), 6. Children's Bureau statistics cited in Lenroot, "Social Responsibility for the Protection of Children Handicapped by Illegitimate Birth," 124.

35. *Pittsburgh Social Survey,* NCWC-USCC, ACUA.

36. Ibid.

37. Alice Padgett, Study of the Catholic Charities of Cincinnati, NCCC, ACUA.

38. St. Joseph's Home, RG 107, File 1, Archives of the Sisters of Charity, Mt. St. Joseph's, Ohio. Sister Mary Lea Mueller, S.C., "The Social Policies of

Şt. Joseph's Infant Asylum and Maternity Hospital, Cincinnati," M.A. thesis, University of Notre Dame, 1939, provides a good history and analysis of the social policies of St. Joseph's, particularly of two base years, 1915 and 1937, showing the shift from earlier open-door policies. See Kunzel for parallel clashes between institutional staff and social workers at the Crittenton homes.

39. *The Cincinnati Sanitary Bulletin,* July 15, 1926, provides death and death rate figures for the city from 1915 to 1925 (8). The average infant mortality rate for Cincinnati and Hamilton County was seventy-seven per thousand. For comparable data, see *Statistical Report of Infant Mortality for 1924 in 667 Cities of the United States* (New York: American Child Health Association, 1915).

40. Alice Padgett, Study of the Catholic Charities of the Archdiocese of Cincinnati, NCCC, ACUA.

41. Florence L. Sullivan to Rev. John O'Grady, 31 Aug. 1926, O'Grady professional papers, NCCC, ACUA. Sister Mary Lea Mueller, S.C., cited the 1934 State Report on St. Joseph's. Although they had added a social worker for placements and adoptions, the 1934 Ohio Department of Welfare report by social worker Joanne Ortella found the load too heavy for only one worker and recommended additional staff. Yet the Sherill survey, cited by Mueller, found the institution had good medical equipment and provided excellent physical care. In 1937 the infant mortality rate was down to 3.3 percent; there were no maternity deaths (Mueller, 39–64).

42. St. Joseph Infant Asylum, RG 107, File 1, Archives of the Sisters of Charity, Mt. St. Joseph, Ohio. Biographical information on the superiors indicates that most were trained as teachers. The NCCC also surveyed Scranton's Catholic agency and institutions in 1926. See Leslie M. Foy to John O'Grady, 21 May 1926, and "Study of the Catholic Charities of the Diocese of Scranton," Administrative File, NCCC, ACUA.

43. *Report of a Case Study of Our Lady of Victory Women's and Children's Hospital and Our Lady of Victory Infant Home of Lackawanna,* NCCC, ACUA. Killip's case sample was from 1921 through 1925.

44. "Social Policy of Institutions Caring for Unmarried Mothers," *Proceedings of the Ninth National Conference of Catholic Charities* (1923), 283–86. By the 1930s students from twenty-one schools of nursing participated in a twelve-week course at the Foundling Hospital on affiliation (Walsh, 93). See also *Report of the Catholic Charities of the Archdiocese of New York,* 1926, NCCC, ACUA. Tinney, "Illegitimacy," 103.

45. McHugh, while commending the good health care provided by the institution, cited the need to decrease the institutional mortality rates, "Survey of the New York Foundling Hospital," 79–84, 129, NCCC, ACUA. The full report filled twelve volumes. Minutes of the Board of Trustees, Catholic Charities of the Archdiocese of New York (hereafter, CCANY), 16 December 1927.

46. Ibid., 7.

47. Ibid., 5. She was particularly referring to the Boarding Out and Placing Out Departments. Significant changes were instituted following McHugh's report. In 1930 a Social Service Department was created. See Walsh, III:93–94.

48. Four received their M.S.W. degree between 1924 and 1930 and another 36 between 1931 and 1940. Thirty of them earned degrees at Catholic University; the others at Fordham and St. Louis University. Fitzpatrick, 51.

49. Special Meeting on Maternity Homes, *Proceedings of the Tenth National Conference of Catholic Charities* (1924), 373.

50. Bryan J. McEntegart to John O'Grady, 19 June 1942, NCCC, ACUA.

51. Donahue, 357–72. See also Morton, 68.

52. Diocesan charities were developing foster home programs, particularly in the Midwest. Alice Padgett to Maud Morlock, Children's Bureau, 26 May 1938, NCCC, RG 76, ACUA. Attached was a list of forty-nine Catholic infant and maternity homes.

53. *Proceedings of the Twenty-fifth National Conference of Catholic Charities* (1939), 143–69. Sister Mary Eileen, C.S.A., had completed her Master's thesis at the Catholic University of America in 1926 on "An Interpretation of the Records of 200 Mothers and Children Under the Care of the Saint Ann Maternity Home, Cleveland, Ohio." Morton offers a fine comparative study of the four maternity homes in Cleveland and their relationship to the Federation for Charity and Philanthropy. She argues that though the homes generally endorsed national standards, their practices lagged behind. What remained unchanged, however, was the homes' mission of moral reinstatement and spiritual reclamation. In 1952 the director of Catholic Charities urged greater publicity for Loretta House so that "more Catholic girls might be directed to our institution instead of to the non-Catholic homes" (Morton, 61–82).

54. O'Grady, 85–86. See Susan Scharlotte Walton, "To Preserve the Faith: Catholic Charities in Boston, 1870 to 1930," Ph.D. dissertation, Boston University, 1983, 80. See also Francis Lane, *American Charities and the Child of the Immigrant: A Study of Typical Child Caring Institutions in New York and Massachusetts Between the Years 1845 and 1880* (Washington: Catholic University of America Press, 1932), 117, 120–21; Susan Whitelaw Downs and Michael W. Sherraden, "The Orphan Asylum in the Nineteenth Century," *Social Service Review* 57 (June 1983): 273–90.

55. O'Grady, 21–31, 72. To support themselves, the Sisters of Charity adopted the three-institutional approach to survival. They tried to establish a "paying" school to support a free school and an orphanage.

56. Catherine J. Ross, "Society's Children: The Care of Indigent Youngsters in New York City, 1875–1903," Ph.D. dissertation, Yale University, 1977, 63–69.

57. See Hyman Bogen, *The Luckiest Orphans: A History of the Hebrew Orphan Asylum of New York* (Urbana: University of Illinois Press, 1992). In Baltimore the Dolan Aid orphanage was an exception and had forty-four

children in 1889–1890. Nurith Zmora, *Orphanages Reconsidered: Child Care Institutions in Progressive Era Baltimore* (Philadelphia: Temple University Press, 1994).

58. Fitzgerald, "'The Perils of Poverty and Passion,'" 54; Lowell, 175–229. LeRoy Ashby, *Saving the Waifs: Reformers and Dependent Children, 1890–1917* (Philadelphia: Temple University Press, 1984) analyzes the Protestant orphanages of the National Benevolent Association.

59. O'Grady, 152–55, 160–62. See also Mary F. Godley, "The Program for Catholic Child-Caring Homes, Its Meaning and Significance," *Proceedings of the Ninth National Conference of Catholic Charities* (1923), 111–12. The Women's Committee of the National Catholic War Council conducted a major survey of numbers of staff and boys and girls in each institution in 1919, Women's Committee, NCWC-USCC, ACUA. Chicago's efforts in meeting the flow of immigrants in the diocesan or parish orphanages is briefly detailed in Edward R. Kantowicz, *Corporation Sole: Cardinal Mundelein and Chicago Catholicism* (Notre Dame: University of Notre Dame Press, 1983), chap. 9. For a comparison of Jewish orphanages, see Reena Sigman Friedman, *These Are our Children: Jewish Orphanages in the United States, 1880–1925* (Hanover: Brandeis University Press, 1994). Jewish administrators faced the same criticisms from public and Jewish social workers.

60. This $255,000 was raised in spite of major strikes in the coal industry and at the Westinghouse plant and riots by railroad workers. *Memoirs of the Pittsburgh Sisters of Mercy* (New York: Devin-Adair, 1918), 36. St. Paul's had added a one-hundred-bed hospital in 1911. Sister M. Jerome McHale, R.S.M., *On the Wing: The Story of the Pittsburgh Sisters of Mercy, 1843–1968* (New York: Seabury Press, 1986), 193–94.

61. *Pittsburgh Social Survey,* NCWC-USCC, ACUA.

62. Ibid.

63. Ibid.

64. Ibid.

65. Kennedy particularly worried that there were no fire drills and, with the crowded conditions, feared panic.

66. To a complaint on skin disease, the sister replied that she "couldn't help it with so many children" (Ibid.). "Herd" skin and eye diseases were constant threats in the large institutions.

67. Ibid.

68. Ibid.

69. Ibid.

70. Ibid. Kennedy reported that St. Michael's Orphan Asylum maintained by the Germans of St. Michael's parish, with only forty-one boys and girls in residence, was generally well run and the children "unrepressed."

71. *Pittsburgh Social Survey,* NCWC, ACUA. A social worker who surveyed placements of St. Paul's, Grace M. Buxton, later wrote a brief history of the orphanage, *They Lived and Loved at St. Paul's Orphanage* in 1968. The

new superintendent, Rev. Henry J. Gilbert, became the first secretary of the Pennsylvania Superintendents of Institutions for Children. The alumni association established at St. Paul's was singled out for special praise by Rev. John M. Cooper as the "finest piece of after care work he had encountered." The Buxton text offers many individual success stories to pair with the tragedies reported by Kennedy; she is as lyrical as Kennedy is critical. See also Sister M. Canice Dolan, R.S.M., "St. Paul's Orphanage: An Historical Study of a Private Sectarian, Child-Caring Institution, Pittsburgh, 1836–1962," M.S.W. thesis, Fordham University, 1963. The Archives of the Sisters of Mercy, Carlow College, Pittsburgh, contains a 1952 survey of St. Paul's by Alice May, a consultant from the Baltimore Catholic Charities. See also John A. Lapp to John Burke, 24 Nov. 1925, Lapp correspondence, Files of the General Secretary, NCWC/USCC, ACUA Archives. By the 1960s 74 percent of the children at St. Paul's were assigned and under the supervision of the courts. After a survey requested of the Child Welfare League and assessing costs, Bishop Wright closed St. Paul's in 1965 (McHale, 198–99).

72. Godley, 111.
73. Conference of Religious, National Conference of Catholic Charities, Report of the Committee on Standards, *A Program for Catholic Childcaring Homes* (Washington: Catholic University of America, 1923); Godley, 114.
74. Godley, 114–15.
75. C. H. LeBlond, "A Complete Program for Catholic Child Care," *Proceedings of the Ninth National Conference of Catholic Charities* (1923), 136.
76. Ibid., 141. Alice Padgett observed in her 1926 report on the Catholic Charities of Cincinnati that "submission" to the director of the Bureau of Catholic Charities that was "not based on genuine conviction will not make for real progress." NCCC, ACUA.
77. "Religious Communities a Progressive Force," *Catholic Charities Review* 11 (Oct. 1927): 312.
78. Walsh, III:117.
79. Sister Miriam Regina, S.C., "Recent Progress in Catholic Child-Care," *Proceedings of the Thirteenth National Conference of Catholic Charities* (1927), 341–43. Walsh, III:117.
80. Ibid., 347.
81. John T. Gillard, S.S.J., *The Catholic Church and the Negro* (Baltimore: St. Joseph's Society Press, 1929), 48–49, 199–201. Curley to Leonard, 18 Nov. 1935, and 7 May 1936, Curley Papers, Archives of the Archdiocese of Baltimore. See also Cyprian Davis, O.S.B., *The History of Black Catholics in the United States* (New York: Crossroad, 1991), and Oates, *The Catholic Philanthropic Tradition in America*, 62–70.
82. Correspondence on the Commonwealth Fund support is in the Mother Miriam Regina Files, Archives, Sisters of Charity Center, Mount St. Vincent-on-Hudson, Bronx, New York. John O'Grady writing to Rev. Robert F. Keegan, 21 July 1926, noted that having the study under the auspices of

the Sisters' Conference "will raise fewer questions than to have the study made under the direction of the Conference as a whole." NCCC, ACUA.

83. John M. Cooper, "The National Study of Catholic Children's Homes," *Proceedings of the Fourteenth National Conference of Catholic Charities* (1928), 240–46. See Karl J. Alter, "The Study of Children's Institutions— What Shall We Do with It?" *Proceedings of the Fifteenth National Conference of Catholic Charities* (1929), 128–33.

84. Mary Irene Atkinson, Superintendent, Ohio State Department of Public Welfare, "Children's Institutions," *Catholic Charities Review* 15 (Nov. 1931): 299–301. It was immediately added to the Five Foot Shelf, a collection of recommended texts for social workers when it was published in 1931.

85. John M. Cooper, *Children's Institutions* (Washington: Catholic University of America Press, 1931), 43, 50.

86. Ibid., 97–98, 103–4, 112–13.

87. Ibid., 119–21, 136–37.

88. Ibid., 151–56.

89. Ibid., 176–78.

90. Ibid., 459–77.

91. Ibid., 559–88, 671.

92. Ibid., 592.

93. Ibid., 622–31.

94. Ibid., 611–18.

95. John M. Cooper, "The Study of Children's Institutions—Report and Comment," *Proceedings of the Fifteenth National Conference of Catholic Charities* (1929), 125. See Rev. Joseph Haley, "Diocesan Organizations of Catholic Charities and Religious Communities," *Proceedings of the Fourteenth National Conference of Catholic Charities* (1928), 379–84, for an instance of the work still to be done in working out relationships between diocesan bureaus and religious communities.

96. *Official Catholic Directory,* 1910–1955. From 1910 through 1929, the *Directory* reported an average of 48,000 children in Catholic orphanages. In 1945 the numbers again rose to 48,329, reflecting war conditions and a paucity of day-care facilities. By 1955 the totals were down to 36,147 children in 328 institutions.

97. The Arizona trip resulted in a spectacular court case, *Foundling Home* v. *Arizona,* 1904. See transcript of Sister of Charity testimony, Tierney-*America* Papers, Georgetown University. Walsh, III:81–89; Elizabeth McKeown and Dorothy M. Brown, "Saving New York's Children," *U.S. Catholic Historian* 13 (summer 1995): 89–95. The Foundling Asylum eventually found it impossible to develop good long-distance after-care and finally limited their placements to New York and the surrounding states. For comparisons see Rev. Hastings H. Hart, "Placing Out Children in the West," in Robert H. Bremner, ed., *Care of Dependent Children in the Late Nineteenth and Early Twentieth Centuries* (New York: Arno, 1974), 171–

77, and Hastings H. Hart, *Preventive Treatment of Neglected Children. Correction & Prevention*, vol. 4 in *Poverty, USA: The Historical Record*, ed. David J. Rothman (New York: Arno, 1971), 221–22.

98. Cited in Hart, *Preventive Treatment of Neglected Children*, 171–72, 221–22. Hart estimated that in the first decade of the century, approximately 1,400 children were placed each year by Roman Catholic agencies in New York City.

99. John Cardinal Farley to Rev. and dear Father, 7 Feb. 1917, Tierney-*America* Papers, Georgetown University. Monsignor Shahan cited as a source of "leakage in the Catholic Church" the "non-Catholic character of a multitude of the homes in which the little children were placed." *Proceedings of the Second National Conference of Catholic Charities* (1912), 291. McEntegart, "Recent Developments in Child Placing," *Proceedings of the Ninth National Conference of Catholic Charities* (1923), 157–58.

100. Ibid., 158–59. Cardinal Farley was worried about a "when practical" clause in the New York City Charter, Chapter 13, Section 664, arguing it provided a defense for "secret enemies of our faith. We must not allow our children to be smuggled out of the Church in this manner." See Farley letter, 7 Feb. 1917. In New York state, if an agency did not make a placement with a family of the same religion, it had to provide a reason for such an exception. In Massachusetts the State Board of Charity Minor Ward department, since 1882, placed children not in institutions but in foster homes. Rev. Michael J. Scanlan, "Child Placing in Massachusetts," *Catholic Charities Review* 1 (Sept. 1917): 200–203. See also Winifred A. Keneran, "Child Guardianship in Boston," *Proceedings of the Eighth National Conference of Catholic Charities* (1922), 158–59.

101. These New York and Massachusetts child welfare laws were only two instances of a state-by-state review of the laws and practices in place to protect children. By 1921 Children's Code Commissions were at work in twenty states. Catholics clearly favored the New York idea that a state functioned best when public and private assistance supplemented each other. Mary C. Tinney, "Children's Code Commissions," *Proceedings of the Seventh National Conference of Catholic Charities* (1921), 66–71; McEntegart, "Religious Standards for Family Homes of Children under Public Care," 155.

102. Mary Tinney, "An Interpretation of Three Thousand Placements by the New York Catholic Home Bureau," *Proceedings of the Fourth National Conference of Catholic Charities* (1916), 181–83.

103. Ibid., 184–85.

104. Walton, "To Preserve the Faith," 92–94.

105. Catholic Charities Folder, Archives of the Pittsburgh Diocese. See also *Proceedings of the Second National Conference of Catholic Charities* (1912), 255–57.

106. Ibid., 82–83. Cincinnati used the same approach, publishing a notice in *The Service Call*, the monthly bulletin of the Catholic Charities League, August 1921, that its children's institutions were filled to capacity.

107. Rev. Joseph Kroha, *Proceedings of the Seventh National Conference of Catholic Charities* (1921), 77–79.

108. Ibid., 78–79.

109. Only one family, visited by social worker M. G. Buston, was cited as giving "evidence of success above average in family of workers." Their home was beautifully furnished; the rooms in "1st class condition." *Pittsburgh Social Survey,* NCWC-USCC, ACUA.

110. Ibid.

111. Ibid.

112. J.F.R. Corcoran, "How Can We Find Good Catholic Boarding Homes?" *Proceedings of the Tenth National Conference of Catholic Charities* (1924), 157–58; John O'Grady to Bryan J. McEntegart, 11 April 1924, NCCC, ACUA. Even McEntegart, however, still raised the question of the motive of the boarding mother at the 1924 NCCC meeting, asking "Is it love for children and a desire to care for them or is it a desire to supplement income?" The New York Foundling Hospital had 581 licensed boarding homes in that same year. *Catholic Charities Review,* November 1929, reported that the Los Angeles Catholic Charities had 119 foster boarding homes. The agency paid a standard monthly rate of $25.00 for each child, though in the case of problem children the payment rose to $30 or $35.

113. *Report of the Catholic Charities of the Archdiocese of New York* (1926), 40–41.

114. U.S. Department of Commerce, Bureau of the Census, *Children Under Institutional Care,* 1923 (Washington, D.C.: Government Printing Office, 1927): 100.

115. Sister Cyrilla is given a more favorable hearing in Walsh, III:96.

116. Ibid., 4–5.

117. "Children's Bureau," *Pittsburgh Social Survey;* U.S. Department of Labor, Children's Bureau; Hastings Hart et al., *Foster Home Care for Dependent Children,* Bureau Publication No. 136 (Washington, D.C.: Government Printing Office, 1924): 36; *Report of the Bureau of Catholic Charities of the Archdiocese of Cincinnati* (1919), 6.

118. For Pittsburgh, see John J. O'Connor, Jr., "Recreation and its Relation to Delinquency," *Proceedings of the Sixth National Conference of Catholic Charities* (1920), 313, and Rev. Cassian Hartl, *Proceedings of the Third National Conference of Catholic Charities* (1914), 259; for Cleveland, M. P. Mooney, "The Scope of Probation," *Proceedings of the Third National Conference of Catholic Charities* (1914), 234–39; for Milwaukee, Steven Schlossman, *Love and the American Delinquent: The Theory and Practice of "Progressive" Juvenile Justice, 1825–1920* (Chicago: University of Chicago Press, 1977), 144; for New York, Franklin C. Hoyt, "Procedure of the Manhattan Children's Court of the City of New York," in Hart, *Foster Home Care for Dependent Children,* 328–32.

119. William I. Thomas, *The Unadjusted Girl* (Montclair, N.J.: Patterson Smith, 1960 [1923]), 290.

120. In 1910 the Protectory cared for 3,000 ("The New York Catholic Protec-

tory: A Sketch," NCCC, ACUA). The Protectory still cared for 1,599 boys in 1938 ("Seventy-sixth Annual Report of the New York Catholic Protectory," 1 January 1938–31 December 1938). Rev. M. J. Scanlan, "Our Industrial Schools for Delinquents and What They Accomplish," *Catholic Charities Review* 1 (Dec. 1917): 51–52. In Baltimore in 1915, three Catholic reformatories cared for 435 delinquents committed by the courts. Catholic African-Americans were not admitted and went to the House of Reformation for Colored Boys. M. Mercedes Murray, "The Child in the Reformatory," *Proceedings of the Fourth National Conference of Catholic Charities* (1916), 107–11.

121. Mary E. Odem, *Delinquent Daughters: Protecting and Policing Adolescent Female Sexuality in the United States, 1885–1920* (Chapel Hill: University of North Carolina Press, 1995), 148. Odem notes that in Los Angeles the House of the Good Shepherd received 30 percent of the institutional cases from the juvenile court. In 1920 the court placed 44 percent of its institutional cases with the House of the Good Shepherd, the Florence Crittenton Home, and the True Love Home for unmarried women.

122. O'Grady, 172–74. Katherine E. Conway, *In the Footprints of the Good Shepherd, New York, 1857–1907* (New York: Convent of the Good Shepherd, 1907), vi; Fitzgerald, "'The Perils of Poverty and Passion,'" 49–50; George Paul Jacoby, *Catholic Child Care in Nineteenth Century New York* (Washington: The Catholic University of America, 1941), 198–202. Although this section focuses on the rehabilitation of girls, the industrial schools for boys also provided for Catholic delinquents. Three of the most famous were the New York Catholic Protectory, the St. Mary's Industrial School of Baltimore (home of Babe Ruth), and Father Flanagan's BoysTown. See Brother Henry, "Industrial Schools," *Proceedings of the First National Conference of Catholic Charities* (1910), 306–10; "The New York Catholic Protectory, A Sketch," "Seventy-Sixth Annual Report of the New York Catholic Protectory," 1 January 1938–31 December 1938; and Scanlan, "Our Industrial Schools for Delinquents and What They Accomplish," 51–52. For statistics on African-Americans in the houses, see Gillard, 202.

123. There were two Good Shepherd orders, which differed not in their mission but in their organization (O'Grady, 172–74).

124. Sister Mary of St. Theresita, R.S.G., *The Social Work of the Sisters of the Good Shepherd* (Cleveland: Cadillac Press, 1938): 9–11.

125. When Mabel Ruth Fernald sought to include fifty cases from the Good Shepherds in her study of women delinquents in New York in 1920, the sisters refused to subject their residents "to scrutiny relative to their past." Mabel Ruth Fernald et al., *A Study of Women Delinquents in New York State* (New York: The Century Co., 1920), 19. Fernald particularly wanted the Good Shepherd's cooperation because it had more cases of older women and those convicted of alcohol-related crimes. Of the 552 cases she investigated in state institutions, 40 percent were Catholic.

126. Sister Mary of St. Theresita, 86. Odem provides a good comparison with Protestant women reformers' attitudes toward fallen women, victims, and the environment as well as Anglo and ethnic concern over protecting the chastity of working women.
127. Ibid., 93–95; Pascoe, 80. Pascoe notes that the Protestant matrons of rescue homes in the West also prepared their clients for domestic service.
128. Pascoe, 99.
129. Joan Ward Mullaney, "Fifteen Treatment Programs Provided by the Sisters of the Good Shepherd in the New York Province with Particular Reference to the Teachings of Mother Euphrasia," D.S.W. dissertation, Catholic University of America, 1963, 38.
130. Conway, 31.
131. "Programs of Catholic Training Schools for Girls," *Catholic Charities Review* 9 (June 1925): 221–24.
132. Leslie Foy to John O'Grady, 31 May 1929, NCCC, ACUA.
133. Kennedy reported that between December 1, 1918, and December 1, 1919, Troy Hill had admitted sixty-five from morals court, eleven from juvenile court, and forty-six from parents (Conway, 24–25, 100–115, 204–5). There were approximately 3,000 Magdalenes in 1938 (Sister Mary of St. Theresita, 129).
134. Report on the Home of the Good Shepherd, Troy Hill, *Pittsburgh Social Survey*, NCWC-USCC, ACUA.
135. Ibid.; see also Sister Mary of St. Theresita, 295.
136. Reformer Miriam van Waters decried "an institutional plant, heavy as a locomotive set on a track and capable of running in only one direction." Miriam van Waters, "Where Girls Go Right: Some Dynamic Aspects of State Correctional Schools for Girls and Young Women," *Survey* (May 27, 1922): 361–76. Margaret Reeves, a field agent for the Russell Sage Foundation, also commended cottage plans in her 1929 study, *Training Schools for Delinquent Girls* (New York: Russell Sage Foundation, 1928). Neither included the houses of the Good Shepherd in their assessments (Odem, 118).
137. "Programs of Catholic Training Schools for Girls," *Catholic Charities Review* 9 (March, April, May, June 1925).
138. Ibid.; see Emma Quinlan, "Cases Cared for by the Chicago Juvenile Court and the House of the Good Shepherd," *Catholic Charities Review* 9 (June 1925): 208–13. Between 1915 and 1919, the Chicago juvenile court committed 660 girls and young women to the House of the Good Shepherd, almost half the total handled by the court. The city paid forty cents per diem for each girl committed [Helen Rankin Jeter, "The Chicago Juvenile Court," United States Children's Bureau Publication No. 104 (Washington, D.C.: Government Printing Office, 1922), 88]. For an account of the casework at admission and after-care at the House of the Good Shepherd in St. Louis, see St. Louis Survey, NCCC, ACUA.
139. Sister Mary of St. Anthony Norris, *The Annals of the Good Shepherd,*

Philadelphia, 1859–1925 (Philadelphia: Sisters of the Good Shepherd), 264–66.

140. Ibid., 266–67; Sister Mary of St. Anthony, 123, 231–32.

141. Sister Mary of St. Theresita, foreword, 10; Mullaney, 38.

142. George Q. Flynn, *American Catholic Charities and the Roosevelt Presidency, 1932–1936* (Lexington: University of Kentucky Press, 1968), 78–102; David J. O'Brien, *American Catholics and Social Reform: The New Deal Years* (New York: Oxford University Press, 1968), 52–53. See the support of NCWC's John A. Ryan, "Economics and Ethics," *Proceedings of the Nineteenth National Conference of Catholic Charities* (1933), 57–72. Editorials, *Catholic Charities Review* 17 (June, September, November 1933): 163–65, 193–94, 285–86.

143. Both the NCCC and the NCWC rushed to defend the sisters, creating a brief confusion over who should "speak for" the church. On the one hand, the industrial and labor issues came under the purview of the NCWC; on the other hand, the institutions of the Good Shepherd were involved in rehabilitation and charity, the domain of the NCCC. When the assistant general secretary of the NCWC sent a letter to the bishops asking their help in obtaining information from the Good Shepherd superiors for the Cotton Garment Code Authority, he faced the wrath of Marcellus Wagner, president of the NCCC, for interference in the business of diocesan charities (Thomas W. Tifft, "Toward a More Humane Social Policy: The Work and Influence of Monsignor John O'Grady," Ph.D. dissertation, Catholic University of America, 1979, 120–29).

144. Sister Mary of St. Stanislaus, Baltimore, to O'Grady, 16 Nov. 1934, and the Sisters of the Good Shepherd, Hot Springs, to O'Grady, 18 Nov. 1934, NCCC, ACUA Archives. O'Grady subsequently wrote to them urging compliance through the pledge and responding to the questionnaire. On 28 Nov. 1934, O'Grady wrote to Edwin L. Leonard, Bureau of Catholic Charities, Baltimore, apprising him that the Baltimore Province was the only one in the country that was refusing to cooperate with the National Sheltered Workshop Committee and warning that if they remained recalcitrant they would have to meet the standards set by the laundry and cotton code authorities. See O'Grady to J. Clarke Murphy, 9 Jan. 1935. NCCC, ACUA.

145. Sister Mary of St. Stanislaus, Peoria, to O'Grady, 25 Sept. 1934; Sister M. Visitation to O'Grady, Denver, 2 Jan. 1934; Sister Mary of St. Lawrence, 3, 19 March, 24 Sept. 1934. Correspondence between L. T. Dwyer of McLaughlin Manufacturing Company, Kokomo, Ind., and O'Grady in July and August 1934 indicates O'Grady's concern with fair pricing. Union pressure is exemplified by correspondence between G. F. Weizenecker of the Laundry & Linen Supply Drivers, Cincinnati, to O'Grady seeking his help in getting the Sisters of the Good Shepherd to pay union wages for the driver at their Price Hill Laundry, 9, 30 Aug. 1935. See John O'Grady to Sisters, 12 March 1935; Msgr. M. J. Lavelle to Msgr. Robert F. Keegan, 22

March 1935; Robert F. Keegan to Lavelle, 25 March 1935. O'Grady also wrote to diocesan directors asking consideration of orphanages and other institutions using the Good Shepherd's work, O'Grady to Ralph Glover, 20 July 1934, NCCC, ACUA. Tifft, 129. Rose K. Golden, "Recent Trends— Present Program of Institutional Care Under the Good Shepherd Sisters," *Proceedings of the Twenty-fourth National Conference of Catholic Charities* (1938), 277–79, sets out improvements in vocational programs and placement. Minutes of the Meeting of Executive Committee, NCCC, 17 May 1935, NCCC, ACUA.

4. Outside the Institutions: Pensions, Precaution, Prevention

1. *Proceedings of the Conference on the Care of Dependent Children held at Washington, D.C., January 25, 26, 1909* (Washington, D.C.: Government Printing Office, 1909), 9–10.
2. Mary C. Tinney, "Remarks on Adequate and Inadequate Relief," Bureau, *Proceedings of the Fourth National Conference of Catholic Charities* (1916), 141.
3. Gwendolyn Mink provides a useful synthesis of the "maternalists'" arguments for mothers' pensions. Gwendolyn Mink, *The Wages of Motherhood: Inequality in the Welfare State, 1917–1942* (Ithaca: Cornell University Press, 1995), 3–53.
4. *Delineator* cited in Theda Skocpol, *Protecting Soldiers and Mothers: The Political Origins of Social Policy in the United States* (Cambridge: Harvard University Press, 1992), 442–45. Hubert LeBlond, *Proceedings of the Third National Conference of Catholic Charities* (1914), 154–56.
5. In recent years there has been an explosion of studies on mothers' pensions and major controversies involving the issues of gender, class, social control, and state polity. See Skocpol; Linda Gordon, *Pitied But Not Entitled: Single Mothers and the History of Welfare, 1890–1935* (New York: Free Press, 1994); Seth Koven and Sonya Michel, *Mothers of a New World: Maternalist Politics and the Origins of the Welfare State* (New York: Routledge, 1993); Molly Ladd-Taylor, *Mother-Work: Women, Child Welfare, and the State, 1890–1930* (Chicago: University of Illinois Press, 1994); and Mink. Several recent dissertations deal with the issue: Joanne L. Goodwin, "Gender Politics and Welfare Reform: Mothers' Pensions in Chicago, 1900–1930," Ph.D. dissertation, University of Michigan, 1991; Libba Gage Moore, "Mothers' Pensions: The Origins of the Relationship Between Women and the Welfare State," Ph.D. dissertation, University of Massachusetts, 1986; Kriste A. Lindenmeyer-Dick, "'A Right to Childhood': A History of the United States Children's Bureau, 1912–1938," Ph.D. dissertation, University of Cincinnati, 1991. See also Grace Abbott, *From Relief to Social Security: The Development of the New Public Welfare Services and Their Administration* (New York: Russell & Russell, 1966).
6. *Record-Herald,* 26 November 1911, and Commissioner Peter Bartzen cited

by Goodwin, 180–81. See also C. C. Carstens, "Public Pensions to Widows with Children: A Study of the Administration in Several Cities," in *Security and Services for Children*, ed. Robert H. Bremner (New York: Arno Press, 1974), 5–36, and Ladd-Taylor, 144–60.

7. Mary E. Shinnick, "Pensioning of Widows," *Proceedings of the Second National Conference of Catholic Charities* (1912), 122–23. See also the comments of Robert Biggs of Baltimore and the overview of David Tilley of mothers' pension legislation in the *Proceedings of the Second National Conference of Catholic Charities* (1912), 278–81, 129–34, 144–49.

8. Lenora Z. Meder, "The Utilization of Municipal Agencies in Relief Work," *Proceedings of the Third National Conference of Catholic Charities* (1914), 273–77. Goodwin points out that "Private agencies and individuals shaped the contours of the policy on mothers' pensions through their role on the citizen's committee" (Goodwin, 188–93).

9. Goodwin, 207, 212, 292; and Goodwin, "An American Experiment in Paid Motherhood: The Implementation of Mothers' Pensions in Early Twentieth Century Chicago," *Gender and History* 4 (autumn 1992): 324–42. Ladd-Taylor in *Mother-Work* (152–56) provides a case study of a Lithuanian widow and the problems of negotiating the new system for her five children.

10. Bogue surveyed ten localities for the Children's Bureau on mothers' pensions in 1927 and found inadequate funding and inadequate administrative staffs. See Bogue, "Ten Years of Mothers' Pensions," *Survey* 49 (Feb. 15, 1923): 633–37.

11. (Mrs.) J. M. Molamphy, *Proceedings of the Third National Conference of Catholic Charities* (1914), 153–54. Her experience paralleled that of other Catholic women on pension boards in Portland, Kansas City, and New York.

12. New York State, *Report of the Commission on Relief for Widowed Mothers*, 1914, in Robert H. Bremner, ed., *Children and Youth in America: A Documentary History*, 2 vols. (Cambridge: Harvard University Press, 1971), II:379–84. "First Annual Report of the Board of Child Welfare of the City of New York," 1 October 1915 to 1 October 1916. Katherine M. Dinan of the AICP reported spending $150,000 yearly and questioned whether the state should add this burden as it already was not meeting its obligations to care for the tubercular, sick, and aged. *Proceedings of the Third National Conference of Catholic Charities* (1914), 134–40, 149–51. New York State, *Report of the Commission on Relief for Widowed Mothers*, 1914, cited in Bremner, *Children and Youth in America*, II:380. The Report was also critical of the opposition of Russell Sage. In keeping with the New York State Board of Charities' tradition of volunteer commissioners, New York's mothers' pensions would be administered by volunteer commissioners appointed by the governor. For a summary of the major arguments of the opposition, see Mary E. Richmond, "Motherhood and Pensions," *Survey* 29 (March 1, 1913) cited in Edna O. Bullock, *Selected Articles in Mothers' Pensions* (White Plains, N.Y.: H.W. Wilson and Co., 1950), 58–72.

13. James E. Dougherty and Thomas W. Hines of the St. Vincent de Paul Society of the Bronx and Brooklyn testified before a Hebbard subcommittee, 22 Jan. 1914, on the need for public funding. Transcript of Hearing, Folder 32, Roll 4, Commission on the Relief for Widowed Mothers, New York State Archives, Albany.

14. For Devine's opposition and a compendium of other contemporary reservations, see Bullock. *Proceedings of the Third National Conference of Catholic Charities* (1914), 154–56.

15. *Survey* 32 (April 4, 1914); "First Annual Report of the Board of Child Welfare of the City of New York," 1 October 1915 to 1 October 1916. The AICP had supported pensions and argued for professional administration.

16. *Survey* 14 (April 3, 1915) cited in Bullock, 57.

17. Emma O. Lundberg, "Aid to Mothers with Dependent Children," *Annals of the American Academy of Political and Social Science* 98 (Nov. 1921): 97–105.

18. Ada Ruth Burns, Secretary, Erie County Child Welfare Board, "Family Life and Mothers' Allowances," *Ninth National Conference of Catholic Charities* (1923), 223–28; Monica C. Keating, Exec. Secretary, Ramsey County Child Welfare Board, St. Paul, "Standards and Tendencies in the Mothers' Allowance Movement in Minnesota"; and Charles J. Tobin, Board of Child Welfare, Albany County, "Standards and Tendencies in the Mothers' Allowance Movement in the State of New York," *Tenth National Conference of Catholic Charities* (1924), 147–54. At the same session, Rev. Robert P. Barry of Boston's Catholic Charitable Bureau presented a "Report on Massachusetts Mothers' Aid Law," 155–57.

19. Burns, 225.

20. Mink, 53–73.

21. Richard A. Meckel, *Save the Babies: American Public Health Reform and the Prevention of Infant Mortality, 1850–1929* (Baltimore: Johns Hopkins University Press, 1990), 214–15; Ladd-Taylor, *Mother-Work*, 188; Robyn Muncy, *Creating a Female Dominion in American Reform, 1890–1935* (New York: Oxford University Press, 1991), 105; "Maternity and Infancy Act," *Catholic Charities Review* 8 (Dec. 1924): 358–59; U.S. Congress, House Committee on Interstate and Foreign Commerce, *On the Extension of Public Protection of Maternity and Infancy. Hearings Before the Committee on Interstate and Foreign Commerce on HR 7555*, 69th Cong., 1st sess., 1926, 23. The opposition of much of the Catholic hierarchy, including O'Connell, was clear on the Child Labor Amendment of 1924 and efforts in the 1930s. See Thomas R. Greene, "The Catholic Committee for the Ratification of the Child Labor Amendment, 1935–1937: Origin and Limits," *Catholic Historical Review* 54 (April 1988): 248–69.

22. The Sisters of Charity opened the first Catholic Day Nursery in New York in 1887. *Proceedings of the First National Conference of Catholic Charities* (1910), 335; Marguerite T. Boylan, "The Catholic Charitable Bureau of Bridgeport," *Catholic Charities Review* 6 (May 1919): 152. Sheila M.

Rothman points out that the number of licensed centers declined from 695 in 1916 to 600 in 1925. Rothman, "Other People's Children: The Day Care Experience in America," *The Public Interest* (winter 1973): 11–19.

23. Ethyll M. Dooley, "The Day Nursery as a Social Agency," *Proceedings of the Ninth National Conference of Catholic Charities* (1923), 127; Alice E. Padgett, "Horizon Lines in the Day Nursery Situation," *Catholic Charities Review* 10 (Nov. 1927): 331.

24. Dooley, 127–28.

25. *Proceedings of the First National Conference of Catholic Charities* (1910), 337, 341. Mrs. Kelley reported that New York City needed hundreds of additional centers.

26. *Report of Catholic Charities of the Archdiocese of New York, 1922* and 1926. St. Benedict's Nursery in Harlem opened in 1923. Gillard lists only three Catholic day nurseries for African-Americans in 1929; the other two were in Baltimore and Milwaukee [John T. Gillard, S.S.J., *The Catholic Church and the Negro* (Baltimore: St. Joseph's Society Press, 1929), 198].

27. Sister M. Gertrude, "A Population Study of Catholic Day Nurseries," *Proceedings of the Twelfth National Conference of Catholic Charities* (1926), 390–401.

28. Dooley, 133–34.

29. Ibid., 133.

30. Ibid. See Mother Marie Gertrude, "A Changing Day Nursery," *Catholic Charities Review* 19 (Dec. 1935): 321–23. Mother Marie Gertrude reported on the Divine Providence nursery's response to a changing neighborhood by contracting its day nursery work while directing its services to the clerical workers through lunch programs, recreation, and spiritual centers.

31. Rev. John M. Cooper, "The School and Social Work," *Proceedings of the Ninth National Conference of Catholic Charities* (1923), 69–70; John M. Cooper, "The School as a Preventive Agency in Juvenile Delinquency," *Proceedings of the Twelfth National Conference of Catholic Charities* (1926), 149–54. Cooper reported little progress. Only one or two of the more than fifty diocesan bureaus had followed his advice. However at the 1937 NCCC meeting, Sister Isabelle, O.S.B., reported on the widespread use of social workers and visiting teachers by the schools. "The Role of the School in Individual Adjustment," *Proceedings of the Twenty-third National Conference of Catholic Charities* (1937), 199.

32. The social worker reported that classes in religion and the Bible were taught in Polish, Slavic, Lithuanian, and Ukranian so that the children could discuss religion with their parents. *Pittsburgh Social Survey*, NCWC-USCC, ACUA.

33. Rev. Cassian Hartl, *Proceedings of the Third National Conference of Catholic Charities* (1914), 260; Rev. Louis J. Fries, "Symptoms of Delinquency and Methods of Dealing with Them," *Proceedings of the Tenth National Conference of Catholic Charities* (1924), 239–45; Sara E. Laughlin, "Preventive Work in Parochial Schools," *Proceedings of the Ninth National*

Conference of Catholic Charities (1923), 196–200; Rev. Moses E. Kiley, "Social Work Through the Schools," ibid. (1923), 65; Rose J. McHugh, "Health Supervision in Parochial Schools," *Proceedings of the Seventh National Conference of Catholic Charities* (1921), 139; Sara E. Laughlin, "Counseling in the Parish Schools," *Catholic Charities Review* 8 (March 1924): 83–91; Sara Laughlin to John O'Grady, May 1922, NCCC, ACUA; John O'Grady, "The School and the Home," *Catholic Charities Review* 6 (April 1922): 113–14; and Sister Miriam Regina, "The Problem Child," *Proceedings of the Seventh National Conference of Catholic Charities* (1921), 64–65. See also Benedict S. Alper, "Progress in Prevention of Juvenile Delinquency," *Annals* 212 (Nov. 1940): 202–6.

34. See papers on the backward, the subnormal, and problem child in the *Proceedings* of the fourth, seventh, and tenth annual meetings of the National Conference of Catholic Charities. Jane M. Hoey, "Understanding the Delinquent: Society in Relation to the Child," *Proceedings of the National Conference of Social Work* (1927), 95.

35. Catholic Charities of New York recognized the need in establishing its clinic in 1922; seventeen years later Cincinnati Catholic Charities established the Catholic Guidance Clinic. See "An Analytical Summary of the Catholic Charities of the Archdiocese of Cincinnati and The Fenwick," 1938, Drawer 23, File 77, McNicholas Papers, Archives of the Archdiocese of Cincinnati.

36. Dr. Leo H. Bartemeier and James Fitzgerald, "The Whole Health of the Child," *Proceedings of the Fourteenth National Conference of Catholic Charities* (1928), 221–39.

37. Margo Horn, *Before It's Too Late: The Child Guidance Movement in the United States, 1922–1945* (Philadelphia: Temple University Press, 1989), 15–27, 102.

38. Frederick A. Moran, "New Light on the Juvenile Court and Probation," *Proceedings of the National Probation Association* (1930), 66; see Charles Brown, "The Relations Between the Juvenile Court and Other Social Agencies of the Community," *Proceedings of the Ninth National Conference of Catholic Charities* (1923), 45–52; and Anthony M. Platt, *The Child Savers: The Invention of Delinquency* (Chicago: University of Chicago Press, 1977), 133–40. Robert M. Mennel, *Thorns & Thistles: Juvenile Delinquents in the United States, 1825–1940* (Hanover, N.H.: University Press of New England, 1973) is particularly helpful in tracing the Catholic struggle to set up its own protectories or at least gain access to the reformatories through Catholic chaplains. See Ellen Ryerson, *The Best-Laid Plans: America's Juvenile Court Experiment* (New York: Hill & Wang, 1978); Katharine F. Lenroot and Emma O. Lundberg, "Juvenile Courts at Work: A Study of the Organization and Methods of Ten Courts," Children's Bureau Publication No. 141 (Washington, D.C.: Government Printing Office, 1925): 123; Evelina Belden, "The Boys' Court of Chicago: A Record of Six Months Work," *American Journal of Sociology* 20 (May 1915): 731–44.

39. Paul Hanly Furfey, "The Juvenile Court Movement," *Thought* 6 (Sept. 1931): 207–9.

40. Ryerson, 47; see "Treatment of Juvenile Offenders in Milwaukee," *Proceedings of the Seventh National Conference of Catholic Charities* (1921), 161–62; Rev. J. W. R. Maguire, "Catholic Work for Dependent Children," *Proceedings of the Seventh National Conference of Catholic Charities* (1921), 57. William I. Thomas, *The Unadjusted Girl* (Montclair, N.J.: Patterson Smith, 1960 [1923]), 152, declared that in the largest cities as many as 80 percent of delinquent children were either foreign-born or first generation. Mary E. Odem, *Delinquent Daughters: Protecting and Policing Adolescent Female Sexuality in the United States, 1885–1920* (Chapel Hill: University of North Carolina Press, 1955), 24–96. John J. O'Connor, Jr., "Recreation and Its Relation to Delinquency," *Proceedings of the Sixth National Conference of Catholic Charities* (1920), 313, noted that although the Catholics comprised only one-third of the population of Pittsburgh and Allegheny County, they averaged more than fifty percent of those in the juvenile court from 1915 to 1918. M. P. Mooney, "The Scope of Probation," *Proceedings of the Third National Conference of Catholic Charities* (1914), 234–39, estimated that although Catholics made up only 40 percent of the population of Cleveland, nearly 60 percent of the delinquent girls were Catholic. Sixty-two percent of the boys in the Cleveland juvenile court in 1922 were Catholic; only 25 percent had attended Catholic school. John S. Becka, "Curative Factors in Delinquency Among Boys," *Proceedings of the Eighth National Conference of Catholic Charities* (1922), 215. The Cleveland statistics seem rather static. In 1914 66 percent of the delinquent boys in the juvenile court were Catholic as were nearly 60 percent of the delinquent girls. In the Buffalo children's court in 1926, 85 percent of the delinquent boys were Roman Catholic. Mooney, 234–39. Joseph M. Hawes, *Children in Urban Society: Juvenile Delinquency in Nineteenth-Century America* (New York: Oxford University Press, 1971), 140, observed: "Policemen, reformers, and philanthropists had long regarded immigrants as the chief source of crime and pauperism."

41. *Proceedings of the Second National Conference of Catholic Charities* (1912), 211–13. See Joseph M. Hawes, *The Children's Rights Movement: A History of Advocacy and Protection* (Boston: Twayne, G.K. Hall, 1991), 18–19, 29–32, 54–65, 211–22, for another review of the developments in psychology, intelligence testing, and mental health.

42. *Proceedings of the Second National Conference of Catholic Charities* (1912), 309, 312–13. Selma Berrol, "Ethnicity and American Children," in Joseph M. Hawes and N. Ray Hiner, eds. *American Childhood: A Research Guide and Historical Handbook* (Westport, Conn.: Greenwood Press, 1985), 343–75, concluded that ethnicity "*did* make a difference in children's lives."

43. Thomas, 209; Julian W. Mack, "The Juvenile Court as Legal Institution," in Hastings Hart et al., *Foster Home Care for Dependent Children,* Bu-

reau Publication No. 136 (Washington, D.C.: Government Printing Office, 1924), 306; Schlossman, 144. Franklin C. Hoyt, "Procedure of the Manhattan Children's Court of the City of New York," in Hart (328–32) notes that 86 percent of the children arraigned were either born abroad or the daughters and sons of immigrants. See Hartl, 259. Hartl noted that in 1914 the Pittsburgh juvenile court dealt with 13 Jews, 217 Protestants, and 279 Catholics. Catholics made up half of the children in juvenile court and only one-fourth of the Pittsburgh population. See also "Causes of Delinquency," *Proceedings of the Second National Conference of Catholic Charities* (1912), 327–31. Bernard J. Fagan, "Why Boys and Girls Go Wrong," *Proceedings of the Tenth National Conference of Catholic Charities* (1924), 52–53.

44. Mary Regina Kelley, "Delinquency and Employment," *Proceedings of the Fourth National Conference of Catholic Charities* (1916), 96–97.

45. Schlossman, 164.

46. Ibid., 191; Fagan, 49. Odem points out that in Los Angeles the families brought in 47 percent of the cases and sought to win a court decision to enable them to keep control of their recalcitrant children (Odem, 158–76).

47. Brown, 49.

48. Charles D. Gillespie, "Juvenile Delinquency," *Proceedings of the Fourth National Conference of Catholic Charities* (1916), 78. Edwin J. Cooley, "The Prevention of Delinquency," *Catholic Charities Review* 8 (Nov. 1924): 311–12, and Rev. Robert E. Lucey, "Adjusting Behavior Problems," *Proceedings of the Thirteenth National Conference of Catholic Charities* (1927), 155, stress character formation. Brother Paulian, "An Aspect of Juvenile Delinquency," *Proceedings of the Fourth National Conference of Catholic Charities* (1916), 82; Patrick Mallon, "Delinquent Children," ibid., 99; John O'Grady to Howard Knight, 26 Jan. 1932, General Administration Files, NCCC, ACUA. See also Ryerson, 25.

49. Mallon, "Delinquent Children," 100; Quille in discussion of "Prevention of Delinquency," *Proceedings of the Second National Conference of Catholic Charities* (1912), 227. This record may have stemmed from the freedom of the parochial school principals to suspend or expel the most unruly students. Rev. Harold J. Markey, "The Delinquent Child," *Proceedings of the Twenty-third Conference of Catholic Charities* (1937), 339.

50. In Brooklyn, Homer Folks observed, the Catholic probation officer had so many children under supervision that home visitation was virtually impossible. Folks quoted by Mack, "The Juvenile Court as Legal Institution," in Hart, 293–317; Folks, "Juvenile Probation in New York," in Hart, 348–57. In Chicago the court tried to secure probation officers of the same ethnicity as the delinquent. See Jeter, 32, and Henry W. Thurston, "The Juvenile Court as a Probationary Institution," in Hart, 336–46.

51. Emma Quinlan, "Detention Homes for Boys and Girls," *Proceedings of the Seventh National Conference of Catholic Charities* (1921), 185, 187–89.

52. Platt, 123–24, 133. See also Mennel, 140–41. For patronage battles when

the probation officers became paid positions, see Goodwin, "Gender, Politics, and Welfare Reform."

53. Miss Alice Carter was the Catholic probation officer. When the court began to pay the salaries of its officers, it retained Miss Carter, who continued to report to the Knights. She was busy. Of the 367 delinquents before the court from January to June, 1919, 235 were Catholic. CSWA-Reconstruction Committee, NCWC-USCC, ACUA.

54. R. Marcellus Wagner, "Working Relations Between Juvenile Courts and Catholic Agencies," *Proceedings of the Tenth National Conference of Catholic Charities* (1924), 247–60. Mallon's salary was originally paid by the St. Vincent de Paul Society, but by 1924 it was paid by the court. Detroit's SVPS hired a trained social worker to deal with the court and Catholic delinquents. Leslie W. Tentler, *Seasons of Grace: A History of the Catholic Archdiocese of Detroit* (Detroit: Wayne State University Press, 1990), 228.

55. Caroline E. Boone, "What Ought We Do in Probation Work," *Proceedings of the Third National Conference of Catholic Charities* (1914), 250.

56. Hans Weiss, "The Child on Probation," *Annual Report of the National Probation Association, 1929,* 94–108. For short surveys on the evolution of probation and the juvenile courts, see Emily E. Williamson, "Probation and Juvenile Courts," *Annals of the American Academy of Political and Social Science* 20 (July 1902), 259–76; Charles L. Chute, "Juvenile Probation," *Annals of the American Academy of American Political and Social Science* 105 (Jan. 1923): 223–28; Charles W. Hoffman, "Trends of Probation," *Annual Report of the National Probation Association, 1930.*

57. Joseph P. Murphy, "Training for Work with Delinquents," Bernard J. Fagan, "Administrative Problems of Probation Work," and Rose J. McHugh, "The Proper Relation Between the Volunteer Worker and the Courts," *Proceedings of the Sixth National Conference of Catholic Charities* (1920), 292–300, 317–25, 274–84. Michael Sheridan, judge of the Milwaukee juvenile court, however, was enthusiastic about the work of the St. Vincent de Paul Society and its representative's work in his court in "Treatment of Juvenile Offenders in Milwaukee," *Proceedings of the Seventh National Conference of Catholic Charities* (1921), 160–70.

58. Edwin J. Cooley, *Probation and Delinquency: The Study and Treatment of the Individual Delinquent* (New York: Catholic Charities of the Archdiocese of New York, 1927), viii; James P. Kirby, "The Future of Probation," *Proceedings of the Twelfth National Conference of Catholic Charities* (1926), 170–80.

59. Edward Roberts Moore, *Roman Collar* (New York: Macmillan, 1950), 139–40.

60. William Kerby, "Protection of Young Girls," *Proceedings of the First National Conference of Catholic Charities* (1910), 241.

61. *Proceedings of the Fourth National Conference of Catholic Charities,* 1916.

62. Jane Addams, *The Spirit of Youth and the City Streets* (Urbana: University of Illinois Press, 1972), 5, 8, 150.

63. Mennel, 172. Also see Odem, 96–118.

64. Mary W. Dewson and Hastings H. Hart, "Schools for Delinquent Girls," in Hastings H. Hart, *Preventive Treatment of Neglected Children: Correction and Prevention,* vol. 4 in *Poverty, U.S.A.: The Historical Record,* ed. David J. Rothman (New York: Arno Press, 1971), 32–33. In the 1920s there were no national statistics on juvenile delinquency, but Katharine Lenroot of the Children's Bureau estimated that the juvenile courts were dealing with three to five times as many boys as girls. Most of the boys were charged with theft or disorderly or mischievous conduct; the majority of delinquent girls were charged with sex immorality or incorrigibility.

65. Michael F. Girten, "Delinquency," *Proceedings of the First National Conference of Catholic Charities* (1910), 195–206; Rev. Harold P. Chilcote, "A Study of the Factors in One Hundred Selected Cases," *Proceedings of the Fifteenth National Conference of Catholic Charities* (1929), 133–38. Chilcote noted that 69 were "probably feeble-minded." He noted it was more important if the mother were feeble-minded for, "if the father is mentally deficient, nobody notices the difference."

66. Hawes, 179. Cyril Burt, *The Young Delinquent,* rev. ed. (Bickley, Kent: University of London Press, 1944), 425, listed sex as the most significant major and minor factors in the delinquency of girls. Mennel, 184.

67. O'Grady, 163. See Addams, 5–9, 67–68. For women in the workforce, see Julie A. Matthaei, *An Economic History of Women in America: Women's Work, the Sexual Division of Labor, and the Development of Capitalism* (New York: Schocken Books, 1982); Leslie W. Tentler, *Wage-Earning Women: Industrial Work and Family Life in the United States, 1900–1930* (New York: Oxford University Press, 1979); and Alice Kessler-Harris, *Out to Work: A History of Wage-Earning Women in the United States* (New York: Oxford University Press, 1982). Caroline Manning in one of the many Women's Bureau publications of the 1920s surveyed *The Immigrant Woman and Her Job,* U.S. Department of Labor, Women's Bureau Bulletin No. 70 (Washington, D.C.: Government Printing Office, 1929). In a special issue of *Annals,* May 1929, Alice Rogers Hager reviewed "Occupations and Earnings of Women in Industry," 69–73. Concern for girls and women workers and their virtue are generally covered in Sheila Rothman, *Woman's Proper Place: A History of Changing Ideals and Practices, 1879 to the Present* (New York: Basic Books, 1975), Nancy Woloch, *Women and the American Experience* (New York: Alfred A. Knopf, 1984), and the contemporary assessment by Sophonisba Breckinridge, *Women in the Twentieth Century: A Study of Political, Social, and Economic Activities* (New York: Arno Press, 1970).

68. "Girls' Welfare," CSWA-Women's Committee, NCWC-USCC, ACUA.

69. John M. Cooper, "Our Girls," *Catholic Charities Review* 4 (Feb. 1920): 53–55; Catherine A. O'Donnell, "The Room Registry of Pittsburgh," *Catholic Charities Review* 2 (March 1918): 89; "New Boarding Homes for Chicago," *Catholic Charities Review* 5 (Oct. 1921): 274. Joanne J. Mey-

erwitz, *Women Adrift: Independent Wage Earners in Chicago, 1880–1930* (Chicago: University of Chicago Press, 1988) provides the definitive study on the Chicago housing problem for women. New York was far in advance of Chicago. The 1918–1919 annual report of the Association of Catholic Charities, the Ladies of Charity of St. Vincent de Paul, listed seven residences in downtown New York City and a vacation house in Tuckahoe, New York. *Catholic Charities Review* 5 (Sept. 1921): 234.

70. Tentler, *Seasons of Grace*, 432.

71. Anna D. Polanek, "The Housing Problem," *Proceedings of the Tenth National Conference of Catholic Charities* (1924), 277–85.

72. Michael J. Curley to John O'Grady, 4 Feb. 1925, 25 Feb. 1925, and To Rev. and dear Father, 6 March 1925, Curley Papers, Archives of the Archdiocese of Baltimore.

73. *Survey,* Girls' Clubs, CSWA-Women's Committee, NCWC-USCC, ACUA. Of the 313 houses listed in the October 31, 1919, report on religious orders engaged in boarding-house work, the Sisters of Mercy managed 69; Sisters of Providence, 41, the Holy Ghost Sisters, 40. Until enough boarding houses were available, Cooper urged Catholic women's associations to redouble their efforts to find lodging in Catholic family homes for working Catholic women.

74. "N.C.C.W. Plans Girls' Welfare Bureau," *Catholic Charities Review* 3 (Nov. 1923): 343. The emphasis was on housing.

75. John M. Cooper, "Some Plans for the Housing of Women Wage-Earners in our Larger Cities," *Proceedings of the Eighth National Conference of Catholic Charities* (1922), 250–53; John M. Cooper, "Girls' Housing: Two Recent Surveys," *Catholic Charities Review* 6 (May 1922): 155–56. Cooper particularly cited the two recent studies of Chicago and New York boarding houses: *Housing of Non-Family Women in Chicago* and *Housing Conditions of Employed Women in the Borough of Manhattan;* Sister Gregory, "Homes for Wage Earners," *Proceedings of the Eighth National Conference of Catholic Charities* (1922), 262.

76. "New Directory of Boarding Homes for Girls and Women," *Catholic Charities Review* 7 (Nov. 1923): 327; Cooper, "Some Plans for the Housing of Women Wage-Earners in our Larger Cities," 252–53. See correspondence on Fontbonne, a residence conducted by the Sisters of Charity in Cincinnati on their program and problem of older residents. Fontbonne, Drawer 15, File 83, McNicholas Papers, Archives of the Archdiocese of Cincinnati.

77. Ibid., 253–54; John M. Cooper, "Mint and Cummin," *Catholic Charities Review* 6 (Feb. 1922): 43, 46–47.

78. *Proceedings of the Seventh National Conference of Catholic Charities* (1921), 243–44.

79. Monsignor Mueller-Simonis, *Proceedings of the First National Conference of Catholic Charities* (1910), 242–44; Lenora Z. Meder, "Care of Young Girls In America," *Proceedings of the Fourth National Conference of Catholic Charities* (1916), 339.

80. Teresa R. O'Donohue, "The Disappearance of Young Girls in Our Large

Cities," *Proceedings of the Sixth National Conference of Catholic Charities* (1920), 364–66. O'Donohue noted that if the girl was missing "to hide her shame," Catholics should take all possible steps to help her, secure in the knowledge that "she can be a good woman, even though she did make one false step."

81. Teresa R. O'Donohue, "The Home and Recreation," *Proceedings of the Twelfth National Conference of Catholic Charities* (1926), 251–53. Mrs. O'Toole's question was raised in 1923. See *Proceedings of the Ninth National Conference of Catholic Charities* (1923), 207.

82. Edward Garesche, S.J., "The Catholic Young Woman: Her Needs and Some Remedies," *Proceedings of the Fourth National Conference of Catholic Charities* (1916), 354–55, 357; "Recreation and Social Welfare," *Pittsburgh Social Survey*, NCWC, ACUA; "New Social Center at Tampa, Fla," *Catholic Charities Review* 7 (March 1923): 103.

83. Hastings H. Hart provides an overview of the National Playground Association and other developments in organized recreation in *Preventive Treatment of Neglected Children. Correction and Prevention.* John Cooper had several articles on play, clubs, and gangs in *Catholic Charities Review* (Feb. 1920, Feb. 1923, May 1924, and May 1925). Rev. J.W.R. Maguire, C.S.V., suggested playgrounds and the regulation of public amusements in "A Community Program for the Reduction of Juvenile Delinquency," *Proceedings of the Sixth National Conference of Catholic Charities* (1920), 302–7. Gertrude Horigan, "Recreation Outside of the Home," and Mary Agnes Flowers, "Recreation Outside of the Home," *Proceedings of the Twelfth National Conference of Catholic Charities* (1926), 258–67, offered a range of suggestions. John M. Cooper, "A Magna Charta for the Girl and Woman in Athletics," *Catholic Charities Review* 9 (Jan. 1925): 3–5.

84. John M. Cooper, "Girl Scouts or a National Catholic Organization?" *Catholic Charities Review* 6 (Nov. 1922): 310–12; Mrs. Carpenter participated in the discussion of scouting in the session of Jane D. Rippin, "The Girl Scout Program," *Proceedings of the Seventh National Conference of Catholic Charities* (1921), 198–200; Peter M. H. Wynhoven, "Opportunities of Girl Scout Leaders," *Catholic Charities Review* 11 (Jan. 1927): 22–25.

85. Charles A. McMahon, "Parents and the Movies," *Catholic Charities Review* 11 (March 1927): 88; Charles A. McMahon, "Cleansing the Movies," *NCWC Bulletin* 2 (Feb. 1921): 19. John J. Daly followed McMahon's "Parents and the Movies" article in the March issue of *Catholic Charities Review* with "The Theater and the Younger Generation" (93) which concluded that the "old folks" couldn't keep youth away from the ultra-sophisticated plays of Broadway. Charles A. McMahon, "The Problem of the Movies," *NCWC Bulletin* 2 (Jan. 1921): 16–17.

86. Moving Picture List, Women's Committee, NCWC-USCC, ACUA. See Lizabeth Cohen, *Making a New Deal: Industrial Workers in Chicago, 1919–1939* (Cambridge: Cambridge University Press, 1990), 120–31.

87. The Cincinnati Catholic Women's Association, May 1923 to May 1924,

annual report. "Resolutions Adopted at 7th Annual Convention of the NCCW," *NCWC Bulletin* 11 (Nov. 1927): 18. Sister Mary Patrice Thaman, *Manners and Morals of the 1920s Reviewed in the Religious Press* (New York: Bookman, 1954) presents a fine survey and analysis of the other denominations' crusades against the movies, beauty contests, and dance halls. Robert Sklar, *Movie-Made America: A Social History of American Movies* (New York: Random House, 1975), 173–74.

88. Addams, 7, 18–19. For a good analysis of the New York City reform efforts, see Elisabeth Israels Perry, *Belle Moskowitz: Feminine Politics & the Exercise of Power in the Age of Alfred E. Smith* (New York: Oxford University Press, 1987), 48–54. "An Experiment with Dance Halls," *Catholic Charities Review* 8 (May 1924): 174. For the Lutherans and other Protestants on dance halls, see Thaman, 70–80.

89. O'Donohue, 366.

90. Ibid., 365; John J. O'Connor, Jr., "Recreation and its Relation to Delinquency," *Proceedings of the Sixth National Conference of Catholic Charities* (1920), 316–17; Helen Phelan and Merrick House, "The Family and the Community," *Proceedings of the Fourteenth National Conference of Catholic Charities* (1928), 345; Bernard J. Fagan, "Why Boys and Girls Go Wrong," *Proceedings of the Tenth National Conference of Catholic Charities* (1924), 50. See also "The Public Dance Hall as the College Boy Sees It," *Catholic Charities Review* 5 (Feb. 1921) and "This Business of Dancing," *Survey* 52 (July 15, 1924): 458–62. See Cohen, 145–47.

91. Sara E. Laughlin, "Protective Work for Girls in Philadelphia," *Catholic Charities Review* 4 (Dec. 1920): 315–19.

92. A. Madorah Donahue, "Preventive-Protective Work," *Catholic Charities Review* 10 (March 1926): 87–90, and Donahue, "Recreation and Social Hygiene," *Proceedings of the Seventh National Conference of Catholic Charities* (1921), 209–13. Hernan's report is in Women's Committee, NCWC-USCC, ACUA.

93. New York's organization was the first organized in 1902. It was also the first to affiliate with the nonsectarian international organization of Big Brothers and Sisters. See Rev. John B. Kelly, "The Catholic Big Brother Movement," *Catholic Charities Review* 3 (April 1919): 115–17; Marcellus Wagner, "The Contribution of the Big Brother and Big Sister," *Proceedings of the Ninth National Conference of Catholic Charities* (1923), 200–207; and "Standards in Catholic Big Brother and Big Sister Work," *Proceedings of the Fourteenth National Conference of Catholic Charities* (1928), 351–53.

94. Catherine McNamee, "Catholic Big Sisters," *Catholic Charities Review* 12 (June 1928): 200; *Report of Catholic Charities of the Archdiocese of New York*, 1927, 39–40; M. Walsh in discussion of Anna Ward, "The Catholic Big Sisters," *Proceedings of the Sixth National Conference of Catholic Charities* (1920), 352; Sara E. Laughlin, "Case Work for Girls," *Proceedings of the Seventh National Conference of Catholic Charities* (1921), 239. See summarized reports and statistics on Big Sisters in New York City,

Philadelphia, and Chicago, *Proceedings of the Ninth National Conference of Catholic Charities* (1923), 268–69.

95. Ward, 345–52; McNamee, 200–201; Laughlin, "Case Work for Girls," 239; Anna E. King, "The Technique of the Big Sister," *Catholic Charities Review* 12 (June 1928): 204. For Catholic Big Brothers, see A. J. McGavick, "Big Brother Work," *Proceedings of the Seventh National Conference of Catholic Charities* (1921), 224–34. The 1928 meeting of the NCCC Committee on Protective Care was on the topic "Standards in Catholic Big Brother and Big Sister Work." It ended with a resolution to appoint a committee to make a study and formulate standards for the work. *Proceedings of the Fourteenth National Conference of Catholic Charities* (1928), 351–53.

96. Margaret Talty, "Plans for the Delinquent Girl," *Proceedings of the Seventh National Conference of Catholic Charities* (1921), 242.

97. Lady Armstrong, vice president of the International Federation of Big Brothers and Big Sisters, reported that the records of the New York Catholic Big Brothers and Sisters indicated that 78 percent of their work was preventive. *Proceedings of the Ninth National Conference of Catholic Charities* (1923), 205.

98. The Big Brothers and Big Sisters of New York worked with almost 4,400 Catholic youngsters in 1927. *Report of Catholic Charities of the Archdiocese of New York, 1927*, 39–40. They claimed that their intervention had avoided court action in 553 cases.

99. Frederick A. Moran to John O'Grady, 6 June 1929, NCCC, ACUA.

100. Frederick A. Moran, "Catholic Big Brothers and Big Sisters," 1929, NCCC, ACUA. Moran had special kudos for the Big Sisters of Cleveland who provided "as good an example of effective Big Sister work as one is apt to find." In 1929 Cleveland Big Sisters had worked with 275 girls. Records detailed that 112 girls experienced difficult home conditions; 20 were homeless; 69 were "definitely delinquent"; of these 18 were immoral; 40 were incorrigible; and 8 had stolen. Three were truants.

101. Moran, 1–8.

102. Ibid. Moran could discover no information on efforts made or results achieved in mounting an effective preventive program to meet the social or religious problems of their young clients.

103. Frederick A. Moran, "Progress Report of the Committee on a Catholic Protective Program," *Proceedings of the Fifteenth National Conference of Catholic Charities* (1929), 209–13.

104. The phrase "muscular Christianity" is used by Edward R. Kantowicz in *Corporation Sole: Cardinal Mundelein and Chicago Catholicism* (Notre Dame: University of Notre Dame Press, 1983), 173. Bernard J. Sheil, "The Challenge of Youth Today," *Proceedings of the Twenty-second National Conference of Catholic Charities* (1936), 142.

105. Moore, 159–60. The actual chair was Bishop Joseph H. Conroy of Ogdensburg, New York. The Catholic Committee was expanded by the 1940s to twenty-two archbishops and bishops and, according to Moore, "became

one of the most authoritative and influential committees of the hierarchy."
For boy guidance and boyology, see Brother Barnabas, "Boy Guidance, the
New Profession," *Proceedings of the Tenth National Conference of Catholic Charities* (1924), 14–20, for the curriculum of the boy guidance M.A.
program. He also spoke on "Boyology" to the National Conference of
Social Work, detailing not only the graduate program at Notre Dame but
also the thirty-hour intensive courses for businessmen. Also see Christopher
J. Kauffman, *Faith and Fraternalism: The History of the Knights, 1882–
1982* (Cambridge: Harper & Row, 1982).

106. John A. Theobald, "Spiritualizing the Scout Program," *Proceedings of the Twenty-first National Conference of Catholic Charities* (1935), 152.

107. Moore, 170–74. The Lutherans soon developed a medal with the Crusaders' Cross and Shield with the inscription: "Pro Deo Et Patria." The Jewish emblem was the Ner Tamid, "The Eternal Light." There was also expansion of Catholic Girl Scout troops throughout this period. See Mrs. N. F. Brady, "Girl Scouting, A Program for Junior Girls," *Proceedings of the Eighth National Conference of Catholic Charities* (1922), 243–49. Like Vincent Ridder, Mrs. Brady held a position on the national board of the Scouts, serving as treasurer, Girl Scouts, Inc.

108. Walter H. Chelminski, "Scouting as the Core of a Diocesan Program," *Proceedings of the Twenty-first National Conference of Catholic Charities* (1935), 155–61. Kantowitz deals with the male culture of Mundelein and Sheil.

109. Sheil, 144.

110. Moore, 148–54. See Tentler, *Seasons of Grace* (430–41) for Detroit's CYO boxing experience.

111. Bernard Sheil, "The Record of the Chicago Catholic Youth Organization Speaks," *Proceedings of the Twenty-first National Conference of Catholic Charities* (1935), 180–83; Sheil, "The Catholic Youth Organization," *Proceedings of the Twenty-third National Conference of Catholic Charities* (1937), 39. Sheil warned that middle-class youth were prey to "The white-collar craving" of "an artificial generation" ("The Challenge of Youth Today," 151).

112. Moore, 141–44. Moore later criticized the Chicago situation as a one-man set-up.

113. Sheil, "The Challenge of Youth Today," 146–51.

114. Jack Elder, "Cooperation Between NYA and WPA and CYO," *Proceedings of the Twenty-third National Conference of Catholic Charities* (1937), 214–18. The CYO could choose which WPA workers were assigned to parishes. Seventy-five parishes had full-time supplementary assistance. There were few complaints from the pastors.

115. Roosevelt to General Watson, 13 Nov. 1939, and FDR night letter to Sheil, 14 May 1941, RG 108, Reel 2, Franklin D. Roosevelt–Roman Catholic correspondence, ACUA. Similarly, the CYO director of Cleveland did not fear Catholic cooperation, insisting that "Catholic young people have a

right to the new services and these services will not be withheld" if the projects are balanced, assist in community planning, and lead to better citizenship. James H. O'Brien, "The Place of Religion in the Catholic Leisure Time Program," *Proceedings of the Twenty-third National Conference of Catholic Charities* (1937), 184–85.

116. Pastoral letter of John McNicholas, 21 March 1935, NCCC papers, ACUA. Rev. William Labodie was appointed executive secretary of the Cincinnati CYO. He saw the central CYO functioning as a service station to aid the parish priests. William Labodie, "Catholic Philosophy and Some Newer Aspects of Leisure Time Needs," *Proceedings of the Twenty-fourth National Conference of Catholic Charities* (1938), 147.

117. Thomas J. O'Dwyer, "The Mobilization of the Resources of the Church Against Delinquency," *Proceedings of the Twenty-first National Conference of Catholic Charities* (1935), 178; see O'Grady to O'Dwyer, 31 October 1935, RG 76, NCCC, ACUA; Bernard O'Shea, "Program for an Urban Parish," *Proceedings of the Twenty-fifth National Conference of Catholic Charities* (1939), 266; William J. Campbell, "Report of Committee on Youth Activities of National Conference of Catholic Charities," *Proceedings of the Twenty-second National Conference of Catholic Charities* (1936), 141. For the NCCC study see John J. McClafferty to John O'Grady, 9 Dec. 1936; O'Grady to Edward R. Moore, 3 Dec. 1936; Executive Committee Minutes, NCCC, 18 Dec. 1936; Moore to O'Grady, 18 March 1937, NCCC, ACUA. Moore, 188.

5. Catholic Charities, the Great Depression, and the New Deal

1. See *Proceedings of the Nineteenth National Conference of Catholic Charities* (1933); *Catholic Charities of the Archdiocese of New York Annual Report*, 1933, 12.

2. Rev. Aloysius J. Hogan, S.J., "The Catholic Church and the Social Order," *Proceedings of the Nineteenth National Conference of Catholic Charities* (1933), 50. See George Q. Flynn, *American Catholics & the Roosevelt Presidency: 1932–1936* (Lexington: University of Kentucky Press, 1968), xi, 17, and David J. O'Brien, *American Catholics and Social Reform: The New Deal Years* (New York: Oxford University Press, 1968), 54.

3. Statistics and examples from Dixon Wecter, *The Age of the Great Depression, 1929–1941* (New York: Macmillan, 1948), 17–19, 36–40; Cabell B. H. Phillips, *From the Crash to the Blitz, 1929–1939* (New York: New York Times Co., 1969), preface, 34–35; Arthur Schlesinger, *The Crisis of the Old Order, 1919–1933* (Cambridge: Houghton Mifflin, 1957), 249–69; Robert S. McElvaine, *The Great Depression: America 1929–1941* (New York: New York Times Books, 1984); Caroline Bird, *The Invisible Scar* (New York: David McKay, Inc., 1966), 34. On Chicago women, see Agnes Van Driel, "Chicago's Unemployed Women," *Catholic Charities Review* 15 (March 1931): 71–74.

4. Cited in William W. Bremer, *Depression Winters: New York Social Workers and the New Deal* (Philadelphia: Temple University Press, 1984), 31.
5. Ibid.
6. Ibid., 31, 69.
7. Josephine C. Brown, *Public Relief, 1929–1939* (New York: Octagon Books, 1971), 63–68, 121–33.
8. Minutes of the Meeting of the Board of Trustees, CCANY, 5 December 1930. Catholic Charities, New York City.
9. *Catholic Charities of the Archdiocese of New York Annual Report, 1930.*
10. In November 1932 Rose McHugh was appointed to the new Committee on Federal Social Work of the American Association of Social Work. Its mandate was to analyze the social work program of the federal government. *Catholic Charities Review* 16 (November 1932): 287.
11. *Catholic Charities of the Archdiocese of New York Annual Report, 1930; Bremer,* 34.
12. William H. Matthews, *Adventures in Giving* (New York: Dodd, Mead & Co., 1939), 182–203; Minutes of the Board of Trustees, CCANY, 7 November 1930, and December 1931, Catholic Charities of New York; *Catholic Charities of the Archdiocese of New York Annual Report, 1930.*
13. Matthews, 182–203. Matthews specifically cites the good work of Father Brennock of the Catholic Charities Family Welfare Division. Minutes of the Board of Trustees, CCANY, 7 November 1930; *Catholic Charities of the Archdiocese of New York Annual Report, 1930.*
14. Andrew Greeley, "What Is Subsidiarity? A Voice from Sleepy Hollow," *America,* Nov. 9, 1985, 292–93. See also Bernard J. Coughlin, *Church and State in Social Welfare* (New York: Columbia University Press, 1965), 31–32.
15. See Mary L. Gibbons, "Home Relief," *Catholic Charities Review* 16 (June 1932): 165–67. Gibbons noted that 80 percent of those who applied for relief in the first three months needed assistance. Fifty percent of the 150,615 applicants in the first months had never requested any form of relief before.
16. *Catholic Charities of the Archdiocese of New York Annual Report, 1931;* Minutes of the Board of Trustees, CCANY, December 1931; Albert U. Romasco, *The Poverty of Abundance: Hoover, the Nation, and the Depression* (New York: Oxford University Press, 1965), 154–55, Bremer, 65. See also Marguerite T. Boylan, *Social Welfare in the Catholic Church: Organization and Welfare through Diocesan Bureaus* (New York: Columbia University Press, 1941). Catholic Charities Division of Families still assisted 18,105 families, including 38,000 children; work relief through the Prosser and Gibson Committees brought $938,080.30 on projects in churches and institutions employing 6,625 men and women; relief funds from the Gibson Committee to Catholic Charities totaled $322,689. Other funding continued to come from parishes, donations, and special funds, the *New York Times Neediest Cases,* and others. Total expenditure of Catholic

Charities, St. Vincent de Paul Society, and the Ladies of Charity for 1931 was $1,256,067.84 in family relief.

17. Bremer, 69–74; *Catholic Charities of the Archdiocese of New York, Annual Report, 1931;* Minutes of the Board of Trustees, CCANY, 27 January 1933.

18. See Harold P. Chilcote, "The Development of Organized Catholic Charities in the Diocese of Cincinnati, Cleveland, and Toledo," M.A. thesis, Catholic University of America, 1926.

19. Mary Luella Sauer, "How Cincinnati Handled the Unemployment Problem During the Winter of 1929," *Catholic Charities Review* 14 (1930): 10.

20. McNicholas letter, 31 March 1932, in *Cincinnati Telegraph.* Wagner speech excerpted in *Cincinnati Telegraph,* 14 April 1932. See McNicholas letter to parishes, 11 April 1931, and Cincinnati Community Chest Tentative Budgetary Allowances, 1931–1932, Drawer 20, McNicholas Papers, Archives of the Archdiocese of Cincinnati.

21. Kenneth J. Heineman, "A Catholic New Deal: Religion and Labor in 1930s Pittsburgh," *Pennsylvania Magazine of History & Biography* 108 (Oct. 1994): 70.

22. Bruce M. Stave, "Pittsburgh and the New Deal," in John Braeman, Robert Bremner, and David Brody, *The New Deal: States and Local Levels* (Columbus: Ohio State University Press, 1975), 376; Heineman, 77.

23. Lawrence A. O'Connell, "The Conference of Catholic Charities," in *Catholic Pittsburgh's One Hundred Years* (Chicago: Loyola University Press, 1943), 175–77.

24. Ibid.

25. Cited in Stave, 392. "Pittsburgh Catholic Charities," *Catholic Charities Review* 16 (December 1932): 314–15.

26. Thomas J. Noel, *Colorado Catholicism and the Archdiocese of Denver, 1857–1989* (Boulder: University Press of Colorado, 1989): 129–30.

27. James F. Wickens, "Depression and the New Deal in Colorado," in Braeman, Bremner, and Brody, *The New Deal,* 270–72.

28. Noel, 106.

29. "Ten Years of Catholic Charities in the Diocese of Denver—1927–1937," *Tenth Annual Report of the Catholic Charities of the Diocese of Denver, Inc., 1936.*

30. John R. Mulroy to John O'Grady, 10 Oct. 1931, NCCC Papers, RG 76, ACUA. *Fourth Annual Report of the Catholic Charities of the Diocese of Denver, Inc., 1931.* The St. Vincent de Paul Society disbursed another $12,937.88. The Denver Diocesan Council of Catholic Women dealt with 1,330 needy cases in their Mexican Welfare work, providing $1,272.40 in relief. The Jewish agencies generally provided a higher standard of aid. Claris Silcox and Galen M. Fisher in *Catholics, Jews and Protestants: A Study of Relationships in the United States and Canada* (Westport, Conn.: Greenwood Press, 1934) provide important comparisons of Jewish and Catholic social provision in their chapter "Relations in Social Work."

31. Wickens, 273–75; *Tenth Annual Report of the Catholic Charities of the Diocese of Denver, Inc., 1936;* Noel, 117–18.

32. Jo Ann E. Argersinger, *Toward a New Deal in Baltimore: People and Government in the Great Depression* (Chapel Hill: University of North Carolina Press, 1988), 2–7, 19–29. See also Dorothy M. Brown, "Maryland Between the Wars," in Richard Walsh and William Lloyd Fox, eds., *Maryland: A History, 1632–1974* (Baltimore: Maryland Historical Society, 1974), 685, 730–36.

33. "Baltimore," *Catholic Charities Review* 10 (March 1926): 108. On the other hand, John O'Grady, with the concurrence of Curley, in October 1928 moved his Board of Catholic Charities in the District of Columbia to accept participation in the community chest. See also Thomas W. Spalding, *The Premier See: A History of the Archdiocese of Baltimore, 1789–1989* (Baltimore: Johns Hopkins University Press, 1989), 336–37.

34. Argersinger, 21–27.

35. Ibid., 27–29. Michael J. Curley to Edwin Leonard, 20 March 1932, and 25 February 1932, Curley Papers, Archives of the Archdiocese of Baltimore.

36. *Baltimore Catholic Review,* Dec. 23, 1932.

37. Argersinger, 24–26. *Baltimore Catholic Review,* Dec. 23, 1932, and Jan. 6, 1933.

38. "Action in the Present Emergency," a paper presented 29 December 1931, to the AALL was published in *Catholic Charities Review* 16 (January 1932): 5–9. See Brown, 82–83, and Thomas W. Tifft, "Toward a More Humane Social Policy: The Work and Influence of Monsignor John O'Grady," Ph.D. dissertation, Catholic University of America, 1979, 42–47.

39. Tifft, 42–47. Tifft cites the similar support of Rev. John A. Ryan for an ambitious public works program. In January 1931 he urged a $5 billion federal appropriation.

40. Tifft, 60. See Jordan Schwarz, *The Interregnum of Despair: Hoover, Congress, and the Depression* (Urbana: University of Illinois Press, 1970), 23–32, 141–46.

41. Gertrude Springer, "Funds for Another Bleak Winter," *Survey* 66 (June 15, 1931): 302; Alice E. Padgett, "Where Is the Money Going?" *Catholic Charities Review* 15 (Nov. 1931): 290–96.

42. An editorial, "Catholic Charities of Chicago and Unemployment Relief," *Catholic Charities Review* 16 (February 1932): 48, reported that the Catholic bureau in Chicago had cared for 20,000 Catholic families, of the 100,000 "clamoring for relief." Without the space to provide relief from the central office, the bureau set up parish stations and sent applicants to their parishes. The St. Vincent de Paul societies dispensed parish funds and then applied to the central office when more were needed.

43. Alice E. Padgett, "The Year in Catholic Charities," *Catholic Charities Review* 16 (January 1932): 9–12; Alice E. Padgett to Rose J. McHugh, 3 March and 29 March 1932, NCCC, RG 76, ACUA. *Survey* was also

printing reports and statistics. See "How the Cities Stand," *Survey* 68 (April 15, 1932): 71–75, for a report on thirty-seven cities. Padgett continued her reports through 1932. The total for January through August 1932 was 208,588 relief families and $2,832,025.55 disbursed. This was an increase of 50 percent over 1931. The St. Vincent de Paul conferences, she estimated would expend approximately $5 million. She noted the figures did not include Baltimore, Boston, and Chicago. It is not clear what percentage of the funds is from public or private sources; however, she estimated that Catholic agencies would have spent at least $12 million for relief in 1932. "Relief Expenditures," *Catholic Charities Review* 17 (January 1933): 20–21.

44. U.S. Congress, Senate, Committee on Manufactures, *Unemployment Relief, Hearings Before a Subcommittee of the Senate Committee on Manufactures on S. 174 and S. 262,* 72nd Cong., 1st sess., 1932: 180–87. See also editorial in *Catholic Charities Review* 16 (January 1932): 16–17. O'Grady reported to Linton B. Swift that Democrats Joseph Robinson, Thomas Walsh, and David I. Walsh, and Republican Senator George H. Moses were conservatives "who might be open to our point of view" (Tifft, 57–59). Swift to O'Grady, 12 Nov. 1931; O'Grady to Swift, 13 Nov. 1931, NCCC, RG 76, ACUA.

45. Tifft, 60. The testimony was summarized in *Catholic Charities Review.* Some agencies were able to accept only 40 to 50 percent of the applicants. A survey of 800 cities indicated the average amount of relief given to the average family each week was $6.02, considerably less than enough for an adequate family diet. Alice E. Padgett, "Who Needs Relief?" *Catholic Charities Review* 16 (March 1932): 78–79. The bishops had issued a statement published November 12, 1931, through the NCWC asserting that "federal and state appropriations for relief in some form will become necessary." They urged a conference of labor, business, and government to deal with the emergency (Flynn, 26).

46. The O'Grady editorial in the September 1932 issue of *Catholic Charities Review* was followed by an article not wholly sympathetic to the Bonus Expeditionary Force, asserting that Congress had "already been more than generous in dealing with the veterans. . . There seems to be no end of the bounties which they were willing to hand out to the veterans."

47. Joanna C. Colcord, "A New Relief Deal," *Survey* 69 (May 1933): 179–81.

48. Searle F. Charles, *Minister of Relief: Harry Hopkins and the Depression* (Syracuse: Syracuse University Press, 1963), 5–38; Harry L. Hopkins, *Spending to Save: The Complete Story of Relief* (New York: W.W. Norton & Co., Inc., 1936); Brown, 182–83.

49. John O'Grady to M. Luella Sauer, 6 May 1933, NCCC, ACUA. In his unpublished memoir, O'Grady credited pressure from the chest movement "who by this time had developed a vast influence in American social welfare" in pressing Hopkins to eliminate voluntary organizations like the St. Vincent de Paul Society from public relief (Colcord, 179–81).

50. Brown, 185–86. Brown notes the "consternation in the ranks of private social workers" and points to "considerable difficulty and delay" encountered in some large cities, citing Baltimore and St. Louis as examples.

51. Charles, 32–33; Hopkins, 100, 104–6; Brown, 71–90, 198–99; *Catholic Charities Review* 17 (September 1933): 199–200.

52. John O'Grady to Robert F. Keegan, 15 April 1933, NCCC, ACUA.

53. O'Grady memoir, 209, NCCC, ACUA.

54. Gene D. L. Jones, "The Chicago Catholic Charities, the Great Depression, and Public Welfare," *Illinois Historical Journal* 83 (spring 1990): 15–20.

55. Ibid., 28–29.

56. M. Luella Sauer to John O'Grady, 25 August 1933, NCCC, ACUA; "Public and Private Agencies in Pittsburgh," NCCC Papers, RG 76, ACUA; and Alice E. Padgett, "Catholic Charities and Public Agencies," *Catholic Charities Review* 17 (September 1933): 206.

57. Argersinger, 30–33. Leonard cited in the *Baltimore Catholic Review,* Dec. 15, 1933. He noted the number of St. Vincent de Paul volunteers had risen to 700.

58. "Maryland Employment Relief Commission of the State Board for Aid and Charities," "Application of Rules and Regulations No. 3 of the Federal Emergency Relief Administration, July 29, 1933," "Application of Rules and Regulations Sent Out by the Federal Emergency Relief Administration to the Citizens' Committee on Relief and Employment St. Louis, Missouri," NCCC, ACUA. O'Grady wrote to John Butler, 16 August 1933, cited in Tifft, 87.

59. John Mulroy wire to John O'Grady, 17 August 1933; O'Grady to Pierce Williams, 17 August 1933; O'Grady to John Mulroy, 17 August 1933; Mulroy to O'Grady, 27 December 1933, NCCC, ACUA. In this December letter, Mulroy reported that Catholic Charities had been receiving $4,700 per month in federal relief orders to assist three hundred families.

60. John O'Grady to Bart Murtaugh, 1, 21 September 1933; Murtaugh to Bishop Francis C. Kelley, 5 September 1933; Murtaugh to O'Grady, 27 September 1933; Murtaugh to Marcellus Wagner, 27 October 1933, NCCC, ACUA.

61. John O'Grady to Robert F. Keegan, 23 August 1933, NCCC, ACUA. See also Tifft, 91.

62. R. Marcellus Wagner to John O'Grady, 21 August 1933. Wagner to Patrick G. Moriarity, 21 Aug. 1933, NCCC, ACUA.

63. Brown, 191–217. O'Grady cheered the short-lived but massive Civil Works Administration which was terminated in April 1934. NCCC's only CWA initiative was an unsuccessful attempt to secure CWA funding for repairs to Catholic institutions (O'Grady, unpublished memoir, 213); Tifft, 136–38. O'Grady's editorial comments on CWA are in *Catholic Charities Review* 18 (March 1934): 65–66. The most thorough analysis of CWA is in Bonnie Fox Schwartz, *The Civil Works Administration, 1933–1934: The Business of Emergency Employment in the New Deal* (Princeton: Princeton Univer-

sity Press, 1994). See also Charles, 46–65; Hopkins, 116–22, 164–65; and Brown, 158–63, 254–56. O'Grady was more successful with the FERA rulings dealing with surplus food through the Federal Surplus Relief Corporation. FERA approved distribution to institutions receiving public aid as long as they did not substitute for the regular purchases for food. O'Grady forwarded to Hopkins a list of Catholic institutions caring for Indian children, noting they had only a food allowance of fifteen cents a day. A letter from Sr. M. Helen, C.S.A., superior of St. Joseph's Orphanage in Baraga, Michigan, to NCCC, 13 Feb. 1934, is a good example of needs and attitudes in an Indian orphanage. NCCC, ACUA.

64. The correspondence from and about Denver spanned from 26 January through 14 June 1934. Mulroy to O'Grady, 26 January, 3, 8, 10 February, 3, 14 March, 17, 19 May, 9 June; O'Grady to Mulroy, 17 March, 13, 14 June; Bishop Urban J. Vehr to Marcellus Wagner, 20 February 1934; O'Grady to Sara Brown, 21 February 1934; O'Grady to Marcellus Wagner, 1 March 1934, NCCC, ACUA.

65. Even in Pittsburgh M. Luella Sauer reported that she had cut Catholic Charities' cooperative caseload from 2,400 to 1,000. Sauer to John O'Grady, 24 January, 14 February, 7, 27 March, 10, 13 April, 16 July 1934; O'Grady to Sauer, 12 April 1934, NCCC, ACUA. Like Mulroy and other diocesan directors, Sauer worked to have sympathetic public officials.

66. Edward M. Farrell to O'Grady, 20 April 1934; O'Grady to Farrell, 7 May, 14 June 1934, NCCC, ACUA. O'Grady believed that if Farrell got the diocesan directors in Illinois to stick together, then the state relief administration would not insist on a change. The Family Welfare Association supported the FERA position that public funds should only be dispersed by public agencies. Like the Chicago social work professionals, the survey team would also take umbrage at the volunteers on the staffs of Catholic Charities and the Salvation Army.

67. R. Marcellus Wagner to John O'Grady, 12 April 1934, NCCC, ACUA.

68. *Proceedings of the Twentieth National Conference of Catholic Charities* (1934), 20–21; *Catholic Charities Review* 20 (Dec. 1936): 300–301.

69. The relief crisis arrived in November as FERA ended. See Ewan Clague, "1932—When Relief Stops—1935," *Survey* 71 (Nov. 19, 1935): 328–29, and Joanna C. Colcord and Russell H. Kurtz, "1932—Relief Policies and Practices—1935," *Survey* 71 (Dec. 1935): 374–76. As they had with FERA, the diocesan directors sought to participate in WPA projects. See O'Grady to the directors, 20 June 1935, NCCC, ACUA, on his negotiations with Hopkins and Williams.

70. Joseph B. Toomey, "Report on Meetings of Diocesan Directors of Catholic Charities," *Proceedings of the Twenty-first National Conference of Catholic Charities* (1935), 300–301. The Continuing Committee minutes of the April 23, 1935, meeting cite the questions raised on funding and the concern that there would be a reversion to the old poor law administration through county boards. A survey of the directors by the Continuing Com-

mittee in 1936 found that a slender majority of those responding favored direct relief as part of the permanent federal program. Members of the Committee saw this as quite a "change in attitude." Minutes of the Continuing Committee, 26 March 1936; "WPA and Relief," 4 March 1936, NCCC, ACUA.

71. The literature on Social Security is extensive. See Walter I. Trattner, *From Poor Law to Welfare State: A History of Social Welfare in America* (New York: Free Press, 1979); Roy Lubove, *The Struggle for Social Security, 1900–1935* (Cambridge: Harvard University Press, 1968); Edward D. Berkowitz, *America's Welfare State From Roosevelt to Reagan* (Baltimore: Johns Hopkins Press, 1991); Martha Derthick, *Policymaking for Social Security* (Washington: Brookings Institution, 1979); and Winifred Bell, *Aid to Dependent Children* (New York: Columbia University Press, 1965). Linda Gordon, *Pitied But Not Entitled: Single Mothers and the History of Welfare, 1890–1935* (Madison: University of Wisconsin Press, 1994).

72. Brown, 204; Tifft, 151–52.

73. For the Catholic position, see Edwin E. Witte, *The Development of the Social Security Act* (Madison: University of Wisconsin Press, 1962), 50–54, 165–71. Frances Perkins, *The Roosevelt I Knew* (New York: Viking Press, 1946). Arthur J. Altmeyer, *The Formative Years of Social Security* (Madison: University of Wisconsin Press, 1966), and Thomas H. Eliot, *Recollections of the New Deal: When the People Matter* (Boston: Northeastern University Press, 1992) have nothing to say on the Catholic role.

74. Following the resignation for health reasons of longtime chief Grace Abbott in June 1934, there had been an extended delay and debate over whether Lenroot or Eliot would be the successor. See Lela B. Costin, *Two Sisters for Social Justice: A Biography of Grace and Edith Abbott* (Urbana: University of Illinois Press, 1983), 216–18.

75. *Social Security in America: The Factual Background of the Social Security Act as Summarized from Staff Reports to the Committee on Economic Security* (Washington, D.C.: Government Printing Office, 1937): 287.

76. Report of the Committee on Economic Security, Hearings, 74th Cong., 1st sess., House, *Economic Security Act. Hearings Before the Committee on Ways and Means on HR 4120* (Washington, D.C.: Government Printing Office, 1935): 48. See also Grace Abbott, *From Relief to Social Security: The Development of the New Public Welfare Services and Their Administration* (New York: Russell & Russell, 1966), 88. The Children's Bureau put its highest priority on the health measures. See Robyn Muncy, *Creating a Female Dominion in American Reform, 1890–1935* (New York: Oxford University Press, 1991), 124–50.

77. Grace Abbott compared benefits under Pennsylvania public relief and the Mothers' Assistance Fund: "One represents the old tradition of pauper relief . . . The other represents the modern conception of relief as a form of social service which will prevent rather than perpetuate pauperism" (Abbott, 88).

78. *Social Security in America,* 233–49; Gordon, *Pitied But Not Entitled,* 257.
79. Brown, 309–10. See also Lindenmeyer-Dick's chapter, "The Roots of Controversy: The Inclusion of Children in the 1935 Social Security Act," and the full discussion by Linda Gordon in *Pitied But Not Entitled,* 185–206, 253–85. Christopher Howard saw the FERA strategy as the CES' understanding that it would need FERA support when the measure reached Congress. He also cites Altmeyer's recollection that "we were much more concerned about allaying opposition to the inclusion of the various maternal and child health and welfare activities in the bill than we were in the question of who would administer ADC." Christopher Howard, "Sowing the Seeds of 'Welfare': The Transformation of Mothers' Pensions, 1900–1940," *Journal of Policy History* 4 (1992): 212–13. Brown became a Roman Catholic during the 1930s. See Emilia E. Martinez-Brawley, "From Countrywoman to Federal Emergency Relief Administrator: Josephine Chapin Brown, A Biographical Study," *Journal of Sociology and Social Welfare* 14 (June 1987): 153–83.
80. *Social Security in America,* 251–58.
81. O'Grady to Glover, 18, 25 Nov. 1936, NCCC, ACUA.
82. Minutes of Special Meeting of Diocesan Directors of Catholic Charities, 29 January 1935, NCCC, ACUA.
83. Ibid.
84. Hearings, 74th Cong., 1st sess., *Economic Security Act: Hearings Before the Committee on Finance, U.S. Senate on S 1130* (Washington, D.C.: Government Printing Office, 1935): 370.
85. This did not deter the NCWC, which did submit this language in its statement at the Senate Finance Committee hearings. *Economic Security Act: Hearings Before the Committee on Finance,* 370.
86. In the law Title II, Section 203 became Title IV, Section 406. Memoranda for Meeting of Diocesan Directors of Catholic Charities, 29 Jan. 1935, NCCC, ACUA. Interestingly Kingsbury had made this same claim in the fight for mothers' pensions in New York.
87. Ibid. Minutes of the Meeting of the Diocesan Directors of Catholic Charities, 29 January 1935.
88. Robert F. Wagner Papers, Georgetown University Special Collections, Washington, D.C.
89. Memorandum attached to the Minutes of the Meeting of the Diocesan Directors, 19 Jan. 1935, NCCC, ACUA. See Lindemeyer-Dick's chapter, "The Roots of Controversy: The Inclusion of Children in the 1935 Social Security Act," for a fine analysis of the strategy and compromises of the Children's Bureau.
90. Witte, 165–71.
91. McEntegart statement in Minutes of the Continuing Committee, Diocesan Directors of Catholic Charities, 13 Feb. 1936, NCCC, ACUA.
92. Keegan to Perkins, 9 Feb. 1935, Chairman's Files, Social Security Administration, Box 125, RG 47, National Archives. Memo O'Grady to Diocesan

Directors, 9 Feb. 1935, NCCC, ACUA. J. Jerome Reddy to Robert F. Wagner, 11 Feb. 1935, Wagner Papers, Georgetown University.

93. Brown, 309–10; Minutes of Meeting of Continuing Committee, 23 April 1935. O'Grady wrote to John Mulroy, 25 February 1935: "As to Mother's aid. . . . Remember, we decided to go along with mothers' assistance program with certain restrictions [degree of kinship]" (NCCC, ACUA).

94. Minutes of the Continuing Committee of Diocesan Directors of Catholic Charities, 23 April 1935, NCCC, ACUA.

95. See Brown, chap. 14. O'Grady to Wagner, 28 May 1935. O'Grady was responding to a letter from Wagner, 24 May 1935, reporting that Mary Godley of the NCSSS was under the impression that O'Grady was insisting on the administration being in the hands of the Economic Security Board rather than the Children's Bureau. NCCC, ACUA.

96. Memo O'Grady to Diocesan Directors, 9 Feb. 1935, NCCC, ACUA. U.S., *Statutes at Large*, 74th Cong., 1st sess., Ch. 531, 14 Aug. 1935.

97. Minutes of the Meeting of the Continuing Committee, 23 April 1935.

98. Marcellus Wagner to McEntegart, 22 April 1935, NCCC, ACUA.

99. Ibid., 167–71. Roosevelt had warned Witte that Catholics might be bitterly opposed to the maternal and child health programs drafted by the Children's Bureau. No such opposition materialized. A bargain was a bargain. At the same time, Witte credited the loyal work of Grace Abbott in galvanizing the Children's Bureau network to pry the bill out of committee (Muncy, 153). See also Monroe Billington and Cal Clark, "Catholic Clergymen, Franklin D. Roosevelt, and the New Deal," *Catholic Historical Review* 79 (Jan. 1993): 65–82.

100. Jane Hoey, "Aid to Dependent Children," *Annals* 102 (March 1939): 74–81. Emma O. Lundberg, *Unto the Least of These: Social Services for Children* (New York: Appleton-Century-Crofts, 1947), 15, updated the figures to February 1946 when 733,632 children were beneficiaries of ADC. For state-by-state statistics in 1942, see Lewis Meriam, *Relief and Social Security* (Washington: Brookings Institution, 1946), 62–63.

101. The recognition of the inadequacy of the ADC payments was apparent in the statement of Lawrence A. Glenn of Duluth at the February 9, 1938, meeting of the diocesan directors in Chicago. He believed that institutions "will get a lot of children from widows who will have to work." The same applied to divorced mothers. They would have to work and send their children to institutions. Minutes of the 9 Feb. 1938 meeting, NCCC, ACUA.

102. Howard, 188, 216. Howard also points out that black families did somewhat better under ADC than under mothers' pensions, comprising 15 percent of ADC recipients by the late 1930s. The inclusion of a year's residency requirement in the legislation also cut out aid to migrant families. Alice Kessler-Harris analyzes how "deeply gendered understandings [create] state policies" in "Designing Women and Old Fools: The Construction of the Social Security Amendments of 1939," in Linda K. Kerber, Alice Kessler-

Harris, and Kathryn Kish Sklar, eds., *U.S. History as Women's History* (Chapel Hill: University of North Carolina Press, 1995), 87–106. Hoey is cited in Blanche D. Coll, *Safety Net: Welfare and Social Security, 1929–79* (New Brunswick: Rutgers University Press, 1995), 105. The "nice families" referred to Edith Abbott's testimony for ADC at the 1935 Social Security hearings. The abuse of the "suitable home" provision is detailed in Bell, *Aid to Dependent Children.* Michael J. Ready of the NCWC did forward a letter to Senator Pat Harrison printed in the hearings of the Senate Finance Committee asking for the inclusion of employees of charitable institutions under Social Security with the extension of this benefit to cover widows and children. The NCWC expressly asked for the continued exclusion of religious. *Hearings before the Committee on Finance, U.S. Senate, 76th Cong., 1st sess. on H.R. 6635:* 363.

103. Derthick, 21. The rapidly expanding literature on the gendering of American welfare or the two-track system of social provision is complex. Beyond Gordon's comprehensive *Pitied But Not Entitled,* see Linda Gordon, "Social Insurance and Public Assistance: The Influence of Gender in Welfare Thought in the United States, 1890–1935," *American Historical Review* 97 (Feb. 1992): 19–54, and Gordon's introduction and "The New Feminist Scholarship on the Welfare State," and the articles by Barbara Nelson and Virginia Sapiro in Linda Gordon, ed., *Women, the State, and Welfare* (Madison: University of Wisconsin Press, 1990). Also see Mary Jo Bane, "Politics and Policies of the Feminization of Poverty," in Margaret Weir, Ann S. Orloff, and Theda Skocpol, eds., *The Politics of Social Policy in the United States* (Princeton: Princeton University Press, 1988). Theda Skocpol in *Protecting Soldiers and Mothers: The Political Origins of Social Policy in the United States* asserts that early in the century U.S. social politics focused more on solidarities of gender than on solidarities of economic class position. An extended exchange by Gordon and Skocpol is in Linda Gordon, "Gender, State and Society: A Debate with Theda Skocpol," and Theda Skocpol, "Soldiers, Workers, and Mothers: Gendered Identities in Early U.S. Social Policy," *Contention* 2 (spring 1993): 139–89. Gwendolyn Mink provides a useful analysis of the "spread of gender bias" in the 1939 amendments. Gwendolyn Mink, *The Wages of Motherhood: Inequality in the Welfare State, 1917–1942* (Ithaca: Cornell University Press, 1995), 123–50.

104. *Proceedings of the Twenty-fourth National Conference of Catholic Charities* (1938), 61.

105. Rose J. McHugh, "Functions of Catholic Charities in Assisting People to Obtain their Rights Under the New Governmental Programs," *Proceedings of the Twenty-fifth National Conference of Catholic Charities* (1939). To put this in context, see Ann Shola Orloff, *The Politics of Pensions: A Comparative Analysis of Britain, Canada, and the United States, 1880–1940* (Madison: University of Wisconsin Press, 1993). Trattner (236–37) asserts that with Social Security "the American people as a whole accepted

the assumption that a large number of people had a right (which could be legally enforced) to public benefits, or at least that failure to provide such benefits was socially and economically shortsighted."

106. Katharine F. Lenroot, "Child Welfare and Social Reconstruction," *Proceedings of the Twenty-first National Conference of Catholic Charities* (1935), 29–38.

107. Mary Irene Atkinson, "The New Front on Child Welfare," *Survey* 71 (Oct. 1935): 294–95.

108. Perkins to McEntegart, 16 August 1935; Martha M. Eliot to McEntegart, 25 Nov. 1935; McEntegart to O'Grady, 27 Nov. 1935, and Lenroot wire to O'Grady, 3 Dec. 1935. Agenda for Meeting of Diocesan Directors of Catholic Charities, 22 Jan. 1936, NCCC, ACUA.

109. Unofficial copy of Report of Advisory Committee on Community Child Welfare Services, confidential memo from Bryan McEntegart for NCCC Continuing Committee, 31 Dec. 1935, NCCC, ACUA. In the June 1935 *Survey,* C. C. Carstens, Child Welfare League of America, wrote "Child Care, Public and Private," also arguing that the private agency still needed to exist, functioning "side by side" with the public agency for the care of children.

110. Minutes of a meeting of the subcommittee of Advisory Committee on Child Welfare Services, Children's Bureau, 15 Feb. 1937, forwarded by McEntegart to O'Grady, 4 March, with the request to keep it confidential. NCCC, ACUA.

111. O'Grady to Lenroot, 18 March 1937; McEntegart to Lenroot, 22 March 1937, Children's Bureau, 15.0.4.4., Box 1004, RG 102, National Archives.

112. Mary Irene Atkinson, "Report to Advisory Committee on Community Child Welfare Services," 7 April 1937, NCCC, ACUA.

113. Lenroot memo 3 May 1937 for distribution to participants. "Discussion of Public and Private Services for Child Welfare," Children's Bureau, 15.0.4.4., Box 1004, RG 102, National Archives.

114. O'Grady "blasted" the quality of the child welfare services of the Children's Bureau in rural areas and again argued against any extension of the child welfare services into urban areas (Coll, 166).

115. Minutes of the 22 January 1936, meeting of the Diocesan Directors of NCCC, NCCC, ACUA; Brown, 326–29.

116. Catholic Agnes Van Driel headed the Technical Training Service of the BPA. McHugh was responsible for the 1941 study of six states investigating restrictive practices at the state level that were blocking ADC reaching needy children (Coll, 111–18).

117. For a good profile of Hoey's efforts to ease state restrictions and her arguments for the extension of services through ADC, see Coll, 106–67.

118. Minutes of Meeting of Diocesan Directors of Catholic Charities, 22 Jan. 1936, NCCC, ACUA. McKinley and Frase cite Hoey's "unusual gifts for dealing with policy problems and in handling state people" but are critical of her administrative skills within the BPA. Charles McKinley and

Robert W. Frase, *Launching Social Security: A Capture-and-Record Account, 1935–1937* (Madison: University of Wisconsin Press, 1970), 138–80.

119. Minutes of Meeting of Continuing Committee, Diocesan Directors of Catholic Charities, 13 Feb. 1936, NCCC, ACUA.

120. Memo to Directors and Executives of Catholic Charities, 24 Feb. 1936, and memo to Directors of Diocesan Catholic Charities re: WPA and relief, 4 March 1936, NCCC Papers, ACUA. Newark's diocesan director Ralph Glover expected a radical change. Catholic Charities and private agencies had cared for dependent children who were ineligible, usually through residence restrictions, for public support and supervision. Lowering the residence requirement to one year would leave few needing private care. Director George Grady in Hartford did not expect Connecticut to qualify for federal funds given its system of municipal, county, and state assistance. Catholic Charities expected to continue to receive municipal funding for the children it placed and supervised.

121. The director of St. Thomas' Orphanage in Lincoln, Nebraska, reported that Catholics had succeeded in having the Nebraska law worded to include payments from county welfare boards for dependent children in Catholic institutions. From Phoenix, executive secretary Eileen Ward cited the willingness of the State Department of Public Welfare to allow Catholic Charities' workers to supervise Catholic dependent children under the Social Security Act. There had even been some discussion of using public funds to pay her for part-time services in developing the Arizona program. There were only two responses from the South. Dependent Children survey, 1936; O'Grady to Flanagan, 2 March 1936, NCCC, ACUA.

122. Dependent Children survey, 1936, NCCC, ACUA.

123. John J. Mulroy, "The Meaning of Coordination in Catholic Charities," *Proceedings of the Twenty-second National Conference of Catholic Charities* (1936), 262–63.

124. Minutes of the Meeting of Continuing Committee of the Diocesan Directors, 26 March 1936, and attached statement. They also reviewed the legislative trends in the states. They found "a rather general apathy" by legislators to deal with administrative details. Most merely empowered the state department of public welfare to submit a plan to the Social Security Board. NCCC, ACUA.

125. Minutes of Meeting of Continuing Committee, Diocesan Directors of Catholic Charities, 22 April 1936. The revised statement is in the July 31, 1936, report of the Continuing Committee, NCCC, ACUA. The Continuing Committee followed the reports on the Child Welfare Services closely. See Memorandum from Lundberg to Martha Eliot and attachment on programs in the states for 1936 as well as Memorandum on Constitutional Limitations on Use of State and Local Subsidies to Organizations Maintained by Sectarian or Denominational Groups, 2 Dec. 1936, Children's Bureau in NCCC, ACUA.

126. Report of the Continuing Committee of Diocesan Directors of Catholic Charities, 31 July 1936, NCCC, ACUA. The NCWC was anxious to contact Hoey also. See Raymond A. McGowan to Linna E. Bressette, 26 May 1936, Social Action Department, NCWC-USCC Papers, ACUA.

127. Minutes of the Continuing Committee of Diocesan Directors, 26 April 1937, NCCC, ACUA. Emma Lundberg wrote to Alice Padgett on August 27, 1936, after speaking in her class at the School of Social Work of Catholic University asking for the activities of diocesan charities bureaus beyond the large cities. She wrote again 19 October 1937, observing that in the State of Washington diocesan activities might become a "real factor in the development of a State-wide program." Children's Bureau, 0.2.6.2., RG 102, National Archives. The NCCC agenda for the meeting of the Executive Committee, 28 Aug. at St. Paul cited the 1933 study of Catholic child-care and noted it had not been kept up to date. NCCC needed to have data on hand in regard to Catholic work in the field of child welfare. Minutes of the Executive Committee meeting, NCCC, 28 Aug. 1937, NCCC, ACUA. That same meeting reviewed the data from a survey of dioceses on the private institutional care of the aged under the Old Age Assistance provisions of Social Security.

128. O'Grady to Ralph J. Glover, 18 Nov. 1936; O'Grady to Diocesan Directors, 10 Jan. 1937, NCCC, ACUA.

129. Edward M. Farrell to O'Grady, 12 Feb. 1937, and O'Grady response, 16 Feb. 1937, NCCC, ACUA.

130. Memorandum for Father Burke: Report on the 1935 Peoria Conference of the NCCC, by Rev. Michael Ready, 15 October 1935, NCWC, ACUA. O'Grady to Glover, 18, 25 Nov. 1936, NCCC, ACUA. O'Grady to Rev. Edward M. Farrell, Peoria, 16 Feb. 1937, states that Msgr. Cummings of Chicago suggested an amendment extending Title IV to foster care, but all of the directors opposed it, believing it would mean that foster care would tend to become entirely public. A confidential memorandum to Continuing Committee, 30 Dec. 1936, on institutional care of the aged summarizes the efforts to secure an amendment to state laws to make it possible for the aged in private institutions to receive public assistance. Lenroot had sent O'Grady information on constitutional limitations on the use of state and local subsidies to sectarian groups. Ibid.

131. O'Grady to Diocesan Directors NCCC, 10 Jan. 1937, contained a seven-page attachment on the implications of Social Security extension to support foster care. McEntegart to O'Grady, 4 May 1938, cites the religious clause record. NCCC, ACUA. The 1939 amendments did include a 50 percent match and raised the age limit for coverage of children attending school from sixteen to eighteen. They did not include an increase in maximum payments to individual children. The major impact on ADC came not from the Title IV but the Title II amendments which created OASI. See Coll, 107–11.

132. Minutes of the Meeting of Diocesan Directors, Seattle. "The Directors and

the Challenge of Youth," *Proceedings of the Twenty-second National Conference of Catholic Charities* (1936), 251–53; John J. Butler, "Presidential Address," ibid., 18–19.

133. See Eileen Ward, "Institutions Change with Changing Times," *Catholic Charities Review* 21 (April 1937): 110–11; Mother Mary of Kevelaer, F.M.M., "Another Institution Redirects Its Program," *Catholic Charities Review* 22 (Sept. 1938): 207–8; H. Jos. Jacobi, "New Institutions for Old," *Catholic Charities Review* 22 (May 1938): 140–42; Margaret Wallace, "Work for the Aged A Challenge!" *Catholic Charities Review* 22 (March 1938): 69–72; Msgr. Thomas J. O'Dwyer, "New Opportunities for Private Charitable Agencies," *Catholic Charities Review* 21 (May 1937): 135–37. Catholic Charities still maintained a modest relief function. See "Catholic Charities Marches On," *Catholic Charities Review* 21 (June 1937): 177, and "Our Sisterhoods in the Twentieth Century," *Catholic Charities Review* 22 (Dec. 1938): 312–14.

134. Albert J. Murphy, "Reinforcing Volunteer Values," *Catholic Charities Review* 21 (Oct. 1937): 249. "The Actual Content of Volunteer Visiting—What Is It?" *Catholic Charities Review* 22 (June 1938): 163–64. Mary Gibbons, "Presidential Address," *Catholic Charities Review* 23 (Sept. 1939): 219.

135. Minutes of the Executive Committee, 8 Feb. 1939, NCCC Papers, ACUA.

136. In 1937 the Catholic bishops of New York were successfully fighting against passage of the Child Labor Amendment in the legislature. They opposed the age limit of eighteen and the "vague" provisions. See Greene, "The Catholic Committee for the Ratification of the Child Labor Amendment, 1935–1937," 256–69.

137. *Proceedings of the Twenty-fourth Conference of Catholic Charities* (1938), 16–27, 38–45.

138. "The New President," *Catholic Charities Review* 22 (Oct. 1938): 252.

139. See *Proceedings of the Twenty-fourth National Conference of Catholic Charities* (1938), 46–68, 120–34.

140. Institute for Women Volunteers file; John O'Grady to Rev. A. J. Murphy, 3 Nov. 1938, NCCC, ACUA.

141. Gibbons, "Presidential Address," 220–21.

142. Rev. Edward Hayes, the director of New York Catholic Charities' Finance Division, organized a session on "Publicity Relations in the Interpretation of the Work of Catholic Charitable Organizations, Institutions, and Agencies." Announcement of John O'Grady to Directors and Executives, Diocesan Catholic Charities, 14 Feb. 1939, NCCC, ACUA. The NCCC followed up with a manual, "Is It News? Private Social Work and Public Relations."

143. Minutes of Executive Committee, 2 March 1939; Report of the Committee on Volunteer Women's Organizations, 1940, RG 76, NCCC, ACUA.

144. Rose McHugh to Jane Hoey, "Study of the Administration of Aid to Dependent Children In Massachusetts," Social Security Board, 52-A-203, A-93, RG 47, National Archives.

145. The Minutes Book of Catholic Charities of the Archdiocese of New York cited in Sister Mary Margaretta Shea, R.S.M., "Patrick Cardinal Hayes and the Catholic Charities in New York City," unpublished Ph.D. dissertation, New York University, 1966, 288.

146. Ibid. O'Grady had assisted in forming a statewide Catholic Welfare Committee in Indiana and a new State Catholic Welfare Committee in California. He convened district meetings of diocesan organizations of Catholic Charities in Boston, Chicago, Rochester, and Cleveland.

147. O'Grady to Vincent Ryan, 7 June 1939, NCCC, ACUA. On the national level, strategies of coordination and cooperation were clearly evident as Catholic organizations developed a position on the national health program proposed by Senator Wagner in 1939. Both NCCC and NCWC representatives had participated in the discussions of the President's Interdepartmental Committee to Coordinate Health and Welfare Activities, chaired by Josephine Roche of the Treasury Department. Catholics believed, from the Interdepartmental Committee discussions, that their positions would be included in the legislation. Shocked and feeling betrayed, they joined with the AMA and the American Hospital Association and scuttled the measure. See testimony in *Catholic Charities Review* 23 (June 1939): 165–77. The complexity of both the support and opposition for S 1620 is detailed by Daniel S. Hirschfield, *The Lost Reform: The Campaign for Compulsory Health Insurance in the United States from 1932 to 1943* (Cambridge: Harvard University Press, 1970), 135–65. See also Christopher J. Kauffman, *Ministry and Meaning: A Religious History of Catholic Health Care in the United States* (New York: Crossroad, 1995), 212–47.

148. Msgr. Robert F. Keegan, "The Responsibility of a Democratic Society for The Care of Children and Youth," *Catholic Charities Review* 23 (May 1939): 132–43. The correspondence of Katharine Lenroot and Keegan gives a sense of their good relationship. See Keegan to Lenroot, 7 Feb., 22 March, 19, 24, 25 April, 1939; and Lenroot to Keegan, 18 April 1939, 8, 9 Jan. 1940, 0–1–0–46, Boxes 658, 659, 660, RG 102, National Archives.

149. Bryan J. McEntegart to Katharine F. Lenroot, 24 March 1939, NCCC, ACUA. On November 30, 1939, he forwarded a final draft of a section on religion to John O'Grady for review, ibid. Jane Hoey also forwarded recommendations to Lenroot. They included John Cooper of Catholic University and Father O'Hara of Notre Dame as the only two Catholics in the education section. Hoey to Lenroot, 15 Dec. 1938, 0–1–0–46, Box 660, RG 102, National Archives.

150. *White House Conference on Children in a Democracy. Final Report. Washington, D.C., January 18–20, 1940*, 184.

151. In the recommendations on maternity care and health and medical services for children was included the principle that "the local community should provide maternity care and health and medical services for children, as needed, as part of its public-health responsibility, utilizing available qualified services and facilities." Ibid., 364–65, 371–73.

Conclusion

1. Bishop Aloisius J. Muench, "Catholic Charities and Parochial Life," *Proceedings of the Twenty-second National Conference of Catholic Charities* (1936), 55–56.
2. William A. O'Connor, "Problems Facing Catholic Charities Today," *Catholic Charities Review* 23 (March 1940): 70.
3. In the 1990s the clerical leadership has been replaced by lay social workers, yet, as one division director of Catholic Charities of Baltimore observed, the new leadership is predominantly white and male. Interview with author, 26 September 1996.
4. Minutes of the meeting of the Committee on Volunteer Women's Organization, 17 Nov. 1940, RG 76, NCCC, ACUA. The diocesan agencies certainly provided supplementary relief when necessary; they directed clients to public agencies for assistance. This enabled them, as Marcellus Wagner had observed, to concentrate on service.
5. Children still comprised 27 percent of the clients of Catholic Charities, with 67,838 supervised in foster or group homes and residential care, Catholic Charities, U.S.A. 1993 and 1994 Annual Survey prepared by the Urban Institute. *Washington Post,* 9 Aug. 1995. For an urban comparison see "Sharing the Spirit," Annual Report, Catholic Charities, Baltimore and the Catholic Charities, 1995 and Directory of Services, Baltimore.
6. Timothy Kelly, "Suburbanization and the Decline of Catholic Public Ritual In Pittsburgh," *Journal of Social History* 28 (winter 1994): 311–30; Mary J. Oates, *The Catholic Philanthropic Tradition in America* (Bloomington: University of Indiana Press, 1995), 131, 142, 166–68. Oates shows that when the bishop provided for parish access to a percentage of the campaign funds or targeted the drive to appealing projects such as the support of retired nuns, Catholics would be generous indeed. For the Catholic Worker movement, see Dorothy Day, *The Long Loneliness: The Autobiography of Dorothy Day* (New York: Harper & Row, 1952); Neil Better, "The Great Depression and the Activities of the Catholic Worker Movement," *Labor History* 12 (spring 1971): 243–58; David J. O'Brien, *American Catholics and Social Reform: The New Deal Years* (New York: Oxford University Press, 1968), 182–211.
7. Blanche Coll, *Safety Net: Welfare and Social Security, 1929–79* (New Brunswick: Rutgers University Press, 1995), 204–76; James T. Patterson, *America's Struggle Against Poverty 1900–1994* (Cambridge: Harvard University Press, 1994), 224.
8. Mary E. Bane, "Politics and Policies of the Feminization of Poverty," in Margaret Weir, Ann S. Orloff, and Theda Skocpol, eds., *The Politics of Social Policy in the United States* (Princeton: Princeton University Press, 1988), 381–96. Most Americans in poverty were, of course, white and almost 50 percent of the poor lived in rural, small-town, or suburban areas (Patterson, 227).

9. The Family Support Act of 1988, while it made AFDC recipients eligible for Medicaid, also established programs of "job opportunities and basic skills." In 1993 Congress expanded the Earned Income Tax Credit for low-income working families (Patterson, 231–38).

10. Patterson, 225; Coll, 283–85.

11. After two years able-bodied adults who could not find private-sector work might be offered community service jobs, if the states and localities established public jobs. The federal welfare appropriations will be cut by $56 billion over a six-year period, cuts partially gained by restricting eligibility for legal immigrants and reductions in food stamps. *Newsweek,* Aug. 12, 1996: 44.

12. *New York Times,* 18 Sept. 1996. Bane's colleagues were Peter Edelman and Wendell Primus. Bane also provides a link to Rose McHugh because both were executives in the state welfare programs of New York.

13. Megan Rosenfeld, "Faith, Politics and Charity," *Washington Post,* Aug. 9, 1995.

14. Catholic Charities, U.S.A. 1994 Annual Survey prepared by the Urban Institute. *Washington Post,* 9 Aug. 1995. "Metro-riding Priest Makes Good Charities Case," *National Catholic Reporter,* March 13, 1992.

Index

Abbott, Edith, 84–85
Abbott, Grace, 172
African-American children, 104–105,
  243n120
Ahern, John F., 34, 41
Aid to Dependent Children, 172–173,
  177–178, 195–196, 270n101; kinship
  provisions and, 176
Allegheny County Emergency Relief
  Board, 166
Alter, Karl (Reverend), 72, 231n107
American Academy of Christian Democ-
  racy, Hot Springs, N.C., 73
Association for Improving the Condition
  of the Poor, New York, 2–4, 37, 123–
  124
Atkinson, Mary Irene, 7, 180, 181–182

Baltimore Catholic charities organiza-
  tions, 59–60, 80, 159–161
Baltimore Community House, 68–69
Baltimore Emergency Relief Committee,
  166–167
Big Sisters and Big Brothers, 142–146,
  259n101
Birth control, 70–71, 223n61, 224n62,
  228n92, 235n29
Blandina Segale (Sister), 67, 88
Boston Catholic charities organizations,
  57–58, 110
Boston College, 73
Boylan, Marguerite, 190–191, 231n105

Boyle, Hugh (Bishop), 55–56, 158
Brace, Charles Loring, 16–18
Brown, Josephine, 173
Buffalo Catholic charities organizations,
  94–95
Burke, John J. (Reverend), 65–66, 70, 70–
  71, 84
Butler, John J. (Reverend), 175, 187

Canevin, Regis (Bishop), 55, 102
Catholic agencies, and Federal Emergency
  Relief Administration, 165–169,
  266n49, 267n63, 267n66
Catholic Charitable Bureau, Boston, 57
Catholic charities, centralization of,
  51–52
Catholic charities organizations, by dio-
  cese: Baltimore, 59–60, 80, 159–161;
  Boston, 57–58, 110; Buffalo, 94–95;
  Chicago, 58–59, 148–150; Cincinnati,
  93–94, 95; Cleveland, 60–61; Denver,
  158–159, 168–169; District of Colum-
  bia, 65; New York, 12–50, 53–55, 88–
  89, 95–96, 112–113, 127–128; Pitts-
  burgh, 55–57, 98–102, 111–112,
  115–116; St. Louis, 136
Catholic Charities Review, 61
Catholic Charities, U.S.A., 9, 194, 197
Catholic Home Bureau, New York, 39,
  109
Catholic University of America, 82–85
Catholic Youth Organization, 147–150

Charities investigations, New York, 13–14; in 1910, 40–42; in 1914–1915, 42–49

Charity Organization Society, New York, 2–3, 16, 124, 208n32

Chicago Catholic charities organizations, 58–59, 148–150

Child guidance clinics, 129

Children's Aid Society, 16, 212n57

Children's Bureau, Department of Labor, 8, 90–91, 102, 124–125; Social Security Act and, 171–176

Children's Institutions (NCCC), 105–108

Children's Law (1875), 24

Cincinnati Catholic charities organizations, 93–94, 95

Citizens Family Welfare Committee, New York, 155

Cleveland Catholic charities organizations, 60–61

Code of Canon Law (1917), 87, 233n5

Coler, Bird S., 34–35

Community chests, 60–61; in Cincinnati, 157; in Pittsburgh, 157–158; in Denver, 159; in Baltimore, 159–161; in New York, 217n11; in Washington, D.C., 264n33

Connolly, Mary Townsend, 19–20, 206n16

Connolly, Richard Barrett, 20

Cook, Clarence Chatham, 22

Cooley, Edwin J., 133

Cooper, John M. (Reverend): *Children's Institutions* (NCCC) and, 105–108; housing for working women and, 135–138

Corrigan, Joseph M. (Bishop), 84, 85

Corrigan, Michael A. (Archbishop), 29–30, 209n36

Croker, Richard, 29

Curley, James Michael (Archbishop), 61, 84, 105

Daughters of Charity, 86

Day nurseries, 126–128

De Lacy, William H., 121, 130

Denver Catholic charities organizations, 158–159, 168–169

Denver City-County Relief Committee, 167

Depression. *See* Great Depression

Devine, Edward T., 45

District of Columbia Catholic charities organizations, 65

Doherty, William J., 43–45

Donahue, A. Madorah, 142

Dowd, Nell, 67–68

Duquesne University, 74

Eliot, Martha, 172, 175

Emergency Work Bureau, New York, 155

Euphrasia, Mother (Mother Mary of St. Euphrasia), 114–115

Farrell, William B., 45–48

Federal Emergency Relief Administration (FERA), 7–8, 163–165, 172–173; and Catholic agencies, 165–169, 266n49, 267n63, 267n66

Felician Sisters, 87

Fitzgibbon, Mary Irene (Sister), 19

Florence Crittenton homes, 91

Folks, Homer: opposition to the New York system, 24–25, 34 ; as City Commissioner of Charities, New York, 36, 212n58, 212n68; Mulry and, 38–39, 212n64; Kingsbury and, 42–43 ; Social Security Act and, 172 ; White House Conference on Children in a Democracy and, 191

Fordham University, 73, 76

Foster care, 108–113, 243n112

Foundling Asylum Society, New York, 20

Gavin, Gertrude Hill, 70, 223n59

Gerry, Elbridge, 32

Gibbons, Mary, 8, 156, 178, 189

Godley, Mary, 103

Great Depression, 153; and Catholic charities, 153, 162–163, 265n43, 265n45; in New York, 154–156, 262n16; in Cincinnati, 157; in Pittsburgh, 157–158; in Denver, 158–159; in Baltimore, 159–161; and the National Conference of Catholic Charities, 161–163

Haas, Francis (Reverend), 72

Hassard, John R.G., 22–23

Hayes, Patrick J. (Cardinal), 46, 53–54
Hebberd, Robert, 46
Hebrew Sheltering Guardian Society, 43
Hoey, Jane M., 7, 73, 79, 178; and Bureau of Public Assistance, 182–183, 185
Home Relief Bureau, New York, 156
Hopkins, Harry, 8, 152; FERA and private agencies and, 164–165; Catholics and IERA in Chicago and, 165–166
Houses of the Good Shepherd, 114–119, 244n125, 245n138; NCWC Troy Hill (Pittsburgh) survey (1919) of, 115–116; *Catholic Charities Review* survey (1925) of, 116–117; National Industrial Recovery Act (1933) and, 118–119, 246nn143–145
Hughes, John (Archbishop), 14, 31
Hurley, Timothy, 113, 132

Illegitimacy, 90–91, 97
Illinois Emergency Relief Commission, 59
Illinois Emergency Relief Administration, 165–166
Industrial and training schools, 113–114, 233n3
Infant and maternity homes, 89–90, 97

Juvenile courts, 113, 130–132
Juvenile delinquency, 252n40, 253n44, 254n54

Keegan, Robert F. (Reverend), 73, 90, 176
Kelly, John, 18–19
Kennedy, Mary Ann, 91–92, 98–101
Kerby, William (Reverend), 63–64, 72, 220n38, 221n39, 232n113
Killip, Irene M., 94–95
Kingsbury, John A., 42–48, 73
Knights of Columbus, 59

Lapp, John A., 102
Laughlin, Sara, 129, 141–142
LeBlond, Hubert, (Bishop), 88, 121, 188–189
Lenroot, Katharine, 172, 175, 180, 181, 191
Leonard, Edwin (Reverend), 68–69, 80, 105
Letchworth, William Pryor, 24
Long, Margaret McGoorty, 66–67

Low, Seth, 36
Lowell, Josephine Shaw, 16, 25
Loyola University, Chicago, 72–73

Mary of St. Euphrasia (Mother), 114–115
McCloskey, John (Cardinal), 18
McCrystal, Teresa Vincent (Sister), 19
McDonald, Barnabas (Brother), 45, 146
McEntegart, Bryan (Reverend), 73; Conference of Religious Standards Committee (NCCC) and, 102; child welfare and, 172, 176, 180, 181, 181, 182 ; White House Conference on Children in a Democracy (1939–1940) and, 191–192
McGlynn, Edward (Reverend), 29–30
McHugh, Rose, 87, 182; survey of Catholic family casework and, 80–81; survey of Catholic social workers and, 81–82, 229n96, 230nn99–101; survey of New York Foundling Hospital (1926) and, 95–96; survey of Placing Out and Boarding Departments of NYFH (1927) and, 112–113; mothers pensions and, 122–123, 228n93; on needs-rights relationship, 179; report on ADC in Massachusetts and, 190
McMahon, Dennis (Monsignor), 41
McNicholas, John T. (Archbishop), 93, 157, 231n107
Metz, Herman, 36–37
Misklow, Edward J. (Reverend), 56, 218n16
Missionaries of the Sacred Heart of Jesus, 87
Mitchel, John Purroy, 13–14, 40–42, 47, 49, 213n73, 215n92
Molamphy, Teresa, 123
Moore, Edward Roberts (Reverend), 148
Moran, Frederick A., 143–146
Moree, Edward A., 46
Morrissy, Elizabeth, 171
Mothers pensions, 34, 41, 120–121; in Illinois, 121–123; in Pennsylvania, 123; in New York, 123–124, 248n12
Movies and dance halls, 140–141
Muench, Aloisius (Bishop), 1, 193
Mulroy, John (Reverend), 158–159, 169, 184

Mulry, Thomas Maurice, 26–28; Folks and, 39–40, 212n64; New York charities investigation and, 46, 48; White House Conference of the Care of Dependent Children and, 120, 188; mothers pensions and, 121, 124

Mundelein, George (Cardinal), 58–59, 218n21, 219n24

National Catholic Community House, Cincinnati, 67–68

National Catholic School of Social Service, 71–72, 82–84, 231nn107–109

National Catholic War Council, 65–66; Women's Committee of the, 66–69

National Catholic Welfare Conference, 69, 87, 174, 223n57; Social Action Department of, 69, 79

National Conference of Catholic Charities, 62–63, 87, 89; Conference of Religious of, 89, 91, 96–97, 102–103; mothers pensions and, 125; Sheppard-Towner and, 125; Youth Committee of, 149–150; New York convention (1933) of, 151–152; Conference of Diocesan Directors of, 152; role in Social Security legislation, 174–177; Social Security implementation and, 179–181, 187–188; Continuing Committee of, and ADC, 183–186, 268n70; National Catholic Welfare Conference and, 186, 246n143, 276n147

National Council of Catholic Women, 70–71

National Industrial Recovery Act (1933), 118–119, 246nn143–145

National League for the Protection of American Institutions, 31–32, 210n44

New Deal: Federal Emergency Relief Administration and, 7–8, 163–165, 172–173; Social Security and, 8, 152, 170, 171–178, 182–183, 185, 195–196, 269n79, 270n101, 273nn120–121, 274nn130–131; New York State Constitutional Convention (1894), 30–32; National Industrial Recovery Act (1933) and, 118–119, 246nn143–145; National Youth Administration and, 149; Catholic agencies, 165–169, 266n49, 267n63, 267n66; Illinois Emergency Relief Administration, 165–166; Allegheny County Emergency Relief Board, 166; Baltimore Emergency Relief Committee, 166–167; Denver City-County Relief Committee, 167; Tulsa FERA, 167–168

New York Catholic Protectory, 21, 207nn21–22, 209n43

New York Foundling Hospital, 202n8; foundation as Asylum, 19–20, 89–90; survey (1926) of, 95–96; survey of Placing Out and Boarding Departments (1927), 112–113

New York Juvenile Asylum, 23, 43

New York Orphan Asylum, 14, 15

New York School of Social Work, 73, 225n73

New York State Catholic charities organizations, 12–50; diocesan survey and reorganization (1919) of, 50, 53–55, 88–89; survey of child-caring institutions (1926) in, 95–96; boarding-out and placement survey (1927) of, 112–113; day nurseries and, 127–128

Norman, Margaret, 78

Oblate Sisters of Providence, 87, 104

O'Brien, Morgan J., 35, 211n52

O'Connell, William (Cardinal), 57, 126

O'Conor, George P. (Reverend), 57–58

O'Donohue, Teresa, 28–29, 138, 139

O'Donohue, Joseph J., 206n17

O'Dwyer, Thomas (Reverend), 187, 188

O'Grady, John (Reverend), 55, 74–75, 77, 89, 91, 102, 191, 191; National Conference of Catholic Charities and, 64–65; Catholic University School of Social Work and, 82–85, 230n103, 232n113; Houses of the Good Shepherd and, 117–119; Great Depression and, 161–162, 163; Hopkins and, 165; Catholic agencies and FERA and, 167–170; Social Security legislation and, 175, 177, 177, 180, 181, 186

Orphan trains, 109, 205n8

Our Lady of Victory Women's and Children's Hospital, and Our Lady of Victory Infant Home, Lackawanna, New York, 94–95

Padgett, Alice, 93–94, 162–163, 232n113
Parochial schools, 14–15, 30–32, 128–129, 210n45
Perkins, Frances, 176
Pittsburgh Catholic charities organizations, 55–57, 98–102, 111–112, 115–116
Pius XI, Pope, *Quadragesimo anno* (1931), 152, 155–156
Planned Parenthood, 194
Potter, Daniel (Reverend), 37–38, 41, 46, 47, 49
Prendergast, William A., 41
Probation and probation officers, 132–133
Program for Catholic Child-caring Homes, A (NCCC), 102–104
Prosser Committee, 154–155, 262n16
Protective care for girls and women, 134–135, 139; and housing, 135–138, 256n70, 256n74
Public School Society, New York, 14, 31

Quadragesimo anno (Pius XI), 152, 155–156

Ready, Michael (Monsignor), 191, 271n102
Regan, Agnes, 70, 71, 85, 191
Relief agencies, 165–169, 266n49, 267n63, 267n66; Illinois Emergency Relief Administration, 165–166; Allegheny County Emergency Relief Board, 166; Baltimore Emergency Relief Committee, 166–167; Denver City-County Relief Committee, 167; Tulsa FERA, 167–168
Religious congregations of women, and child-care, 86–89; Sisters of Charity of Emmitsburg, 19–20; Sisters of Charity of Cincinnati, 67, 93–94; Daughters of Charity, 86; Sisters of Charity of New York, 86, 87, 89; Ursuline Sisters (French), 86, 88; Oblate Sisters of Providence (African-American), 87, 104; Sisters of Mercy (Irish), 87, 98–102; Sisters of Notre Dame (German), 87; Felician Sisters (Polish), 87; Missionaries of the Sacred Heart of Jesus (Italian), 87; Sisters of Notre Dame of Cleveland (Czech), 87; Sisters of Char-

ity of St. Vincent de Paul, 89; Sisters of Charity of St. Augustine, 97; Sisters of the Good Shepherd, 114–119
Richmond, Mary, 77
Ring, Charlotte, 68
Roman Catholic Benevolent Society, New York, 20–21
Roman Catholic Orphan Asylum, 15
Roselia Foundling Asylum and Maternity Home, Pittsburgh, 91–93
Russell Sage Foundation, 43, 81
Ryan, James Hugh (Bishop), 83–84, 230n103
Ryan, John A. (Reverend), 69

St. Anne's Hospital, Cleveland, 97
St. Joseph's Industrial Home, New York, 23
St. Joseph's Maternity and Infant Hospital, Cincinnati, 93–94, 237n41
St. Louis Catholic charities organizations, 136
St. Louis University, 73
St. Mary's Training School, Chicago, 58
St. Patrick's Cathedral, New York, 22
St. Paul's Roman Catholic Orphan Asylum, Pittsburgh, 98–102, 239n71
St. Rita's Home for Infants, Pittsburgh, 91, 92–93
Sanger, Margaret, 70–71
Sauer, (Mary) Luella, 56, 157, 166, 190
Schuyler, Louisa Lee, 16
Scouting, 139–140, 146–148
Sheil, Bernard (Bishop), 147–150
Shinnick, Mary, 122
Sisters of Charity: Emmitsburg, 19–20; Cincinnati, 67, 93–94; New York, 86, 87, 89; St. Vincent de Paul, 89; St. Augustine, 97
Sisters of Mercy, 87, 98–102
Sisters of Notre Dame, 87
Sisters of the Good Shepherd, 114–119
Slattery, Agnes (Mrs. Francis E.), 126
Social Security, 8, 152; Social Security Act and, 170; Committee on Economic Security and, 171, 269n79; Children's Bureau and, 171–172; Aid to Dependent Children and, 172–173, 176, 177–178, 195–196, 270n101; Child Welfare Services and, 172, 174, 175; NCCC

Social Security *(continued)*
response to, 174–177, 273nn120–121,
274nn130–131; Bureau of Public Assistance and, 182–183, 185
Social work education, Catholic, 75–79,
226n79, 227nn86–88
Social worker survey, Catholic, 81–82
Social work programs, Catholic: American Academy of Christian Democracy,
Hot Springs, N.C., 73; Boston College,
73; Catholic University of America, 82–
85; Duquesne University, 74; Fordham
University, 73, 76; Loyola University,
Chicago, 72–73; St. Louis University,
73; Trinity College, Washington, D.C.,
72; Xavier University, New Orleans,
225n71
Society for the Prevention of Cruelty to
Children, New York, 33–34; Society of
St. Vincent de Paul, 25–26; Mission of
the Immaculate Virgin, Staten Island,
and, 26, 45, 46; Catholic Home Bu-
reau, New York, and, 39 ; Knights of
Columbus and, 59–60; White House
Conference on the Care of Dependent
Children and, 62; National Conference
of Catholic Charities and, 62; centen-
ary celebration and, 151; Baltimore
Catholic charities and, 159–161
State Board of Charities, New York, 24,
208n28; New York State Constitutional
Convention (1894) and, 32–33, 34,
210n48, 211n53; charities investigation
(1914–1915) and, 44–45
State Charities Aid Association, New
York, 16, 37, 46

Strong, Charles H., 44, 49
Strong Commission, 44–45, 47, 48–49,
214nn81–82
Sullivan, Florence L., 94
Swanstrom, Edward (Reverend), 190

Tammany Hall, 18–19, 26, 202n11
Temporary Emergency Relief Administra-
tion, New York, 156
Tierney, Richard H., 47
Tinney, Mary C., 91, 109
Trinity College, Washington, D.C., 72
Tulsa Federal Emergency Relief Admini-
stration, 167–168
Tweed, William Marcy, 18, 205n10

Ursuline Sisters, 86, 88

Vehr, Urban (Bishop), 158

Wagner, Marcellus (Monsignor), 157,
169–170, 175
Wagner, Robert F., 176
Walsh, Miriam Regina (Sister), 89, 104
Wastl, Francis S. (Reverend), 74
White House Conference on the Care of
Dependent Children (1909), 62, 120
White House Conference on Children in a
Democracy (1939–1940), 191–192
Williams, Pierce, 167
Wiretapping, 47, 215n89
Witte, Edwin, 175, 270n99

Xavier University, New Orleans, 225n71